A Sociophilological Study of Late Latin

UTRECHT STUDIES IN MEDIEVAL LITERACY

10

UTRECHT STUDIES IN MEDIEVAL LITERACY

General Editor

Marco Mostert (University of Utrecht)

Editorial Board

Gerd Althoff (Westfälische-Wilhelms-Universität Münster)
Michael Clanchy (University of London)
Peter Gumbert (University of Leiden)
Mayke de Jong (University of Utrecht)
Rosamond McKitterick (University of Cambridge)
Arpád Orbán (University of Utrecht)
Armando Petrucci (Scuola Normale Superiore di Pisa)
Richard H. Rouse (UCLA)

A SOCIOPHILOLOGICAL STUDY OF LATE LATIN

by
Roger Wright

BREPOLS

British Library Cataloguing in Publication Data

Wright, Roger, 1947-
  A sociophilological study of late Latin. – (Utrecht studies in
  medieval literacy ; 10)
  1.Latin language, Medieval and modern 2.Latin language, Medieval
  and modern – Social aspects 3.Romance languages – History
  I.Title II.Rijksuniversiteit te Utrecht
  478

  ISBN 2503513387

© 2002, Brepols Publishers n.v., Turnhout, Belgium.

All rights reserved. No part of this publication may be reproduced, stored in a
retrieval system, or transmitted, in any form or by any means, electronic,
mechanical, photocopying, recording, or otherwise, without the prior
permission of the publisher.

D/2003/0095/13

ISBN 2-503-51338-7

Printed in the E.U. on acid-free paper

Contents

This Book

Sociophilology is a word which I invented in 1996 in order to refer to an approach to the linguistic study of texts from the past which attempts to combine traditional philological analysis with the insights of modern sociolinguistics. This requires as careful a knowledge as can be acquired of the historical and intellectual circumstances of the scribes and authors who have provided the evidence for us. Although sociophilology applies by definition to the linguistic history of literate communities, and historical linguistics has often preferred to concentrate on languages with little or no written history, or the prehistory of subsequently literate languages, it is important for the two to complement each other without contradictions. It is thus difficult. The successful sociophilologist has to attempt to understand several academic fields at once as well as be acquainted with a wide range of data. In the Latin-Romance field, central to the whole project is an appreciation of the nature of medieval literacy, which is why I am very pleased that the *Utrecht Studies on Medieval Literacy* have agreed to include this book in its series.

'Late Latin' is the language which, when written, is traditionally regarded as a kind of Latin, but when spoken, is often regarded as being 'Early Romance'. Speech and writing are seen here as being two modalities of the single language of Late Latin. The chronological period examined extends from the late Roman Empire to the first Romance texts in each Romance-speaking community. The study of the way Latin developed from being a single language in the Roman Empire into several living Romance languages, as well as into the 'dead' language which we now call 'Medieval Latin', is both complex in itself and confused by several centuries' worth of competing scholarly analyses. A sociophilological perspective gives us a chance of clarifying the picture, and cutting a number of Gordian knots in the process.

I have already published one collection of selected articles, mostly with particular reference to the Iberian Peninsula, under the title of *Early Ibero-*

Romance: twenty-one studies on language and texts from the Iberian Peninsula between the Roman Empire and the Thirteenth Century (Newark, 1995). Many of these were in effect detailed sociophilological analyses *avant la lettre*. The present book is based on twenty-five other previous studies on the development of Latin. Some are printed almost unchanged, but most have been revised to a greater or lesser extent, and in some cases abbreviated to avoid too much repetition. Of these six were originally published in Spanish, two in Italian and two in French, and these have been translated into English by myself. They have been arranged mainly into chronological order of subject matter rather than of composition. One of them (Chapter 9) was actually published before my *Late Latin and Early Romance in Spain and Carolingian France* (Liverpool, 1982), but most of them are relatively recent, and collectively they present a wide perspective on the topic. Full publication details of the papers concerned are included at the start of each chapter of this book.

Section A

Latin, Medieval Latin and Romance

The four studies in this section take a long view, examining how the Latin of the Roman Empire developed and came to be thought of as being several different languages by the end of the thirteenth century. Latin and Romance are a special case in historical linguistics, in that the standardization of Medieval Latin as an international, but "dead", language, seems to be related to the way in which its living descendants fragmented into the several Romance languages. Thus the first chapter traces the way in which Latin eventually became a foreign language for us all, even in Romance-speaking areas, while the second looks at the reasons for linguistic divergence, concentrating in this case on the Iberian Peninsula. The validity of linguistic periodization is discussed in chapter three, also mainly with reference to the Iberian Peninsula, suggesting that our understanding of internal linguistic changes are distorted by any desire to divide language history into periods, but that the nature of written texts can change with relative suddenness for contextual reasons; a sociophilological approach is of particular relevance in such cases, in which a language can even change its name.

The main chronological turning point is seen to be the period of the Carolingian "*renouatio*" of intellectual life, around the year 800 A.D.. This idea was first presented in detail in my 1982 book *Late Latin and Early Romance in Spain and Carolingian France*, and it still seems to me to be essentially right, even though it was only the later Twelfth-Century Renaissance that validated a general Latin-Romance distinction. Since 1982, however, this field has been transformed and revitalized by the work of Michel Banniard, in particular by his book *Viva Voce* of 1992; and it has thus seemed sensible to include in this initial overview the review article dedicated to *Viva Voce* in 1993.

Chapter 1

How Latin Came to Be a
Foreign Language for All

L atin was originally the native language of the inhabitants of the area of Latium (modern Lazio), around the city of Rome. By the end of the Middle Ages, it was taught and learnt as a foreign language even by those who spoke as their native language one of the Romance languages that had developed out of spoken Latin. The process by which this language became foreign even to those who spoke evolved versions of it is a complex one and not yet entirely understood by the historical linguists, although many details in the process have become clearer in recent years.

From the earliest stages of the spread of their political and military influence outside their home territory the Romans came into contact with speakers of related Italic languages, such as Oscan, more distantly related Indo-European languages, such as Celtic, and languages of other families entirely, such as Etruscan. In order to prosper or even survive in the expanding Roman state, native speakers of these other languages had to learn Latin. By the height of the Roman Empire, Etruscan and Oscan and other languages once spoken on the Italian Peninsula seem to have been spoken no more. The Latinization process seems to have been so successful as to lead to a largely monolingual peninsula (ignoring, for the moment, Greek-speaking communities in the south and in Sicily). But we have no record of any pedagogical method that was then

This chapter is a reprint with minor changes of: "The study of Latin as a foreign language in the Early Middle Ages", in: *History of the Language Sciences*, I, ed. S. AUROUX e.a. (Berlin and New York, 2000), pp. 501-510. We are grateful to Jennifer Mand, on behalf of Mouton de Gruyter (Berlin), for permitting the reprint.

used to teach, learn and study Latin as a foreign language. Probably the language was learnt in living circumstances rather than at school or in night classes; traders in the markets, soldiers in the armies, slaves in Roman households and others needed a knowledge of spoken Latin and acquired it informally *in situ*. The Romans probably had no coherent plan to stamp out the languages they met, but of these only Greek had any prestige at all, and it is unlikely that outside special circumstances a native Latin-speaker would have learnt any other language than Greek. In all newly-conquered areas we can surmise the existence of bilingual communities for many decades, but in most places, after the initial contact period, subsequent generations increasingly learnt Latin as a first language, or as one of two first languages, in a native manner. For the evidence that we have, suggests that the teaching of Latin in schools and academies was designed to increase the literary skills of those who already spoke Latin, rather than teach Latin to those who did not yet know it.[1]

As the Roman State expanded out of the Italian Peninsula it encountered and dominated speakers of many other languages, including Phoenician, Berber languages, Iberian, Celtic, Germanic, Greek, Aramaic, Syriac and Coptic. But although we know of the existence of schools, the only documentary clues that survive for us concerning the practice of teaching and learning Latin as a foreign language during these centuries come from the Greek-speaking areas at a somewhat later time, and even that evidence is hard to assess. In some areas, such as the British Isles, knowledge of Latin seems rarely to have been monolingual, with the result that the pre-existing Celtic continued to flourish, although a knowledge of spoken Latin may well not have died out entirely, as used to be thought. Harvey argues convincingly for its survival to some extent not only in Britain but also in Ireland, which was never part of the empire.[2] St Patrick wrote in Latin there in the late fifth century, and a knowledge of Latin literacy can be seen behind the elaboration of Ogam as the written form of Irish. In other areas, such as Gaul, the hold of Latin became stronger, and eventually (in the Early Middle Ages) may have ousted Celtic; but although Latin must have been learnt at some time by hundreds of thousands of people in these areas who already spoke some other language, we cannot say to what extent it was taught to them in any formal sense as an object of study.

Some surviving bilingual Latin-Greek papyri found in the sands of North Africa seem to attest to linguistic school exercises, probably, at least in some

---

[1] J.P.V.D. BALSDON, *Romans and Aliens* (London, 1979).
[2] A. HARVEY, "Latin, literacy and the Celtic vernaculars around the year A.D. 500", in: *Celtic Languages and Celtic Peoples*, ed. C.J. BYRNE e.a. (Halifax, 1992), pp. 11-26.

cases, designed for Greek-speakers learning Latin, although not necessarily in a formal classroom setting.[3] In his study of the "Bu Njem" tablets of the 250s, Adams argues that Phoenician-speaking soldiers learnt colloquial Latin in the army in an unstructured manner.[4] We have there rare examples of first-generation Latin-learners who have been taught to write, largely with the help of whole model words and phrases, but who display unusual mistakes characteristic of second language learners. The graffiti of the originally Celtic-speaking potters of La Graufesenque are another case.[5] The bilingual Greek-Latin word-lists known as *Hermeneumata* are often ancient in origin and pre-Christian in content, and may have had a function similar to the papyri. But they seem to be largely a Western phenomenon, that is, mostly destined for Latin-speaking Greek-learners (about whom we know rather more).[6] There is a late fourth-century grammarian called Dositheus whose *Ars Grammatica*, in Latin, seems to have been prepared, perhaps from the start, with a companion translation in Greek.[7] Presumably the translation was made to aid Greek-speaking Latin students, but we need not assume that that was Dositheus's original intention. There undoubtedly were students of this type at the time, such as those attending the law schools in Beirut once Greeks were declared to be subject to Roman Law in 212 A.D., but even in the Eastern end of the Empire the main reasons for learning Latin were the simple practicalities of international life, such as the need to survive in the army, or the desire to gain employment elsewhere, perhaps in Rome itself. Even in the Greek-speaking area there seems not to be anything we could call a pedagogical or intellectual tradition of 'Latin as a foreign language'. When Priscian, in the early sixth century (between 512 and 528), turned his attention to an attempt to explain Latin syntax to the predominantly Greek speakers of Byzantium, his intellectual inspiration and written sources were to be found in the local grammars of Greek, since the study of Latin syntax (as opposed to morphology) had not yet been broached, but Greek

---

[3] A. WOUTERS, *The Grammatical Papyri from Graeco-Roman Egypt. Contributions to the Study of 'Ars Grammatica' in Antiquity* (Brussels, 1979).

[4] J.N. ADAMS, "Latin and Punic in contact? The case of the Bu Njem ostraca", *Journal of Roman Studies* 84 (1994), pp. 87-112.

[5] P. FLOBERT, "Les graffites de la Graufesenque: un témoignage sur le Gallo-latin sous Néron", in: *Latin vulgaire – latin tardif* III, ed. M. ILIESCU and W. MARXGUT (Niemeyer, 1992), pp. 103-114.

[6] A.C. DIONISOTTI, "From Ausonius' schooldays? A schoolbook and its relatives", *Journal of Roman Studies* 72 (1982), pp. 83-125. EADEM, "Latin grammar for Greeks and Goths", *Journal of Roman Studies* 74 (1984), pp. 202-208.

[7] H. KEIL, *Grammatici Latini*, 7 volumes (Leipzig, 1885-1880; reprint Hildesheim, 1961), VII, pp. 376-436.

syntax had been being analysed since the second century. Even educated speakers of Greek saw no particular reason to learn Latin before the general adoption of Christianity. Greek culture could satisfy most literary tastes. Even Plutarch had claimed to have learnt only a little Latin, in an informal manner, and was probably told of material in his Latin sources by his colleagues. But in the fourth century the Church hierarchy in Constantinople, Antioch, Alexandria and elsewhere needed translators for practical purposes, such as ensuring they had accurate records of Councils, and many Greek speakers may have been eager to learn Latin.[8] The fourth-century Greek Claudian wrote in Latin; this is also the date of most of the bilingual papyri. Yet even Jerome and the other Biblical translators of the fourth century (translating from Greek into Latin) seem not to have established a continuing tradition of Latin being taught in a regular pedagogical manner to native speakers of Greek; conversely, we also know of Latin texts that were then translated into Greek (including Saints' Lives by Jerome himself).

The reasons for this apparent lacuna are not hard to appreciate; in general there can be no effective tradition of the study of a foreign language until there already exists a native monolingual tradition of what we would now call 'descriptive linguistics'. It takes linguists of genius to perceive the organizational principles of their native language in such an objective way that they can be presented as objects of study to others, and a tradition of analysis of the nature of Latin linguistics took a long time to be established even in the native-speaker intellectual context. Varro, Quintilian and others were mines of ideas and information for advanced study, but the basics of the language did not really begin to be codified into a coherent form suitable for elementary study until the work of Aelius Donatus in the fourth century A.D. (although he may have drawn on some previous work now unknown to us). Donatus (Jerome's teacher) compiled a short *Ars Grammatica*, usually known as the *Ars Minor*, and a longer one known as the *Ars Maior*. The *Ars Minor* seems unsatisfactorily uncomprehensive to us now (lacking, for example, reference to what have come to be called the fourth and fifth declensions, or to exceptions to the main paradigms), but it included a great deal of basic morphological information in a moderately accessible structure. Gaps were progressively filled by the many commentators in subsequent centuries who used the *Ars Minor* as the starting point for their own further elucubrations, and collectively their analyses formed the basis of the educational tradition of Latin language-study that has

---

[8] E.A. FISHER, "Greek translations of Latin literature in the fourth century A.D.", *Yale Classical Studies* 27 (1982), pp. 173-215, p. 175.

lasted in many respects to the present day. Pinkster's grammar was the first serious attempt to start again for over sixteen centuries.[9] The *Ars Maior* was longer than the *Ars Minor* because it contained extra material that would be classified now as literary rather than linguistic. Thus it was the *Ars Minor* that came to be the basis for all subsequent linguistic education in Latin.[10]

Donatus, however, was writing for the benefit of those who knew the language already, and his focus was on written language alone (which is what *Grammatica* originally meant). That is, Donatus saw his brief as being to help his students to write, and understand the written form of, the language which they already spoke. The ability to write 'correctly' at that time (understandably, although to the eternal disappointment of all subsequent philologists) did not rest on the ability to provide a phonetic transcription of vernacular morphosyntax, but to spell words as the ancients did, using the morphology and syntax which they had used in earlier texts. This appears to have seemed to Donatus and his colleagues to imply a need above all for long lists of morphological paradigms, particularly of nouns and pronouns. This concentration in turn appears to imply that not all the nominal endings lovingly illustrated could be trusted to come naturally to the mind of the contemporary native speaker; a deduction which fits the conclusion, reached by the Romance philologists who aim to reconstruct the nature of spoken Latin at this time, that nominal morphology was then simplifying in the speech of all. An ability to recognize the separate paradigms and inflectional morphemes was taken to be essential for the correct writing and understanding of texts; and it is probably here that we find the origin of the Early Medieval grammatical habit of regarding the nominal word endings (such as *-m*) as forming part of the study of orthography, rather than of syntax or of pronunciation.

No Latin grammarian before Priscian had much to say about syntax, and since Donatus was writing for the native-speaker alone, he included no instructions on pronunciation either, and very few on vocabulary. Not many of his predecessors or contemporaries mentioned pronunciation either, and there is no documentary evidence for the belief of some modern Romance philologists working in the Reconstruction tradition – that is, reconstructing Proto-Ro-

---

[9] H. PINKSTER, *Latin Syntax and Semantics* (London, 1990).

[10] L. HOLTZ, *Donat et la tradition de l'enseignement grammatical: étude sur l'Ars Donati et sa diffusion (IVe-IXe siècle) et édition critique* (Paris, 1981), made the development of this tradition much easier to trace, but the outstanding modern study of the grammatical work of the Early Middle Ages is: M. IRVINE, *The Making of Textual Culture: "Grammatica" and Literary Theory, 350-1100* (Cambridge, 1994). See also: V. LAW (ed.), *History of Linguistic Thought in the Early Middle Ages* (Amsterdam, 1993).

mance from the evidence of the several subsequently-attested Romance languages – that there existed a separate educated 'Latin' pronunciation at that time, consciously differentiated from the normal Early Romance pronunciations that were beginning to be part of everybody's speech throughout the late Empire. That is, the balance of probability now seems to be that in essence many of the reconstructed pronunciations did indeed exist then, such as a vocalic system based on quality rather than length, but that archaic alternatives were not also in use at the same time (until they were reinvented much later by the Carolingians, when they established Medieval Latin *grammatica* as a consciously distinct international clerical standard: see below). Those who read Donatus, taught classes with his help, or learnt from him in such classes, continued to speak with their existing Early Romance pronunciation, but were in addition studying to read and write their own language with greater certainty of being 'correct'.

Since instruction concerning vocabulary and pronunciation is of immediate importance and relevance to the learner of a foreign language, Donatus's work cannot have been easy to use by a non-Latin speaker. As Servius, Pompeius,[11] Isidore of Seville,[12] and others eclectically elaborated and expanded the tradition set by Donatus, grammatical studies became more comprehensive, more discursive and more closely entwined with the analysis of prestigious texts; but these developments in themselves would not have assisted the foreign learner. Previous grammars largely disappeared from view. There was, for example, apparently no Medieval circulation of Varro's *De Lingua Latina*. Outside Byzantium, the Early Romance-speaking community, including within it the Latin-studying community, remained essentially monolingual for centuries yet; but the influence of Donatus came to be unavoidable. As Irvine phrases it, "to escape Donatan or late Imperial *latinitas*, Gregory would have had to stop writing" (that is, Gregory the Great, Pope from 590 to 604).[13] In the wide Early Romance speaking area there were naturally sociolinguistic, stylistic and geographical variations and complexities, but their study of *grammatica* remained in the Early Middle Ages the study of the elevated and educated registers of their own language. The arrival of Priscian's *Institutiones Grammaticae* onto

[11] Both well studied in: R. KASTER, *Guardians of Language: the Grammarian and Society in Late Antiquity* (Berkeley, 1988).

[12] M.C. DÍAZ Y DÍAZ, "Introducción general", in: *San Isidoro de Sevilla: Etimologías*, ed. J. OROZ RETA, 2 volumes (Madrid, 1982: Biblioteca de Autores Cristianos), pp. 1-257. See also: J. FONTAINE and J.N. HILLGARTH (ed.), *Le septième siècle: changements et continuités* (London, 1992).

[13] IRVINE, *The Making*, p. 194.

the European higher education curriculum, from the early ninth century on-wards, as the standard textbook for higher education, to be studied subsequent to the study of Donatus and his commentators as the standard textbooks at a simpler level, and the adoption of the Anglo-Saxons' practice of pronouncing the texts with a sound for each written letter of standard spellings, together provided the inspiration needed to establish the process that was to turn the study of Latin into a foreign-language study for speakers of Romance languages as well.

This analysis of the pre-Carolingian Romance-speaking communities as being complex but monolingual is still in some respects controversial, despite fitting what evidence there is. The earlier view, which sees a clear distinction even at that early time between 'Romance' and 'Latin' as conceptually separate language systems, still has many adherents. Kaster is particularly pessimistic about the abilities of the unlettered, but the studies in McKitterick's collection suggest we can be more bullish.[14] The monolingual view does not imply a lack of linguistic evolution in these communities. In particular, most of the phonetic developments which are generally declared by modern philologists to be characteristic of Romance rather than of Latin were well under way even by the end of the Roman Empire. The traditional spellings of words continued to be taught as correct, naturally, for phonetic script had not been invented yet, and would not have been thought desirable if it had. But the gradually increasing divergences, between correct orthography and any intuitions which we can envisage them as having had concerning phonetic details, do not seem to have worried Romance speakers. In practice, it may be reasonable for us to suggest that the teaching of spelling was done on an increasingly logographic basis – that is, word by word (as in modern Britain) rather than merely sound by sound. In the same way, the ubiquitously employed abbreviations, and the 'Tyronian' short-hand as used in particular by notaries, naturally referred to the lexical word rather than to its phonetic constituents. Thus there were details of writing that did not apply to speech, but there always are, in any literate community. We can deduce, for example, from the phrasing of the orthographical instructions that Cassiodorus gave to his monks in sixth-century Italy, that the addition of a final -*m* to a noun was seen as a matter of written correctness alone.

Written language had variations in style too, of course. By the mid-eighth century, at least, several writers had the sophistication to adjust the register level of their compositions to suit the intended audience (for example, in the

---

[14] KASTER, *Guardians*, p. 38. R. MCKITTERICK (ed.), *The Uses of Literacy in Early Medieval Europe* (Cambridge, 1990).

preparation of those Saints' Lives that were intended for recitation to the congregation rather than for private monastic study). In a series of remarkable studies, stemming from his thesis and then book entitled *Viva Voce*, Michel Banniard has established beyond much reasonable doubt that even writers of such intellectual standing as Augustine, Gregory, Isidore and the eighth-century hagiographers expected their texts to be generally intelligible when read aloud; and indeed most texts were read aloud.[15] The implications we can draw from this are that not only did the *lectores* deliver phonetically evolved forms of words that were easily recognizable by an unlettered Romance audience, but that the traditional morphology and syntax used in the texts were not yet baffling to the general public. That is, the morphological and syntactic changes which we identify now as taking place from 'Latin' to 'Romance' took much longer to complete than the phonetic changes, because the older usages often remained in general passive comprehension competence for centuries after the arrival of the newer alternatives that seem in retrospect to have neatly taken their place.[16] And such a complex yet monolingual situation could have continued to be the case for a long time yet but for the advent of what has come to be known as the Carolingian 'Renaissance'.

Some of the expertise acquired by bilingual Latin-Greek speakers, and some of the texts prepared on the basis of their experience, seem to have survived in the Western Empire, as Dionisotti's acute studies of the *Hermeneumata* and glossaries suggest, where they would not have been used directly to teach Latin as a foreign language.[17] Sometimes we can glimpse Romance-speaking commentators on Donatus using Eastern expertise. Indeed, the manuscripts of these Latin-for-Greeks works tend to survive in the West rather than the East; all three surviving manuscripts of Dositheus are tenth-century copies from St Gall.[18] And Greek-based expertise did contribute to the initial stage of the general transformation of the study of Latin in the West from the textual study of a known language to the learning of an unknown and foreign one,

---

[15] M. BANNIARD, *Viva Voce: communication écrite et communication orale du IVe au IXe siècle en Occident latin* (Paris, 1992). IDEM, "Latin tardif et français prélitteraire: observations de méthode et de chronologie", *Bulletin de la Société de Linguistique de Paris* 88 (1993), pp. 139-162.

[16] J.N. GREEN, "The collapse and replacement of verbal inflection in Late Latin / Early Romance: How would one know?", in: *Latin and the Romance Languages in the Early Middle Ages*, ed. R. WRIGHT (London, 1991; reprint, Penn State, 1996), pp. 83-99.

[17] A.C. DIONISOTTI, "On Bede, grammars and Greek", *Revue Bénédictine* 92 (1982), pp. 111-141, as well her studies in n. 6.

[18] DIONISOTTI, "From Ausonius' schooldays?", p. 84.

when the revival of Latin study began to take place in the British Isles. Vivien Law's masterly book on the Insular Latin Grammarians made the process easier to follow.[19] And although details of the way in which Irish writers learnt to use Latin remain unclear, it was certainly based on textual traditions rather than native contacts in Ireland itself, such that their usage seemed archaic in vocabulary and style when Irish scholars moved to the Continent.[20] The most productive intellectual impulse in the Anglo-Saxon area seems to have come in the seventh century, at least partly from the Greek-speaking Eastern Mediterranean, rather than from the Augustinian mission in the sixth. The credit for the growth of interest in Latin study in Britain can be allotted to two emissaries from the papacy who travelled to the Isles in 669 A.D.: Theodore, a Greek scholar who had worked and studied and learnt Latin in Greece, initially as a foreign language, and Hadrian, a colleague of the Pope's (Pope Vitalian). It is possible to reconstruct that some general expertise in the practice of teaching and learning Latin as a foreign language was provided at that point by Theodore. Even though he did not bring with him all of Priscian's *Institutiones*, which were at a higher intellectual level than was needed at that time, practical advice was clearly forthcoming, and books came with him – not necessarily all the way from the East – probably including some of the more elementary Latin grammatical works compiled for Greeks, such as the briefer Priscian extract known as the *Institutio de nomine et pronomine et verbo*. We can also glimpse a habit of textual analysis from surviving Latin to Anglo-Saxon glosses from seventh-century Canterbury. Thus from the start the type of Latinity that educated Anglo-Saxons began to have contact with came from Italy rather than from Gaul. Aldhelm of Malmesbury, for example, was a personal pupil of Theodore's. Even so, despite the initial impulse from these personal contacts, Insular studies of Latin were to be primarily text-based rather than supplied by native-speaker expertise. Meanwhile, Irish latinity at this time continued, as it had been hitherto, to be essentially based on the Bible, and despite the renewal of contacts the teaching of Latin to both Celtic and Germanic speakers was more directly related to the study of texts than to a need for colloquial inter-

---

[19] V. LAW, *The Insular Latin Grammarians* (Woodbridge, 1982). And subsequently: EADEM, *Grammar and Grammarians in the Early Middle Ages* (London, 1997).

[20] M.W. HERREN, "Hiberno-Latin philology: the state of the question", in: *Insular Latin Studies*, ed. M.W. HERREN (Toronto, 1981), pp. 1-22. D. O'CRÓINÍN, "The Irish as mediators of antique culture on the continent", in: *Science in Western and Eastern Civilization in Carolingian Times*, ed. P.L. BUTZER and D. LOHRMANN (Basle, 1993), pp. 41-51.

course. Richter's study of Irish culture at this time, indeed, stresses the vital nature of the native oral traditions in comparison to the stilted Latin texts.[21]

The linguistic works that survive from the pen of Insular scholars attest to a pedagogical and scholarly tradition that began with Bede (673-735). Bede kept what seems to be a teacher's notebook, in which he progressively noted down all kinds of useful details valuable to the teacher of Latin; unfortunately this work has been given the title of *De orthographia*, but in effect it covers all linguistic levels.[22] Subsequent Insular grammarians that we know of include Tatwine, Boniface, and the authors of the anonymous grammars named after the libraries where their manuscripts are preserved (Berne and Amiens). This last has some Biblical quotations from the *Vetus latina* rather than the Vulgate, which suggests ancient source material, probably from Gaul.[23] Even so, they can all be seen to belong in Bede's educational tradition, although Boniface, who exported Insular expertise to the Germanic-speaking continent, seems to have been more influenced in his own Latinity by Aldhelm. Irish grammars, probably including the impressive one now known as *Anonymus ad Cuimnanum* which contrasts ancient and standard Latin and also manifests a knowledge of Greek, continued to have a partly separate tradition. The preferred vocabulary of Insular Latin-speakers was that of the Bible, whether or not it sounded archaic in the Romance world. For they spoke and recited Latin – Bede even seems to have expected his *Historia* to be read aloud – but they met it in written form from the start. They therefore encountered the registers and styles of the language in a most non-native order. On the Western Romance-speaking Continent, native speakers acquired colloquial styles first, naturally, as children, and only learnt to read and write later, if at all. On the British Isles, those who learnt this language met the written registers from the start, and colloquial styles probably never, unless they crossed the Channel. The result was the acquisition of a stilted level of Latinity which at times was unrecognizable on the Continent. Conversely, Pope Gregory II's Roman vernacular was not totally comprehensible to Boniface. In particular, the Insular Latinists developed the practice of pronouncing Latin words in the way that we all do now, that is, on the basis of giving a specified sound to each already written letter (or digraph) of the standard spelling of the words. This probably explains why the Anglo-Saxons called Grammar "*staefcraeft*" ("lettercraft"). This strange and

---

[21] M. RICHTER, *The Formation of the Medieval West: Studies in the Oral Culture of the Barbarians* (Dublin, 1994).

[22] IRVINE, *The Making*, pp. 288-290. DIONISOTTI, "On Bede".

[23] IRVINE, *The Making*, p. 114.

unnatural practice led to great differences between the way they pronounced Latin, in effect reading texts aloud as if they were in phonetic script, and the pronunciations that had become normal in the native Romance-speaking world, where many spellings were learnt and taught logographically rather than phonographically. In particular, the Anglo-Saxons' near neighbours in Gaul had by then come to employ varieties of speech which had undergone many sound changes, often dropping whole syllables from the phonetic form that had originally inspired the orthographic shape of the words a millennium earlier.

By the seventh and eighth century the motives for learning to understand and compose texts in Latin in the British Isles were more likely to be religious than literary.[24] The Insular teachers, and others, felt a need to Christianize their didactic material. Vivien Law, for example, studied a variant of Donatus, used and even perhaps prepared, by Paul the Deacon in Italy, in which the text is slightly Christianized, in that the morphologically paradigmatic examples of feminine, neuter and common gender nouns have been changed to "*ecclesia*" (from "*musa*"), "*templum*" (from "*scamnum*") and "*fidelis*" (rather than "*sacerdos*", which to the pagans had indeed been a common gender noun, whereas Christian priests had to be male). Isidore, Bishop of Seville, in early seventh-century Spain, seems to have begun his academic life with a priestly distrust of pagan literature that came to be increasingly diluted as he developed his career as polymath and gradually appreciated its fascination. The Christianized Donatus tradition seems also to have been known in the British Isles.

Donatus did his best, as did his commentators, to work out what actually happened in the language of the Latin texts they admired and respected. Priscian did his best to adapt the conceptual techniques he found in his Greek sources to the study of Latin, and on the whole Priscian's analyses of Latin syntax are impressive and often convincing. Both Donatus and Priscian were essentially descriptive in motivation, trying to establish what actually happened. Unfortunately, as the centuries went by, and the grammatical details found in ancient texts and in these grammarians' analyses began to correspond to only a few of the available variants in the morphology and syntax of Romance speech, the descriptive came to be seen as prescriptive. That is, teachers assumed that what Donatus and Priscian had said was the case, was what they themselves ought to be doing, and, more significantly, that any variant which Donatus and Priscian had not mentioned was one which teachers ought not to be recommending, using or writing. By taking this extra step, they were introducing the moral dimension into grammar which has been so destructive and

---

[24] P. RICHÉ, *Education et culture dans l'occident barbare, VIe-VIIe siècles* (Paris, 1962).

still tends to dominate linguistic teaching. Thus 'correct' Latin slowly came to be uniquely defined by this combined tradition, and the books of Donatus, his commentators, and Priscian were appealed to in order to instruct even the native-speakers about what they ought now to be doing themselves, rather than merely about what others before them had, as a matter of fact, been doing when preparing texts.

Written Latin was thus already by the time of the so-called Carolingian 'Renaissance' – their own word was *"renovatio"*[25] - in danger of becoming a foreign language for its supposed native-speakers. But this dissociation was not inevitable, and with a little flexibility the old monolingualism could probably have carried on for centuries (as it has in China, and as it still is, if precariously, in the English-speaking world now).[26] The decisive catalyst in the long process can be seen at the moment when the two systems clashed, the Insular and the native Romance. More precisely, the key moment can be seen in retrospect to have been the appointment by Charlemagne of an Englishman, Alcuin of York, who had been schooled in the Bede inheritance, to reform the Carolingian education system. Several Insular grammarians were already known on the Continent, and Alcuin inherited their prestige. He first arrived in 782, but his linguistic studies seem to have extended in the 790s, when he was working at Tours on his standard Biblical text, his grammar, and the *De orthographia* which aimed to establish correctness in both speaking and writing;[27] and Alcuin, unlike his other compatriots, also studied there Priscian's *Institutiones*. Alcuin had no interest in any vernacular, not even his own. Among many other aspects of the educational reforms he inspired there seems to have been a desire to encourage all those in the church to pronounce Latin words in the stilted Anglo-Saxon way, a sound for each letter, rather than in the normal local evolved manner as the clergy had used naturally hitherto. This would have made the language seem foreign indeed. Banniard even suggests that Alcuin wanted to insist that all parishioners spoke the Anglo-Saxon way when confessing to their priests, but since it proved difficult to do, and difficult to understand if done correctly, that plan lapsed. If Banniard is right in this, it is easy to envisage the annoyance caused there by the arrival of a foreigner telling them that they did not know their own language. In 813, after Alcuin's death, the Carolingian church also decided that the formal pronunciation need not apply

[25] J.J. CONTRENI, "The Carolingian Renaissance: education and literary culture", in: *The New Cambridge Medieval History*. II. *c.700-c.900*, ed. R. MCKITTERICK (Cambridge, 1995), pp. 709-757.

[26] R. MCKITTERICK, *The Carolingians and the Written Word* (Cambridge, 1989).

[27] IRVINE, *The Making*, pp. 313-333.

to sermons, whose function lay in their very intelligibility. But in the long run, this reform took root with all the other aspects of Alcuinian *grammatica* that laid the foundations for later medieval culture. At first maybe it was normal practice only at Alcuin's home base of Tours, and centres influenced by Tours; for theirs was not in practice a centralized state, and cultural variations continued. But subsequently Alcuin's star pupil, Hrabanus Maurus, Abbot of Fulda and eventually Bishop of Mainz, who was the centre of a huge web of intellectual contacts, seems to have been a key figure in promoting the general use of the newly standardized *grammatica*, conceptually separate from Romance, within the clerical education system. In the Romance world, other centres managed to continue the new system, including Fleury, where the Visigoth Theodulf (abbot from 798 to 818) had established the Alcuinian model, Odo of Cluny had revived it (abbot from 937) and the library maintained an excellent grammatical collection throughout. When the educational world began to expand again with the 'Twelfth-Century Renaissance', the reformed non-vernacular pronunciations, at least in their essential requirement that every letter deserved to be given some sound – even if that sound was sometimes going to vary from place to place as the Romance phonetics varied – survived together with the requirements of 'correct' morphology, syntax and vocabulary usage, as an essential part of the *grammatica* that was generally taught and learnt as the basis of all education, in Romance areas as well as non-Romance. The study of *grammatica* as a wholly separate language spread then to Romance-speaking areas that were not in the Carolingian realms (in the Iberian Peninsula, Sardinia, Southern Italy, but not, it seems, Rumania), such that by the height of the 'Twelfth-Century Renaissance' Latin had come to be studied generally as a foreign language wherever the classes were. The new universities of the thirteenth century then developed the tradition to a higher intellectual level, but it had been Alcuin and his colleagues who brought the study of Latin to a sufficiently objective level for the new universities to exploit.

The establishment in this way of Medieval Latin as a conceptually separate language from everyone's vernacular meant, in addition, that it became in due course necessary to invent new written systems for non-reformed Romance. Texts in experimental Romance orthographies, in which the letter-sound correspondences of the new system were employed to represent spoken morphology, syntax, word order and vocabulary, turn up in all Romance areas as a direct consequence of the adoption of the reformed Latin system, because the educational reform meant that texts written in the old style could no longer necessarily, as before, be read aloud easily in the vernacular intelligible manner, particularly by native Germanic speakers. The metalinguistic context, consequent on the conscious categorization of the stylistic differences into two languages in the same geographical area rather than just one, changed with the advent of the two 'Renaissances', the Carolingian and the Twelfth-Century.

Renaissances often run the risk of destroying by fossilization what they claim to want to preserve, or at the least confining it to a small élite.[28] In the event the consequences of Alcuin's prejudices were largely pernicious in the Romance-speaking lands, since the Reform not only drove wedges between those who did and those who did not master the new system, it led, as a necessary consequence of their exclusively phonographic obsession, to the need to elaborate different new spelling systems in different kingdoms, which in turn abetted the growing poison of divisive nationalism within what had once been an international Romance-speaking whole. The new Romance spellings were not elaborated for the illiterate, of course, who could no more cope with the new spelling than with any other. All the earliest written Romance texts come from centres of expert Latinity. For a long time anyone literate in the new Romance written systems would have been trained first in reading (and perhaps also writing) Latin, so at first written Romance might well have been harder for many of them to operate than the traditional Latin. But once there was a sizeable group of people literate in their new local written Romance form but not in Latin – which happened in the thirteenth century – old-style written Latin forms could start to seem foreign even to the literate, and the change was for practical purposes complete.[29]

The Anglo-Saxon tradition had inspired the transformation of the study of *grammatica* from instruction in how to write the language of Early Romance speakers into a guide to the learning of a foreign language, separate from the vernacular of all, and through the ninth century scholars from the British Isles (including Ireland) still had the authority to go to the Continent and give advice on how to proceed with the linguistic reforms. But the developing continental tradition, with its input from Priscian, was becoming more sophisticated than the British one already by the time when the Scandinavian invasions of the ninth century disrupted the Insular traditions. In the following century, we find that the Continental scholars now had the authority to come to the Isles and tell aspiring scholars what to do. Abbo of Fleury, for example, went to Ramsey in

---

[28] Compare Contreni's question, "who would train the rural clergy?", in: "The Carolingian Renaissance", p, 714.

[29] J. HERMAN, *Du Latin aux langues romanes* (Tübingen, 1990). M. SELIG e.a. (ed.), *Le passage à l'écrit des langues romanes* (Tübingen, 1993).

985-987, at a time when Fleury was a renowned centre of intellectual and linguistic expertise, welcoming scholarly visitors from every direction. Abbo wrote his *Quaestiones Grammaticales* as an answer to questions posed to him by his Anglo-Saxon speaking students, and as a result the work is informative about Anglo-Saxon, as well as about differences in the Latinity of the two communities.[30] The questions answered tend to cover matters not dealt with in the Alcuinian rules, such as the positioning of stress in polysyllables. Germanic-speaking scholars on the Continent continued to be influential after the Carolingian age, however, and since they naturally saw all forms of Latin and Romance as foreign, and often learnt how to read reformed Latin without learning to speak Romance, they helped the dissociation process to continue. This seems the best explanation in context for the elaboration of a Latin-based Romance spelling in the late ninth-century *Cantilena Eulaliae* from St Amand during Hucbald's abbacy.[31] Richter, however, argued that literacy was not an important feature of Germanic society until after the twelfth century. In Moslem Spain there are many written Latin texts from the ninth century, but hardly any thereafter. It looks as though the Christians there, in view of the increasing dissimilarity between the Visigothic linguistic traditions that they inherited and the manner of their Romance speech, decided, possibly even consciously, to reserve their literacy for the Arabic they needed to know anyway in their society, despite continuing to be bilingual Arabic-Romance in speech. The Arabic-speakers usually knew Romance, but it is unlikely they studied Latin.[32]

All periodizations are, of course, administrative fantasies; but if we are searching for a means of distinguishing chronologically the Early Middle Ages from the High Middle Ages, the point at which Latin became in effect a foreign language for everybody is as distinctive a turning point as any other.

---

[30] A. GUERREAU-JALABERT (ed.), *Abbo Floriacensis: Quaestiones Grammaticales* (Paris, 1982).

[31] R. WRIGHT, *Late Latin and Early Romance in Spain and Carolingian France* (Liverpool, 1982), pp. 128-135.

[32] D.J. WASSERSTEIN, "The language situation in Al-Andalus", in: *Studies on the Muwassah and the Kharja*, ed. A. JONES and R. HITCHCOCK (Oxford, 1991), pp. 1-15. See also chapter 11 below.

Chapter 2

Why the Romance Languages
Are Not All the Same

Roman armies found themselves in the Southern and Eastern Iberian Peninsula at the end of the second Punic War, in the late third century B.C.; and after an initial period of indecision, Rome decided to stay there. The Iberian Peninsula thus saw some of the earliest occupation by the Romans outside Italy itself, but their effective pacification of the entire peninsula took another two centuries, and the effect was to prove geographically variable.[1] The south-eastern half seems to have become generally Romanized by the first century A.D., but the northern areas bordering the Bay of Biscay may never have been genuinely romanized at all (at least until the second millennium A.D.). The Western Roman Empire collapsed politically in the fifth century A.D., but most of the inhabitants remained where they were, speaking the Latin of the time, as did the Visigoths who eventually filled the political vacuum until the arrival of the Moslems in the early eighth century. At that time, and probably later, the Romance-speaking areas of the former Western Empire can be seen as still forming a single wide speech-community, although naturally there was a great deal of internal variability of a stylistic, geograph-

This chapter is a reprint with minor changes of: "Latin in Spain: early Ibero-Romance", in: *The Origins and Development of Emigrant Languages*, ed. H.F. NIELSEN and L. SCHØSLER (Odense, 1996), pp. 277-298. We are grateful to Professors Hans Frede Jensen and Lene Schøsler, on behalf of NOWELE (North-West European Language Evolution) and Odense University Press, for permitting this reprint.

[1] A. GARCÍA Y BELLIDO, "La latinización de España", *Archivo Español de Arqueología* 40 (1967), pp. 3-29.

ical and sociolinguistic nature. Their language was still thought of as being Latin, and within the Peninsula, throughout both Moslem and Christian Spain, it continued to be seen as a monolingual, though complex, unit until the twelfth century. Eventually, however, separate political units patronized different standardizations of detail out of the wide general variability, which is how Romance came to be written in different ways in different places.

Possible external causes for the geographical divergence of linguistic features have often been sought, but only a few stand up to serious scrutiny. In the present case, the first of these concerns the effect of the Pre-Roman languages spoken in the Peninsula. The Peninsula seems to have contained at least twenty-five different nameable groups at the time of the conquest, with a complex ethnic mix that had already developed over many centuries. The Iberian Peninsula might seem a natural cultural unit, but it contained great diversity then (as Europe does now, to the probable surprise of historians millennia into the future). Roman writers naturally saw pre-Roman inhabitants as essentially uncivilized and barbarous, and this unbalanced perspective has had unfortunate consequences, in that many modern historians still refer to them as "tribes" or even "barbarians". This evaluation is unjustified; we must not confuse shortage of evidence with absence of civilization. Robert Knapp calls the groups "states", indeed,[2] often independent from each other as much as from the Romans, who for a long while were just one large factor in a multifactored political and military stew that had long included other pre-Roman Mediterranean contacts as well. Many different languages were spoken there, for the Peninsula contained groups whose ancestors can be traced back to Celtic travellers from Northern Europe, Phoenician colonists from the Middle East, Carthaginians from Africa (themselves ultimately of partly Phoenician origin), Greeks, and descendants of pre-Indo-European peoples whose ultimate origins are now largely untraceable, many of whom are lumped together under the label "Iberians". The Iberians had already been drawn into the Mediterranean cultural world. We know more now about the Iberians and their interaction with the Phoenicians than we used to, as Richard Harrison's book makes clear.[3]

There may have been Celtic influence on the development of Latin in Spain, but it was more evident in other areas, most noticeably Gaul. Even if Celtic-Latin bilinguals can be blamed for the intervocalic voicing of plosive consonants in Western Romance, as has been suggested but can hardly be proved, no particularly Hispanic feature can be attributed to them. There were,

---

[2] R.C. KNAPP, *Aspects of the Roman Experience in Iberia, 206-100 B.C.* (Alava, 1977).
[3] R.J. HARRISON, *Spain at the Dawn of History* (London, 1988).

in any event, different Celtic languages in Spain.[4] A similar geographical inde-terminacy would apply to any postulated influence of Phoenician. Any feature of Latin that could be attributed to Phoenicians or Carthaginians is unlikely to have locally Hispanic inspiration or consequences.

Iberian may have had some influence on Hispanic Latin, but if so it was almost certainly merely lexical. This field is a controversial one, however, for Iberian was a written language (or more than one), and Iberian 'texts' – that is, coins, plaques, inscriptions, labels, inscribed silverware and pottery, tablets – from a period of some eight centuries, and ranging from Provence to the Algar-ve, have been found in seven separate alphabets, including the Greek and Ro-man.[5] Thanks to careful and rational research by Gómez Moreno, since refined by several others,[6] these data can be mostly read, in the sense that we can make a good guess at the phonetics represented in the symbols, but they still cannot be understood. The Iberian coins only date from after the Roman invasion, and seem to attest Iberian-Roman collaboration, in frontier areas, rather than inde-pendence and antagonism. Iberian writing dies out during the first century A.D.. So does written Phoenician, which is in fact the language of the oldest surviv-ing written evidence from the Peninsula, and which Koch has shown to be still of considerable importance even in the first century A.D..[7] The Iberian areas were among the first to be Romanized, and thus, probably, to lose their own languages. The most impressive testimony to written Iberian is on the famous lead tablet from Alcoy, near modern Alicante, which has been interpreted imaginatively as a list of very local placenames with transparently motivated morphology. Román del Cerro thereby claimed to have added semantics to the already known phonetic equivalents of the signs.[8] Even though he speculatively offered new Iberian etyma for the Latin words "*campus*", "*custos*" and "*basi-um*", plus Spanish "*hueco*" and "*salpicar*",[9] the field of toponymy, plus per-

---

[4] A. TOVAR, "La inscripción del Cabeço das Fráguas y la lengua de los lusitanos", in: *Actas del III Coloquio sobre lenguas y culturas paleohispánicas*, ed. J. DE HOZ (Salamanca, 1985), pp. 227-253.

[5] J.M. ANDERSON, *Ancient Languages of the Hispanic Peninsula* (Lanham, 1988), p. 26. IDEM, "Structural elements of Ancient Iberian", *Hispanic Linguistics* 2 (1989), pp. 179-190.

[6] M. GÓMEZ MORENO, "La escritura ibérica", *Boletín de la Real Academia de la Historia* 112 (1943), pp. 257-281. ANDERSON, *Ancient Languages*, chapter 2.

[7] M. KOCH, "Observaciones sobre la permanencia del sustrato púnico en la Península Ibérica", in: *Actas del I Coloquio sobre lenguas y culturas prerromanas de la Península Ibérica*, ed. F. JORDA e.a. (Salamanca, 1976), pp. 191-199.

[8] J.L. ROMÁN DEL CERRO, *El desciframiento de la lengua ibérica en "La Ofrenda de los Pueblos"* (Alicante, 1990).

[9] ROMÁN, *El desciframiento*, p. 29, p. 103, p. 109, p. 172 and p. 119.

haps anthroponymy, still provides the only established Iberian source for modern Spanish lexis.

Unfortunately, Román invited scholarly derision by a subsequent attempt to ally his deciphered Iberian with modern Basque.[10] Scholars thought that this practice – what Harrison calls "this burlesque" – had been long since debunked.[11] A look at any map of the pre-Roman peninsula shows that the Vascones were not in the Iberian area, three hundred miles and many other groups away from Alcoy.[12] The great Luis Michelena spent a lifetime studying all the available evidence, and sadly concluded that Basque and Iberian were not closely related, despite a few likely lexical borrowings and shared personal names;[13] less close than, say, Danish and English. Only those who do not know Basque – as Román unfortunately does not – have been tempted to believe otherwise. A similar attempt, to revive the ancient hypothesis of a link between Basque and some or all of the forty Caucasian languages, is meeting similar and equally deserved derision from the poor Basque specialists, who have more to do with their time than defend their subject from such ill-informed fantasies.[14]

I would also suggest, more controversially perhaps, that the same scepticism should be applied to the postulated effect of Basque on the development of Hispanic Latin. This has often been proposed, but the more that modern scholars know about Basque, the less such influence they can see. The fact that Basque survived, and no other peninsular pre-Roman language seems to have outlasted the Empire – although a survival of Celtic in the North-West cannot be ruled out – is certainly interesting. It suggests that the ancient Basque-speakers were not overwhelmingly romanized. The Romans did not themselves see the Basques as particularly hostile or uncooperative. Augustus's famous attacks were on the Gallaeci, Astures and Cantabri, many miles further to the West. As Michelena and Collins have pointed out,[15] the Basques were more

---

[10] J.L. ROMÁN DEL CERRO, *El origen ibérico de la lengua vasca* (Alicante, 1993).

[11] HARRISON, *Spain*, p. 141. A. TOVAR, "Discurso inaugural", in: *Actas del I Coloquio sobre lenguas y culturas prerromanas de la Península Ibérica*, ed. F. JORDA e.a. (Salamanca, 1976), pp. 11-24.

[12] For instance: KNAPP, *Aspects*, p. 222. L.A. CURCHIN, *Roman Spain: Conquest and Assimilation* (London, 1991), p. 220.

[13] L. MICHELENA, "La langue ibère", in: *Actas del II Coloquio sobre lenguas y culturas prerromanas de la Península Ibérica*, ed. A. TOVAR e.a. (Salamanca, 1979), pp. 23-39; reprinted in: IDEM, *Lengua e Historia* (Madrid, 1985), pp. 341-356. IDEM, "Sobre la posición lingüística del ibérico", in: IDEM, *Lengua e Historia*, pp. 334-340.

[14] R.L. TRASK, *The History of Basque* (London, 1997), pp. 404-408.

[15] L. MICHELENA, *Sobre historia de la lengua vasca* (San Sebastián, 1988). R. COLLINS, *The*

antagonistic to the later Franks and Visigoths than they were to the Romans. The Romans seem in effect to have ignored the Basques, as most modern historians of Roman Spain also do, which suggests that in practice the Basques survived by being seen as essentially insignificant. Being to some extent unromanized, unassimilated and ignored, therefore, we could conclude that their language was less likely than many of the others in the Peninsula to have affected the Latin of the Iberian Peninsula during the Empire, except, of course, in the mouths of bilinguals in their own small area.

Yet Basque did survive, and becomes significant to our theme almost by accident. The language we now call Spanish is in fact the modern form of the indigenous Romance speech of the area of Old Castile, in the central Northern part of the Peninsula, and in North-Eastern Old Castile in the crucial period of the early and central Middle Ages there do seem to have been a significant number of bilingual Basques. That is, although we cannot seriously ascribe general features of Hispanic Romance to the Basques, any more than we can ascribe features of American English to Mohawk, such an explanation for a few specifically Old Castilian features might in principle have more initial plausibility. Yet for the very same reason, the Basque influence need not be old. Lexical borrowings from Basque to Castilian Romance could as well have been made in the fourteenth century as in the first.[16] Even in the vocabulary, though, such hypotheses are slowly losing their appeal, for fewer general Spanish words are now attributed by etymologists to Basque than used to be the case. The revised edition of Corominas and Pascual's etymological dictionary, for example, effectively discounts a Basque origin for Spanish "*zorra*" ("fox"), a word that still tends to turn up on lists of Spanish words borrowed from Basque even though the Basque word for "fox" is actually of Roman origin.[17] Local Romance borrowings from Basque are plentiful, of course, as the Linguistic Atlas of the region shows.[18]

Unfortunately, in the late 1970s and 1980s, Basque influence was often invoked to explain particular features of Spanish grammar, although again this was only done on any scale by those who were not specialists in Basque. Ángel

Basques (second edition; Oxford, 1990).

[16] Compare: R. WRIGHT, "Semicultismo", *Archivum Linguisticum* 7 (1976), pp. 13-28, concerning the word "*sapo*" ("toad").

[17] J. COROMINAS and J.A. PASCUAL, *Diccionario Crítico Etimológico Castellano e Hispánico*, 6 volumes (Madrid, 1980-1991), VI (1991), pp. 113-116, p. 114. R. PENNY, *A History of the Spanish Language* (Cambridge, 1991), p. 258.

[18] See: R.M. CASTAÑER, *Estudio del léxico de la casa en Aragón, Navarra y Rioja* (Zaragoza, 1990).

López García, for example, wrote an article claiming fourteen points of important influence of Basque grammar on Castilian grammar.[19] If this were true, it
would be extremely significant. Larry Trask, a renowned specialist in Basque
syntax, then pointed out that all fourteen of those suggested influences were
either non-existent or highly debatable.[20] For example, it is a striking aspect of
the development of Castilian that it has been and still is undergoing a process
of blurring the surface distinctions between direct and indirect object, but,
contrary to López García's claim of Basque causation for this development,
Basque is in fact a prime example of a language that keeps direct and indirect
objects clearly distinct. López García had, however, just written a best-selling
paperback claiming that Castilian was not so much in origin the Romance
speech of Castille as Basque grammar given Romance vocabulary, used originally as a Northern Peninsular *koine* way beyond the borders of Castille,[21] and
he wrote an immediate reply.[22] But it is possible that Trask has helped dampen
the enthusiasm for such direct equations of Old Castilian and Basque syntax.
María Teresa Echenique's book on the topic is in comparison admirably
calm,[23] largely downplaying the role of Basque in the distinctive development
of Castilian, even in the modern Basque country itself. She has pointed out, for
example,[24] that the Castilian now spoken in the Basque areas tends noticeably
to omit pleonastic clitic pronouns found elsewhere, but that Basque cannot
itself be the cause of this peculiarity because Basque uses such pronouns regularly (which are pleonastic in the sense of their function being already marked
in the verb). Professor Echenique's work is an admirable corrective to the
former hysteria. She is a Basque-speaker, a former pupil of both Lapesa and
Michelena, and the main investigator still studying the effect of Basque on
Romance. The reverse effect, of Romance influence on the development of
Basque (particularly in recent times), may be marginally more plausible, but
even so, the immediate reaction of anyone who knows both languages is to
exclaim how very different the grammars are.

[19] A. LÓPEZ GARCÍA, "Algunas concordancias gramaticales entre el castellano y el euskera",
in: *Philologica Hispaniensia in Honorem M. Alvar*, II (Madrid, 1985), pp. 391-405.

[20] R.L. TRASK and R. WRIGHT, "El 'vascorrománico'", *Verba* 15 (1988), pp. 361-373.
TRASK, *The History*, pp. 415-429.

[21] A. LÓPEZ GARCÍA, *El rumor de los desarraigados: conflicto de lenguas en la Península
Ibérica* (Barcelona, 1985).

[22] A. LÓPEZ GARCÍA, "Respuestas a algunas preguntas no formuladas a propósito del
'vascorrománico'". *Verba* 15 (1988), pp. 375-383.

[23] M.T. ECHENIQUE ELIZANDO, *Historia Lingüística Vasco-Románica* (second edition;
Madrid, 1987).

[24] ECHENIQUE, *Historia*, p. 87.

As regards phonetics, it used to be claimed that Basque had caused the Castilian development of initial [f-] to [h-] in words such as Latin *"facere"*, in which the initial consonant aspirated: Old Castilian *"fazer"* was pronounced [hadzér]; and subsequently became lost, to leave modern *"hacer"*, pronounced [aθér]. The arguments against the proposed Basque causation of this development have been expressed convincingly by Izzo, less clearly by Torreblanca, and magisterially by Trask, and probably no specialist seriously maintains that theory any more.[25] A hypothesis of a more indirect nature, however, remains respectable, as in the authoritative overview of the question presented by Paul Lloyd.[26] For it is possible that Latin had variable realizations of the /f/ phoneme, some of them sounding more aspirated (less completely occluded) than others, probably including the [ɸ] still found in some Northern Peninsular areas, and that the Basques preferred to use the existing more aspirated variants in their own Latin speech. The same kind of preference in a variable situation has been invoked, *mutatis mutandis*, for the later development of the medieval Castilian sibilants to a system not unlike that of Basque;[27] it is generally accepted within sociolinguistics that bilingualism can influence the choice made between existing variants.[28] All such theories are at least preferable to that proposed by Salvador to the effect that this change ([f] > [h]) was due to the absence of fluoride in the water of the Basque provinces, which caused all their teeth to fall out, so that they could not pronounce labiodentals at all.[29] Since modern Basques can indeed pronounce initial [f-], and almost all areas of the Peninsula have negligible amounts of fluoride in the water, this theory is no less unconvincing than Salvador's more recent theory that people in Spain could hardly talk at all between the sixth and the tenth centuries.[30] The subsequent career of initial [f-] and [h-] in Castilian has been excellently traced by

[25] H. IZZO, "Pre-latin languages and sound-change in Romance: the case of Old Spanish /h/", in: *Studies in Romance Linguistics*, ed. M.P. HAGIWARA (Rowley, 1977), pp. 227-253. M. TORREBLANCA, "La 'f' prerromana y la vasca en su relación con el español antiguo", *Romance Philology* 37 (1984), pp. 273-281. TRASK, *The History*, pp. 424-428.

[26] P.M. LLOYD, *From Latin to Spanish*, I (Philadelphia, 1987), pp. 218-223.

[27] LLOYD, *From Latin*, I, pp. 267-273.

[28] For instance: C. SILVA CORVALÁN, *Language Contact and Change: Spanish in Los Angeles* (Oxford, 1994).

[29] G. SALVADOR, "Hipótesis geológica sobre la evolución F- > h-", in: *Introducción Plural a la Gramática Histórica*, ed. F. MARCOS MARÍN (Madrid, 1982), pp. 11-21.

[30] G. SALVADOR, "Lexemática histórica", in: *Actas del I Congreso Internacional de Historia de la Lengua Española*, ed. M. ARIZA e.a. (Madrid, 1988), pp. 635-646. R. WRIGHT, "Versatility and vagueness in Early Medieval Spain", in: *Hispanic Linguistic Studies in Honour of F.W. Hodcroft*, ed. D. MACKENZIE and I. MICHAEL (Oxford, 1993), pp. 207-223.

Penny, and their word-internal development by Pensado.[31] From all this we conclude that the distinctiveness of Hispanic Romance cannot be attributed to Basque.

Another theory which is advanced from time to time, to explain some of the distinctively Hispanic developments of Latin, is based on the non-Roman provenance of a majority of the original soldiers and settlers. It is undoubtedly true that by the time of the Roman expansion into the Peninsula their civilization was already ancient, and their language variable. Related Italic languages, particularly Oscan and Umbrian, were still spoken, and although Oscan and Umbrian themselves may hardly ever have been spoken in the Peninsula, any peculiarities of Oscan Latin or Umbrian Latin would have. Menéndez Pidal proposed an important influence here, making particular reference to the town of Huesca, Latin "*osca*", in Aragón. This theory had already by then been largely undermined by Rohlfs, but even so, Lapesa's cautious discussion leaves this possibility open.[32] Elerick's attempt to revive it was unhelpful,[33] partly because some of the features he adduces are neither particularly Hispanic nor early, partly because most of the features adduced in his study do not in fact survive in the Italian dialects of the original Oscan-speaking areas, and partly because his main evidence comes from the list called the *Appendix Probi*, which he apparently believed to be from the south of Italy in the third century A.D., but which has been known since 1963 to be from further north in the seventh century A.D..[34] Osca was in any event not a new foundation but already an "important native town in its own right".[35] In short, postulating a connection between Huesca and Oscan Latin seems as tenuous as arguing that the English

---

[31] R. PENNY, "Labiodental /f/, aspiration and /h/-dropping in Spanish: the evolving phonemic value of the graphs *f* and *h*", in: *Cultures in Contact in Medieval Spain: Historical and Literary Essays presented to L.P. Harvey*, ed. D. HOOK and B. TAYLOR (London, 1990), pp. 157-182. C. PENSADO, "Sobre el contexto del cambio F > *h* en castellano", *Romance Philology* 47 (1993), pp. 147-176.

[32] R. MENÉNDEZ PIDAL, "Colonización suritálica de España según testimonios toponímicos e inscripcionales", in: *Enciclopedia Lingüística Hispánica* I, ed. M. ALVAR e.a. (Madrid, 1960), pp. 49-68. G. ROHLFS, "Oskische Latinität in Spanien?", *Revue de Linguistique Romane* 19 (1955), pp. 221-225. R. LAPESA, *Historia de la Lengua Española* (eighth edition; Madrid, 1980), pp. 101-103.

[33] C. ELERICK, "Italic bilingualism and the history of Spanish", in: *Spanish and Portuguese in Social Context*, ed. J. BERGEN and G.D. BILLS (Georgetown, 1983), pp. 1-11.

[34] C.A. ROBSON, "L'*Appendix Probi* et la philologie latine", *Le Moyen Age* 69 (1963), pp. 39-54.

[35] KNAPP, *Aspects*, pp. 147-148.

spoken in the Australian state of New South Wales is based on that of Southern Welsh English in Britain (or basing the speech of New York on that of York).

Historically, a more promising candidate for such non-Roman Italic causalities seems to be the city of Italica, near Sevilla, which was founded specifically to house non-Roman Italians. But here too the women were largely from the Peninsula and the settlers' descendants were thus of mixed descent, and in any event, even if non-Roman Romance traits came to exist there, that area has seen such vastly shifting subsequent populations that we cannot expect such traits to remain visible.

The crude Oscan explanation for Hispanic features cannot stand, but a related theory could, that of a possible 'interdialect'. Peter Trudgill has studied what happens when different but mutually comprehensible forms of the same language come into prolonged contact with each other, as in armies whose troops are recruited from a variety of regions, or in colonial settlements.[36] Within two generations, as a result of speakers' natural desires to accommodate to their listeners by reducing dissimilarities along their shared continuum, a recognizably different local emigrant dialect emerges as a kind of highest common factor of the contributory dialects, involving simplification of irregular paradigms in morphology and phonology, choosing unmarked variants rather than marked, concentrating on shared items of vocabulary, preferring transparent affixation and compounding to synthetic opaque lexical items, removing complexities of limited functional load, and coming up eventually with a local speech that not only has a distinctive nature from all of the contributory dialects but is also easier to learn. Thus the first generation community has a complex dialect mixture, but their children share eventually a new more coherent and unified dialect, focussed and identifiable if necessary. Trudgill deduces this as a generalization mainly from detailed study of the English spoken in the southern hemisphere. Penny has applied it illuminatingly to the history of Castilian Spanish, where population movements from many sources into the successively established Castilian capital cities of Burgos (in the 880s), Toledo (after 1085), Sevilla (after 1248) and Madrid (after 1561) could help explain why the history of Castilian is indeed one largely of progressive simplification (except, perhaps, in the lexicon).[37] This combination of levelling and simplification is close to what has been called 'koineization' with reference to Latin America, where the Spanish is not, as is often thought, exactly the same as that of Andalucía, but a kind of highest common factor of Euro-

---

[36] P. Trudgill, *Dialects in Contact* (Oxford, 1986).
[37] R. Penny, *Patterns of Language Change in Spain* (London, 1987).

pean Spanish dialects.[38] Following this train of thought, then, it is possible to suggest that in the first two centuries B.C. Oscan Latin, Umbrian Latin, Faliscan Latin, the Latin spoken by Greeks, or any other kind of Latin could have all been contributors to the primordial Latin mix in the Iberian Peninsula, from which distinctive features of Romance could eventually emerge.

Overall, this theory is attractive. It helps explain why Romance in general is simpler than Latin. It implies that the areas from which the emigrants left will now have more complicated speech than the areas they moved into, which is on the whole true for the relative complexity of Italian dialects compared to those in the Iberian Peninsula, and the relative complexity of Northern Spanish dialects compared with those of the south, largely formed from a mixture of speeches of emigrants from the north; and indeed, the dialects of Britain compared with those of the former British colonies. This interdialect theory is certainly preferable to the idea that Romance emerged as the result of creolization, as if the non-Roman inhabitants of the Empire had had at one point to operate with pidgins, and were never able to operate satisfactorily in the Latin spoken by everyone in Italy. The most recent exposition of this depressingly patronizing theory (by De Dardel and Wüest) even suggests that the inhabitants of Rome itself were in effect not native speakers of Latin, and incapable of using noun morphology in speech.[39]

One limitation of the interdialect hypothesis, however, is that it can offer little explanation for the features that eventually differentiate the Romance speech of one emigrant area from that of another, because interdialects, as Trudgill shows, are liable to be much the same wherever they are. But this aspect of the theory is, in the event, one of its advantages when applied to the time of the Roman Empire itself, because scholars have been increasingly coming to the view that the spoken Latin of the final period of the Western

---

[38] H. IZZO, "Andalusia and America: the regional origins of New World Spanish", in: *Studies in Romance Linguistics*, ed. E. PULGRAM (Michigan, 1984), pp. 109-131. M.B. FONTANELLA DE WEINBERG, *El español de América* (Madrid, 1992). J. LIPSKI, *Latin American Spanish* (London, 1994). J. LÜDTKE (ed.), *El español de América en el siglo XVI* (Frankfurt, 1994).

[39] B. SCHLIEBEN-LANGE, "L'Origine des langues romanes: un cas de créolisation", in: *Langues en contact, Pidgins - Creoles*, ed. J.M. MEISEL (Tübingen, 1977), pp. 81-101. J. WÜEST, "Latin vulgaire et créolisation", in: *Actes du XXe Congrès International de Linguistique et Philologie Romanes*, II (Tübingen, 1993), pp. 656-661. R. DE DARDEL and J. WÜEST, "Les systèmes casuels du protorroman: les deux cycles de simplification", *Vox Romanica* 52 (1993), pp. 25-65. The theory has also been discredited with regard to American Spanish: E. MARTINELL GIFRE, "Formación de una lengua hispánica en América", in: *Actas del Primer Congreso Anglo-Hispano. I. Lingüística*, ed. R. PENNY (Madrid, 1993), pp. 3-24.

Roman Empire was probably more geographically homogeneous than it had been four centuries earlier. That is, that the Empire, overall and on average, was a time of linguistic convergence rather than divergence. This is not to imply that there was a lack of evolution – evolution, particularly phonetic evolution, had come a long way by the fifth century A.D. – but that there was a lack of significant divergence, in that the main lines of development were essentially empire-wide. Herman's work on the epigraphic evidence in particular shows that trends may have started in one area, but then tended to spread more widely.[40] As Herman and Varvaro have pointed out, the geographical trends that can be traced for the imperial period in this evidence are not, as a result, the direct ancestors of the trends found in the differentiation of the Romance languages at a later stage.[41] For example, the geographical distribution of inscriptions lacking word-final -*s* is unrelated to the distribution of the Romance languages that eventually dropped final [-s] (and despite the useful evidence of some of Gaeng's studies this perspective seems to be largely right).[42] This discovery seems to imply that the interdialect formed in the extra-Italian areas of the Empire came to be a general Empire-wide Early Romance, a single language despite normal internal variability, which in due course was even influencing Italy itself, much in the same way as Mexican and Argentinian Spanish are currently influencing the Spanish of Spain, and Australian and American English are currently affecting Britain; through sheer demography, rather than necessarily any linguistic or cultural superiority.

Clearly, by the time that the Western Roman Empire crumbled (in the fifth century), there was wide linguistic variation, geographical as well as sociolinguistic; but it was seen as language-internal, and confined to distributional statistics, which is part of the reason why it is usually impossible to locate texts of the time on linguistic features alone. Under this scenario, any initial influence of Iberian, or of Basque, or of non-Roman settlers in the Iberian Peninsula, diminishes with time, and is unlikely to be still applicable at the much later period of Romance differentiation. This gradual lessening of the effects of external influence is not at all surprising; Arabic influence is less in Spanish now than it was in 1250, for example.

---

[40] J. HERMAN, *Du latin aux langues romanes* (Tübingen, 1990).

[41] HERMAN, *Du latin*. A. VARVARO, "Latin and Romance: fragmentation or restructuring?", in: R. WRIGHT (ed.), *Latin and the Romance Languages in the Early Middle Ages* (London, 1991; reprint, Penn State, 1996), pp. 44-51.

[42] For instance: P.A. GAENG, "La morphologie nominale des inscriptions chrétiennes de l'Afrique", in: *Latin vulgaire – latin tardif*, III, ed. M. ILIESCU and W. MARXGUT (Tübingen, 1992), pp. 115-132.

Differentiation to any important extent between the emigrant Romance languages must have occurred much later than the fifth century and for different reasons. The Twentieth International Conference of Romance Linguistics and Philology, held at Zürich in April 1992, had a special section and a Round Table devoted to the *"Fragmentation linguistique de la Romania"*. Herman and Wüest's *"Présentation de la Section"* in the Acts, and Herman's conclusion, both show that not many contributors to the section were really interested in the conceptual or metalinguistic aspects of the fragmentation,[43] but Herman's own remarks demonstrate that he is still the master in the field, and those collected papers of the section are probably still the best place to find recent scholarly approaches to the topic.[44] Historical and textual evidence of several kinds suggests that the Romance of the Iberian Peninsula forms part of a geographically wider unit which we can call 'Early Romance', quite possibly into the second millennium A.D. There is no academic difficulty in accepting this, but there is a practical problem, in that this approach clashes totally with that of the Romance Reconstruction tradition,[45] which reconstructs diagnostic divergences between Romance languages as already existing during the Roman Empire itself, envisaging, for example, Proto-Ibero-Romance and Proto-Gallo-Romance as being identifiably separate entities on their tree diagrams for about a thousand years earlier than seems reasonable or necessary. This comment is not designed to cast scepticism on the usefulness of reconstruction techniques in general as applied to pre-literate communities, merely on the way they have been applied to Early Romance communities that remained in contact with each other and remained literate throughout, with extensive textual data that the reconstructionists intentionally ignore.

Ralph Penny aims to demolish the concept of Romance tree-diagrams altogether.[46] One of Penny's main arguments is that the tree image lays far too much stress on the distinctive features of the so-called standard languages, and in real life there is still even now essentially a spoken continuum in the Romance world, unless the groups concerned had actually lost touch with each other – as might well have applied to speakers of Old Rumanian – or undergone mass migrations – as in the southern half of the Iberian Peninsula after the

---

[43] J. HERMAN and J. WÜEST (ed.), "La fragmentation linguistique de la Romania", in: *Actes du XXe Congrès International de Linguistique et Philologie Romanes*, II (Tübingen, 1993), pp. 335-698, pp. 335-344 and pp. 694-698.

[44] Also: R. WRIGHT, *Early Ibero-Romance* (Newark, 1995).

[45] As in: R.A. HALL Jr, *Proto-Romance Phonology* (New York, 1976).

[46] R. PENNY, "El árbol genealógico: ¿modelo lingüístico desfasado?", in: *Actas del III Congreso Internacional de Historia de la Lengua Española* (Madrid, 1996), pp. 827-839.

Reconquest. The chronological consequences of this view are that the effective differentiation of the Romance languages from each other occurs only as late as the twelfth and thirteenth centuries A.D., when the standard languages were being constructed in different ways in different places. By this time, any useful distinction between Italy, as the point of origin, and elsewhere, as being emigrant communities, is no longer of great significance, even though Italy is indeed rather a special case for other reasons.

We cannot blame any Hispanic distinctiveness on the Germanic once spoken by the Visigoths, who ruled most of the Peninsula for most of the time between the Romans and the Moslems, because they already spoke Latin at the time they arrived. Visigothic Spain in the seventh century was in fact the area of Western Europe with the most impressive Latin culture, and has even been described as the area with the "best Latin", on the evidence of the skilful language of many of the surviving texts,[47] although that is now generally interpreted as being merely a consequence of their having had a better education system than elsewhere. A few distinctive features of Northern French can probably be attributed to the Franks, who were indeed 'barbarians' compared with the Visigoths; the long survival in France of distinctive nominative and accusative morphology, for example. There is not even a resulting lexical distinctiveness in the Peninsula, for the few Germanic words in Spanish tend to be pan-Romance anyway, probably dating back to Imperial times. The place taken in French vocabulary by Germanic, and in Rumanian vocabulary by Slavonic, is taken in Spanish vocabulary by Arabic, although about half of the roughly four thousand words of Arabic etymology found in medieval Spanish texts do not seem to have become rooted enough to last, and many may just have been nonce-borrowings, locally or authorially stylized. Arabic influence on phonetics and syntax in the Peninsula is negligible, except probably on the Romance spoken by the many bilinguals in Moslem Spain, and in several of the many thirteenth-century written translations from Arabic into Castilian (at a time when written Castilian syntax was still quite fluid and largely unstandardized).

The differentiation scenario that seems most plausible is one of a wide monolingual Romance-speaking community, which during the second half of the first millennium A.D. acquires more and more internal variation. Phonetic evolution affects all speakers and produces recognizable local accents, but probably did not yet lead to serious mutual incomprehension among speakers from different areas. Morphological and syntactic developments occurred, and

[47] A.J. CARNOY, *Le Latin d'Espagne d'après les inscriptions: étude linguistique* (Brussels, 1906).

evolved forms turned up in the speech of all, but in general the old morphological forms remained intelligible when heard in texts read aloud, as most were, and, as Green pointed out, these forms took a long time to die out altogether.[48] For Michel Banniard has established that, at least until the late eighth century, normal written texts were generally expected to be intelligible to all when read aloud, whether the listeners were literate or not.[49] This perspective implies that there did not after all then exist the '*apartheid*' between literate and illiterate that some historians envisage even now. McKitterick, in fact, argues for textual comprehensibility in France well into the tenth century.[50]

This phenomenon is not at all incompatible with the postulation of reconstructable morphosyntactic evolutions. In morphology and syntax, as the reconstruction tradition seems not to have appreciated, the advent of new features does not in itself lead to the immediate loss of the older features that the new ones in retrospect might seem to have neatly replaced. We can envisage a long period of flexibility and versatility in which differences between the available variants, old or new, could be exploited by speakers for pragmatic and even semantic contrasts: variation, for example, between the absence and presence of a definite or indefinite article, between the use of naked nominal morphology and the presence of clarifying prepositions, between the old analytic and the new synthesising futures, between accusative plus infinitive and *quod* clauses, et cetera. If we can liberate ourselves from the mirages of the periodizable existence of entire linguistic systems, we can draw the simple conclusion that much of what we now call Romance phonetics had ousted earlier features long before the earlier Latin morphosyntactic features disappeared. In sum, that different linguistic levels evolve in different ways and at different rhythms, with syntactic change being the slowest of all (as also argued for later Castilian by Ridruejo).[51] There was not a single unitary change of whole systematic languages. The vocabulary was probably increasing

---

[48] J.N. GREEN, "The collapse and replacement of verbal inflection in Late Latin / Early Romance: How would one know?", in: WRIGHT, (ed.), *Latin and the Romance languages*, pp. 83-99.

[49] M. BANNIARD, *Viva Voce: communication écrite et communication orale du IVe au IXe siècle en Occident latin* (Paris, 1992). IDEM, "Latin tardif et français prélittéraire: observations de méthode et de chronologie", *Bulletin de la Société de Linguistique de Paris* 88 (1993), pp. 139-162. And see chapter 4 below.

[50] R. MCKITTERICK, "Latin and Romance: an historian's perspective", in: WRIGHT (ed.), *Latin and the Romance Languages*, pp. 130-145.

[51] See: A. LÓPEZ GARCÍA, *Cómo surgió el español* (Madrid, 2000). E. RIDRUEJO, "¿Un reajuste sintáctico en el español de los siglos XV y XVI?", in: *Actas del Primer Congreso Anglo-Hispano. I. Lingüística*, ed. R. PENNY (Madrid, 1993), 49-60.

through this period, not only with borrowings but through affixation and compounding.[52] On the other hand, words take a long time to die out of vocabulary, particularly since they often remain largely intelligible in texts even if hardly surviving in speech, and that very intelligibility implies that they still have a genuine place in the language. Modern worldwide English is in a state broadly similar to that of early medieval Romance, in that it is a flexible and varied monolingual unit, growing all the time, with a generally shared wide passive lexical and syntactic comprehension competence; what Banniard, for Early Romance, calls "*polymorphisme*", Wüest describes as "*anarchique*", and Kiss as a "*koine*".[53]

This Early Romance flexibility and versatility had its advantages, but by the ninth century or so the speech community was becoming ripe for the next step. For eventually these larger units become naturally unwieldy, and speakers start unconsciously to specialize in some of the variants and discard others. Different cultural areas are then likely to see their speakers making different choices from out of the same wide gamut of available possibilities. Thus the different available ways of indicating determinacy via a so-called 'definite' article, with "*ille*" or "*ipse*", or of indicating possession, et cetera,[54] probably existed to some extent in every part of the Early Romance world in the eighth century, but in due course speakers in different places chose differently when they came to decide which variants they preferred to keep; as when some Catalan areas chose "*ipse*" for definite article use, and almost all other areas did not. Such decisions were often likely to be based on existing statistical regularities, of course, so the fact that some areas were going to keep "*illorum*" for third person plural possessive use (as eventually in French "*leur*", Italian "*loro*") while others preferred "*suus*" (as in Castilian "*su*"), may conceivably be visible in distributional statistics concerning the forms at an earlier time. But the textual existence of the other form, the one that was not due to become standardized in the area of that text, is not usually to be taken as evidence of early influence or borrowing between one dialect and another, but instead as a

---

[52] For instance: H. MEIER, *Notas Críticas al DECH de Corominas/Pascual* (Santiago de Compostela, 1984). Y. MALKIEL, "The Spanish nominal augments reconsidered", *Romance Philology* 43 (1989), pp. 90-112.

[53] BANNIARD, "Latin tardif". WÜEST, "Latin vulgaire". S. KISS, "'Solutions parallèles' dans l'histoire des langues romanes et interprétation des textes tardifs", in: HERMAN and WÜEST (ed.), "La fragmentation", pp. 651-655.

[54] M. SELIG, *Die Entwicklung der Nominaldeterminanten im Spätlatein* (Tübingen, 1992). C. LYONS, "On the origin of the Old French strong-weak possessive distinction", *Transactions of the Philological Society* (1986), pp. 1-41.

symptom of native internal variation. Indeed, the whole concept of 'borrowing' within a continuum is inappropriate, for this reason. A further implication is that we should not use linguistic features to locate texts definitely until after the period of standardization in the thirteenth century.

There is nothing at all adventurous in this view. According to Jean Aitchison,[55] this scenario represents the normal case. At one stage "multiple options arise in a language". At a later stage "these options are whittled down, due to psycholinguistic, typological, intralingual and social factors", and some option becomes dominant. This chronological sequence fits the Romance case, although we need to be sceptical of typology even as a classificatory device, let alone as a causal factor, and we can prefer to see the reasons for the 'whittling down' as being (from a linguistic viewpoint) to a large extent accidental. This remains the most likely explanation, even if they may with hindsight be explicable on semantic criteria.[56] In fact, if there were anything serious to be said for typological explanations of linguistic change, the divergence of cognate languages should not happen at all. As it is, it happens everywhere. Neither French "*leur*" nor Castilian "*su*" is intrinsically preferable to the other on linguistic grounds. There came a time when speakers wanted to reduce the options, and they just happened to choose differently in different places from the same available variants.

In practice, the most significant variations in these local choices were probably lexical. If different areas use different words and morphemes, that has the potential to impede communication far more than details of phonetics within the pronunciations of the same lexical item, while differences in syntax only rarely cause any practical problems whatever in real life, however distressing to normative linguists. It could be that studies of lexical developments from the eleventh to the thirteenth centuries in different areas will unlock secrets here, if medieval Latinists can be encouraged to help the Romance philologists in such tasks.

In these centuries, there are two allied divergences to consider; the conceptual separation of Romance languages from each other, and the conceptual separation of Latin from Romance. Their dating, however, seems to be close, and the two processes were probably connected. Both are widely thought nowadays to be linked to the establishment of separate methods of writing. On the

[55] As quoted by: W. VAN DER WURFF, "Gerunds and their objects in the Modern English period", in: *Papers from the 10th International Conference on Historical Linguistics*, ed. J. VAN MARLE (Amsterdam, 1993), pp. 363-375.

[56] As it is in Van der Wurff's case.

one hand, Michel Banniard has argued that the conceptual distinctiveness of Romance must have preceded the writing of texts in an intentionally new written shape.[57] Maria Selig and her colleagues at Freiburg took that relative chronology for granted, but it certainly cannot be just assumed.[58] The Swedish Latinist Tore Janson thinks that the conceptual separations (of both types) can only have followed, rather than preceded, the establishment of regular distinctions in writing systems, and even suggests that they were inspired by them.[59] Janson's perspective is preferable, in my view, and indeed my own date for the conceptual separation of Latin from Romance (*c.*800 A.D.) is now more often criticized for being too early than for being too late.[60] In 1982, I saw these distinctions as being consequences of the linguistic reforms of the scholars of the Carolingian Renaissance.[61] I still think they started then, but they took a long time to be generally intuited, probably not before the so-called 'Twelfth-century Renaissance', although Posner sees the conceptual separations between Latin and the different Romance languages as a phenomenon of the sixteenth century (*sic*) – that is, two millennia later than extreme reconstructionists such as De Dardel.[62]

This question could be empirically solvable, though. The existence of Latin-Romance and Romance-Romance translations is a crucial indication that there were genuine conceptual distinctions made between these as separate languages, and such translation is a phenomenon of the 'Twelfth-Century Renaissance' and no earlier, which in the Iberian peninsula effectively means of the thirteenth century.[63] Translations were not needed before precisely because the distinctions between separate languages were not felt, and texts in the traditional forms continued to be accessible (at least in oral presentation). Then, in the first two decades of the thirteenth century, officials in royal chanceries, and

---

[57] For instance: M. BANNIARD, "Rhabanus Maurus and the vernacular languages", in: WRIGHT (ed.), *Latin and the Romance Languages*, pp. 164-174.

[58] M. SELIG e.a. (ed.), *Le passage à l'écrit des langues romanes* (Tübingen, 1993).

[59] T. JANSON, "Language change and metalinguistic change: Latin to Romance and other cases", in: WRIGHT (ed.), *Latin and the Romance Languages*, pp. 19-28.

[60] R. WRIGHT, "Introduction: Latin and Romance, a thousand years of incertitude", in: WRIGHT (ed.), *Latin and the Romance Languages*, pp. 1-5.

[61] R. WRIGHT, *Late Latin and Early Romance in Spain and Carolingian France* (Liverpool, 1982).

[62] R. POSNER, "Latin to Romance (again!): change or genesis?", in: VAN MARLE (ed.), *Papers from the 10th*, pp. 265-279. R. DE DARDEL, *A la recherche du protoroman* (Tübingen, 1996).

[63] R. WRIGHT, "Translation between Latin and Romance in the Early Middle Ages", in: *Medieval Translation Theory and Practice*, ed. J. BEER (Kalamazoo, 1997), pp. 7-32.

other teams that prepared important documents in France, England, Italy, Navarra, León, Castile, Portugal and Catalonia, all started producing at least some documents in their own particular separate new written Romance orthographies – as it seems had already happened to some extent in Provence. This practice led eventually to standardizations on a kingdom-wide basis, rather than the previous more local scribal habits so illuminatingly unveiled for us in the French case by the computerized thirteenth-century data of Dees and his Amsterdam colleagues.[64] Each kingdom wanted to have its own standardized form, and to some extent may have set out deliberately to write differently from its neighbours and even thereby deliberately hinder general Romance-wide intelligibility, such that by the year 1300 we suddenly find that there are a large number of different written standards. Up to the twelfth century, the old written traditions were still taught and learnt all over the Romance-speaking area, used very much more commonly than the still esoteric experiments of what we call written Old French; this was reflecting still a conceptually monolingual state. By 1300 we find several different orthographies in use. But mere language changes in themselves did not cause all this apparent divergence, for the motivation for separate new standardizations, and the elevation of geographical language labels such as Castilian, Galician and so on, was essentially self-conscious and political. The change, in Le Page's terms, was thus one from a diffuse linguistic community tolerant of wide variability to several competing communities, each with its own 'focus'. These extralinguistic considerations accelerated a process that may well have already been under way, the local simplification out of the wide variation in the Romance continuum. But the early Medieval Romance variation itself was the result of natural intralinguistic processes of evolution, and hardly ever attributable to extrinsic causes even in minor details. Thus I conclude that the origins of the emigrant languages of Spain lie in the first millennium B.C., that their development has been continuous, and their individuality is only consecrated in the second millennium A.D..

---

[64] A. DEES, *Atlas des formes et des constructions des chartes françaises du 13e siècle* (Tübingen, 1980).

Chapter 3

Periodization

It is apparently natural for historical linguists to want to divide up the history of Latin and the Romance Languages into subsections, often named after chronological periods.[1] Most Hispanists, for example, are happy to refer to 'Latin', 'Late Latin', 'Ibero-Romance', 'Old Spanish', 'Medieval Spanish', 'Golden Age Spanish', 'Modern Spanish', and so on. But the linguists do not want to imply that there were clear historical dividing lines between these entities, nor that the states of language referred to were intrinsically invariable or even necessarily coherent. Periodizations in historical linguistics are in effect the chronological counterpart of the nearly necessary fictions used in dialectology. We all know that in real life there are usually transition zones on the ground between cognate dialects, and that the geolinguistic dialect continuum is the default case, but nonetheless Hispanists all continue to talk and write cheerfully about Leonese, Asturian, Riojan, Aragonese, et cetera, as if the fact that these areas are clearly delimited politically implies that they are also clearly delimited linguistically at those political borders. Until the thirteenth century, postulating such metalinguistic divisions at all is anachronistic. It is simpler to cut the Gordian knot and leave the label relatively vague, by calling

This chapter is a reprint with minor changes of: "Periodization and how to avoid it", in: *Essays in Hispanic Linguistics Dedicated to Paul M. Lloyd*, ed. R. BLAKE e.a. (Newark [Delaware], 1999), pp. 25-41. We are grateful to Professor Thomas Lathrop, on behalf of Juan de la Cuesta Hispanic Monographs (Newark, Delaware, USA) for permitting the reprint.

[1] This chapter was inspired by: P. LLOYD, "On the naming of languages (and other things)", in: R. WRIGHT (ed.), *Latin and the Romance Languages in the Early Middle Ages* (London 1991; reprint, Penn State, 1996), pp. 9-18.

the language of that period 'Ibero-Romance'. This chapter will propose that we would be best advised to resort to similar constructive vagueness in our chronological divisions as well.

All Romance historical linguists know that the question 'when did Latin change into Romance?' (or into any of the Romance languages) cannot be given in terms of a date. The phrasing of the question is inappropriate; not merely because the linguistic changes involved took a longer time than such a question implies, and not merely because languages change all the time anyway; it has also fallen victim to what we can call the 'structuralist fallacy'. This is the assumption that if there happens to exist now a single name for a linguistic state in the past, there must have existed then a complete single language system which that name is used to refer to. But the linguistic system in which everything is held in its place by the paradigmatic opposition of everything else (*"où tout se tient"*), the structuralists' perfect synchronic state, is as much of an idealization as the 'ideal speaker-hearer', who is not only ideal but idealized to the point of non-existence. The metaphor of a language as a 'structure' has been extraordinarily powerful. It has seemed obvious to many investigators in recent decades that if there is a change in the syntax of a language, then what has happened is that one complete synchronic grammatical structure has been superseded by the next.[2] But this image is misleading. In real life all individual linguistic changes involve a period in which both the old and the new phenomenon are used, and both are understood. During this period the identity of the language being spoken is correspondingly less clear.

For several centuries during the development from Latin to Romance it is not immediately obvious which of the two names is most appropriate. For example, Romance historical linguists are used to thinking of the use of "*de*" to mean "of" as being part of the structure of Romance, and of synthetic genitives as being a part of the structure of Latin, so they can be baffled by finding both in close proximity in the same text. In this example (taken from a will drawn up in Salamanca in 1163),[3] "*... illa mea vinea de la Costa et quinta mea parte de meas oves et de meos porcos. Ad canonicos Sancte Marie mando ...*",

---

[2] David Lightfoot is explicit about this: "if G_1 is a grammar of a language at time t, and G_2 is a grammar of the same language at a later stage of development t + 1 ... the grammars of two *adjacent* stages of some language ... G_1 and G_2 may differ only minimally ..." (Lightfoot's italics). D. LIGHTFOOT, *Principles of Diachronic Syntax* (Cambridge, 1979), pp. 14-16.

[3] R. WRIGHT, "Reading a will in Twelfth-Century Salamanca", in: *Latin vulgaire – latin tardif* V, ed. H. PETERSMANN and R. KETTEMANN (Heidelberg, 1999), pp. 505-516. Also: IDEM, *El Tratado de Cabreros (1206): estudio sociofilológico de una reforma ortográfica* (London, 2000), pp. 19-22.

we have three uses of *"de"* as "of" followed by the genitive of *"Sancte Marie"*; ostensibly Romance *"la"* and ostensibly Latin *"illa"* are both used here in the same noun phrase. So which language is this? In the same way as it is convenient to cut the Gordian knot in early medieval dialectology with the geographical vagueness of the word 'Ibero-Romance' rather than the unhelpful precision of 'Aragonese', et cetera, it is best to refer to texts of that period with a term that implies neither a clearly distinguished 'Latin' nor a clearly distinguished 'Romance'. Nor does it help to refer to a 'mixture' of the two, as is sometimes proposed, although it is impossible to envisage what this could have meant in practice. We should use a language name that implies a monolingual state versatile enough to include both the older and the newer phenomena. And once again, this time for chronological reasons, 'Ibero-Romance' seems to be an appropriate label for us to use now, even though it is a phrase never used at the time.

'Latin' was once an acceptably vague term also. During the Empire it was used to refer collectively to the spoken and written usage of Plautus, Apuleius, Claudius Terentianus, the soldiers at Vindolanda, Cicero, Vergil and everybody else. Contemporary grammarians such as Aulus Gellius, Velius Longus and Donatus were in their original context concentrating on keeping alive the expertise in reading and understanding literature. Their work was also useful for teaching students high styles of writing. But over the long run, the Grammarians increasingly got hold of the educational and intellectual tradition, and the *Ars minor* of Donatus in particular came to be used prescriptively with the implication that any feature not found there was *ipso facto* incorrect. Subsequent grammarians usually tell their readers which of the variant features of spoken language were acceptable, and the result in the Late Latin (Early Romance) context was to narrow considerably the range of the linguistic features which could be used in writing. Eventually, in the Carolingian curriculum, acceptable Latin grammar was uniquely defined as that which Donatus and Priscian had said it was.

One consequence of this restriction was that a phenomenon which under a normal relaxed meaning of the word would have been said to be 'Latin' – for example, the use of *"quod"* and the indicative after a verb of saying – came to be thought of as not being 'Latin' at all; in this case, because the grammatical tradition led people to believe that such clauses ought to involve an accusative and infinitive construction. Yet such *"quod"* clauses had been an available alternative all along. Similarly, the use of *"de"* to mean "of", which can also be glimpsed as existing in real life from earlier times, comes to be thought not to be 'Latin', rather than just not being the usual embodiment of that meaning in the more formal registers. Since Donatus and Priscian established the tradition which in essential respects continued through to every pedagogical grammar,[4] Latin is now usually thought of as comprising those and only those features which these grammars say it includes, and thus by definition nothing else. So tetchy editors misguidedly 'correct' genuine Late Latin manuscript readings in order not to offend Donatus, as Lindsay did to poor St Isidore's *Etymologiae*.[5] Michel Banniard accepts the existence of complex monolingualism in the Early Middle Ages, but periodizes three separate stages of spoken Late Latin, which reintroduces the same kind of conceptual over-schematization that his support for the monolingual perspective has helped to dispel.[6]

The term 'Romance' never suffered such referential impoverishment. That is why it is and was a useful term. Because of its vagueness, rather than in spite of it, it was used to refer to the common language in use before the conceptual fragmentation of Romance into separate Romance languages – that is, it was in use once coherent texts first began to be written intentionally in a new way, before such geographical labels as 'French' or 'Castilian'. Latin and Romance had become separate concepts only after – and, in most places, not even immediately after – the arrival of the reformed Latin which we now call 'Medieval Latin' for use in Church contexts. In the Peninsula, outside Catalonia, this was introduced in the late eleventh century. Gradually the conceptual distinction spread, and once the idea of having available two alternative ways of writing also became acceptable, the idea that Latin and Romance were two different languages became more general. It was as yet just Latin and Romance, however; for example, the Treaty of Cabreros of 1206 survives in versions from both the Leonese and the Castilian chancery, being in each of them the first important document drawn up in Romance rather than Latin, but the linguistic details cannot be labelled as respectively 'Leonese' and 'Castilian'. We can also deduce that no general agreed 'Castilian' method of writing existed yet, given the detailed orthographical differences between the Castilian version of the Treaty, the 1207 Cortes document from Toledo, and the *Poema de Mio Cid*.[7]

The Latin-Romance distinction does not seem to be made explicitly in the Peninsula before that century. The sequence of words "*latinum circa roman-*

---

[4] At least until: H. PINKSTER, *Latin Syntax and Semantics* (London, 1990).

[5] W.M. LINDSAY, *Etymologiarum sive Originum libri XX* (Oxford, 1911; third edition, 1962).

[6] M. BANNIARD, *Du Latin aux langues romanes* (Paris, 1997), p. 30.

[7] WRIGHT, *El Tratado*, pp. 78-98.

çum", which was used out of context and anachronistically by Avalle as a label for texts of earlier times, in fact comes from a Toledan text translated from Arabic in 1290.[8] The words do not in fact constitute a noun phrase, as can be seen in context:

> ille est vituperandus qui loquitur latinum circa romançum, maxime coram laicis, ita quod ipsi met intelligunt totum; et ille est laudandus qui semper loquitur latinum obscure, ita quod nullus intelligat eum nisi clerici; et ita debent omnes clerici loqui latinum suum obscure in quantum possunt et non circa romançium.[9]

"*Circa romanç(i)um*" is here an adverbial phrase, contrasted to "*obscure*", and "*latinum*" a separate noun phrase, the object of "*loquitur*".

It seems natural for people in a literate society to identify the existence of as many cognate languages as there are writing systems. In Castile, Latin and Romance after 1206 corresponded to two such; the subsequent systematization of geographically separate written forms of Romance is a phenomenon of the later thirteenth century. Berceo, writing in the Riojan monastery of San Millán between 1230 and 1252, told us he was writing Romance rather than Latin, but that was as far as his sub-divisions went. Thus in the following phrase in his *Milagros*, "*dissoli un latino la raíz profundada*", the word "*latino*" is used as a noun to mean a "Latin-speaker" in Constantinople (another manuscript reads here "*cristiano*", which shows how closely related the new standard Latin was to the Christian church). The cleric so addressed replies to this "*latino/cristiano*" with the words "*Laudetur Deus e la Virgo gloriosa*" (that is, in Latin, not in Romance).[10] So for Berceo, Medieval Latin and "*romanz*" existed, distinguishable from each other, but Romance had no geographically restricted subcategories yet. He used the words "*castellano*", "*leonés*" and "*riojano*", but only to refer to people: for instance: "*essa gent castellana*",[11] "*ir sobre leoneses*",[12] "*sonó la buena fama a los riojanos*".[13] He would probably have been aware of language-internal variability, but without thinking of any geograph-

---

[8] D'A.S. AVALLE, *Latino "circa romançum" e "rustica romana lingua"* (Padua, 1965). Interestingly, Roy Harris, in his review of Avalle's book, referred to the text as a "late Ibero-Romance source": *Medium Aevum* 36 (1967), pp. 52-54.

[9] Quoted from R. MENÉNDEZ PIDAL, *Orígenes del español* (Madrid, 1926; seventh edition, 1972), p. 459.

[10] Gonzalo de Berceo, *Milagros*, 701c. Quotations from Berceo are taken from the edition by: B. DUTTON (ed.), *Gonzalo de Berceo, Obras Completas*, 5 volumes (London, 1967-1981).

[11] Gonzalo de Berceo, *Vida de Santo Domingo de Silos*, 274d.

[12] Gonzalo de Berceo, *Vida de San Millán de la Cogolla*, 407b.

[13] Gonzalo de Berceo, *Vida de San Millán*, 41a.

ical limits as constituting diagnostic isoglosses for separating complete systems. Berceo was writing after the establishment in the 1220s of written Romance as an officially acceptable alternative to Latin, but before the imminent arrival in the later 1250s of the Castilian nationalism embodied in Alfonsine metalinguistics.[14] So he did not say he was writing in "*riojano*", or in "*castellano*", but "*en romanz*" (contrasted explicitly with "*latino*"):

> Quiero fer una prosa en romanz paladino
> en qual suele el pueblo fablar con su vezino
> ca non só tan letrado por fer otro latino.[15]

Lanchetas glossed this phrase, misguidedly, as "*en castellano puro, neto, claro*".[16] Berceo refers to his own work with the same word at the start of the *Martirio de San Lorenzo*, "*en romanz qe la pueda saber toda la gent*",[17] and at the end of *Los Loores de Nuestra Señora*, "*qui est romance fizo fue tu entendedor*".[18] The verb "*romançar*" is also used self-referentially at the start of the *Vida de Santa Oria*, "*De esta santa virgen romançar su dictado*".[19] Lanchetas glosses this too as "*poner en romance, en castellano*".[20] But there is no sense in which we can say that Berceo was writing "*castellano*". He was not Castilian, he was not in Castile, and, as Penny puts it, "even by Berceo's time, written language was far from standardized on the Burgos-Toledo model".[21] The grammarians' Latin was still there, as used by "*letrados*" who knew how to define it, and now Romance also existed as a written alternative, gloriously undefined and unsubdivided as yet.

We can base periodizing labels on external criteria, then, for the language used in texts in the Central Northern Iberian Peninsula.[22] The monolingual Ibero-Romance continuum separated out into co-existing "*romance*" and Medieval Latin only after the new orthography was developed there in the early

---

[14] F. MÁRQUEZ VILLANUEVA, *El concepto cultural alfonsí* (second edition; Madrid, 1995).

[15] Gonzalo de Berceo, *Vida de Santo Domingo*, 2a-c.

[16] R. LANCHETAS, *Gramática y vocabulario de las obras de Gonzalo de Berceo* (Madrid, 1900), p. 668.

[17] Gonzalo de Berceo, *Martirio de San Lorenzo*, 1d.

[18] Gonzalo de Berceo, *Los Loores de Nuestra Señora*, 232b.

[19] Gonzalo de Berceo, *Vida de Santa Oria*, 2b.

[20] LANCHETAS, *Gramática*, p. 667.

[21] R. PENNY, "The language of Gonzalo de Berceo, in the context of peninsular dialectal variation", in: *The Medieval Mind: Hispanic Studies in Honour of Alan Deyermond*, ed. I. MACPHERSON and R. PENNY (London, 1997), pp. 327-345.

[22] F. MARCOS MARÍN, *Reforma y modernización del español* (Madrid, 1979).

thirteenth century, even though the origins of this rift had been ultimately introduced by the change of rite in 1080. Only later do the noun phrases "*romance
castellano*" and "*castellano*" turn up to specify "*romance*" further. Both these
phrases are used by scholars at the Court of Alfonso X (1252-1282) to refer to
their own language, but so, still, are unqualified "*romance*" and even "*nuestro
latín*".[23] The use of geographical adjectives as substantival names for languages
spread during the second half of the thirteenth century in the whole Romance
world, not only in the Iberian Peninsula, as emerging Romance-speaking states,
who had previously been content to share a great world language, wished to
boost their national virility by writing differently from each other and thus
being able to claim to have their own national language. The Leonese lost a
trick here. Even two decades after the time when Alfonso X was establishing
written Castilian as a separate entity and national symbol, the *De Preconiis
Hispaniae*, written in 1278-1282 by the Franciscan, Paris-educated, Leonese
scholar Juan Gil de Zamora (and which concentrates on the Western part of the
Peninsula) includes Romance works among its sources but is nonetheless written in the old form.[24] In Márquez Villanueva's phrase, [*castellano*] "*si había de
afirmarse frente al latín, precisaba también de hacerlo frente a los otros
dialectos iberorrománicos*".[25] After establishing written Castilian in the 1250s,
Alfonso X was happy to do the same for Galician by writing his lyric poems in
Galician in the 1270s;[26] but the original official establishment of written Castilian prose was a conscious option chosen for a political purpose,[27] in the same
way as the original distinction between Latin and Romance had been deliberately created in Carolingian France.[28] As Janson points out, in these cases the
change of language name was consequent on the establishment of separate
writing systems, which had in turn been caused by external historical events
and circumstances, rather than being the result of an internal diachronic development.[29] Contingential language-planning leads to plausible periodization in
these cases, of a type which was not to occur in the Peninsula again until the

[23] H.-J. NIEDEREHE, *Alfonso X, El Sabio, y la lingüística de su tiempo* (Madrid, 1987).

[24] M. CASTRO Y CASTRO, *Fray Juan Gil de Zamora: De Preconiis Hispanie* (Madrid, 1955).

[25] MÁRQUEZ VILLANUEVA, *El concepto*, p. 39.

[26] MÁRQUEZ VILLANUEVA, *El concepto*, p. 13 and p. 40.

[27] MÁRQUEZ VILLANUEVA, *El concepto*, p. 127: as part of "*la magna recimentación cultural
iniciada por el Rey Sabio*", and which would not have just happened otherwise. Compare:
IBIDEM, pp. 36-37.

[28] R. WRIGHT, *Early Ibero-Romance* (Newark, 1995), chapter 3.

[29] T. JANSON, "Language change and metalinguistic change: Latin to Romance and other
cases", in: WRIGHT (ed.), *Latin and the Romance Languages*, pp. 19-28.

age of those modern Spanish *autonomías* that want to establish their own individual writing norms and language names for similar reasons. These events are contingential, rather than inevitable, because the importation of the foreign rites, and the Alfonsine hunger for a distinctive writing system, were not logically necessary in any sense. And despite all this, *Romance* continued to be an available name for the language even as late as in the title of Bernardo de Aldrete's treatise of 1606, *Del origen y principio de la lengua castellana o romance que oi se usa en España.*

Periodization on the basis of internal developments in speech, however, is dubious for several reasons. Not all levels of language change at the same rate, nor at the same time. For example, the phonology of Latin changed at a faster rate than the syntax; this relative speed may even be a universal truth.[30] Those linguists who think phonological change is the more significant for these purposes will ascribe the label of 'Romance' (or 'Proto-Romance') to an earlier date than those who prefer to base such judgments on syntax. De Dardel and Hall, for example, propose the existence of 'Sardinian' as an identifiably separate language from the rest of Romance, as well as from Latin, by the second century B.C., on entirely phonetic grounds.[31] If we think syntax is more important, the essential differences between what we like to call Latin and what we like to call Romance seem not to have arrived until much later, and even then at a variable rate that baffles the structuralists who instinctively wish to see the structure changing all at once. Noun morphology became what we would call 'Romance', for example, before verb morphology did.[32] Lexical change can be almost instantaneous, but semantic change tends to be long, gradual, and often unnoticed by grammarians, which is why words that look like Latin (from their orthography, morphology and syntax) can appear in Early Medieval texts with their evolved meaning unbanished. Even if we want to come up with a global date for Latin turning internally into Romance, we have to accept different dates for different diachronic phenomena, and the global date would be no more than some kind of average.

There is a further internal theoretical reason for this absence of clear chronological boundaries. Although it is true that linguistic changes can be directly related to each other, for structural or other reasons, that does not usually in itself imply that such related changes happened at the same time. 'Pull-chains'

---

[30] Compare: A. LÓPEZ GARCÍA, *Cómo surgió el español* (Madrid, 2000).

[31] R.A. HALL Jr, *Proto-Romance Phonology* (New York, 1976). R. DE DARDEL, *A la recherche du protoroman* (Tübingen, 1996).

[32] J. HERMAN, *Vulgar Latin* (Penn State, 2000).

of related changes, which take time to operate, seem more generally plausible than 'push-chains', which (if they ever occur) are causally sequential but chronologically close. Chains of related changes that spread up a strength hierarchy can even last for millennia, as Harris-Northall's study of consonant weakening in Spanish made abundantly clear.[33] Consonant weakening is part of the history of Latin, Romance, Ibero-Romance, Medieval Castilian, Modern Spanish, and almost certainly of the Spanish of the future as well, and this is not a mere concatenation of coincidences but a symptom of the fact that the divisions implied by the separate language-names are artificial. Postulated pull-chains of semantic changes can also spread over more than a millennium.[34] In the Iberian Peninsula it has been the same language, in effect, all along, since it was first substantially introduced there in the late third century B.C., regardless of the fact that it has not developed the same way elsewhere (Italy, for example, saw consonant strengthening more often than weakening). Thus although, as sociophilologists can deduce, written texts demonstrate periodizability as a result of external events, the internal nature of the spoken vernacular is better understood without erecting such barriers.

There is no reason why any internal changes should necessarily have occurred coincidentally with the development and official acceptance of the new alternative orthographies around 1200. Changes in written texts need not coincide with any change at all in speech. This is obvious, but tends to be overlooked. Many features that we want to categorize generally as Romance are already visible in the texts of previous centuries, as Bob Blake tirelessly points out.[35] Less obvious, perhaps, is the converse: several features that we might wish to classify as Latin rather than Romance still exist, after the split, in texts written in the new form, and could have been still there in speech also. Not all the words which we think of as Latinisms in Berceo, for example, need actually be Latinisms at all. Sala has already pointed this out with regard to the word *"cras"* ("tomorrow") as used in *"Esti viernes que viene, de cras en otro día"*,[36] and on eight occasions in Berceo's *Milagros*.[37] Some of these ostensible

---

[33] R. HARRIS-NORTHALL, *Weakening Processes in the History of Spanish Consonants* (London, 1990).

[34] For instance in Romance words for "cut": WRIGHT, *Early Ibero-Romance*, chapter 8.

[35] For instance: R. BLAKE, "Squeezing the Spanish turnip dry: Latinate documents from the Early Middle Ages", in: *Linguistic Studies in Medieval Spanish*, ed. R. HARRIS-NORTHALL and T.D. CRAVENS (Madison, 1991), pp. 1-14.

[36] Gonzalo de Berceo, *Vida de Santo Domingo*, 720a.

[37] R. SALA, *La lengua y el estilo de Gonzalo de Berceo* (Logroño, 1983), p. 46. R. PELLEN, *Los milagros de Nuestra Señora: étude linguistique et index lemmatisé* (Paris, 1993), p. 90.

Latinisms appear in the *Poema of the Cid* too, including, on nine occasions, "*cras*". Some may be words that died out of the vernacular only in the later thirteenth century. Several moribund lexical items probably did suffer merciful release coincidentally with the establishment of the new written forms, however. Steven Dworkin has pointed out that the sequence of events presented in this present book implies that a large number of words fell from general competence at the time of the establishment of alternative orthographies.[38] This is right; and the reason for this exodus is probably that apprentice writers were no longer told by their teachers to use in writing several words and inflectional morphemes which had hitherto been commonly used, in the old written form, but had largely fallen out of spoken usage. Similarly, if English spelling were reformed, not every word now found in more formal written registers would then necessarily go on to be used in new written 'Californian', et cetera.

In this scenario, the advent of new texts in written Romance form represents the development of an alternative orthography to replace that of Late Latin, rather than of a new language; the new language in that context was Medieval Latin. But even though written Romance was in essence only a new orthography, it was that which precipitated the metalinguistic idea of a new language name.[39] For the change in written form cannot have been directly inspired by any internal development. Changes in spoken syntax, for example, need no concomitant change in the writing system. We can write words in any order we like, or with whatever choice from the available morphological repertoire we wish, regardless of what the orthographical system may be. Changes in spoken morphology in the Romance case had involved the loss of several older inflectional morphemes, rather than the advent of new ones (which might have been more problematical). Writers certainly did not need any systematic change in orthography in order to refrain from writing *-orum* or *-amini*, or to extend the textual functions of "*de*", "*ad*", "*est*", "*habere*", "*ille*", "*se*", et cetera, for these words already had well-known standard written forms. Only entirely new words, and in particular Proper Names, had the potential to cause orthographical doubts. These had turned up regularly in the old orthography in the twelfth century, and were usually spelt by analogy with existing words with

---

[38] S.N. DWORKIN, "Latín tardío y romance temprano: implicaciones léxicas de una hipótesis controvertida", in: *Actas del Primer Congreso Nacional de Latín Medieval*, ed. M. PÉREZ GONZÁLEZ (León, 1995), pp. 489-494.

[39] See also: F. SABATINI, "Dalla *scripta latina rustica* alle *scriptae* romanze", *Studi Medievali* 9 (1968), pp. 320-358. A. EMILIANO, "Latin or Romance? Graphemic variation and scripto-linguistic change in medieval Spain", in: WRIGHT (ed.), *Latin and the Romance Languages*, pp. 233-247. JANSON, "Language change".

similar pronunciations. The traditional orthography had not approximated to a phonetic transcription for many centuries. But the co-existence of standard spellings with non-isomorphic pronunciations did not usually matter there in practice before 1200 any more than it does now in Modern Britain, since spelling could be taught by the word (that is, logographically). The old writing system had carried on being usable for a long time, and could have continued for longer, just as the present English and French anisomorphic orthography will probably last well into the future, despite all the changes in speech. A problem only arose when it became important to signal the distinction between Medieval Latin and Romance pronunciations of the same words, after the Carolingian reforms. This is perhaps the only envisageable motive for an alternative orthography to have been elaborated, and then established. Since it is apparently normal to think there are as many languages as there are orthographies, this development became metalinguistically crucial. But it was external and contingent, even so. Thus the new orthographical system indeed marks a period, but not for any internal reason.

If Romance and Hispanic historical linguists wish to base successive periodizations on internal considerations alone, there seems to be no good reason to have any periodizations at all. Maybe that would be for the best. It is easy to be mesmerized by the differences and fail to see the great continuities. Latin is really very like Old Spanish, and Old Spanish is very like Modern Spanish. Latin is far more like Modern Spanish than, say, Basque or Aymara or Arabic. Many of the lexical items and much of the phoneme inventory, for example, are the same. If it was not for the external water-muddying factors considered above, Latin could still now be being called 'Latin' all over the Romance-speaking world, rather than by the present range of locally restricted names such as 'Portuguese', 'Galician', 'Castilian', 'Catalan', 'French', et cetera, in the same way as Greek is still called 'Greek' despite having suffered many internal developments. The Italian habit of calling the Romance Languages "*le lingue neolatine*" is entirely appropriate. Probably everyone who uses phrases such as 'Medieval Spanish' realizes that this is an administrative convenience rather than a clear concept, that there is no internally-motivated clear linguistic boundary at either end of the Middle Ages (even if we think we know when the Middle Ages began and ended), that thirteenth-century and fifteenth-century Castilian texts are both indeed medieval but recognizably different, and – perhaps less consciously – that in the middle of the Middle Ages there was never a period of linguistic stability and immobilism.

These questions were brought into sharp focus in a 1991 article by Rolf Eberenz. Eberenz, intriguingly, proposes to periodize via giving labels to periods of related changes, rather than to periods of stability;[40] which is the opposite of the more usual approach. Arguing from internal data, but also inspired by a desire for Spanish to have as many periodizations as French, Eberenz suggested the establishment of the idea of a *"castellano medio"*, located between 1450 and 1650. These views have been favourably received,[41] for Eberenz expresses well several of the problems inherent in the traditional chronological sub-categories. But by reorganizing the periods, rather than abandoning the idea of internally-founded periodization at all (a possibility he does in fact consider),[42] he reacts to this dissatisfaction in the wrong direction. Many related changes indeed were occurring then, but some began much earlier than 1450, and not even Eberenz manages to make all the relevant internal phonetic, syntactic and semantic developments which characterize the proposed *"medio"* period, coincide closely. Indeed, some of the Spanish phenomena adduced by Eberenz were also used by Pountain to elaborate a convincing pull-chain, which in Pountain's view stretched from roughly 1140 to 1520.[43] This was a chain of connected and "crucially ordered" changes essentially inspired by the increasing use of *"haber"* as a perfect auxiliary. Thus a start for this chain in the Late Latin period seems plausible.

Eberenz praises Paul Lloyd for presenting change as continuous, and individual changes as dynamic,[44] despite the apparently periodized labels that appear in Lloyd's chapter headings. Overall he is more successful in casting doubt on the periodizations used by others than in building his own. For it is not necessary to have them at all, other than for mere administrative convenience. And as Eberenz notes himself, Menéndez Pidal himself did not like periodizing,[45] given his vision of the lengthy *"estado latente"* of a linguistic

[40] R. EBERENZ, *"Castellano antiguo y español moderno*: reflexiones sobre la periodización en la historia de la lengua", *Revista de Filología Española* 71 (1991), pp. 80-106. R. WRIGHT, "Status Quaestionis: el estudio diacrónico del español", *Lingüística* 5 (1993), pp. 77-126, p. 112.

[41] For instance by: E. RIDRUEJO, "¿Un reajuste sintáctico en el español de los siglos XV y XVI?", in: *Actas del Primer Congreso Anglo-Hispano*. I. *Lingüística*, ed. R. PENNY (Madrid, 1993), pp. 49-60.

[42] EBERENZ, *"Castellano antiguo"*, pp. 94-97.

[43] C.J. POUNTAIN, "Copulas, verbs of possession and auxiliaries in Old Spanish: the evidence for structurally interdependent changes", *Bulletin of Hispanic Studies* 62 (1985), pp. 337-356.

[44] P.M. LLOYD, *From Latin to Spanish*, I (Philadelphia, 1987).

[45] In: MENÉNDEZ PIDAL, *Orígenes*.

change, which seems so sensible now and seemed so odd at the time to scholars instinctively attracted by neat and tidy categories.[46]

To conclude, language-planning can lead to chronologically valid periodization. Changes in language names tend to be based on such external changes. In the Iberian Peninsula, perhaps only the literally epoch-making political events of the thirteenth century qualify. Periodization in vernacular speech, however, is a mirage, whether based on external or internal causes. The modern habit of naming language states by centuries, as in the phrase 'Fifteenth-Century Spanish', is merely desperate. Those who use the term should find some other words instead, preferably not using a noun phrase at all, for they cannot wish to imply that the language changed identity on the 31st of December 1399, and then again on the 31st of December 1499. External causes for changes in language labels, and thus for periodizations between the changes, need to be more than mere chronological accidents. The best conclusion, even if it is a counsel of perfection, would be that historical linguists should try to avoid using language names at all; not to write, for example, that "in Medieval Castilian they said '*beso*' with a [z]" but to write instead that "in Castile, between at least the ninth and fifteenth centuries, native-speakers usually pronounced the word spelt as '*beso*' with a [z]" (if that is what we mean). If we can in this way refer to times with temporal expressions ("between the ninth and fifteenth centuries", rather than "in Medieval Spanish"), and refer to places with locative phrases ("in Castile" rather than "in Castilian"), and thereby eliminate the hypostatization implicit in the use of language labels, we will avoid more confusion than we cause. That is a worthwhile ambition, and in at least some contexts it can be achieved.

---

[46] As can still be seen in the frighteningly over-determined schemata of: P. KOCH, "Pour une typologie conceptionnelle et médiale des plus anciens documents/monuments des langues romanes", in: *Le passage à l'écrit des langues romanes*, ed. M. SELIG e.a. (Tübingen, 1993), pp. 39-81.

Chapter 4

Viva voce

Review Article: Michel Banniard, *Viva voce: communication écrite et communication orale du IVe au IXe siècle en occident latin* (Paris, 1992).

Michel Banniard's magnificent book will become a standard and generally respected work in a field where divergence, misunderstanding, and recrimination are not unknown. For the sociolinguistic nature of the Latin-speaking community of western Europe in the period between the Roman and Carolingian empires has recently been the subject of a remarkable diversity of scholarly research and opinion. The most noticeable divide has been between the textual historians and the Romance historical linguists, who have often preferred to ignore each other. Banniard belongs to the first camp by training and instinct, but is a professor of Medieval French language, and manages to combine expertise in many relevant areas. That in itself is encouraging; and this book surpasses expectations, in that a detailed examination of the most appropriate texts, although confined to northern France, Rome, and southern Spain, is allied to an intelligent appreciation of the nature of grammatical change and linguistic aptitudes in those societies.

The core of the book consists of seven careful and leisurely analyses of what we can learn about the nature of contemporary communication from the

This chapter is reprint with very few changes of: "Review article: Michel Banniard, *Viva Voce: Communication écrite et communication orale du IVe au IXe siècle en occident latin*. Paris, Institut des études augustiniennes, 1992", *Journal of Medieval Latin* 3 (1993), pp. 77-92. We are grateful to M. Luc Jocqué, on behalf of the *Journal of Medieval Latin* and Brepols publishers (Turnhout) for permitting the reprint.

works of Augustine, Gregory the Great, Isidore, Merovingian hagiographers, Alcuin and the Carolingian reformers, and the loquacious Christian writers of Moslem Spain. Later Italian and Byzantine Greek evidence is summarized in an appendix. At one stage, apparently, Banniard was planning to include a great deal more, even considering every writer of the period. Perhaps he still will, for he is a scholar of inexhaustible energy. But this work, in origin a thesis, represents twenty years of thought and measured consideration, and we can be glad not to have to wait for it any longer (as it is, it spent many years in press).

The focus of the analysis throughout is on what he calls "*communication verticale*"; that is, how educated people can write in such a way as to be intelligible to the illiterate when their works are read aloud. Every chapter has copious textual quotations, both cited and sensitively translated. The earliest writer considered in detail is Augustine (chapter 2), who gives the impression that he could write in an intelligible enough way to communicate to any congregation, when his text is read aloud. The question arises, naturally, who the intended audience can be. Banniard shows convincingly that it can be anyone and everyone, even if some of the works are more obviously aimed at intellectuals: "*les illettrés et les demi-lettrés ont accès à un texte lu à haute voix et traitant de questions difficiles*" (p. 83). There is thus linguistic continuity into the fifth century. This seems so straightforward a conclusion that it comes as a shock to remember (p. 87, n. 68) that the opposite view is widely held, that Christian Latin was an intrinsically novel linguistic entity. This begins to seem not so much a linguistic point as a spiritual one.[1]

The chapters on Gregory and Isidore have the same effect: that writing and speech may not be identical – in the same way as there are considerable differences between the two modes of Modern French or English – but reading aloud is a practical process uniting the two:

> ...Grégoire le Grand qui établira le contact avec ses auditeurs exactement selon les modalités augustiniennes, et il y a tout lieu de penser que la situation ne sera pas différente en Espagne isidorienne. Toute solution de continuité entre la lettre et la parole est encore exclue. (pp. 95-96)

Banniard concludes that written and spoken language could not be sharply distinguished at that time. Gregory (chapter 3) in particular comes alive as a human being. He works in a context where written language was merely the

---

[1] See for instance: C. MOHRMANN, *Études sur le latin des chrétiens*, 4 volumes (Rome, 1961-1977), 4, pp. 367-404 (with the appendix by: J. SCHRIJNEN, "Charakteristik des altchristlichen Lateins").

textual counterpart of spoken language. Of course, the written evidence cannot be interpreted by us as if it were in detail a precise transcription of speech; but then it never can, in any community. Banniard's arguments succeed in casting considerable doubt on Herbert Grundmann's view that the sixth or seventh-century *"litteratus"* in Italy possessed, by virtue of his literacy, a separate non-native language then in the same way as a contemporary *"litteratus"* did in England, or in Italy in the twelfth century. If the acoustics permitted, at least (p. 154), Gregory's audiences could understand his texts when they were read aloud. József Herman came to a similar conclusion in a 1988 article which could already be described as 'classic'.[2]

This conclusion also effectively challenges a line taken by Adalbert de Vogüe in his 1978 edition of the *Dialogues,* to the effect that the uneducated audience would not have understood Gregory.[3] For the differences between speech and writing at that time should not be exaggerated. Some linguists have been tempted to argue that several common linguistic features found in texts did not exist in contemporary speech (see below). But even the most extreme of the Romance reconstruction theorists envisage a spoken language which has much in common with the texts (including much of the vocabulary), and Banniard may be wrong to assume, as he seems to, that Romance linguists in general will not like his conclusions. Gregory's *Dialogues* are carefully written, of course, but then carefulness is an aid to intelligibility, rather than a hindrance. It is entirely rational to postulate that there were different levels of care to be found within the speech of that community, naturally, because that is true of all societies. To make this point, Banniard often refers to the linguistic *"ensemble"* of the time (which makes his determination nevertheless to distinguish between *"latin"* and *"roman"* rather confusing). The conclusion drawn is that the non-literate of Gregory's time were not for that reason inherently cut off from educated culture, provided that the texts were read aloud. This perspective at once restores some dignity to the many inhabitants of the age who have been assumed by later historians to be untouched by literate culture, and implies that many modern assessments of the intellectual state of these centuries are needlessly pessimistic (see p. 233, n. 193). Banniard will have been encouraged, however, by the historical studies in the collection edited by Rosamond McKitterick, which are comparatively cheerful in this respect despite their disappoint-

---

[2] H. Grundmann, "Litteratus – illiteratus," *Archiv für Kulturgeschichte* 40 (1958), pp. 1-65. J. Herman, "La situation linguistique en Italie au vie siècle", *Revue de linguistique romane* 52 (1988), pp. 55-67.

[3] A. de Vogüe (ed.), *Grégoire le Grand: Dialogues*, 3 volumes (Paris, 1978-1980: *Sources chrétiennes* 259, 260 and 265).

ing lack of any linguistic analysis.[4] As Banniard points out (p. 139), Caesarius of Arles, fifty years earlier, had recommended the rich to hire *"lectores"* to read to them, but it seems reasonable to argue that such methods of communication were not the exclusive preserve of the rich.[5] In any event, a simple perusal of the evidence makes it clear that in Gregory's Italy no translator was required for his work to reach a normal public. It sufficed to have a reader. When, early in his papacy, Gregory sent a letter to Sicily, he said *"scripta mea ad rusticos quae direxi per omnes masses fac relegi"* (p. 146, n. 162; *Epistle I*, 42, of May 591; *MGH Epistolae* 1, pp. 61-69, at p. 69, l. 4). Furthermore, there is still no necessary conflict between being correct and being intelligible: *"on peut au VIIe siècle se faire entendre et lire de tous en s'exprimant avec correction"* (p. 179), even when Gregory was preparing a homily on Ezekiel. Banniard makes this all seem so obvious – the main virtue of accurate grammar is precisely that it helps make the speaker's meaning clear – that it is again a shock to remember that British scholars, in particular, used to the idea that Latin was necessarily a foreign language in Anglo-Saxon England, tend to assume that it was foreign rather than vernacular on the 'Latin' Continent as well. But this is not a specifically British misapprehension, for some French scholars – particularly Ferdinand Lot – have proclaimed it as well.[6]

Chapter 4, on Isidore of Seville, is similar, and similarly convincing. Since the work of Jacques Fontaine and Manuel Díaz y Díaz, it has become easier for investigators to see a real person at work here, rather than an abstract name appended to texts.[7] The chapter begins, surprisingly but with total relevance, with a discussion of the annotated slates, mostly from Salamanca province, that

[4] R. McKitterick (ed.), *The Uses of Literacy in Early Medieval Europe* (Cambridge, 1990).

[5] G. Morin (ed.), *Sancti Caesarii Arelatensis sermones*, 2 volumes (Turnhout, 1953: *Corpus Christianorum. Series Latina* 103-104), I, pp.31-32, from no. 6, 1: " *Primum est, quod lectionem divinam etiamsi aliquis nesciens litteras non potest legere, potest tamen legentem libenter audire"*; 2: *"novimus enim aliquos negotiatores, qui cum litteras non noverint, requirunt sibi mercennarios litteratos"*; 3: " *nemo ergo dicat: non possum aliquid de id quod in ecclesia retinere. Sine dubio enim, si velis, et poteris: incipe velle, et statim intelleges"*. The phrase *"mercennarios litteratos"* reappears in Sermon 8 and, as Banniard suggests, seems to imply the existence of such a profession.

[6] R. Coleman, "Vulgar Latin and the diversity of Christian Latin", in: *Latin vulgaire – Latin tardif*, ed. J. Herman (Tübingen, 1987), pp. 37-52. F. Lot, "A quelle époque a-t-on cessé de parler latin?", *Archivum latinitatis medii aevi* (= *ALMA*) 6 (1931), pp. 97-159.

[7] M.C. Díaz y Díaz, "Introducción general", in: *San Isidoro de Sevilla: Etimologías*, ed. J. Oroz Reta, 2 volumes (Madrid, 1982: *Biblioteca de Autores Cristianos*), pp. 1-257. J. Fontaine, *Isidore de Séville et la culture classique dans l'Espagne wisigothique* (second edition; Paris, 1983).

probably date from seventh-century Spain.[8] Like Gregory, Isidore believed that texts would be generally intelligible if read aloud (for instance: *"Homiliae autem ad vulgus loquuntur"*, *Etymologiae* 6.8.2). Banniard suggests that Isidore made a conscious effort to research the local speech, but that would not have been necessary: Isidore spoke the local language naturally, for his family were from Cartagena and he was probably born in Seville. Isidore had an academic interest in language, but showed no awareness of a Latin-Romance conceptual distinction, instead contrasting the Latin-Romance *ensemble* with other languages entirely, such as Hebrew and Greek (*"Tout montre donc qu'il n'y a pour Isidore qu'un seul langue en usage, le latin"*, p. 211). Banniard suggests here, somewhat confusingly, that the reason for this metalinguistically monolingual assessment by Isidore is that *"le roman n'était pas encore apparu"*. It only becomes clear in the last chapter of *Viva voce* that what Banniard means by this is that a large number of individual linguistic traits subsequently identifiable (by us) as Romance had undoubtedly appeared, but that the older linguistic features with the same function had not yet disappeared and were still in competition with them, such that the conceptual invention of both a new language name and of a difference between Latin and Romance lay in the future, and the whole was still, in the seventh century, a single conceptual unit. If Banniard had meant by this explanation what he initially appears to mean – that the speech of seventh-century Seville had not changed since imperial times – this book would thereby have lost credibility. Fortunately, Banniard explains here (p. 230), as again later, that monolingualism does not imply either lack of variation or chronological immobilism: indeed, sociolinguists see variation as integral and even essential to the smooth functioning of a community. Thus the fact that Isidore counsels *"lectores"* to be clear has no particular linguistic significance beyond that implied by similar advice given in modern France. Nor is there a need to agonize at length before reaching the simple conclusion that *"la langue parlée est une base suffisante pour apprendre a lire, sans qu'il soit besoin d'étudier spécialement la langue écrite"* (p. 236; writing, as one would expect, became hard to master long before reading did). Isidore is thus shown to have been a sophisticated communicator.[9]

At this point readers might be tempted to foresee that Banniard's conclusion will be the same for every context studied. Chapter 5 (*"Échanges linguisti-*

---

[8] See: I. VELÁZQUEZ SORIANO, *Las pizarras visigodas: edición crítica y estudio* (Murcia, 1989).

[9] It is difficult to accept the disparaging comment that "Isidore's personal understanding of the subject [i.e. rhetoric] is poor": G.A. KENNEDY, "Rhetoric", in: *The Legacy of Rome: A New Appraisal*, ed. R. JENKYNS (Oxford, 1992), pp. 269-294.

ques en Gaule mérovingienne"), however, shows linguistic complications beginning to develop (reminiscent of those of the modern English-speaking world). What Banniard likes to call the *"prise de conscience"*, of a linguistic difference between writer and unsophisticated listener which gradually comes to be ever harder to bridge, was growing through the eighth century in the Merovingian area, and was eventually made worse by Alcuin's clumsy attempts to solve it through the reform of everyone else's practice to conformity with his own. As Banniard argues, from many examples, Merovingian saints' lives, if the style was kept simple, were still understood when read aloud (here Banniard, like everyone else, is indebted to the trail-blazing work of Marc van Uytfanghe).[10] Their authors' practicality in keeping the style simple, though, has unfortunately made both contemporary and subsequent scholars tend to criticize them for their success in achieving the grammatical straightforwardness needed for communication in that context rather than producing imitations of Cicero. The writer of the preface to the *Vita Eligii*, among others, sees how hard it is to please both audience and grammarians; and the so-called pseudo-Germain writes in such a way *"ut nec rusticitas sapientes offendat, nec honesta loquacitas obscure rusticis fiat"* (p. 261). Even in the eighth century, *"rusticitas"* and *"grammatica"* were not yet identified as separate languages; there was not yet a scenario in which each linguistic feature was classified as belonging to one or the other, as would happen later, but they were now beginning to "crystallize" into two separate categories within the same language.

The conceptual distinction comes with *"Alcuin et les ambitions d'une restauration ecclésiale"* (chapter 6). There is still room for modern scholarly argument over some of the details of the attempted restorations (see below), but the encounter between the English scholars' Latin, grammatically learned as a foreign language, uniquely defined by those grammars, and the versatility and flexibility of the native speakers' Romance, is now beginning to be accepted as the catalyst that led to the conceptual distinction.[11] Banniard expresses the contrast as follows:

---

[10] For instance: M. VAN UYTFANGHE, "Le latin des hagiographes mérovingiens et la protohistoire du français", *Romanica Gandensia* 16 (1976), pp. 5-89. IDEM, "L'hagiographie et son public à l'époque mérovingienne", *Studia patristica* 16 (1985), pp. 54-62.

[11] See, for example, several of the papers in: R. WRIGHT (ed.), *Latin and the Romance Languages in the Early Middle Ages* (London, 1991; reprinted, Penn State, 1996), and the review-article of that volume by: C. VERSTEEGH, "The debate concerning Latin and Early Romance", *Diachronica* 9 (1992), pp. 259-285. R. WRIGHT, *Early Ibero-Romance* (Newark, 1995), chapter 9.

> Naturellement, la langue parlée par les locuteurs continentaux dépourvus d'instruction présentait une image sonore très déformée (et donc fautive) du latin d'école qui avait nourri Alcuin. (p. 348)

Banniard is not an apologist for Alcuin; rather, there is an unblinking acceptance here of how obnoxious Alcuin must have been, compared with the diverse but on the whole sympathetic characterization given to Augustine, Gregory and Isidore. Alcuin's self-contradictory determination to achieve both grammatical correctness ("*goût de la norme*") and effective widespread preaching, two desiderata hitherto combined by intelligent compromise from native speakers, led eventually – and after his death – to the conceptual crystallization between two languages often said by modern scholars to be attested in the Council of Tours of 813 (see below).

The reformed Latinity gradually became, in formal contexts, the ideal, and even the practice, of much of the post-Carolingian realm. Banniard traces this process no later than the 820s in *Viva voce*, but, in a subsequent neat article, sees the increasingly positive attitude taken by Alcuin's pupil Hrabanus Maurus towards the German language's qualifications to be given written form as a major precipitating factor in the final separation in different written guises of Romance and Latin.[12] Chapter 7 ("*Illusions et realités d'une réforme culturelle laique*") traces how the extreme form of the planned relatinization of society fell through, inevitably, and consequentially

> on ne pouvait, à la fois, employer une langue de plus en plus difficile à comprendre par les fidèles illettrés et exiger leur participation accrue à la vie réligieuse du royaume. (p. 406)

The Carolingian intellectuals were prepared then to accept that the liturgy would become less generally intelligible (p. 376, n. 28), whereas the sermons again came to be delivered in an accessible manner (pp. 411-413), and the priests were once again allowed to accept the Creed from their parishioners in unvarnished vernacular (p. 378, n. 35). Banniard sums this process up neatly: "*la* grammatica *et la* rusticitas, *après une longue osmose, se trouvèrent en conflit*" (p. 398). To a linguist, the obvious culmination of this chapter would have been a consideration of the methods by which a separate Romance orthography was invented (probably in the ninth century, although that traditional dating can be challenged in favour of a later one).[13] A very brief discussion emerges in the

---

[12] M. BANNIARD, "Rhabanus Maurus and the vernacular languages", in: WRIGHT (ed.), *Latin and the Romance Languages*, pp. 164-174. This was written in 1989, but after *Viva voce*.

[13] R. POSNER, "Latin to Romance (again!): change or genesis?" in: *Papers from the 10th*

conclusion, but on the whole Banniard unfortunately feels that it is beyond his brief. Perhaps he is right, for he appears slightly ill at ease even when only briefly considering the relationship among phonetics, phonology, and spelling.

Most cultural historians of the period would stop there. Not the least of the admirable features of this book is Banniard's decision to devote a chapter (8) to ninth-century Córdoba, a notoriously awkward topic here tackled in an adventurous way. His attempt to analyze the views on communication of Eulogio, Álvaro, and Samson is valuable, but his attempt to see them as representative of ninth-century Spain in general is not convincing. Eulogio and Álvaro were fundamentalists, presented by several modern scholars as being little short of insane.[14] And even if this assessment is less than fair, these two writers were certainly not representative of ninth-century Córdoba, Córdoba was not representative of Moslem Spain in general, nor was Moslem Spain representative of Spain as a whole. The comments on Eulogio are further vitiated by his apparent lack of awareness of the consequences of the fact that the surviving text is one substantially rewritten by Ambrosio de Morales in the sixteenth century. Sometimes Banniard claims that there was Carolingian influence in intellectual Christian circles at Córdoba; more often, and far more persuasively, he claims that there was no real connection (referring to their "*insularité linguistique*", p. 490). The consequences of their deliberately heightened style were not, as the consequences of Alcuin's requirements had started to do further to the northeast, to lead eventually to conceptual and written separation between a formal and an informal language; soon the Romance speakers of Al-Andalus were to be giving up literacy in their Latin-Romance ensemble entirely, for, while remaining bilingual (with Arabic) in speech, they seem to have been mostly literate in Arabic alone by the late tenth century. Meanwhile, though, Banniard makes valuable and acute observations. To these scholars, writing involved "*expoliendi*" (p. 434, n. 42), polishing their natural language "*à la lime du connaisseur*" rather than translating it into a different one; achieving their aims "*sententiis per artem Donati politis*" (p. 438), which is what Gregory said he was not going to do. It is also interesting to observe that the fourth-century grammar of Donatus was still the guide, rather than the seventh-century works of Isidore or Julian of Toledo, even in an area where Visigothic culture was still strong. Álvaro and Eulogio thus still saw a monolingual Latin-Romance ensemble, but with very wide internal stylistic variations. Their own attitudes were

International Conference on Historical Linguistics, ed. J. VAN MARLE (Amsterdam), pp. 265-279.

[14] K.B. WOLF, *Christian Martyrs in Moslem Spain* (Cambridge, 1988).

aggravating these variations rather than alleviating them. Yet as Álvaro says in the most famous passage of his *Indiculus luminosus*,[15] most speakers of *latina lingua* could not achieve the high style of their own language, so his own ability to do just that shows that he can hardly be seen as representative even of the more sophisticated members of the Christian community; and, as Banniard says, these texts were almost certainly not intended to be read aloud in public (partly because in Moslem Córdoba that would have been illegal).

The deductions that Banniard draws from Samson's attack on Hostegesis in the 880s, however, are untenable. This magnificently pedantic controversy over written style is thought by Banniard to prove the existence of a realization that Latin and Romance were separate. The interpretation cannot be accepted in so bald a form, if only because the features of Hostegesis's usage criticized by Samson cannot be seen with any consistency to be features of the spoken Early Romance of that time and place. Early Spanish Romance did not include the word "*idolatrix*", one of the words used by Hostegesis and criticized by Samson, for example, any more than the standard written language did.[16] The linguistic naiveté of Banniard's section on Samson, undermined as it is by Banniard's own demonstration that Samson's phonetics were probably Romance, and by the total absence of evidence for Banniard's unnecessary assertion that Samson criticizes Hostegesis's "*phonétique*" (p. 478), contrasts strangely with the sophistication of the previous 470 pages. Banniard even makes the wider and wilder deduction, based only on the unreliable and at best obscure comments of these hyperactive evangelists suffering from what Fontaine called "*autointoxication*", that a general conceptual break into separate languages occurred in Córdoba between 850 and 880. This implausible over-extension of his method can be forgiven, however, for the excellent translations provided for so many impenetrable texts, and for the welcome fact that he treats the Cordoban writers seriously.

With the exception of one small and one large detail, to be discussed below, the picture presented in *Viva voce* is considerably more persuasive than most of the alternatives hitherto on offer. The various disciplines of intellectual history, sociolinguistics, and historical linguistics are currently combining into an unexpectedly coherent whole, more than Banniard realized until the conference called in 1989 – after *Viva voce* went to press – to consider the question from

---

[15] J. GIL (ed.), *Corpus Scriptorum Muzarabicorum*, 2 volumes (Madrid, 1973), 1, pp. 314-315.

[16] *Corpus Scriptorum Muzarabicorum*, 2, pp. 569-572.

interdisciplinary perspectives.[17] Scholars from a variety of backgrounds have come to support the view, acquired in Banniard's case from close textual analysis, that the pre-Carolingian 'Latin' West was a monolingual ensemble: Romance philology has still to be entirely persuaded, but I am doing my best there.[18] Only inertia can prevent a sophisticated version of this view from seeming like obvious common sense in due course, and Banniard's work in particular will be regarded as seminal.

Michel Banniard himself will be surprised to read this effusive assessment, since, at the time of preparing the final version of this text at least, he seemed to be under the impression that his views disagree strongly with those expressed in my *Late Latin and Early Romance* of 1982 (henceforth *LLER*). He thought the same in his valuable review-article.[19] But, except for the two details to be discussed below, some of the views attributed to me (for instance: p. 250, n. 249; p. 269, n. 56; et cetera) are not ones I expressed in *LLER*, or since, or even before. He criticizes my 1976 article (p. 43, n. 135) precisely for attacking the monolingual view, which it in fact supports.[20] In particular, Banniard thinks I support the diglossic interpretation of the period, even asserting that "R. Wright, *Late Latin ... pousse l'application du concept à ses ultimes conséquences*" (p. 507, n. 76). In fact, I argued against the application of the concept of diglossia to the period in question as early as the second page of *LLER*, and have very often done so since.[21] Banniard's final accurate comment that the Carolingian reform sees the start of a diglossia rather than the breakup of an already existing one is what I have been saying with irritating monotony for years, rather than being "*contrairement aux assertions de R. Wright*" (p. 532, n. 174; Banniard may have confused me with Helmut Lüdtke, who indeed thinks precisely that).[22] On the other hand, on two occasions (p. 365, n. 248; p. 428) Banniard sums up my views with total accuracy, in a manner that appears to be self-contradictory with other references.

There remain the two matters on which we still disagree (there are other details on which this book has changed my mind). The less important concerns the occasional remarks that Banniard makes on non-Moslem Spain after the

---

[17] The papers are printed in: WRIGHT (ed.), *Latin and the Romance Languages*.

[18] For instance: WRIGHT, *Early Ibero-Romance*, chapters 2 and 4.

[19] R. WRIGHT, *Late Latin and Early Romance in Spain and Carolingian France* (Liverpool, 1982), reviewed by: M. BANNIARD, "Vox agrestis", *Trames* (1985), pp. 195-208.

[20] R. WRIGHT, "Speaking, reading and writing Late Latin and Early Romance", *Neophilologus* 60 (1976), pp. 178-189.

[21] For instance: WRIGHT, *Early Ibero-Romance*, chapters 1 and 3.

[22] H. LÜDTKE, *Geschichte des romanischen Wortschatzes* (Freiburg, 1968).

invasion. The comments on the Riojan glosses (p. 61, n. 237; p. 482) are merely wrong, and could have been omitted; for example, he follows the old dating to the tenth century, while referring in a note (p. 482, n. 201) to the work in which Díaz y Díaz established that they are of the eleventh.[23] But at least he is aware that not all of Spain was under Moslem rule at that time: not all medievalists know that.

The second matter is less peripheral, and concerns pronunciation. Banniard says very little indeed about pronunciation, despite its centrality to any assessment of communication, and much of what he says is sensible enough. In particular, concerning the pre-Carolingian period, he says:

> Il est certain, notamment, que la communication verticale n'a pu fonctionner que parce qu'il n'y eut pas de divergences exagérées entre l'élocution des orateurs et des lecteurs et la prononciation spontanée des illettrés. (p. 520, n. 131)

Vertical communication could be successful only because there were no real differences between educated and uneducated phonetics. This is precisely right; the fact that texts were intelligible when read aloud not only implies passive competence in the audience, that is, an ability on the part of listeners to understand the syntax and the words used, but also suggests that there was no great difference between the pronunciation of literate and illiterate. This is not what Romance philologists have tended to believe, particularly in France,[24] and this important assessment could perhaps have been highlighted earlier than page 520. And yet Banniard, who explains so incontrovertibly the linguistic reforming instincts and practices of Alcuin (*"la profondeur et l'ampleur du changement voulu – mais aussi vécu – par Alcuin"*, p. 394), decides that pronunciation was probably not involved in these reforms. Indeed he almost seems to be wishing to give the impression that Latin pronunciation was never introduced into the Romance world at all. But that is impossible to believe. Certainly, by the so-called Twelfth-Century Renaissance at the very latest, there was a phonetic difference between such related words as Latin *"fragilis"* and the French word which had developed from that, *"frêle"* (to take a standard textbook example). The question to be resolved is not whether there existed such a difference, but the period in which such systematic differences can be thought to have begun. Many scholars have assumed, vaguely for the most part, that it must have begun

---

[23] M.C. DÍAZ Y DÍAZ, *Las primeras glosas hispánicas* (Barcelona, 1978), pp. 26-36.

[24] F. DE LA CHAUSSÉE, *Noms demi-savants (issue de proparoxytons) en ancien français* (Toulouse, 1987), assumes throughout that there is a systematic phonetic distinction in the fourth century.

during the first half of the first millennium A.D. Banniard and I seem to be in agreement that it cannot have begun before Alcuin, at least. The postulation of a pronunciation reform instigated by Alcuin (or, at least, by someone at about that time), to be used in formal contexts, based largely on the provision of at least some sound to every already written letter in the word's standard spelling, is not original with me; see, for example, Jackson, Allen, Norberg, and Lüdtke.[25] If any historian wishes to argue for a later date for the introduction of these systematic phonetic distinctions into the Romance-speaking world – explaining in detail who standardized the Latinate pronunciation of such words, and when and why and how and where – they may be able to convince us; but none has attempted to do this hitherto, and the arguments in favour of the Carolingian scholars as the source of such systematic distinctions still seem more realistic.

In *Viva voce* Banniard states on several occasions (for instance: p. 503, n. 65) that Alcuin makes no comments on pronunciation. Yet Banniard himself quotes the comment in Alcuin's *Dialogus de rhetorica* that "*verba sint passim et aequabiliter et leniter et clare pronuntiata, ut suis quaeque litterae sonis enuntientur*" (p. 363: quoted from Karl Halm; "...so that every letter should be pronounced with its own sound").[26] To Alcuin, as we see from this comment, every letter should have its own sound. This attitude sees pronunciation as essentially based on spelling, as though all talking were a variety of reading aloud. Native speakers of a language, however, do not pronounce on such a basis; we need to be aware of the difference between (a) the pronunciation habits of a native speaker (of any language, including Latin), who internalizes whole words lexically one at a time with the normal pronunciation, regardless and usually in ignorance of the 'silent' letters included in the traditional spelling, and (b) the foreigner, such as Alcuin, who has learnt the language in question "as a foreign language" from texts, and has been taught to produce an individual sound for each written letter. This latter approach is almost certainly

---

[25] K. JACKSON, *Language and History in Early Britain* (Edinburgh, 1953), p. 254. W.S. ALLEN, *Vox Latina* (second edition; Cambridge, 1970), p. 106. D. NORBERG, *Manuel pratique de latin médiéval* (Paris, 1968), pp. 50-54. LÜDTKE, *Geschichte*, chapter 5.

[26] K. HALM, *Rhetores Latini minores ex codicibus maximam partem primum adhibitis* (Leipzig, 1863), 16, "Disputatio de rhetorica et de virtutibus sapientissimi regis Karli et Albini magistri", pp. 523-550, at p. 546. The full context is: "*ne verba sint inflata vel anhelata vel in faucibus frendentia nec oris inanitate resonantia, non aspera frendentibus dentibus, non hiantibus labris prolate, sed pressim [sic] et aequabiliter et leniter et clare pronuntiata, ut suis quaeque litterae sonis enuntientur ...*". The precise phonetic phenomena that Alcuin refers to here have never been worked out.

what happened in Anglo-Saxon England – where apprentices met Latin words in written form from the start – and is what everyone now does automatically when reading Latin aloud (the language being now 'foreign' to us all).[27] Alcuin would still for the most part have pronounced words that way at Tours, when we know he was promoting linguistic reforms of other kinds, and when he was (almost certainly) preparing his list of comments on orthography and correct pronunciation subsequently entitled, though not by him, *De orthographia*.[28]

It is difficult to understand why, in such a huge book as *Viva voce*, Banniard ignores this work of Alcuin's. He asks:

> Faut-il en outre admettre que les moines eurent à parfaire leur diction, c'est-à-dire que la réforme eut des aspects proprement phonétiques? Il est très difficile de répondre. (p. 358)

On the contrary, the answer is straightforward: Alcuin would have liked them to do so. Banniard further comments that

> gageons que si Alcuin ou l'un de ses élèves avait composé des guides concrete de pronunciation, il nous serait parvenu au moins un fragment. (p. 365)

But the work has survived in better shape than a fragment; it plays a starring role in Vienna 795 (Vienna, Osterreichische Nationalbibliothek, MS 795) one of the most interesting of all Carolingian manuscripts. Alcuin's treatise was studied by me in detail in 1981.[29] Rather than argue against the conclusions offered there, Banniard seems to have consciously chosen not to investigate the text at all. His only comment on it concerns this heading, found in many of its manuscripts:

> Me legat antiquas vult qui proferre loquelas
> Me qui non sequitur vult sine lege loqui

(with a variant: "*Me legat antiquas cupiat qui scire loquelas // me spernens loquitur mox sine lege patrum*"). According to Banniard, the words "*loqui*" and "*loquela*" should not be interpreted as referring to anything oral (p. 338, n. 138; p. 339, n. 144). This startling *ex cathedra* comment is undermined immediately

---

[27] See: WRIGHT, *Early Ibero-Romance*, chapter 9.

[28] Alcuin's work subsequently entitled *De orthographia* is printed in: J.P. MIGNE (ed.), *Patrologia Latina* 101, pp. 901-920; H. KEIL, *Grammatici Latini*, 7 volumes (Leipzig, 1855-1880; reprint Hildesheim, 1961), 4, pp. 295-312. A. MARSILI, *Alcuini Orthographia* (Pisa, 1952); S. BRUNI, *Alcuino "De Orthographia"* (Firenze, 1997).

[29] Reprinted as chapter 9 of this volume.

by the many occasions even in this book on which Banniard himself translates *"loqui"* as *"parler"*; for instance, from Alcuin himself: *"Quid dulcius debet esse quam Deum audire loquentem?"* translated as *"... que d'entendre parler Dieu?"* (p. 319, n. 49); and from Theodulf, *"... his quos ad loquendum aetas minime perduxit"*, rendered as *"ceux que leur âge empêche de parler"* (p. 374, n. 24; in his *Capitula ad presbyteros parrochiae suae*); where both translations are clearly correct.[30] Even if we think Alcuin might have had his own private semantics, and did not mean "speak" by *"loqui"*, a close examination of the text of the so-called *De orthographia* shows that there can be no doubt that Alcuin was concerned with both spelling and pronunciation, and that many of the changes he made with respect to his main source (Bede) were precisely designed to add comments concerned with pronunciation and omit whole entries that display no such concern. The *De orthographia,* may not, however, have spread to the curriculum of other centres than Tours. One point can easily be conceded to the sensible criticisms of my 1981 study made by McKitterick and the more sweeping ones made by Adams:[31] that this work indeed represents what Alcuin wanted people to do, but we need not see it as an exact guide or reflection in detail of what subsequent Carolingian Latin-readers actually did. As the comments of Abbo of Fleury demonstrate, not all of Alcuin's prescriptions struck root, but at the very least the presumption survived that – in Sidney Allen's words – "every letter should be given *some* pronunciation".[32]

Banniard implies that this presumption came later. But many allied phenomena are easier to understand if we can accept that the Latinate pronunciation, a sound for each letter of the standard spelling, arose by the early ninth century. Most notably the nature of the Latin sequence, structurally based on one linguistic syllable in the reformed pronunciation per musical note, and the new Romance orthography of the ninth century, structurally based – in theory – on one written letter (or digraph) for each Romance sound, seem to depend on the previous existence of such equivalences. Indeed, it is not clear why Romance orthography could not have been used for absolutely everything in the Romance-speaking realms, once it had been invented, if there was not by then

---

[30] Alcuin's Letter 296, ll. 29-30, ed. E. DÜMMLER, *Monumenta Germaniae Historica, Epistolae,* 4, p. 455. Theodulf's *Capitula* are in: J.P. MIGNE (ed.), *Patrologia Latina* 105, pp. 187-206.

[31] R. MCKITTERICK, *The Carolingians and the Written Word* (Cambridge, 1989), p. 12. J.N. ADAMS, review of: WRIGHT, *Late Latin,* in: *Liverpool Classical Monthly* 14 (1989), pp. 14-16 and pp. 34-48 (particularly section V).

[32] A. GUERREAU-JALABERT (ed.), *Abbo Floriacensis: Quaestiones Grammaticales* (Paris, 1982), pp. 209-260. ALLEN, *Vox Latina,* p. 106.

a separate Latinate non-Romance pronunciation used by at least some of the literate. These are among the *"indices"* that Banniard claims he cannot find:

> Le latin post-carolingien n'offre pas d'indices sûrs d'une véritable uniformisation articulatoire. Échec d'une tentative? Plutôt absence de celle-ci. (p. 366, n. 249)

Banniard sees the phonetic aspects of the reform as at best *"toilette"* (p. 365), but we must remember the uncontrovertible truth that not only were ninth-century vernacular pronunciations of words in France usually different from the reformed Latinate pronunciation of the same words, but in some cases very different, with whole syllables having disappeared, even in ecclesiastical words sometimes said to be influenced by clerical pronunciation, such as *"episcopus"* (French *"évêque"*). So much else in the reforms involved structural reorganization rather than mere tidying-up, that the increasingly fashionable view, that the non-vernacular Latinate pronunciation, which must have begun at some time, in fact began at this time, is actually strengthened by the other aspects of Banniard's impressive argumentation (in particular, that serious phonetic reforms could not have happened before 768 at the earliest). This timetable is certainly not incompatible with Banniard's reconstruction of other events. All scholars in the field could provisionally agree that the conceptual distinction between Romance and Latin took a long time to become universally intuited; agree, that is, with McKitterick, Van Uytfanghe, Zumthor, Posner, and also Nelson, who established (in 1985) that the whole of Nithard's *Histories* (*De dissensionibus filiorum Ludovici Pii*), not merely the Strasbourg Oaths, were meant to be read aloud intelligibly.[33] Banniard's remark that *"la restauration du langage n'était qu'à ses débuts en 813"* (p. 501) thus rings truer than his apparently contradictory comment that

> nous savons au contraire que c'est très précisément en ce début du IXe siècle que s'est établie avec netteté dans la conscience commune des lettrés, comme dans leur vocabulaire, la distinction entre langue latine et langue romane. (p. 273)

The latter remark agrees more with the views expressed in *LLER,* and the former agrees more with the more nuanced process I have come to envisage since

---

[33] McKitterick, *The Carolingians and the Written Word*, passim. Posner, "Latin to Romance". M. van Uytfanghe, "Les expressions du type *quod vulgo vocant* dans des textes latins antérieurs au concile de Tours et aux serments de Strasbourg", *Zeitschrift für romanische Philologie* 105 (1989), pp. 28-49. P. Zumthor, *Langue et technique poétique à l'époque romane (XIe-XIIIe siècle)* (Paris, 1963), passim. J. Nelson, "Public *histories* and private history in the work of Nithard", *Speculum* 60 (1985), pp. 251-293, pp. 257-266.

then. Indeed, the fact that I still think that the verb *"transferre"*, as used in canon 17 of the Council of Tours (813), means "change" (that is, that it is used to refer to something much less precise than "translate"), while Banniard still sees it categorically and specifically as "translate", shows that Banniard, in some moods at least, envisages an even clearer "crystallization" of the two entities under Alcuin than I do.[34]

All that has happened is that, despite his acuity over grammatical matters, Banniard has not yet had the chance to consider in detail the relationship between phonetics and orthography, which is at the forefront of debate in contemporary historical linguistics. In general terms, the connection between the two is not necessarily close;[35] indeed, some languages use contentedly an orthography that has little or even no connection with pronunciation at all. Banniard is quite right to comment, of a Merovingian author, that *"il a naturellement transcrit la prononciation vulgaire avec le système orthographique traditionnel"* (p. 297), for there was then no alternative. He knows that spelling is not now and was not then a phonetic transcription (p. 364, n. 245). Yet he can adopt a contradictory view on occasion, and draw improbable implications from spelling, such as:

> ... il est possible d'affirmer qu'il comporte – sauf, évidemment, du point de vue phonétique, parce que l'orthographe latine est préservée – autant de traits protoromans que de traits latins. (p. 286, concerning Chrodegang's *Regula canonicorum*.)

This *non sequitur* is unfortunate. Perhaps it needs to be pointed out yet again, that people who spell well do not thereby necessarily speak in an archaic way. It could well be that some of the contradictions referred to here are the result of the enormous gestation time of the book, with the consequence that later ideas have been added to incompatible earlier ones, rather than replacing them.

The significance and achievement of *Viva voce,* however, are great. In particular there may now be a real chance of bridging the gap of misunderstanding between historical linguists and linguistic historians of this period. For as well as the textual analysis Banniard offers both an initial and a final chapter in which he makes a brave assessment of several aspects of Romance historical

---

[34] The documents of the Council of Tours of 813 are in: *Monumenta Germaniae Historica, Legum* 3, *Concilia* 2.1, pp. 286-293. Canon 17 (p. 288) ends as follows: *"... ut easdem omelias quisque aperte transferre studeat in rusticam Romanam linguam aut Thiotiscam, quo facilius cuncti possint intellegere quae dicuntur"* (see chapter 9 of the present volume).

[35] For consideration of this question in the Latin-Romance world, see: WRIGHT, *Early Ibero-Romance*, chapter 13.

linguistics. He has a low opinion of Romanists, on the whole. The majority of those he knows are French (for instance Brunot, Lot, Straka) or write in French (for instance De Dardel and Wüest, who are both Swiss), and the modern ones among these are scholars working in the reconstruction tradition.[36] This seems to be why he regularly calls Early Romance *"protoroman"* ("Proto-Romance"), a word usually only used within reconstruction theory (for instance by De Dardel). Some of the investigators consulted by Banniard indeed have firmly held views on the earliness of Romance evolution and divergence from Latin. For example, by application of the reconstruction techniques (originally devised to make some kind of guess at Proto-Indo-European), based in this case on comparative analyses of the separate medieval Romance languages, they manage to envisage a genuine bilingual distinction within the Roman Empire itself, or even, in De Dardel's case, long before it. De Dardel is thoroughly determined not to take texts into account at all, and even criticizes Herman for doing so.[37] Banniard is right to point this out with genuine astonishment (p. 515, n. 113), but wrong to think that this school represents modern Romance historical linguists in general. It does not. One of the leaders in the field for the last twenty years has been Alberto Varvaro of Naples, whose voluminous work has unfortunately only rarely been translated out of Italian, but whose vision of the fragmentation and restructuring of Romania is similar to and compatible with Banniard's own.[38] Banniard does not mention him. This only partial perception of the field may underlie Banniard's failure to realize that the perspectives of my *LLER* largely agree with his own. I am a Romance linguist, and whereas Banniard (and McKitterick) call the Latin-Romance ensemble of the period between 410 and 813 'Latin', I prefer to call it 'Early Romance'. The point at issue is the same, however; we are not envisaging an early conceptual split, and we are both referring to a single linguistic state containing essentially the same linguistic elements.

[36] F. BRUNOT, *Histoire de la langue française* (second edition; Paris, 1966). LOT, "A quelle époque". G. STRAKA, *Les sons et les mots* (Paris, 1979). R. DE DARDEL, *Esquisse structurale des subordonnants conjonctionnels en roman commun* (Geneva, 1983). J. WÜEST, *La dialectalisation de la Galloromania* (Bern, 1979).

[37] B. BAUER, *Du latin au français: Le passage d une langue SOV à une langue SVO* (Nijmegen, 1992), supports De Dardel in this, but is even so justifiably sceptical of his syntactic reconstructions (p. 69).

[38] See: A. VARVARO, "Latin and Romance: fragmentation or restructuring?", in: WRIGHT (ed.), *Latin and the Romance Languages*, pp. 44-51, for a unique study of his in English. See also: J. HERMAN, *Du latin aux langues romanes: études de linguistique historique* (Tübingen, 1990).

Some of the linguistic features of the time are ones which we can identify individually from our later vantage point as being 'Latin' – that is, as having also existed in the language of the Roman Empire (such as the 'synthetic' one-word pluperfect, originally *-veram*, which still existed in tenth-century France and still exists today in twentieth-century Portugal) – and others are ones which we can now identify as 'Romance' in that they seem not to have been normal practice in the Empire but became so later in many of the subsequently separately identified Romance languages as a whole (such as the 'analytic' two-word pluperfect, formed with "*habebam*" plus past participle, whose descendants form the normal Romance pluperfect except in modern Portugal). The language of the post-Roman pre-Carolingian period also included, of course, features that existed both in the Roman Empire and in at least some of the Romance languages (including a majority of the words, however pronounced), and also indeed included the occasional baffling item unique to the period, recognizable neither from earlier nor later standardizations. This combination of elements is well explained in Banniard's chapter 9, with perfectly reasonable guesses as to when individual linguistic features fell out of active use. Banniard (pp. 520-522) considers the details of this kind of competition between old and new, and identifies ten relevant phenomena within the noun phrase (including the loss of the neuter gender, the loss of noun cases other than the nominative and accusative, and the appearance of the new definite article, "*ille*", "*ipse*"[39]), eight of the verb phrase (including the loss of the future perfect forms, of the original future forms, of the 'synthetic' one-word passive forms, and of the imperfect subjunctive), and six syntactic phenomena (including the loss of "*ut*" clauses, the increased use of prepositions with infinitives, and closer constraints on permissible word order).

As Banniard realizes, to characterize their language as being a mixture of earlier Latin and subsequent Romance is unsatisfactory, because the language of the period had a coherence of its own. All language stages are transitional between those of earlier and later periods, but it makes little sense to describe (for example) twentieth-century English as being a mixture of the English of the sixteenth century and that of the twenty-third century. Most speakers have no idea of what the former was or of what the latter is going to be, even though the seeds of much of twenty-third-century usage are probably with us now. Similarly, the language of the pre-Carolingian European West deserves not to be called either corrupted Latin, or incipient Romance, or a mixture of the two, but

---

[39] See: M. SELIG, *Die Entwicklung der Nominaldeterminanten im Spätlatein* (Tübingen, 1992).

to be seen as a coherent unit of its own, despite its variability. For that reason, when discussing it, I have consistently tried to use the term 'Early Romance' (or 'Late Latin', when referring to texts), and not to use the single word 'Latin' at all to refer to this ensemble.[40] My view of the linguistic nature of the age, as opposed to the name which we should give to their language, is extremely close to that which Banniard recounts in his final chapter (schematized neatly on pp. 520-522, far better than I have ever done). He calls it *"polymorphisme"*; as detailed above, there is a co-existence for centuries, within the same language, of old, new, and continuing grammatical features, both morphological and syntactic. Even if the new features initially arose early in this period, or during the Empire (which is a probable chronology for their initial occurrence in several cases), the old features with which they were in competition for the same function dropped out of active usage only later; and it is likely that the old-fashioned phenomena dropped entirely out of the passive understanding of those who heard texts read aloud very much later still. John Green, for example, studies the loss of the synthetic passive, to the benefit of its co-existing alternatives, and comes to this conclusion.[41] It was not compulsory for the old features eventually to fall into decline at all, particularly if a slight difference in meaning or conditions of usage turned up which enabled a functional contrast to be exploited between old and new.[42] Furthermore, those that eventually did disappear did not disappear from speech all at the same time in a single cataclysmic structural convulsion. Latin 'turns into' Romance in a long series of stages, rather than all at once. Trying to identify a single chronological transitional point for losing all the old features and gaining all the new features at once is a misrepresentation of what was historically a lengthy and staggered process (we might wish, however, to see the late eighth century as the time when the 'new' features collectively came to be heard on more than fifty per cent of the occasions of use of such competitors). This perspective also means that we can legitimately conclude that many of the pronunciation changes were consummated earlier than the morpho-syntactic ones, but were for a long time common to the whole Early Romance area (this is broadly the view of Herman and Varvaro). Thus the early date of some individual pronunciation changes in the reconstruc-

---

[40] See: WRIGHT, *Early Ibero-Romance*, chapter 1.

[41] J.N. GREEN, "The collapse and replacement of verbal inflection in Late Latin / Early Romance: How would one know?", in: WRIGHT (ed.), *Latin and the Romance Languages*, pp. 83-99.

[42] See: R. WRIGHT, "Versatility and vagueness in early medieval Spain", in: *Hispanic Linguistic Studies in Honour of F.W. Hodcroft*, ed. D. MACKENZIE and I. MICHAEL (Oxford, 1993), pp. 207-223.

tionist scenario remains acceptable, but the theory of a very early divergence into separate languages (geographically, that is, as well as of Latin and Romance) is no longer tenable at all. Banniard manages to find support in a minor but valuable study by Gustav Beckmann, and an aging one by Louis Sas,[43] but he has more support in the linguists' camp than he realizes (or realized at the time of writing), and in particular from the master himself, József Herman. Herman has recently pointed out that confusion over names of languages was as common then as it is now, so perhaps it is time at last to be clear.[44]

To conclude: the nature of the pre-Carolingian monolingualism which Banniard argues for so convincingly in the seven central chapters would perhaps be clearer to appreciate in the first and last chapters if he gave it a name of its own, but that is a secondary issue. The whole book is entirely to be recommended to anyone interested in the language of the period, whether linguist, philologist, Latinist, Romanist, historian, textual critic, or even (in the circumstances) theologian. There are far more interesting details in *Viva voce* than can be referred to even in a long review-article, and this work just cannot be ignored. Banniard's excellent *Genèse culturelle de l'Europe* turns out to have been merely a hors d'oeuvre.[45]

[43] G. BECKMANN, *Die Nachfolgekonstruktionen des instrumentalen Ablativs im Spätlatein und im Französischen* (Tübingen, 1963). L.F. SAS, *The Noun Declension System in Merovingian Latin* (Paris, 1937). Also: H.F. MULLER, *A Chronology of Vulgar Latin* (Halle, 1929). IDEM, *L'époque merovingienne* (New York, 1945).

[44] J. HERMAN, "Spoken and written Latin in the last centuries of the Roman empire: a contribution to the linguistic history of the western provinces", in: WRIGHT (ed.), *Latin and the Romance Languages*, pp. 29-43.

[45] M. BANNIARD, *Genèse culturelle de l'Europe (Ve-VIIIe siècle)* (Paris, 1989).

Section B

Texts and Language in Late Antiquity

The language spoken in the Romance area from the fifth to the ninth centuries has been viewed by modern scholars from a wide variety of perspectives. Sometimes it is essentially characterized as a decadent or barbarous kind of Latin. Sometimes it is seen as an incipient or hesitant kind of Romance (or 'Proto-Romance'). Often both Latin and (Proto-)Romance are thought to have coexisted at the time as separate entities, sometimes in a diglossic relationship. It has also been seen as a combination or mixture of the two. But it is preferable to try to analyse the language and the texts of the time in their own terms, rather than with reference to the past or the future. If we consider the advances made recently in the sociolinguistic understanding of variation, there is no good reason to see the presence of both older and newer linguistic features in the speech of the time as indicating any kind of bilingualism or diglossia; there just existed linguistic variation of an essentially normal kind.

Even so, this is also the period when the ingredients of the future standardized Medieval Latin were gradually coming into being, both as regards the expansion of the grammatical tradition and the extension of Latin to Christian communities of other native languages. The consequence was an increasingly perceptible difference between the Latin of native speakers and that of others. This was not crystallized into any explicit idea that the two were different languages, but it was capable not only of causing slight difficulties in face to face communication but of leading to noticeable differences in small details in written texts, particularly in the genre of rhythmic verse, which depended more than most on features of speech.

The four chapters in this section consider all these aspects. Chapter 5 looks at the grammarian Priscian, who worked at the Emperor's Court in Constantinople and finished his huge *Institutiones Grammaticae* in *c*. 527. The nature of this work is explained by its sources and original circumstances, rather than its future. He was not to know that the work would, three centuries later, become elevated to the status of indisputable authority in a quite different historical context, founding a tradition out of whose shadow scholars have only very recently managed to escape. This was particularly unfortunate in that his analyses were not always indisputably the correct ones.

Chapter 6 looks at the complex but monolingual state of the Early Romance speech communities in the West in the seventh century, where it seems reasonable to suggest that old and new morphosyntactic features coexisted in the variable whole, but all speakers used evolved phonetics.

The seeds for the eventual Medieval conceptual separation of Latin (as used by non-native speakers) from native-speakers' Romance lie in the eighth century, when the two traditions occasionally met. Chapter 7 looks in particular at the meeting between the Anglo-Saxon Latinist Wynfreth (later called Boniface) and the native Roman Pope Gregory II, probably in 722, when Wynfreth preferred for serious matters to communicate with the Pope in writing, even though they could in general converse successfully orally. This chapter also considers, and rejects, the likelihood of any kind of Carolingian-style linguistic reform having taken place in the eighth-century Papacy.

Chapter 8 considers whether perceptible differences in the genre of 'rhythmic' poetry can be attributed to the native vernacular of authors from different areas, and suggests that as regards a few details of alliteration, rhyme, diphthongs, synaloepha, syncope, stress, prefixation, adonic rhythm and the prothetic [e-] vowel, such a distinction can be sensibly made, but on the whole only before the advent of the Carolingian reformed Latin into the author's own community.

Thus the linguistic nature of these centuries is not easy to assess, and much more research needs to be done, but some light can indeed be shed by such a sociophilological approach which combines close analysis of textual detail with an understanding of both historical context and modern sociolinguistics.

Chapter 5

The Role of Priscian

It has long been realized that linguists do not only use language as their data; they also use other linguists. Some compilers of dictionaries, for example, devote as much time to investigating other dictionaries as they do to studying linguistic corpora. The equivalent in the Late and Vulgar Latin period was the glossary, materials for which were normally provided by existing glossaries, which is why they tended over time to get increasingly remote from the normal linguistic usage of the compiler's own time. Many of the most remarkable cases of linguists being led astray by reliance on other linguists concern Renaissance grammarians who tried to make European languages fit the morphological patterns of Latin, which is why even now, for example, some Spanish linguists categorize Spanish with such terms as accusative, optative and middle voice, the use of which tends to create more confusion than it solves. In the Latin case, though, the most startling example must be the analysis made by some of the Roman grammarians of the phonological accent. Most Latinists now accept the view, which might of course be wrong after all (but is probably right), that Latin never had a pitch accent, even though respected grammarians such as Quintilian said it did.[1] If we are right in this view, and the Latin grammarians were, as we suspect, merely assuming that Latin must have worked in the way that Greek did, then we are positing a remarkable situation; these lin-

This chapter is a reprint, with minor changes, of: "Even Priscian nods", in: *Acts of the Sixth International Conference on Late and Vulgar Latin*, ed. H. SOLIN (Hildesheim, 2002). We are grateful to Professor Heikki Solin and Dr Peter Guyot, on behalf of Georg Olms Verlag (Hildesheim), for permitting the reprint.

[1] J. HERMAN, *Vulgar Latin* (Penn State, 2000), pp. 35-36.

guists were saying things that were, it would seem, self-evidently untrue. And this is not a matter of abstruse deep structure, whose nature and very existence are not self-evident, but a phenomenon so high on the surface that it cannot even be recovered from the written mode.

Respect for the Greek grammatical tradition was natural, and deserved. In this case, of course, the Greek linguists were right about Greek. And it cannot have seemed at all obvious, even to the most acute of the Roman linguists, which linguistic features were effectively universals (or, at least, common to both Italic and Greek), and which features could vary from language to language. Vowels, and to a large extent the intuited notion of syllables, are indeed universal, so it probably seemed instinctively natural to take the accentual system to be universal as well, being based, as it is, on the syllabic vocalic nucleus. And if a Roman linguist happened to notice that real people did not use these pitch accents, well, that was just the speakers' mistake. Grammars were primarily written in order to indicate what should be the case, rather than to describe what was actually done, and were only marginally interested in speech at all.

It took a remarkably long while, as it seems to modern specialists in retrospect, for an explicit and autonomous systematic understanding of elementary Latin morphology to arise, but when it did, beginning with Aelius Donatus in the fourth century, it came to dominate the pedagogical aspects of the grammatical tradition. This comment is not designed as a claim that Donatus was particularly brilliant, nor that his *Ars Minor* verged on the exhaustive, because, as Vivien Law has often pointed out, he omitted many categories that now seem necessary, including what later came to be thought of as the fourth and fifth declensions.[2] But a swathe of commentators expanded that tradition, and eventually it did indeed become more or less all-inclusive, in particular as regards inflectional nominal morphology. This emphasis can be taken as a sign that most of the students of grammar in the Late Latin period were increasingly uncertain about at least some of the noun inflections, which was why this basic information was thought to be both important and useful. It is not at all surprising to note that the spread of explicit information about nominal morphology seems to have coincided with the period when parts of it were becoming increasingly unstable in actual usage.[3] Because of the same lack of instinctive knowledge, the Latin-as-a-foreign-language students in the eighth-century

---

[2] V. LAW, *Grammar and Grammarians in the Early Middle Ages* (London, 1997).

[3] HERMAN, *Vulgar Latin*, pp. 49-68. R. WRIGHT, *Late Latin and Early Romance in Spain and Carolingian France* (Liverpool, 1982), pp. 38-43.

British Isles, and then eventually the whole Carolingian higher education system, took Donatus as their elementary textbook. In this case, Donatus's lists can be accepted as essentially correct, even if not all-inclusive; Greek morphology did not substantially distort his analyses.

But outside Constantinople, the Grammarians of the Late and Vulgar Latin period are all but silent on syntax. Maybe they did not know it existed. From the fact that Donatus said almost nothing about syntax (and a great deal about morphology), we can probably deduce that the syntax found in texts was not normally a barrier to their proper understanding in his time; several aspects of word order were still essentially unpredictable, and a knowledge of morphology alone could help here, as inflections, if identifiable, could suffice for disambiguation. Yet there was another reason for the lack of explicit concentration on syntax; new constructions were coming into general spoken usage, but it seems clear that even so in many cases the old ones that they competed with were not yet disappearing, and for a long while both old and new usages were alive. The old functions and structures were also common in texts, and would still be generally understood passively for centuries after Donatus. Thus obsolete vocabulary, and defunct inflections, might stymie a reader, but obsolescent syntax probably would not. For this reason the help given by Donatus came to be increasingly augmented in pedagogical contexts by the use of lexical glosses on texts. But in the Romance-speaking area, at least, syntactic glossing, indicating in particular the normal vernacular word order, or which of a choice of noun phrases was the subject of the verb, only began to be practised several centuries later, as in the famous eleventh-century glosses of the monastery of San Millán. Donatus's own aim, and that of his Early-Romance-speaking commentators, was the elucidation of the textual register, not the explicit classification of structures that were in real life unproblematical for students.

Greek grammarians, on the other hand, belonged to a more philosophical tradition, and had been studying Greek syntax for centuries. When the time came for Greek students to want to learn and study Latin seriously, particularly after the Emperor moved East, these Greek students of Latin needed to be told about syntactic details that the Early-Romance speaking students did not. One consequence of this development was that when Priscian, in early sixth-century Constantinople, became the first Latin-speaking grammarian, so far as we know, to undertake a serious and comprehensive analysis of Latin syntax (*De Constructione*), he had Greek grammarians before him as role models, such as, in particular, Apollonius Dyscolus (second century A.D.). Apollonius Dyscolus's work may perhaps have been known in Rome,[4] but it seems to have started no tradition there of syntactic study. Later, Dositheus prepared a Latin grammar with a Greek translation, probably for the use of Greeks learning Latin, but without venturing beyond the Donatan tradition.[5] In the intervening years the fourth-century grammarians Charisius and Diomedes, at Constantinople, had also been experts in the Greek grammatical tradition, although largely inspired by now-lost treatises by Varro and Palaemon.[6] But in any event they had gone into less detail than Priscian did; the syntactic analyses included in Priscian's huge eighteen-book *Institutiones Grammaticae* (finalized in 526-527), mostly, but not only, in the last two books, are thus simultaneously adventurous and even spectacular within the line of Latin grammarians, but are even so not always original work based on his own analysis of Latin data. He too studied other grammarians as well as, or sometimes rather than, his own language. And there can be no doubt, after Ballaira's brief but pungent analysis,[7] that Priscian was indeed a native Latin-speaker from Mauretania, who probably fled before the Vandals to reach Constantinople before 500, and gained his higher education there within the Greek system.

Priscian was in a position of authority, being probably the main State-employed linguist (at least with respect to Latin) at the courts of the Emperors Anastasius, Justin and Justinian himself. And the decisions that Priscian took in his grammatical analyses were eventually to have remarkable resonance down the ages. Further West, his work was known initially only in excerpted form until Alcuin studied the *Institutiones* in detail and with fascination at Tours in the late 790s; particularly, it seems, in order to learn more about Greek.[8] The influence of the *Institutiones* is visible in Alcuin's own grammatical works, and he also produced an abridged version which omitted the Greek. As Luhtala suggests,[9] it was almost certainly Alcuin's initiative that led to Priscian's *Institutiones*, described by Vivien Law as "a University-level grammar if ever there was one",[10] being added to the official Carolingian higher

---

[4] M. BARATIN, *La naissance de la syntaxe à Rome* (Paris, 1989).

[5] H. BERSCHIN, *Greek Letters and the Latin Middle Ages* (Washington, 1988).

[6] According to: M. IRVINE, *The Making of Textual Culture: "Grammatica" and Literary Theory, 350-1100* (Cambridge, 1994), p. 56.

[7] G. BALLAIRA, *Prisciano e i suoi amici* (Turin, 1989).

[8] J. O'DONNELL, "Alcuin's *Priscian*", in: *Latin Script and Letters, A.D. 400-900*, ed. J. O'MEARA and B. NEUMANN (Leiden, 1976), pp. 222-235.

[9] A. LUHTALA, "Syntax and dialectic in Carolingian commentaries on Priscian's *Institutiones Grammaticae*", in: *History of Linguistic Thought in the Early Middle Ages*, ed. V. LAW (Amsterdam, 1993), pp. 145-191.

[10] LAW, *Grammar*, p. 155.

education curriculum in the role of the advanced textbook (even though it was by then some three hundred years old), to follow on from the *Ars Minor* of Donatus (which by then was almost five hundred years out of date). And these two, accompanied by the Germanic spelling-pronunciation system which artificially gave a sound to every letter, created the monolithic register of Church Medieval Latin, whose invention and gradual spread from the ninth century marks the end of the previous stylistically versatile Late and Vulgar Latin period. This officially decreed assumption that archaism was *per se* desirable had some disastrous consequences; in the words of Ian Wood: "A new set of fissures within the Latin language was introduced with the search for linguistic purity pursued by the Carolingians and their Christian advisers, which resulted in the newly cleansed Latin of the élite being separated off from the proto-Romance of the majority of the population".[11]

At this point I indulge in a brief uncharitable digression to observe that there is considerable truth in the view that, if the Carolingian reforms had been as successful as Alcuin wanted, they would have created a kind of cultural and grammatical police state. Intellectual pluralism did not appeal to Alcuin any more than did the sociolinguistic variation ("*rusticitas*") of the Early Romance that surrounded him at Tours. But fortunately for all but himself, Alcuin died in 804, and some realism could return. As Michel Banniard pointed out,[12] Alcuin may well have wanted all Christian confessions to be made in this new archaic kind of Latin, with every letter sounded out. It is not clear to what extent this ever actually happened, but in any event that would have been impossible to police, and the requirement for sermons to be read aloud in this self-defeating style was relaxed at the Council of Tours in 813 for the sake of intelligibility, and the reciters of sermons could revert to their normal Romance reading, or, where appropriate, change into Germanic. Alcuin's own linguistic work was not canonized; his *De Orthographia* stopped being copied by the 830s, it seems, and his grammar did not in the end become a set book. Hrabanus Maurus had been Alcuin's star pupil, but even so Hrabanus reissued that seventeenth canon of the Council of Tours verbatim on his accession as Bishop of Mainz in 847. Furthermore, as Banniard pointed out, Hrabanus was interested in the use and promotion of Germanic, while Alcuin seems to have had

---

[11] I. WOOD, "Modes of communication: an afterword", in: *East and West: Modes of Communication*, ed. E. CHRYSOS and I. WOOD (Leiden, 1999: *The Transformation of the Roman World* 5), pp. 279-282.

[12] M. BANNIARD, *Viva Voce: communication écrite et communication orale du IVe au IXe siècle en Occident latin* (Paris, 1992), chapter 6.

absolutely no intellectual interest in his own mother tongue.[13] But Priscian himself had become an *auctor* whose word could not be doubted. In turn, Hrabanus's star pupil, Lupus of Ferrières was academically "concerned with establishing and clarifying the whole text" of the *Institutiones*.[14] It may be that Alcuin's death was comparable to the deposition of Margaret Thatcher, or the death of general Franco, in that much of the drive for uniformitization and the intolerance of diversity weakened with his absence. But his promotion of Priscian as an *auctor*, presenting a kind of *ex cathedra* official Latin that needed admiration and close annotation, stuck. Thus the fact that Donatus and Priscian were describing a stage of the language used in the far distant past, and the newly prescribed spelling-pronunciations of almost every word did not correspond to anybody's contemporary vernacular, was not seen as a disadvantage within this register. Consequently, objective analysis of actual spoken language as used in real life fell out of fashion; and as Dionisotti pointed out,[15] a later Carolingian scholar as distinguished as Remigius of Auxerre was able to misunderstand what Priscian had said about Greek. Grammar became part of philosophy rather than an empirical investigation, in Gibson's words: "such endless editorial apparatus merely promoted a command of Priscian's text, without either assessing it or putting it to use".[16]

A great deal is now known about the way in which Priscian's *Institutiones* spread all over the Carolingian intellectual area from Alcuin's base at Tours. My former Liverpool colleague, the late Margaret Gibson, traced the location of Priscian manuscripts in the ninth century and, to some extent, later.[17] The importance of Priscian's decisions, in fixing the explicit doctrine of what correct Latin was, was so seminal that it is still with us. Basic Latin textbooks even now contain details whose formulation can be traced back to Donatus and Priscian, even though we now live in the post-Pinkster age and can see the

[13] M. BANNIARD, "Rhabanus Maurus and the vernacular languages", in: R. WRIGHT (ed.), *Latin and the Romance Languages in the Early Middle Ages* (London, 1991; reprint, Penn State, 1996), pp. 164-174.

[14] M. GIBSON, "Milestones in the study of Priscian, circa 800 – circa 1200", *Viator* 23 (1992), pp. 17-33.

[15] A.C. DIONISOTTI, "Greek grammars and dictionaries in Carolingian Europe", in: *The Sacred Nectar of the Greeks: The Study of Greek in the West in the Early Middle Ages*, ed. M. HERREN (London, 1988), pp. 1-56.

[16] GIBSON, "Milestones", p. 20.

[17] GIBSON, "Milestones". Also: M. PASSALACQUA, *I codici di Prisciano* (Rome, 1978). IDEM, "Priscian's *Institutio de nomine et pronomine et verbo* in the ninth century", in: LAW (ed.), *History*, pp. 193-204. R. HOFMAN, "Glosses in a ninth-century Priscian MS probably attributable to Heiric of Auxerre († *ca.* 876) and their connections", *Studi Medievali* 29 (1988), pp. 805-839.

contextual limitations of Alcuin's assembled authorities.[18] But despite the spread of his ideas throughout the Western World, and the knowledge we now have from the studies of Margaret Gibson, Vivien Law, Martin Irvine and others about the use of Priscian in the Central Middle Ages, no scholar since Hertz, in the edition published by Keil in the *Grammatici latini* (volumes II-III, 1855-1859), has undertaken the by now very necessary task of re-editing the text.[19] And no modern scholar has systematically checked against other available evidence, from other texts and from the discoveries of historical Romance linguistics, to see if everything that Priscian said about Latin was right, or if, on the other hand, he sometimes described Latin in terms which were true of Greek, but not, in fact, of Latin.

There is no time here for a full analysis, but I can offer you two specific misconceptions of this type. The first arises from the fact that the Greek word ἄνθρωπος could be used to refer to both men and women, and that it was possible to use the feminine article with it, ἡ ἄνθρωπος, meaning "the human" when in context referring to a woman. The ending of the noun did not change, and grammarians indicated the presence of the female gender in such cases with the use of the feminine article. The Latin grammatical tradition was naturally unable to indicate gender, number or case in exactly this way, since there was no article in Latin in the fourth century. Donatus instead accompanied nouns with the relevant form of *"hic"*, *"haec"*, *"hoc"*, in order to indicate the gender category which the noun belonged to. For this reason, when Diomedes wanted to indicate that the Latin word *"homo"* could be used to refer to both men and women, he included the word *"haec"*, mistakenly (and perhaps without meaning to do so) implying that *"hic homo"* and *"haec homo"* were both acceptable noun phrases: *"sunt enim communia duum generum ex masculino et feminino, ut hic et haec homo et hic et haec sacerdos"*.[20] Priscian then says the same, but it is only in Priscian that we can work out why he claims *"haec homo"* to be acceptable, since he explicitly compares the case to Greek ἡ ἄνθρωπος:

quae communia esse tam ipsa natura quam exempla Graecorum nobis demonstrare possunt, apud quos vel communia vel mobilia haec inveniuntur, ut hic et haec homo, ὁ ἄνθρωπος καὶ ἡ ἄνθρωπος, hic et haec latro, ὁ λῃστὴς καὶ ἡ λῃστής.[21]

---

[18] H. PINKSTER, *Latin Syntax and Semantics* (London, 1990).
[19] H. KEIL, *Grammatici Latini*, volumes 2 and 3 (Leipzig, 1855 and 1859).
[20] KEIL, *Grammatici Latini*, 1, p. 301, ll. 10-12.
[21] Priscian, *Institutiones Grammaticae*, 5, 10. KEIL, *Grammatici Latini* 2, p. 146, ll. 5-9.

A neat study by Demyttenaere traces a theological problem mentioned in passing by Gregory of Tours back to this grammatical misconception (which seems also to be wrong for the word "*latro*").[22] Apparently merely because Priscian says so, modern dictionaries seem also to imply in passing that "*homo*" could be linguistically feminine (as well as just being usable to apply to female people), but no example has convinced me yet of this. Egeria refers to herself generically as "*homo*" ("one", as French "*on*"), granted, but there is no sign there that this is linguistically feminine (".. *si tamen labor dici potest ubi homo desiderium suum compleri videt*", "if it can be called work when one sees one's desires fulfilled").[23] Lewis and Short misleadingly refer to a use of the noun phrase "*homines feminae*" in Augustine's *City of God*,[24] but the reference is to a use in the ablative which strikes me as being undoubtedly a linguistically masculine noun phrase: "*an deos fas est hominibus feminis, mares autem homines deabus misceri nefas?*",[25] with "*feminis*" being used as Spanish "*hembra*" (or English "*female*") can be now, to show that a masculine noun phrase actually has a female referent; that is, the actual noun phrase "*haec homo*" was never acceptable usage among native speakers.[26] In Romance, this word, as Spanish "*hombre*", Italian "*uomo*" and French "*homme*", can still be used to refer in context to a woman (meaning "human being"), but it does not thereby become grammatically feminine gender, and I do not believe that it did in the sixth century either. The assumption that Greek and Latin had the same grammar could also lead to similar Carolingian misconceptions in the other direction: Carlotta Dionisotti mentions an elementary Carolingian grammar of Greek which wrongly stated that Greek ἱερεύς is both masculine and feminine, just as its Latin counterpart "*sacerdos*" was.[27]

[22] Gregory of Tours, *Historiae*, ed. B. KRUSCH and W. LEVISON (Hannover, 1951: *Monumenta Germaniae Historica. Scriptores rerum Merovingicarum* 1) 8, 20. A. DEMYTTENAERE, "Qu'une femme ne peut être appelée homme. Questions de langue et d'anthropologie autour du concile de Mâcon (585)", in: *Spoken and Written Language: Relations between Latin and the Vernaculars*, ed. M. MOSTERT (Utrecht, 2002: *Utrecht Studies in Medieval Literacy* 4).

[23] Egeria, *Peregrinatio Aetheriae*, ed. P. MARAVAL, *Égérie, Journal de voyage (Itinéraire)* (Paris, 1997: *Sources chrétiennes* 296), 13. 1.

[24] C.T. LEWIS and C. SHORT, *A Latin Dictionary* (Oxford, 1879).

[25] Augustine, *De Civitate Dei*, ed. B. DOMBART and A. KALB (Leipzig, 1928-1929: *Bibliotheca scriptorum Graecorum et Romanorum Teubneriana*), 3, 3.

[26] Du Cange offers "*homo nostra*" in a Belgian document of 1241, meaning "our feudal vassal", referring to a dead vassal's widow: C. DU CANGE, *Glossarium Mediae et Infimae Latinis* 4 (Paris, 1885), p. 224.

[27] DIONISOTTI, "Greek grammars", p. 32.

The second case concerns the use of reflexive syntax with non-agentive semantics.[28] Discussing the reflexive pronoun in Book 13. 22, Priscian decreed as follows, using, as he usually did, the genitive as the citation form of the pronoun:

> *Sui* solum apud Latinos reciprocum fit in eadem tertia persona, quod Graeci ἀντανάκλαστον vocant, id est quando ipsa in se actum reflectit persona, ut eadem sit et agens et patiens, potest significare ἑαυτου *sui*. Nam τὸ ἐμαυτου et σαυτου, quod est primae et secundae personae, non habemus, sed pro eis simplicibus primitivis utimur, quae tam in reciprocatione quam in transitione poni possunt, ut *mei misereor* et *mei misereris*, similiter *tui misereris* et *tui misereor*.[29]

This is not a bad definition of the reflexive, that the same person is both agent and patient.[30] Priscian notes rightly that "*se*" is the only specifically reflexive pronoun in Latin, and that, unlike in Greek, semantically reflexive first and second person usages have no specific separate pronouns available in Latin, using both "*mei*" and "*tui*" for both reflexive and non-reflexive uses. He has indeed noticed a real difference between the two languages here. (This comment is in the *Institutiones* section on pronouns, but is not included in the abbreviated *Institutio de nomine et pronomine et verbo*).[31] It can be seen that Priscian's analysis of the third-person reflexive is not couched in syntactic terms. Nowadays we would define a reflexive as (to quote Trask) "denoting a construction in which two noun phrases are understood as having the same referent".[32] Priscian defines it in semantic terms, as when someone turns an act onto her or himself, "*in se*", in such a way that the same person is both the agent and the patient of the action, thereby correctly rendering the value of the Greek reflexive "ἑαυτου".

Reflexives had apparently not interested native Latin-speaking grammatical analysts before. This section of Priscian's Grammar is largely inspired by Apollonius Dyscolus' account of transitivity ("*in transitione*" in the passage quoted). Priscian's assessment is certainly an advance on Pompeius, who had

---

[28] Studied in more detail in: R. WRIGHT, "La sintaxis reflexiva con semántica no agentiva", in: *Actas del primer congreso nacional de latín medieval*, ed. M. PÉREZ GONZÁLEZ (León, 1995), pp. 415-431.

[29] Priscian, *Institutiones Grammaticae*, 13, 22. KEIL, *Grammatici Latini*, 3, p. 14, ll. 17-24.

[30] It is at least preferable to that of Woodcock's influential school grammar, which states that "*se*" is used when "a speaker is referring to himself"; that is, of course, the definition of the first person pronoun, not of the third person reflexive: E.C. WOODCOCK, *A New Latin Syntax* (London, 1959), p. 24.

[31] KEIL, *Grammatici Latini*, 3, p. 449, l. 7 - p. 450, l. 11.

[32] R.L. TRASK, *A Dictionary of Grammatical Terms in Linguistics* (London, 1993), p. 233.

said that all verbs must either *"agere"* or *"pati"*; himself using the non-personal non-agentive verb phrase *"se habet"* in the process, thereby proving himself wrong:

> scire debes quod omne verbum quod est in rerum natura aut agere aut pati nos ostendit. Et re vera ipsa natura rerum sic se habet.[33]

It is also preferable to the confusion of syntax with semantics which had earlier led Macrobius (*c.* 400) to claim that reflexives were philosophically impossible, since nobody could be both agent and patient at once; and, astonishingly, Macrobius too neatly confounded his own argument by including perfectly formed syntactic reflexives in his own denunciation of semantic reflexives:

> Numquam, inquit [*sc.* Aristotle], fieri potest, ut circa unam eandem rem uno eodemque tempore contrarietates ad unum idemque pertinentes eveniant; scimus autem quia movere facere est et moveri pati est: ei igitur quod se movet simul evenient duo sibi contraria, et facere et pati, quod impossibile est: anima igitur non potest se movere.[34]

Unfortunately, Priscian's analysis in terms of agent and patient is only partly accurate, being over-zealous in two respects. In reality, the entity referred to with the Latin word *"se"* need not be a person, and need not be the agent of the action, although in each case these represent the statistical majority. There are many examples in Latin, from earliest times onwards, of *"se"* being used with a non-personal subject, including:

> nam hanc se bene habere aetatem nimiost aequius.[35]
> caveat ne labitur columella .. denuo eodem modo facito ne se moveat.[36]
> quarum omnium commune est aliter se corpus habere atque consuevit.[37]
> Quo maior vis aquae se incitavisset, hoc artius illigata tenerentur.[38]
> Atque haec eo pertinet oratio ut, perditis rebus omnibus, tamen ipsa virtus se sustentare posse videatur.[39]

---

[33] KEIL, *Grammatici Latini*, 5, p. 213, ll. 23-25.

[34] Ambrosius Theodosius Macrobius, *Commentarii in Somnium Scipionis*, 2. 14. 25. Also discussed by: LUHTALA, "Syntax and dialectic", pp. 158-159, who makes no further reference to reflexive syntax.

[35] Plautus, *Mercator*, l. 549.

[36] Cato, *De Agricultura*, 20. 1.

[37] Celsus, *De Medicina*, 2. 2. 1.

[38] Caesar, *De Bello Gallico*, 4. 17.

[39] Cicero, *Epistola familiaris*, 6. 1. 4. Many other cases are referred to by: H.F. MULLER, "The passive voice in Vulgar Latin", *Romanic Review* 15 (1924), pp. 68-93, pp. 87-88. WRIGHT, "La sintaxis reflexiva", pp. 427-428; and indeed elsewhere.

"*Se*" was also commonly used with non-human referents after prepositions, as in the phrase "*per se*"; compare the discussion of intransitive verbs by Priscian himself, "*quae ex se in se ipsa fit intrinsecus passio, ut 'rubeo', 'ferveo', 'caleo'*", et cetera.[40] There has even so arisen a tradition of referring to such non-personal usages as being necessarily metaphorical, and unavoidably personifying the subject,[41] yet the textual examples that have been unearthed usually seem in practice to be both boringly literal and unpersonified. Flobert's brief analysis, however, does make the necessary distinction between the metaphorically agentive and the agentless usages.[42] Thus the agentive implication in the use of Latin "*se*" was not obligatory. But since Priscian and his academic descendants said that it was, some modern scholars have even suggested that where the subject of the reflexive verb happens to be inanimate, the putatively intrinsic agentive meaning implies some kind of primitive animism in the mind of the author, who must therefore have been attributing agentive power to an inanimate entity.[43] Since the authors in question include Cicero, Caesar, Horace, Pliny the Elder, Varro, Vergil, Quintilian, Livy, Cato, and several grammarians (including Pompeius), it is surely preferable to adjust the grammatical definition of the reflexive, rather than to label such distinguished and rational authors as primitive animists.

The point at issue is that in Latin the referent of the reflexive has to be the patient of the action, certainly, but not necessarily the agent; "*se*" is as indeterminate for semantic agentivity as it is for gender and number. That is, as regards agentivity, Latin functioned like Modern English, in which a stressed use of the reflexive object pronoun does seem to imply an agentive subject, and is thus unavoidably metaphorical if the subject is inanimate; as when an estate agent remarks that "the housing market is so buoyant that these houses are selling themselves", with a strong stress on "selves", [sélvz], a remark which all concerned know is not literally true. On the other hand, an object reflexive is unstressed in perhaps as many as a fifth of modern English uses, without semantic implications of agentivity. A neat example could be heard on the BBC Radio 4 News of 3 November 1997: "Liberty's Store in London has put

[40] KEIL, *Grammatici Latini*, 2, p. 378, ll. 12-13.
[41] Discussed by: J.N. GREEN, "The collapse and replacement of verbal inflection in Late Latin / Early Romance: How would one know?", in: WRIGHT (ed.), *Latin and the Romance Languages*, pp. 83-99.
[42] P. FLOBERT, *Les verbes déponents latins des origines à Charlemagne* (Paris, 1975), pp. 386-390.
[43] For instance: A. RONCONI, *Il verbo latino: problemi di sintassi storica* (second edition, Firenze, 1968), pp. 19-25.

itself up for sale. The directors took the decision ...", where the subject of the reflexive verb is explicitly stated not to have been the agent. Such clitic non-agentive reflexives even appear quite often with a personal subject; as in "I found myself on a train", meaning "I was on a train, but I don't know how I got there". In such unstressed cases the reflexive does not even imply that there was an agent (although there might have been), whereas the paradigmatically competing passive construction ("I was found on a train") implies the existence of an agent ("somebody found me") even if that agent is not mentioned explicitly. As several modern studies have shown, Latin usage was in essence similar to this; even the non-agentive use accompanying a personal subject appears in the *Cena Trimalchionis* (*"nec medici se inveniunt"*, "and no doctors can be found"),[44] although the next example which Latinists have found of such a non-agentive personal subject is much later, in Gregory the Great's *Dialogues*, when he refers to the prophet Habbakuk, who suddenly found himself (*"se invenit"*) being transported, with his lunch, to a different country and back again:

> propheta ex Iudaea sublevatus, repente est cum prandio in Chaldea depositus. Quo videlicet prandio prophetam refecit, seque repente in Iudaea iterum invenit.[45]

Greek ἑαυτου was always stressed, and probably for that very reason always implied an agentive subject. So the Greek grammatical tradition had had no occasion to consider the possible usage of unstressed reflexives. But Latin *"se"* could be either stressed or unstressed, and, as Pederson has argued,[46] it may even be a universal fact of language that unstressed reflexives, and only the unstressed, can be used as a deagentivizing device, or what Michela Cennamo, following Haspelmath, calls an "anticausative".[47] Romance languages have subsequently extended the deagentivizing usage extensively, such that, for example, French *"se brûler"* and Spanish *"quemarse"* mean "to get accidentally sunburnt", whereas intentional burning would have to be specified with the further addition of the stressed form of the pronoun, French *"soi"*, Spanish

---

[44] Petronius, *Cena Trimalchionis*, 47. 2.

[45] Gregory the Great, *Dialogi*, ed. A. DE VOGÜE, *Grégoire le Grand: Dialogues*, 3 volumes (Paris, 1978-1980: *Sources chrétiennes* 259, 260 and 265) , II, c. 22.

[46] E.W. PEDERSON, *Subtle Semantics: Universals in the Polysemy of Reflexive and Causative Constructions* (doctoral thesis; Berkeley, 1991).

[47] M. CENNAMO, "The loss of the voice dimension between Late Latin and Early Romance", in: *Historical Linguistics 1997*, ed. D. STEIN *e.a.* (Amsterdam, 1999), pp. 77-100. M. HASPELMATH, *Transitivity Alternations of the Anticausative Type* (Cologne, 1987).

"*sî*".[48] Much ink has been spilt on the rise of this supposedly Romance construction, but it was in fact in Latin all along, even if infrequent in comparison with Romance, as Muller's study clearly established in 1924;[49] deagentivized reflexives were an unremarkable feature of Latin, so unremarkable that no grammarians remarked on them. Indeed, they had probably already existed in Indo-European.[50]

There are many further interesting facets of the development of the reflexive constructions in Latin, but the only other syntactic (rather than morphological) aspect covered by Priscian concerns cases in which the object in a subordinate clause is co-referential not with the subject of that clause but with the subject of the main clause, as in his own invented example "*rogat Turnus Aeneam ut sibi parcat*", "Turnus begs Aeneas to spare him[self]": that is, to save Turnus.[51] And since Priscian mentioned this minor point, while omitting other major aspects of the use of the reflexive, some subsequent pedagogical grammars mention this and omit the others similarly.

The uncertainty is not confined to syntax. Frédérique Biville has also shown how Greek phonology could mislead Priscian into wrongly analyzing Latin phonology, particularly as regards the voiced velar consonants.[52] And Priscian did not necessarily need Greek models to cause him to nod; a further case concerns Priscian's comment to the effect that prefixed words with the roots *inde* and *quando* had proparoxytonic stress:[53]

> *deinde, subinde, perinde, exinde, proinde,* quae omnia antepaenultimam habent acutam ....
> ut *siquando, nequando*; nam *aliquando,* differentiae causa ab *aliquanto* .. acuit
> antepaenultimam.[54]

Except perhaps for "*deinde*", this comment is merely wrong, which suggests that the other words were no longer part of his active speech. And Carolingian

---

[48] A.G. HATCHER, *Reflexive Verbs: Latin, Old French, Modern French* (Baltimore, 1942), discusses this case, although she was wrong to imply that it was a recent development.

[49] MULLER, "The passive".

[50] WRIGHT, "La sintaxis reflexiva", p. 424.

[51] Priscian, *Institutiones Grammaticae*, 17, l. 134. KEIL, *Grammatici Latini*, 3, p. 176, l. 6.

[52] F. BIVILLE, "Tradition grecque et actualité latine chez les grammairiens latins: l'approche phonique de la langue", *Ktéma* 13 (1988), pp. 155-166. IDEM, "Réflexions sur la notion d'interférence et ses realisations: le cas du grec et du latin", in: *Contatti linguistici e storia del latino*, ed. J. HERMAN and L. MONDIN (Tübingen, 2002).

[53] Priscian, *Institutiones Grammaticae*, 15, 10. Discussed by: D. NORBERG, *L'Accentuation des mots dans le vers latin du Moyen Age* (Stockholm, 1985), pp. 18-19.

[54] KEIL, *Grammatici Latini*, 3, p. 67, ll. 10-12 and 17-19.

and later writers of rhythmic poetry were misled by this, as Norberg pointed out.

My first point has been that even Priscian nods; that is, even Priscian, a linguist of genius, could be guilty of following his intellectual role-models rather than investigating the data of his native language directly. And my second point is that it is unfortunate that the authority of his analyses became set in stone by their apotheosization in the Carolingian education system, the event that effectively turned Latin into a foreign language even for its native speakers. I am not the first to rebel, of course. In his splendid reanalysis of Latin grammar as a whole, effectively the first for 1400 years, Harm Pinkster does not explicitly deal with reflexive constructions, but he does helpfully reanalyse the idea of the agentive, in the terms of Dik's functional grammar, as "control".[55] There may well be other cases in which Priscian's reliance on the correct analysis of Greek as the analogue for his own description of Latin led to misconceptions; but if so, it seems that they have still not been noticed, because it is astonishing to realize how little work has been done by modern linguists on what the most voluble of all the ancient grammarians actually said.

---

[55] PINKSTER, *Latin*, p. 17.

Chapter 6

The Latin-Romance 'Ensemble'
of the Seventh Century

It is generally accepted that the Romance-speaking area in the seventh century was in a transitional stage between the Latin of the Empire and the later Romance Languages. Michel Banniard has used the word "*ensemble*" to refer to the language of the time, and I have adopted that here.[1] Banniard showed that in Gaul up until the eighth century writers expected that a listening audience would understand their text if it was read aloud. He has further elaborated the implications of this through what he calls "*sociolinguistique retrospective*".[2] Examination of texts from the Iberian Peninsula suggests that this complex monolingualism continued there up until the twelfth century in Christian Spain, although in Moslem Spain the ability to use and understand written Latin texts seems largely to have disappeared by the tenth century.[3] The present chapter will analyse more closely the nature of this Latin-Romance 'ensemble' in the seventh century.

This chapter is a translation of: "L'Ensemble latin-roman du septième siècle", in: *Latin vulgaire – latin tardif* IV, ed. L. CALLEBAT (Hildesheim, 1995), pp. 103-112. We are grateful to Professor Louis Callebat and Dr Peter Guyot, on behalf of Georg Olms Verlag (Hildesheim) for permitting the reprint. The translation into English is my own.

[1] M. BANNIARD, *Genèse culturelle de l'Europe (Ve-VIIIe siècle)* (Paris, 1989).

[2] M. BANNIARD, "La voix et l'écriture: émergences médiévales", *Médiévales* 25 (1991), pp. 5-16. IDEM, "Latin tardif et français prélittéraire: observations de mhode et de chronologie", *Bulletin de la Société de Linguistique de Paris* 88 (1993), pp. 139-162.

[3] R. WRIGHT, *Early Ibero-Romance* (Newark, 1995), chapters 9-18.

Phonetics

We can accept the early dating that is usually given to many of the phonetic developments which are now thought of as forming part of Early Romance. There is no way we can give precise dates to a linguistic change, for
changes take a long time to complete; but the study by Cravens shows that even
a small percentage of orthographical errors can be enough to indicate the existence of a phonetic development in progress.[4] Even so, we need not presuppose
that these evolutions imply wide geographical divergence at an early time.
Several studies by József Herman have suggested that the final stages of the
Roman Empire in the West saw some phonetic convergence, in that several
phonetic developments that had begun in a particular area came to spread more
generally.[5] We can also deduce that such geographical variation as did exist
posed no serious barriers to spoken communication in the seventh century.
Romance-speakers managed to travel long distances within Romania without
feeling the need for translators; for example, St. Martin of Braga came all the
way from Pannonia in the East to preach in Gallaecia in the West.

The phonetic developments are to some extent hidden from us by the traditional spellings, which continued to be taught to scribes as being the correct
way to write. Modern philologists would have preferred them to aim for a
phonetic transcription of their speech, but instead they continued to aim to
produce the standard spelling for each word. This meant, as Varvaro, Emiliano
and other scholars have pointed out, that the teaching of orthography had to
become increasingly logographic, as happens in Modern French.[6] That is, the
apprentice scribe learnt separately the whole form of many words, and in the
seventh century as in the twenty-first, there was as a result often a great difference between the standard written form of a word and its phonetic transcription.

Everyone used the evolved forms in speech. Thus Saints' Lives and other
texts that were read aloud could be generally understood.[7] This implies that all

---

[4] T.D. CRAVENS, "Phonology, phonetics and orthography in Late Latin and Romance: the
evidence for early intervocalic sonorization", in: *Latin and the Romance Languages in the Early
Middle Ages*, ed. R. WRIGHT (London, 1991; reprint, Penn State, 1996), pp. 52-68.

[5] J. HERMAN, *Du latin aux langues romanes* (Tübingen, 1990).

[6] A. EMILIANO, "*Latín y romance* en las Glosas de San Millán y de Silos", in: *Actas del I
Congreso Anglo-Hispano. I. Lingüística*, ed. R. PENNY (Madrid, 1993), pp. 235-244. A.
VARVARO, "Latin and Romance: fragmentation or restructuring?", in: WRIGHT (ed.), *Latin and
the Romance Languages*, pp. 44-51.

[7] M. VAN UYTFANGHE, "L'hagiographie et son public à l'époque mérovingienne", *Studia*

the speakers in a particular area used similar phonetics, whether literate or not. The *"lectores"* were supposed to read in a careful manner, of course, as Isidore of Seville explicitly required them to in seventh-century Spain, but that was still a careful style within the repertoire of their own monolingual 'ensemble' of styles; Isidore never told his trainee readers to aim to reproduce archaic or old-fashioned phonemes. In the Early Romance-speaking world they do not seem yet to have followed the system that was going to be recommended in France two centuries later, the system which we know of as Medieval Latin (in which a reader was supposed to base his reading pronunciation on the individual letters of the standard written forms). In the seventh century this method of reading Latin aloud probably as yet only existed in the British Isles.

Morphology and Syntax

The texts that were read, or sung, aloud were of several types: sermons, hymns, Saints' Lives, administrative and legal documents, letters, epitaphs, et cetera. In that century writers more commonly used papyrus than parchment, for it seems that the trade in papyrus remained active until the Moslem expansion of the last part of the century.[8] Papyrus, like wax tablets and wood, is biodegradable, so not many papyrus texts have survived. They also used other writing surfaces at the time, such as the slates found in a rural area of the Iberian Peninsula, examined exhaustively by Isabel Velázquez Soriano.[9] These show that the ability to use writing was not confined to the clerics. The style used by those who composed texts in the seventh century was often fairly straightforward, with the exception of some of the Visigothic writers, who seem deliberately to have preferred not to be too comprehensible, but in each case the style fitted into the general 'ensemble'.

It is likely that the syntax had not changed greatly between the fifth and seventh centuries. The differences that can now be reconstructed between the style of many texts and the vernacular of the time were probably viewed at the time as being cases of stylistic variation within the 'ensemble', for there is no reason to suppose that they impeded communication. For example, the increasingly common use of the words *"ille"* and *"ipse"* with a reduced deictic force

Patristica 16 (1985), pp. 54-62.

[8] H. PIRENNE, "De l'état de l'instruction des laïcs à l'époque mérovingienne", *Revue Bénédictine* 46 (1934), pp. 165-177.

[9] I. VELÁZQUEZ SORIANO, *Las pizarras visigodas: edición crítica y estudio* (Murcia, 1989).

(as analysed by Selig),[10] the increasing use of "*quod*" clauses rather than the accusative and infinitive, the use of the originally pluperfect subjunctive instead of the imperfect, et cetera, did not mean that the older usages had become incomprehensible at all. It is normal in all literate communities for there to be a stylistic difference between writing and speech. This is not what Riché said, but, as Banniard points out, Riché did not appreciate the difference between active and passive competence;[11] we can all understand many relatively archaic usages when we hear them, even if we no longer use them much in active speech.

It could be that morphology posed more problems than syntax did. Herman showed that the traditional verbal morphology seemed more accessible to seventh-century scribes in Gaul than the old nominal morphology did.[12] This may have been the general case; as it is, for example, in the ninth-century *Crónica de Alfonso III* from Oviedo.[13] Herman also showed that inflections could be confused with other inflections within the same paradigm, but that there is usually no confusion between verb and nominal inflections. For example, the use of *-um* instead of correct *-o* is only found with nouns and adjectives, and never in the first person singular of verbs. This indicates that the confusion cannot have been just phonetic. Indeed, *-om* and *-u* are both much rarer than *-um* and *-o*. One conclusion that can be drawn from this is that the written inflections were learnt as separate whole units, in this case as morphographic units rather than logographic; that is, the scribes knew that *-um* and *-o* were correct endings, but were unsure about when to use which.

We can be sure that many other evolved morphosyntactic phenomena that were not recommended in the *Artes Grammaticae* also existed in speech, and had done even in the Empire itself. Those which can also be found in Plautus had been there for centuries, of course. We can feel fairly certain that, to express several meanings, the use of a preposition with a noun in an oblique case was in the seventh century already more common than the use of a noun in an oblique case without a preposition. We can be sure that the relative commonness of analytical future tense forms was increasing at the expense of the origi-

---

[10] M. SELIG, *Die Entwicklung der Nominaldeterminanten im Spätlatein* (Tübingen, 1992).

[11] P. RICHÉ, *Education et culture dans l'Occident barbare, VIe-VIIe siècles* (Paris, 1962). M. BANNIARD, *Viva Voce: communication écrite et communication orale du IVe au IXe siècle en occident latin* (Paris, 1992), p. 61.

[12] J. HERMAN, "Sur quelques aspects du latin mérovingien: langue écrite et langue parlée", in: *Latin vulgaire – latin tardif* III, ed. M. ILIESCU and W. MARXGUT (Tübingen, 1992), pp. 173-186.

[13] WRIGHT, *Early Ibero-Romance*, chapter 11.

nal synthetic future forms. This would have been the case with everybody. Indeed, as Adams showed in his study of the future as expressed in the works of the Grammarian Pompeius, and as I showed in a study of the use in Latin of reflexive syntax without reflexive meaning, the Grammarians themselves did not always manage to follow their own prescriptions in their discursive text.[14]

In the case of morphology and syntax, there is no need to suppose that older forms disappeared at the same time as newer forms with similar functions arrived. Rather than a neat and quick subsitution of one for the other, it seems more probable that, for example, both the newer uses with prepositions and the older uses without them could be heard within the seventh-century 'ensemble'. Manuel Díaz y Díaz has described this kind of variation as sometimes being a kind of competition ("*variables alternativas, acaso en lucha*");[15] but there is no need to see such coexistence as implying a struggle for supremacy. Both old and new could co-exist. Herman has pointed out, for example, that the use of "*quod*" and the indicative after verbs of saying seems to have developed for a specific and limited pragmatic purpose, rather than as a generally available rival for the traditional accusative and infinitive.[16] And the growing desire to use prepositions, instead of relying on oblique cases alone to convey the same meaning, seems to have begun with the ablative, long before the Roman Empire itself, rather than being particularly a Romance innovation. As Silvia Luraghi showed, the Empire coincides with a very long transitional period in which the combination of a preposition and an inflection together expressed with some redundancy the required meaning.[17] The old semantic values of the nominative, accusative, genitive and dative have survived with perfect comprehensibility in the pronouns even to this day, and it seems entirely reasonable to suppose that words endowed with those traditional nominal inflections would still be generally understood when heard read aloud. Even endings such as *-orum* and *-ibus*, pronounced by a reader in a Romance fashion, naturally, would have

[14] J.N. ADAMS, "Some neglected evidence for Latin *habeo* with infinitive: the order of the constituents", *Transactions of the Philological Society* 89 (1991), pp. 131-196. R. WRIGHT, "La sintaxis reflexiva con semántica no agentiva", in: *Actas del Primer Congreso Nacional de Latín Medieval*, ed. M. PÉREZ GONZÁLEZ (León, 1995), pp. 415-431.

[15] M.C. DÍAZ Y DÍAZ, "El latín de España en el siglo VII: lengua y escritura según los textos documentales", in: *Le septième siècle: changements et continuités*, ed. J. FONTAINE and J.N. HILLGARTH (London, 1992), pp. 25-40, p. 37.

[16] J. HERMAN, "Accusativus cum infinitivo et subordonnée à *quod*, *quia* en latin tardif – nouvelles remarques sur un vieux problème", in: *Subordination and other topics in Latin*, ed. G. CALBOLI (Amsterdam, 1989), pp. 133-152.

[17] S. LURAGHI, "The relationship between prepositions and cases within Latin prepositional phrases", in: CALBOLI (ed), *Subordination*, pp. 253-272.

been recognizable, even when they were decreasingly being used spontaneously in speech.

Verb morphology was more complex in itself, but then it was evolving more slowly. Here too old and new could co-exist. Green, for example, showed that in order to express passive meaning both the old synthetic forms and the new analytic or ostensibly reflexive forms were available, existing side by side in the one 'ensemble'.[18]

Thus the forms which readers and listeners encountered in texts from the past corresponded to only a subsection of those that were available in their own linguistic competence. The *Artes Grammaticae*, which were still used in an uninterrupted pedagogical tradition, had only chosen some of the available forms to be recommended in writing, omitting the rest. The inevitable result of the Grammarians' prescriptions was that the syntax and morphology of written texts came to be impoverished in comparison with the vitality and flexibility that seems to have characterised the Latin-Romance speech of the seventh century. Details of the old morphology came to form part of orthographical training, as well as being explained at length in the Grammars,[19] which is how the scribes knew what the endings were. In this way, verb forms that might even have completely fallen from normal speech could still be generally understood; we can compare this situation with that of the "*passé simple*" of Modern French, rarely used in speech, regularly used in writing, and just one part of the Modern French "*ensemble*". So there is no reason to be surprised by the idea that the syntax and morphology of written texts could have been generally intelligible when these were read aloud; that was part of their passive competence.

Vocabulary

New words come into a language, and old ones fall out of use, all the time. But it is more common for new ones to come in. New words are always being used, sometimes borrowed from other languages, sometimes created via derivational morphology from existing resources. This phenomenon has often been studied. Rather less common are studies of the converse process, lexical loss,

---

[18] J.N. GREEN, "The collapse and replacement of verbal inflection in Late Latin / Early Romance: How would one know?", in: WRIGHT (ed.), *Latin and the Romance Languages*, pp. 83-99.

[19] DÍAZ Y DÍAZ, "El latín de España", p. 25.

although Steven Dworkin has considered the process in some detail in Span-ish.[20] In fact, it is always hard to decide whether a particular word has fallen out of use entirely from passive comprehension, and has thus become unintelli-gible. Yet if there was in the seventh century a real barrier to the comprehen-sion of written texts when they were read aloud, it is most likely to have ex-isted at the lexical level. On the other hand, the readers were aware of this possibility. For example, they would often insert words into the margin of their texts which had just such a practical purpose, to help them explain words in the text which the readers have themselves understood but which their audience might have trouble with.

There was another possible cause of confusion which they might never have realized themselves; semantic changes. The semantic value of many words had modified over the centuries. This had happened, for example, to "*ille*", "*ipse*", "*quod*", "*habeo*", "*de*", "*ad*", et cetera. Any context in which these words maintained their old sense ran the risk of leading both readers and listeners to misunderstandings. Isidore of Seville realized this problem, at least as regards the most obvious cases, and a large part of Isidore's own works are dedicated to the clarification of potentially ambiguous usages. But even Isidore of Seville, the most active intellectual of this age, was sometimes mistaken, because his language too belonged to the 'ensemble' of his time.

Early Romance

Many modern specialists have fallen into the habit of separating conceptu-ally the Latin language, as one systematic unit, from the Romance languages, conceived of as conceptually separate complete systems distinct from Latin. Specialists in 'Proto-Romance' reconstruction tend to make this distinction with reference to the time of the Roman Empire, or even earlier. Their phonetic (and even phonological) reconstructions seem to be essentially correct. But unlike these specialists, I believe it is more rational to see the reconstructed pronunciations as applying to the speech of the whole population, including the literate. In this I disagree also with Michel Banniard's conclusion that edu-cated people in the seventh century spoke with a noticeably different phonol-

---

[20] For instance: S. DWORKIN, "Studies in lexical loss: the fate of the Old Spanish post-adjectival abstracts in -*dad*, -*dumbre*, -*eza* and -*ura*", *Bulletin of Hispanic Studies* 66 (1989), pp. 335-342.

ogy from the rest.[21] Whereas I do agree with Michel Banniard and József Herman and others that many of the morphosyntactic features of the Latin of the
Roman Empire were still there, even if only as part of the passive competence
of listeners, until the eighth century or later; that is, during the period which
Banniard calls "*l'antiquité tardive finissante*".

These conclusions are not incompatible. We know that most texts could
still be generally understood when read aloud, in the seventh century. This can
be attributed to the fact that in a particular area they all spoke with the same
evolved phonetics, whether educated or not. We can call that the 'Proto-Romance' phonetics or phonology of the time, if we like, more or less as it has
been reconstructed by modern specialists. For this reason the listening public
could recognize the words. In addition, the syntactic organization of these
words in the text remained accessible on the whole. There were indeed new
features in their 'ensemble', but most of the old ones had not left it yet; the
'ensemble' was, as Banniard also describes it, a case of "*polymorphisme*".[22] It
was only very much later, in the ninth century – or even, if Rebecca Posner is
right, the twelfth century[23] – that scribes systematically tried to distinguish
between two separate languages, standard Latin and vernacular Romance. At
that later time they were going to have to decide which of the forms in their
pre-existing 'ensemble' belonged to which of the two languages separated in
that way, but there was no need even to think of doing that yet in the seventh
century.

One of the problems that the modern reconstruction specialists have lies
here: they feel a need to discover a complete change from one whole complete
linguistic system to another. There is no need to assume that this is necessary,
and in the Latin-Romance case this possibility is only an illusion. It is true that
several phonetic phenomena which we would like to think of as being
'Romance' certainly existed in the West during the time of the Roman Empire,
but there is no reason to draw the conclusion from this that therefore there was
at the time a clear distinction between Latin and Romance. The reconstructable
evolutions, and the geographical divergence which these were seen to imply
even for this early time, motivated the construction of tree diagrams which
envisaged the existence of several Romance languages already by the seventh

---

[21] See above, chapter 4.

[22] BANNIARD, *Viva voce*, chapter 9.

[23] R. POSNER, "Latin and Romance (again!): change or genesis?", in: *Papers from the 10th
International Conference on Historical Linguistics*, ed. J. VAN MARLE (Amsterdam, 1993),
pp. 265-279.

century.[24] The rationale behind such tree diagrams is phonetic. It would be more difficult to design such diagrams on the basis of morphology and syntax, and even if we did, they would not necessarily be exactly the same as those that have a phonetic basis. For example, the existence of an isolated language which we could call 'Sardinian' would probably not seem as early as it does in the present phonetically-based trees.

Some of the developments which led to the definitive abandonment of several morphosyntactic phenomena from general passive competence seem to be locatable to the second half of the eighth century – although Rosamond McKitterick proposes an even later dating[25] – but this conclusion is independent of the chronology of the phonetic changes. There is no need to presuppose that all linguistic levels change at the same time, at the same rate and in the same way. Indeed, it seems to be increasingly accepted that we can date the most important periods for the phonetic and morphosyntactic developments to different times altogether.[26]

The language of the seventh century was not the Latin of the Roman Empire, and it was not the Romance of a later age, just as contemporary French is not sixteenth-century French nor twenty-fifth-century French. It would thus be best not to refer to it as either 'Latin' or 'Romance', *tout court*. It would be absurd, however, to refer to it as a 'mixture' of Latin and Romance, unless we are happy to see contemporary French as a 'mixture' of sixteenth and twenty-fifth-century French. The language in the seventh century was a coherent single language; varied, variable, flexible, yes, and it knew the 'predialectalization' that Banniard has spoken of, but there was as yet no attempt made to separate all the linguistic phenomena of the age out into one or other of two conceptual entities to be called Latin and Romance, and still less between different regional dialects. This 'ensemble' was a genuine language of its own, and deserves its own name. Michel Banniard, who likes periodizing, has called the language of this age *"latin parlé tardif phase deux"*. I have tended to call it 'Early Romance' ("roman précoce" in French, "romance temprano" in Spanish). All rigid chronological periodizations are a mirage, of course. The 'ensemble' in 700 A.D. was not the same as in 600. Languages are always changing,

[24] WRIGHT, *Early Ibero-Romance*, chapter 4.

[25] R. MCKITTERICK (ed.), *The Uses of Literacy in Early Medieval Europe* (Cambridge, 1990).

[26] BANNIARD, "Latin tardif", pp. 149-150. E. ITKONEN, "Un conflit entre facteurs phonétiques et facteurs fonctionnels dans un texte en latin mérovingien", *Neuphilologische Mitteilungen* 70 (1969), pp. 471-484. J. HERMAN, *Vulgar Latin* (Penn State, 2000). A. LÓPEZ GARCÍA, *Cómo surgió el español* (Madrid, 2000), pp. 34-39.

and changes can be slow, so our attempts to pin them down, to classify them, and to define their grammar, are often no more than temporary approximations.

Those who spoke this Early Romance but could not read, participated, even so, in the culture of their time, to a greater extent than has generally been appreciated by modern specialists in the age. It was not difficult, and certainly not impossible, for the educated and the uneducated to talk to each other, no more then than it is now; they shared the same culture in the same society. This is more or less the case in Modern France and Modern Britain as well; nothing unusual is being proposed here. The conclusion is that historical linguists and other interested investigators need to present a rather more generous view of the Early Romance-speaking communities of the seventh century. As Jacques Fontaine has pointed out,[27] for a century or more now we have seen a gradual retreat among scholars from the prejudices that the Enlightenment had against 'Gothic barbarism', and linguists can share in the reevaluation. This was not a time devoid of culture; theirs was a speech community of considerable vitality, which still operated on a basis of written legal documentation.[28] Texts were still intelligible when read aloud, as most were, since readers and listeners shared the same evolved Early Romance phonetics and a grammar that combined old and new morphological and syntactic features in a single monolingual 'ensemble': the Early Romance of the Seventh Century.

[27] J. FONTAINE, "Allocution d'ouverture", in: *L'Europe héritière de l'Espagne Wisigothique*, ed. J. FONTAINE and C. PELLISTRANDI (Madrid, 1992), pp. 5-7.
[28] H. ATSMA and J. VÉZIN, *Chartae Latinae Antiquiores*, XIII (Zürich, 1981).

Chapter 7

Foreigners' Latin and Romance: Boniface and Pope Gregory II

I am not the first Anglo-Saxon specialist in Latin linguistics to have gone to talk in Italy and be somewhat embarrassed by my insufficiency in spoken *"romanzo italiano"*. In the early eighth century the Anglo-Saxon scholar Wynfreth felt the same way when he went to Rome to meet Pope Gregory II in 722. He was asking for the Pope's blessing for his own plans to spread the Christian mission into Germanic lands, and before giving this the Pope wanted him to undergo an oral examination concerning his Christian credentials. Wynfreth, however, was unwilling to do that, and arranged instead to present his understanding of the Christian faith in writing. He passed that written examination with flying colours. Whereupon Gregory changed Wynfreth's name to Boniface, and, under his new Christian name, Boniface then set out to spend three successful decades as the founder of German Christianity.

At no point did Boniface himself inform posterity of his uncertainties about this proposed oral examination. Neither did Gregory, even though several of the letters that these two subsequently exchanged have survived for us. Nor is it mentioned in the relevant section of the *Liber Pontificalis*, Gregory II's *Vita*. The only reason that we know about it now is because Boniface's younger contemporary Willibald included this detail in his biography of Boniface. This fact strongly suggests that the story is true, since in itself it reflects

This chapter is a translation of: "Latino e Romanzo: Bonifazio e il Papa Gregorio II", in: *La preistoria dell'italiano*, ed. J. HERMAN (Tübingen, 2000), pp. 219-229. We are grateful to Professor József Herman and Max Niemeyer Verlag (Tübingen) for permitting the reprint. The translation into English is my own.

no great credit on Boniface's abilities and would hardly have been invented *ex nihilo*. Much later the tale is picked up and elaborated, in words that derive only in part from Willibald, by the eleventh-century monk of St Emmeran in Regensburg, Otloh. Levison's edition of these biographies also includes four others composed in between; these four mention the meeting, but do not mention Boniface's reluctance to be examined through the medium of the spoken language.[1]

Willibald's *Vita Bonifatii* was written before 768, on the basis of first-hand information from Boniface's colleagues. In this account, the Pope and Boniface have already met personally and conversed three years before,[2] so presumably they already knew by then that they were largely intelligible to each other. The second meeting is initiated when Boniface receives a Papal letter while he is North of the Alps:

> cumque sanctus vir adlatas legisset litteras, carptim se invitatum ad Romam intellexit, festinusque summum oboedientiae gradum implere temptavit ...[3]

> When our holy man read the letter that had been brought to him, he gradually came to realize that he had been invited to go to Rome, and he hurriedly did his best to carry this out with total obedience.

The word "*carptim*" here is intriguing; perhaps at first he did not really understand that he was being summoned, and the general tone suggests that it might well have been inconvenient; but in any event he went. When he arrived in Rome, he was at once put up in the visitors' hostel ("*cenodochiam*"), and then:

> Adveniente itaque oportuno conlocutionis eorum die et ad basilicam beati Petri apostoli adventante glorioso sedis apostolici pontifici confestim hic Dei famulus invitatus est. Et cum paucis ad invicem ac pacificis se salutassent verbis, iam de simbulo et fidei ęcclęsiasticae traditione apostolicus illum pontifex inquisivit. Cui mox hic vir Dei humiliter respondit, dicens: "Domine apostolicę, novi me imperitum, iam peregrinus, vestrae familiariţatis sermone; sed queso, ut otium mihi, tempus conscribendae fidei concedas, et muta tantum littera meam rationabiliter fidem adaperiat". Qui etiam protinus consentit et, ut festine hanc scripturam deferret, imperavit. Cumque, aliquanto temporis evoluto spatio, sanctae trinitatis fidem urbana eloquentiae scientię conscriptam detulisset, reddiditque praefato pontifici.[4]

---

[1] W. LEVISON (ed.), *Vitae Sancti Bonifatii archiepiscopi Moguntini* (Hannover and Leipzig, 1905: *Monumenta Germaniae Historica. Scriptores rerum Germanicarum in usum scholarum*).

[2] Willibald, *Vita Bonifatii*, ed. LEVISON, *Vitae*, pp. 1-58, c. 5, p. 21.

[3] Willibald, *Vita Bonifatii*, c. 6, p. 27, ll. 26-28.

[4] Willibald, *Vita Bonifatii*, c. 6, p. 28, ll. 6-22.

So when a convenient day for their interview arrived, this servant of God was invited at once to the Church of the Apostle St Peter, the glorious seat of the Pope. They greeted each other with a few friendly words, and then the Pope started to ask him about the beliefs and traditions of the faith of the Church. But he humbly replied that: "My Lord, I realize that as a foreigner I am not an expert in using your usual spoken language, and I request that you give me the time and the opportunity to expound my faith more thoughtfully, in silent written form". The Pope agreed to this, and told him to bring the written text to him soon. When, a little time later, he brought back his account of his faith in the Holy Trinity, written in a polished style, he gave it to the Pope.

The Pope liked what he read, and they continued discussing religious matters for the rest of that day:

> Multa quoque alia de relegione sanctitatis et fidei veritate sciscitando profert, ita ut omnem pene diem pariter conloquendo alternatim ducerent.[5]

There are many intriguing details in this account. We should note first that they were not mutually unintelligible speakers at all. They spoke to each other in 719, and again in 722 before the question of the oral inquisition arose, and they also seem to have chatted away cheerfully again afterwards. But mutual intelligibility does not in itself imply linguistic similarity. For a matter of such extreme importance to Boniface as the testing of his religious beliefs, he was not sure that he would be able to follow every nuance of what the Pope was going to say to him, nor that he would be able to express intelligibly every nuance of what he wished to say to the Pope. The written mode had less scope for possible misunderstandings, as both men realized. They had a linguistic relationship in which the "*muta littera*" provided a secure link that might perhaps be broken by the "*familiaritatis sermo*", but even so, within a short time they were both communicating orally on allied complex topics ("*pariter conloquendo alternatim*").

The account by Otloh was composed three centuries later, but is still worth investigating, to see how he interpreted these interactions. He was asked by some of the monks at Fulda to compose an easier version of the *Life*; Otloh's own phrase is:

> postulabar a quibusdam eiusdem monasterii fratribus ut Sancti Bonifacii Vitam, difficili stilo editam, aliquid facilius ederem.[6]

---

[5] Willibald, *Vita Bonifatii*, c. 6, p. 29, ll. 1-3.
[6] LEVISON, *Vitae*, p. lxiii.

Otloh may have had other sources in addition to Willibald, so the extra details may even be true. According to Otloh, when Wynfreth first arrived it was the Pope himself who greeted him and arranged the accommodation:

> Deinde, conperto sancti viri adventu, statim venerabilis papa Gregorius illum ad se invitavit et verbis familiaribus salutatum honorifico xenodochio deputavit.[7]

Otloh uses the phrase "*verbis familiaribus*", cognate with Willibald's "*familiaritatis sermo*", which again hints at Wynfreth's surprise that the Pope had not used the highly polished Latinity that he was accustomed to himself, and which the Pope's secretary had used in the letters which had been sent to him. Then mutuality is actually mentioned as accompanying the initial remarks at their interview: "*cum se mutuis ac pacificis satiassent colloquiis*".[8] Wynfreth then replies to the Pope's plan for an oral inquisition, using different words, but with the same meaning in Otloh as in Willibald:

> Quia, domne apostolice, inquisitioni tantae in communi sermone idoneus non sum respondere, quaeso, ut fidei, quam a me exigis, conscribendae tempus mihi concedas sicque mutis tantum litteris denudatam agnoscere valeas.[9]

> Since, my Lord, I am not in a position to answer such questions in normal speech, I ask that you give me time to write down the profession of faith that you ask for, and thus that you can forgive the fact that it has been made clearer by the use of silent letters.

What Wynfreth here calls "*communis sermo*" seems to appear to him to be much harder to achieve than the written form of the language, which seems in comparison straightforward and unadorned ("*denudata*"). Then in this account also the Pope is pleased by what Wynfreth has written:

> sanctae atque catholicae fidei sententiam omni convenientia et eloquentia prolatam literis,[10]

and once again they then set to chatting the whole day:

> multa quoque de religione spiritalis vitae cum illo conferens, ita ut interdum integrum pene diem colloquendo ducerent.[11]

---

[7] Otloh of St Emmeram, *Vita Bonifatii*, ed. LEVISON, *Vitae*, pp. 111-217, I, c. 12, p. 126, ll. 35-39).

[8] Otloh of St Emmeram, *Vita Bonifatii*, I, c. 12, p. 127, ll. 2-3.

[9] Otloh of St Emmeram, *Vita Bonifatii*, I, c. 12, p. 127, ll. 5-10.

[10] Otloh of St Emmeram, *Vita Bonifatii*, I, c. 12, p. 127, ll. 13-15.

[11] Otloh of St Emmeram, *Vita Bonifatii*, I, c. 12, p. 127, ll. 18-21.

In each version, the Pope then changes Wynfreth's name to Boniface, and Boniface makes his oath of allegiance. This oath turns up as no.16 in his collected letters, but Otloh presents him as reciting it directly aloud on the spot.[12]

Modern scholarship suspects that the authors of these accounts have conflated events of his first visit to Rome in 719 with his second visit in 722, but for present purposes that does not matter. Nor is it really significant if Otloh, or even Willibald, have elaborated with poetic licence. The account can be taken to be essentially accurate, but even if it was not true it must have seemed plausible.

Sociophilology can help us to understand this episode. The native Romance-speaking world of the early eighth century was still essentially a monolingual speech community; this world included the Papacy, but not Britain. Within the Romance-speaking area there were, of course, natural linguistic variations of a geographical and sociolinguistic kind, but these were still felt to be language-internal. Thus Romance-speakers could move around within the linguistic community and be understood, as English-speakers can in the modern English-speaking world, even if there were noticeable differences between the speech of different places and groups. Refugees came from the Iberian Peninsula to Italy and to Gaul after the Arab invasion of the peninsula in 711, for example, and were able to communicate with their new neighbours. Merchants, craftsmen, soldiers, scholars, et cetera, travelled and worked together with no need for interpreters. They shared the great advantage of a single written mode for their varied styles of speech, which could shelter any amount of colloquial variability. The existence of a single mode of writing maintained the conceptual unity of the language. Contemporary texts, wherever written, could be read aloud to any interested Romance-speaking audience with an expectation that they would be understood.

This conceptual unity of the Romance speaking world was as yet not split between the two subsequent separate metalinguistic concepts of Latin and Romance. Such a distinction was to come later, as a consequence of the educational and linguistic reforms promoted by Anglo-Saxon and Germanic scholars at the Court of Charlemagne. But we see here, in Boniface's meeting with Gregory II, a glimpse of why it was eventually going to be thought advisable to make this distinction, between Latin and Romance. Boniface – or rather, Wyn-

---

[12] E. EMERTON, *The Letters of Saint Boniface* (New York, 1940: reprint 1973). R. RAU (trans.), *Briefe des Bonifatius – Willibalds Leben des Bonifatius* (Darmstadt, 1968: *Ausgewählte Quellen zur deutschen Geschichte des Mittelalters* 4B). Otloh, *Vita Bonifatii*, c. 14, pp.128-129.

freth – did not feel at ease with the *"communis sermo"*, the *"familiaritatis sermo"*, even of the Pope himself. Levison points out in his edition of Willibald's biography of Boniface that Willibald had earlier used the phrase *"vulgarica Romanorum lingua"*,[13] the spoken language of the Romans, to refer to the fact that Gregory II was generally known in Rome as Gregory the Younger (*"qui et vulgarica Romanorum lingua dicitur iunior"*). The native speaker of Romance, including Gregory, who was a native of Rome, learnt to speak first – learning the *"communis sermo"*, the *"familiaritatis sermo"*, the *"vulgarica Romanorum lingua"* – and then only learnt to write later, if at all. For the native Romance-speaker, the written forms of words were no more than that, written forms of Romance words, pronounced in the same way when they were read aloud as they would have been in natural speech (as happens in every living language). Gregory's speech was that of a native. On duty he probably often spoke carefully, but this manner of speaking was still a high register of Romance rather than any separate language in itself.

Wynfreth, however, had learnt his Latin exactly the other way round. He was a native speaker of Anglo-Saxon, born in *c.* 675, probably near Exeter in South-West England. Willibald's biography makes it clear that his interest in the Latin language was inspired by religious enthusiasm. As an adult he worked in the Benedictine monastery at Nursling in Hampshire, within the intellectual tradition recently inspired by Aldhelm of Malmesbury. Aldhelm's influence has been detected in Wynfreth's early writings, and also in Willibald's *Vita*. Talbot, the English translator of the *Vita*, describes the style as "inflated and obscure, due no doubt to his attempt to model himself on St Aldhelm's writings",[14] the style which Otloh's colleagues were to find so difficult three centuries later.

Aldhelm himself had been for a brief while a student at Canterbury, being taught by Theodore and Hadrian, the two scholars who had been sent to England by an earlier Pope (Vitalian) and had arrived in 669. Even so, Aldhelm seems not to have maintained direct contacts with native speakers of Romance after that, while he read very widely, with the result that his own work was full of cheerfully convoluted and unnaturally high-flown constructions more reminiscent of the most voluble and learned of the contemporary Visigothic scholars than of the humdrum documentation of the Papacy. There did exist some direct personal contacts between Britain and Rome at this time, but they were from further North, from Bede and his companions in Northumbria, who seem

---

[13] Willibald, *Vita Bonifatii*, c. 5, p. 21, ll. 11-12.
[14] C.H. TALBOT, *The Anglo-Saxon Missionaries in Germany* (London, 1954).

not to have been themselves in close contact with their contemporaries in the South of Britain. The Latinity of Wynfreth and his contemporaries in Southern England was, therefore, essentially textual rather than learnt from native speakers.

Wynfreth had written a Latin grammar,[15] and was already an experienced scholar, before he left Britain for the first time in 716, at the age of *c.* 41. This Latin grammar, like all those of the period, includes no syntax, phonology or vocabulary, but is just a long, careful and illustrated list of morphological detail, arranged according to parts of speech and buttressed by Classical sources, in the tradition that ran from Aelius Donatus and was then being adapted for pedagogical use for non-native speakers in the British Isles.[16] That is, among its features are copious lists of inflections that were by then becoming rare in contemporary native active speech on the Romance-speaking continent of Europe, but were still found everywhere in texts. Wynfreth also wrote metric verses,[17] including the thirty-eight lines that form the preface to his grammar, and a brief general account of Latin metrics.[18] In this the analysis of metres, feet and vocalic length suggests that he had no direct experience of the contemporary Romance abandonment of phonemic length, delight in syncope, and the palatalization of short front vowels. There is no reference made there to so-called rhythmic verse.

Wynfreth's Latin was therefore in the first place the written language. He used Anglo-Saxon as his own language of "*familiaritas*". When he first arrived on the Continent, not long before he went to Rome for the first time, he would thus have spoken a kind of Latin whose antiquated morphology would still be largely intelligible, because people heard it read aloud in liturgical and other texts all the time, but whose pronunciation can only have seemed very strange to the native speaker, being based on the artificial system that he had learnt at home, in which every letter of a word's written form was given a sound. This Anglo-Saxon variety of Latin would have been most markedly unlike the native speech of Gaul, where oblique nominal morphology was hardly used in active speech any more, and syncope and apocope were becoming increasingly fash-

---

[15] G.J. GEBAUER and B. LÖFSTEDT (ed.), *Bonifatii (Vynfreth) Ars Grammatica* (Turnhout, 1980: *Corpus Christianorum. Series Latina* 133B).

[16] V. LAW, *Grammar and Grammarians in the Early Middle Ages* (London, 1997), pp. 169-199.

[17] Willibald, *Vita Bonifatii*, c. 2, p. 9, ll. 16-17: "*Metrorum medullata facundiae modulatione*".

[18] GEBAUER and LÖFSTEDT, *Bonifatii*, pp. 109-113. Discussed in: LAW, *Grammar*, pp. 107-109.

ionable in the seventh century, as Alcuin was to find out to his horror a little later. In Italy, on the other hand, most Romance words still had the same number of syllables as they had had in the Roman Empire, and as they appeared to have in writing, but the nominal morphology was simplifying even further than in Gaul, to just a single form for the singular and another for the plural. We can, then, reconstruct Wynfreth's mode of speech in Rome as a kind of spoken Latin based directly on the most traditional written forms, whereas Gregory's was his natural language, learnt when young, long before he became literate at all.

It is interesting to see that, in both Willibald's and Otloh's account of their meeting, the word "*eloquentia*" is only used to refer to Wynfreth's written submission: "*urbana eloquentiae scientiae conscriptam*",[19] "*omni convenientia et eloquentia prolatam literis*".[20] The word "*eloquentia*" was etymologically related to "*loqui*" ("speak") of course, but no longer synchronically. "*Eloquentia*" was not, it seems, thought of as being a property of natural speech. Wynfreth had used the word in the prologue to his Grammar:

> Priscorum quippe consuetudines, qui multa aliter in eloquentia observasse dicuntur, quam moderna urbanitas canonicum esse adprobat.[21]

Law translates this as "the usage of the ancients (who observed very different customs in speech from those which modern eloquence regards as legitimate)".[22] But it seems likely, in the light of both the literary and the historical context, that the written mode is the one at issue here, rather than speech or eloquence, and that "*eloquentia*" and "*urbanitas*" refer to written language, both in this prologue and in the biography.

Wynfreth may perhaps have felt like a country bumpkin when he first came to the Holy City. But this feeling was not going to be reinforced by hearing a higher stylistic level of Latin language in Gregory's mouth than in his own. Wynfreth naturally found writing to the Pope easier than talking to him, since they shared the same written standard with the same regulations; but, with a little practice, at least, they were also able to communicate socially. For important matters, though, in the light of the linguistic differences there were in their spoken habits, he was naturally going to feel more at ease in writing, which was effectively his native register. Law comments on this episode that "the oral

---

[19] Willibald, *Vita Bonifatii*, c. 6, p. 28, ll. 20-21.
[20] Otloh of St Emmeram, *Vita Bonifatii*, I, c. 12, p. 127, ll. 14-15.
[21] GEBAUER and LÖFSTEDT, *Bonifatii*, p. 10, ll. 39-42.
[22] LAW, *Grammar*, p. 174.

competence of even so accomplished a stylist as he was at best shaky".[23] In the event, the stylistic level that he had achieved was precisely what made normal Romance speech hard for him to operate with. It was as if a modern Englishman went to Rome and spoke the language of Boccaccio, or a Japanese were to come to London and try to communicate orally in best Miltonian English.

What we have here is a foreshadowing of the later contrast between Medieval Latin and Romance, *avant la lettre*. It was not conceived of in this way at the time; but the contrast was going to become established during the following century. Medieval Latin was going to be based on the Latin skills of the Anglo-Saxon and Germanic speakers. The Latin of these Germanic speakers was heavily influenced by the traditions that Boniface himself established over the following thirty years. The Romance half of the contrast would be the normal native speech of Romance speakers. One of the seeds of that aspect of the Carolingian Reforms might even have been planted at these interviews in Rome in 719 and 722. We can catch in these accounts some of the bewilderment felt by Wynfreth at discovering that not even the Pope spoke Latin the way that Wynfreth had prescribed in his own grammar and spoke himself. Boniface learnt, of course, from experience; there is no sign of this problem arising again when he next came to Rome, in 737, to see the succeeding Pope Gregory III.

The Papacy did not produce grammarians. Gregory the Great (Pope Gregory I, 590-604) had written a great deal, of course, but he was not a linguist. He saw himself as part of the same textual community as his flock; for example, as Banniard pointed out, he wrote letters which were intended to be read aloud intelligibly to a non-specialist public.[24] And yet, despite the lack of a grammatical tradition, from a more pragmatic and secretarial point of view, the Papacy was probably the centre of the fullest tradition of practical literacy that Romance-speaking Europe knew between the fifth and ninth centuries. This was a matter of political practicalities, rather than intellectual quality, for literacy was involved in the exercise of power. As Noble pointed out, the archives, the letters, the brief biographies of the Popes in the *Liber Pontificalis*, et cetera, were not works of intellectual brilliance or even stylistic grace, but they are none the less impressive evidence of simple practical competence in recording their own language on papyrus.[25] Although these texts have often seen their

[23] LAW, *Grammar*, p. 189.

[24] M. BANNIARD, *Viva Voce: communication écrite et communication orale du IVe au IXe siècle en Occident latin* (Paris, 1992), pp. 105-179.

[25] T.F.X. NOBLE, "Literacy and the papal government in Late Antiquity and the Early Middle Ages", in: *The Uses of Literacy in Early Medieval Europe*, ed. R. MCKITTERICK

language insulted by modern scholars, apparently in the belief that if they did not write like Cicero then they did not, by definition, write well, they have never seen their language seriously studied.[26] And since they did still use papyrus, the biodegradability of that material implies that it is very likely that a large amount of the everyday documentation produced in those centuries did not survive.

If we wish to study the language of Gregory II himself we could, of course, choose to look at his extant letters, written to Boniface, among others. Gregory was a skilled and ambitious diplomat,[27] and according to his biographer in the *Liber Pontificalis* had actually run the Papal library, or archive, before his accession,[28] and was thus probably at ease with the written mode. But in the event it seems likely that these letters were actually drawn up by secretaries in his chancery, rather than by himself, and are more likely to disguise his own linguistic peculiarities than to represent them directly. Instead, it will be more illuminating to compare the two recensions that we have of his biography, the *Vita* within the *Liber Pontificalis*, to see if there are any signs of an incipient linguistic reforming movement in the Papacy during the eighth century, which would thus antedate the Carolingian reforms.

The *Vita* of Gregory II is not an autobiography, but drawn up by a trained cleric (or more than one) in the Papal chancery; that is, a member of the Papal staff likely to have had similar native speaking habits to the Pope himself. We do not, however, know the name of any of the Papal biographers.[29] It is unusual for a Papal biography to come in two recensions. Indeed, in this case there may have been more, for an early version was available in Gregory's lifetime for Bede to use before 724. That cannot itself be either of the versions that we now have, since both these go up to his death in 731. The final version was drawn up some twenty years after Gregory's death, in the 750s. It has been suggested that the existence of the later recension is evidence of a desire for linguistic improvement of the original text; this is implied, at least, by Davis's comment on this *Vita* – which is the ninety-first in the sequence – that:

(Cambridge, 1990), pp. 82-108.

[26] As Noble also points out: T.F.X. NOBLE, "A new look at the Liber Pontificalis", *Archivum Historiae Pontificiae* 23 (1985), pp. 347-358, p. 352.

[27] T.F.X. NOBLE, *The Republic of St Peter: The Birth of the Papal State, 680-825* (Philadelphia, 1984).

[28] L. DUCHESNE, *Le Liber Pontificalis* (Paris, 1886-1892; reprint, 1955), p. 396, ll. 6-7: "*bibliothicae illi est cura commissa*". (The first ever reference to such a post).

[29] NOBLE, "A new look", p. 354.

In some cases, manuscripts show a strong tendency to regularize spelling and grammar to accord wih classical norms. For lives 91 to 99, the most serious textual variants are in 91, which exists both in its original form and in a much revised version, produced perhaps 20 years later.[30]

This is in itself a most interesting possibility. If it were true, we would then have unexpectedly early evidence in the Papal records for that desire to restore the classical norms of Latinity which is associated with the Carolingian reforms, half a century later and much further north. The revisions would then be parallel to the changes that came over the Frankish Annals[31] and the upmarketed version of the Benedictine Rule, and all the other texts whose language was shortly due to be changed by the Carolingian scholars to accord with their anachronistic belief of what ought to have been the original text. The possibility of such a reform in the Papal chancery has never been studied with any clarity, and if reforms on this scale really existed there in the 750s, as Davis suggests, our chronology for the conceptual separation of Latin and Romance would be radically affected.

But the texts of the Life of Pope Gregory II, at least, do not support Davis's view that the later version evinces a "strong tendency to regularize spelling and grammar to accord with classical norms". This *Vita* was published by Duchesne in a parallel edition, with the two recensions side by side.[32] This parallel presentation is most helpful for the present purpose. Each of the versions of this *Vita* survives in three groups of manuscripts, the early one in the groups that Duchesne labels A, C and G, and the later one in those grouped as B, D or E. The later version is longer; that is because it includes many details of fact absent, or insufficiently accurate, in the first version. These additions mention the building repairs that Gregory oversaw in the Papal properties, meteorological peculiarities, a few anti-Lombard sentiments, and brief details of the rebellion by a certain Petasius. There is also a complete rephrasing of the comments on the Moslem invasion of Spain, which corrects one historical inaccuracy at the expense of introducing another.

In each recension, Duchesne usually prints every word in his main text in the grammatically and orthographically most 'correct' version that he finds in the three manuscript traditions he is working with. Fortunately, however, he also includes the copious manuscript variants in the apparatus. It is immedi-

---

[30] R. DAVIS, *The Lives of the Eighth-Century Popes* (Liverpool, 1992), p. xiv.

[31] As explained by: J. ADAMS, "The vocabulary of the *Annales Regni Francorum*", *Glotta* 55 (1977), pp. 257-282.

[32] DUCHESNE, *Le Liber*, pp. 396-410.

ately clear from this apparatus that the spelling of both textual versions varies widely even within their own manuscript traditions; this assures us that orthographical correctness cannot have been a prime purpose of the rewrite. The average orthography of the later text is only marginally more accurate than that of the first, and there are many cases in which the first version's orthography is self-evidently preferable. For example, the word "*antistes*" ("bishop") in the second paragraph,[33] is always spelt correctly this way in manuscripts of the first text, according to the apparatus, but appears as all of "*antistes*", "*antestis*" and "*antistis*" in manuscripts of the second text, as well as once undergoing the non-linguistic promotion to "*episcopus*". The form "*antistes*" is the recommended one, and the other two cannot be the result of any "tendency to regularize spelling".

Many of the changes in spelling involve nominal morphology. These written inflections often seem, in both versions, to have been chosen at random (Boniface would have had a fit, if he had seen them). This is far more true of nouns and adjectives than it is of verbs, as is usual in texts written by Romance speakers in these centuries, since in real life the nominal inflection system simplified further and earlier than did the verbal. For example, when Gregory established the old people's home, the direct object of the verb, the first manuscript tradition presents two alternative lexemes in "*gerocomium*" and "*gerontocomium*", both in the grammatically correct accusative case after "*instituit*"; and the second tradition offers us all of "*gerocomium*", "*gerochomium*", "*gerecomium*", "*cerocomium*", "*gerocomio*" (three times), and "*ierochomio*".[34] The treatises of the time entitled *De Orthographia* often included sections on nominal endings, which we tend now to see as a branch of syntax but which Cassiodorus and others saw as a branch of spelling, since they had, in most of the cases concerned, little direct counterpart in natural speech. Some of the supposed emendations of the second text are merely wrong under any perspective, of language or content, as when a prepositional phrase unanimously written as "*contra imperatoris iussionem*" in the manuscripts of the earlier text becomes "*contra imperatorem iussionem*" or "*contra imperatorem iussioni*" (once each), and also "*contra imperatorum iussionem*" when there can only have conceivably been one emperor in question. Davis translates this as "in resistance to the emperor's mandate".[35] There are also occasional changes of word order, that do not seem to result overall from any notion of

[33] DUCHESNE, *Le Liber*, p. 396, l. 21. DAVIS, *The Lives*, p. 3.

[34] DUCHESNE, *Le Liber*, p. 397, l. 19.

[35] DUCHESNE, *Le Liber*, p. 404, l. 19. DAVIS, *The Lives*, p. 11.

syntactic correctness. This is hardly surprising, since word order is not discussed in the available grammars of the time.

The evidence of the texts does not support the idea that the second version was inspired by a desire to improve the language of the first one, for it is not in general a linguistically more accurate text. We can glimpse a more plausible motivation in the first part of section 3, the only one in which Boniface is mentioned. We find in the first version:

> Hic in Germania per Bonifatium episcopum verbum salutis praedicavit et gentem illam sedentem in tenebris doctrina lucis convertit ad Christum, et maximam partem gentis eiusdem sancti baptismatis lavit unda.[36]

Duchesne mentions variants of "*super*" for "*per*", "*lavi*" for "*lavit*" and "*undam*" for "*unda*", and two mis-spellings of Boniface as "*Onifatium*" and as "*Bonifacium*". In the second version we find:

> Hic in Germaniam per Bonifatium episcopum verbum salutis praedicavit et gentem illam sedentem in tenebris doctrina lucis convertit ad Christum,

in which "*Germaniam*" is less correct than "*Germania*", the non-Classical Romance use of "*sedere*" for "to be" is unchanged between the two, and "*doctrina*" has a grammatically inexplicable manuscript variant in "*doctrinam*" – that is, it is only orthographically explicable, in that the ending is thought of as an alternative form rather than as a morphosyntactic marker. There is also the final textual emendation, in this case the omission of an embarrassing piece of self-evidently incorrect hype. The purpose of this emendation is not linguistic. Although the reason for having a second version at all is unclear, substantive changes of this latter kind must have been the significant motivation for the elaboration of the new text, rather than a desire for improvement of any linguistic deficiencies.[37]

This lack of a desire for strict grammatical correctness is not the result of mere general linguistic inadequacy at the Papal court. They had there, in the early eighth century, a working knowledge of Greek, for example, as Noble

---

[36] DUCHESNE, *Le liber*, p. 397, ll. 10-14.

[37] It is also interesting to see here that both redactors reckoned that the Pope was preaching to the Germans through Boniface, rather than making Boniface the agentive subject of the verb "*praedicavit*".

established.[38] Gregory II (or his secretaries) wrote to the emperor in Greek.[39] Gregory III, the next Pope, is thought to have read Greek, at least,[40] and his successor Zacharias was of Greek origin.[41] But even though Eastern clerics continued to come regularly to Rome, these cultural connections with the Byzantines were beginning to weaken from the time of Gregory II onwards. That was the period when the Papacy began deliberately to cut its direct links with the Emperor,[42] and started instead to cooperate more closely with the Franks. But for most of the eighth century they were not in as receptive a mood as they would be later to participate in Frankish cultural reforms. Referring to the eighth century, Noble concluded that "Papal Rome, for reasons that are quite understandable in the circumstances, evinced none of the self-conscious classicism of the Carolingian Renaissance".[43] This feature of Papal culture helps to explain the initially rather surprising fact that Charlemagne chose to entrust his educational and linguistic reforms to an Anglo-Saxon scholar, Alcuin, rather than to an Italian, even though in general he was collaborating closely with the Papacy at that point and actually met Alcuin in Italy, in 781.[44] It may well be true that Papal documentation acquired a marginally less pedestrian level of Latinity as the century progressed, but Davis comments accurately of all the eighth-century *Vitae* that "their style, their grammar and their vocabulary are not such as would pass muster with the scholars of the Carolingian Renaissance".[45] Noble said of the *Liber Pontificalis* in general that "the work is distinguished neither by elegance of style nor sophistication of philosophical conception".[46] And these comments are as true of Gregory II's second *Vita* as of the first one. But this style need not be seen as a problem, nor even as an inadequacy. Elsewhere Noble calls it "clear, direct and unadorned ... fresh and immediate",[47] which is a more favourable assessment than is usually given to bureaucratic registers. Roman education in general seems to have been

[38] T.F.X. NOBLE, "The declining knowledge of Greek in Eighth- and Ninth-Century Papal Rome", *Byzantinische Zeitschrift* 78 (1985), pp. 56-62.

[39] NOBLE, "The declining", p. 57.

[40] DAVIS, *The Lives*, p. 19.

[41] DAVIS, *The Lives*, p. 35.

[42] NOBLE, *The Republic*, pp. 28-40.

[43] NOBLE, "The declining", p. 61.

[44] W. LEVISON, *England and the Continent in the Eighth Century* (Oxford, 1946), pp. 154-155.

[45] DAVIS, *The Lives*, p. ix.

[46] NOBLE, "Literacy", p. 97.

[47] NOBLE, "A new look", p. 352.

attached to the Lateran,[48] and if, as Noble suggests,[49] these works were actually read aloud to the trainees in the Papal chancery, and used as a school text in Papal Rome, then this simplicity had a practical value that would have been completely lacking, for example, in any work by Aldhelm. This stylistic simplicity, in turn, shows that the trainees were not being trained to operate any other written form than that which was the traditional counterpart of their spoken language. They were being trained for practical reasons, to work in the secretariat, to operate the written mode of the native language they already had, rather than another language entirely. And Gregory II himself was one of these trainees, for his *Vita* tells us that he was "*a parva aetate in patriarchio nutritus*".

The conclusion that can be drawn, from such evidence as there is, then, is that in the first half of the eighth century the distinction between Latin and Romance had not arisen within the Papacy, as it had not in other areas of Romance speech. And even if the contrast between the ways in which Wynfreth and Gregory spoke could perhaps be described anachronistically as a contrast between Latin and Romance, that was because Wynfreth spoke in a Latin way and Gregory spoke in a Romance way, not *vice versa*.

---

[48] NOBLE, "The declining", p. 60. IDEM, "A new look", p. 352.
[49] NOBLE, "Literacy", pp. 97-98.

Chapter 8

Rhythmic Poetry and the Author's Vernacular

Latin 'rhythmic' poetry was a genre in which the pattern of stressed and unstressed syllables created the verse form, rather than the pattern of long and short syllables. One aspect of the analysis of any Latin rhythmic poem that needs to be continually borne in mind concerns the native language of the author. Sometimes, of course, we may not know what that language was, but in most cases we can make a reasonable guess. It is probably a safe assumption, for example, that poems from those lands which are now Romance-speaking were composed by native speakers of Latin (or Early Romance), while poems from lands which are now Germanic or Celtic-speaking were composed by writers who had learnt Latin as a foreign language. This simple dichotomy becomes confused by the Carolingian linguistic reforms of the late eighth century, whose eventual implementation led to Latin becoming a foreign language for everybody, even for those who were native speakers of a Romance language directly descended from it. For this reason, only those poems can be taken as evidence of Romance which come from areas as yet unaffected by these reforms. For most of France and Italy, the reforms date to the late eighth century. In the Iberian Peninsula, however, apart from Catalonia, these reforms were not implemented until the late eleventh century at the earli-

This chapter is a reprint with very few details changed of: "Rhythmic poetry and the author's vernacular", in: *Poetry in Early Medieval Europe: Manuscripts, Language and Music of the Latin Rhythmical Texts*, ed. E. D'ANGELO and F. STELLA (Firenze, SISMEL, 2002), pp. 337-351. We are grateful to Professor Francesco Stella and SISMEL – Edizioni del Galluzzo (Firenze) for permitting the reprint.

est (and in many centres not until the late twelfth, or even the thirteenth century), so we can, for example, consider the poems written there by the Christian scholars of ninth-century Córdoba, and those of the tenth-century Rioja region, as being from a pre-reform milieu. Several of the examples adduced here come from Paulo Álvaro, who was writing in Córdoba in the 850s.

The reason why the native language of the author of a rhythmic poem is significant to our understanding of its nature derives from the fact that the ability to read and write ("*Grammatica*") was of necessity taught in different ways in different language communities.[1] The teaching of "*Grammatica*" was usually based on the *Ars Minor* of the fourth-century grammarian Aelius Donatus. Donatus was originally writing for a public who spoke the natural fourth-century Latin vernacular of their time, which already included a number of the features now often described as being 'Vulgar Latin'; and essentially the subject he was teaching was the written mode of the language that his students spoke. There was no need, for example, for him to give them elementary instruction about phonetics or vocabulary, since they knew about those already. Conversely, the fact that he devoted so much attention to the listing of nominal morphological forms suggests that the general ability to use these forms in the old way was becoming less secure at the time, a chronology which accords with the Romance philologists' reconstruction of the speech of the time. Written "*rithmi*" composed by native speakers of Latin, therefore, are evidence of the way in which their vernacular language was influenced by their pedagogical instruction. When the resulting text looks like a kind of hybrid between natural and educated registers, as it occasionally does even in poetry (though more commonly in prose, especially in legal documents), that inconsistency is evidence of the extent to which the author's natural spoken language has been influenced by the pedagogy involved in their training to write, as has been well studied by Sabatini, Emiliano and others.[2] That is, the inconsistency is not, as is still sometimes said, evidence that their written language has been influenced by their spoken language, but of the precise reverse. In these cases, therefore, we may often be able to explain some particular details of a poem on the basis of the native vernacular tendencies of the author, and to explain other details on the basis of what they had been told in their grammatical training. Unfortu-

---

[1] R. WRIGHT, *Early Ibero-Romance* (Newark, 1995), chapter 9.

[2] For instance: F. SABATINI, "Prospettive sul parlato nella storia linguistica italiana", in: *Italia linguistica: Idee, Storia, Strutture*, ed. F.A. LEONI e.a. (Bologna, 1983), pp. 167-201. A. EMILIANO, "Latin or Romance? Graphemic variation and scripto-linguistic change in Medieval Spain", in: *Latin and the Romance Languages in the Early Middle Ages*, ed. R. WRIGHT (London, 1991; reprint, Penn State 1996), pp. 233-247.

nately, the converse argument is less likely to be illuminating, in the event; often we may not be justified in deducing specific details about the author's speech from the details of his rhythmic poetry, since all verse is to some extent unnatural, particularly if set to music.

The nature of the evidence is quite different for poems composed outside the Romance-speaking communities. When non-Romance speakers began to study Latin as a foreign language, they had a different problem. They had no native vernacular instinct or intuitions; so every aspect of the language needed to be taught. But precisely because they indeed had no such intuitions, they did not need the techniques for turning native vernacular into writing which was the essence of the existing Donatan tradition. Donatus was thus of limited use to them. Latin works by native Greek speakers who had learnt Latin as a foreign language are not considered here, although it is worth pointing out that it was two Greek-speakers (Theodore and Hadrian) who introduced the objective scholarly study of Latin into the British Isles, from the perspective of non-native speakers. When the scholars of the British Isles, including Ireland, studied Latin, they did so in a most non-native order; they had written texts to study from the start, and learnt the high-style written registers of the language first. The native vernacular registers of spoken Latin were not necessarily learnt by scholars in the islands at all, and if they were, that would almost necessarily occur subsequent to their mastering the techniques of reading the language, and perhaps also of writing it.[3] Bede was the main pioneer in adapting the Romance-speakers' tradition for Anglo-Saxon use. Boniface, indeed, compiled a Latin grammar before he left for the Continent (when he was still called Wynfreth), and he almost certainly filled his own Latin speech with many manifestations of inadvertently outdated morphology and phonetics. When Charlemagne met Alcuin in Italy and arranged for him to oversee the forthcoming educational reforms, neither of them may have realized what would be the unfortunate consequences of this difference in the two educational traditions. But in the long run that single administrative appointment led to the regrettable over-standardization of spoken Latin which, in turn, led to the separation of Medieval Latin from normal vernacular Romance and to the need for it to be learnt as a foreign language even by Romance speakers. The linguistic features that can be deduced from rhythmic poetry composed in non-Romance speaking Lands, therefore, will really only be evidence of native non-Romance speech, although here too, of course, we can glean details of what happened in the

---

[3] See for instance: V. LAW, *The Insular Latin Grammarians* (Woodbridge, 1982). EADEM, *Grammar and Grammarians in the Early Middle Ages* (London, 1997).

writer's training. There are valuable syntactic and lexical data in the rhythms, naturally, as there are in all genres,[4] but the only data peculiar to rhythmic poetry are phonetic data, so they are the ones considered here.

Alliteration

One neat and well-known example of these differences in educational practice, and of what can be deduced from them, concerns alliterative verse. In the British Isles they were taught to pronounce Latin on the basis of the written forms of the words, and gave each written letter a standardized sound in performance. Thus in their verse compositions, Germanic and Celtic speakers were able to alliterate words with an initial letter *c* regardless of the following vowel. Bede and Alcuin both did this themselves, indeed, alliterating respectively *"celsa"* and *"caritas"*, *"curva"* and *"certe"*.[5] Howlett's edition of Aldhelm's octosyllabic *Carmen Rhythmicum* helpfully highlights the intended alliterations,[6] as in the following eleven lines which alliterate [k] sounds which have both back and front following vowels:

5.	Ymnista carmen cecini
16.	Conuexi caeli camara
53.	Quae cateruatim culmina
55.	Neque caelorum culmina
83.	Zodiacus cum caetera
84.	Cyclus fuscatur caterua
94.	Late per caeli culmina
98.	Procedit conlidentibus
128.	Celebramus concentibus
141.	Quando cernebant lumina
161.	Scissa caeca caligine

Celtic authors could do the same, and in this instance, the fact that Celtic authors based their Irish orthographic practice on that of Latin supports this anal-

---

[4] See for instance: G. SERBAT, "Quelques traits d'oralité chez Anthime, *De Observatione Ciborum*", in: *Les structures de l'oralité en Latin*, ed. J. DANGEL and C. MOUSSY (Paris, 1996), pp. 85-91.

[5] See: D. NORBERG, *Introduction à l'étude de la versification latine médiévale* (Stockholm, 1958), p. 52. IDEM, *Manuel pratique de latin médiéval* (Paris, 1968), p. 48. R. WRIGHT, *Late Latin and Early Romance in Spain and Carolingian France* (Liverpool, 1982), p. 100.

[6] D. HOWLETT, "Aldhelmi Carmen Rhythmicum", *Archivum Latinitatis Medii Aevi* (= *ALMA*) 53 (1995), pp. 119-140.

ysis.[7] These alliterations could not happen in such verse from Romance areas. Here manifestations of a letter *c* before a back vowel, where it was still articulated as a velar [k] in Romance, represented a separate phoneme from that represented by a letter *c* before a front vowel, where the articulation became palatal, usually [ts]. Accordingly, the evidence from the texts of non-Romance speakers can tell us in such cases about their pronunciation of Latin as a foreign language, and probably something about their own native Germanic or Celtic, but only the poems of the Romance speakers tell us something about real spoken Latin (Early Romance). The Carolingian reforms were intended to introduce the Anglo-Saxon tradition of Latin pronunciation even into Romance lands, so after their implementation even there all words beginning in writing with a letter *c* could alliterate together in the fashion that was previously normal only in non-Romance areas. This is what we find in Hucbald of St Amand's virtuoso late ninth-century poem in praise of baldness (*Egloga de Calvis*),[8] in which every word begins with the letter *c* throughout 146 hexameter lines, whatever the subsequent sound might be. These lines include the same lexical items *cels-* and *cert-* as were alliterated with the initial velar [k] of other words by Bede and Alcuin; in line 25, "*Coniubilant calvi celso clamore canori*", and line 40, "*Catholicum canon certum conscribere curant*". Another verse form created by the Carolingian reforms of Latin pronunciation was the standard Sequence, with its isomorphy of written vowel, sung syllable and musical note.[9] Hucbald is also the most likely candidate to be the author, or at least the elaborator of the revolutionary orthography, of the Romance Sequence *Cantilène de Sainte Eulalie*.[10]

Rhyme

Alliteration concerns consonants, and is only relevant to our present theme in a few cases, since alliteration is rarely intended to apply, as it is in the *Egloga de Calvis*, to one hundred per cent of all potential cases. Early Romance vowel sounds can be invoked more regularly, however, to explain a number of features. One of these, naturally, is rhyme. Rhyme always in principle requires

[7] Pace: P. ZANNA, "Lecture, écriture et morphologie latines en Irlande aux VIIe et VIIIe siècles", *Archivum Latinitatis Medii Aevi* (= *ALMA*) 56 (1998), pp. 180-191.

[8] Hucbald of St Amand, *Ecloga de Calvis*, ed. P. WINTERFELD (Berlin, 1899: *Monumenta Germaniae Historica. Poetae Latini Aevi Carolini* IV, 1), pp. 267-271.

[9] J. SZÖVERFFY, *A Concise History of Medieval Latin Hymnody* (Leiden, 1985), pp. 2-3.

[10] WRIGHT, *Late Latin*, pp. 128-135.

identity of the vowel sounds from the final stressed syllable onwards, whereas the assonance common in at least some native Romance popular verse makes no such requirement for identical consonants. It has long been realized, for example, that Romance-speaking poets of the sixth and seventh centuries, such as Eugenio de Toledo in the Iberian Peninsula and Venantius Fortunatus in Gaul, felt no problem in assonating all [o] vowels together, whether spelt with a letter *o* or *u*, and assonating all [e] vowels together, whether spelt with a letter *e* or *i*. The Insular writers did not do this, since their phonetics were based on the traditional spelling.[11] There are no such cases in the assonance or rhyming patterns in the two hundred lines of Aldhelm's *Carmen Rhythmicum*, for example. It was naturally the insular pattern that prevailed when rhyming practice was standardized systematically by the Carolingian scholars, most notably by Godescalc.[12]

Glide reduction

Since the main requirement of rhythmic verse was the stipulation of a regular number of syllables per line, a second relevant phenomenon which seems exclusive to pre-reform Romance speakers concerns the reduction of high vowels to semivocalic on-glides before another vowel. Resulting combinations of semi-vowel and following vowel thus became syllabic rising diphthongs in ordinary speech, rather than a disyllabic pair of independent vowels. This was an early development in the evolution of Romance, and, as Norberg showed a long time ago, the consequences are even visible in Saint Augustine's alphabetical psalm.[13] One of the words in question is "*ecclesiam*", pronounced apparently as a trisyllable with the final syllable being [sja], and this is yet more strong evidence against the peculiar assumption which used to be made by several Romance philologists to the effect that ecclesiastical words did not undergo sound changes ("*mots savants*").

[11] NORBERG, *Introduction*, pp. 47-48.
[12] As pointed out by: F. STELLA, "Gotescalco, la 'Scuola' di Reims e l'origine della rima mediolatina", in: *Il verso europeo*, ed. IDEM (Firenze, 1995), pp. 159-165.
[13] NORBERG, *Introduction*, p. 29.

Synaloepha and Syncope

Another feature of the vowel sounds of Romance is much more slippery to determine in this context. As has always been realized, the evidence of old-fashioned quantitative poetry as practised by the Classical poets implies that it was already normal at that time to elide a vowel at the end of one word with a vowel that began a following word. For these purposes a final letter *m* at the end of the first word and an initial letter *h* at the start of the second could be disregarded, and this fact has always been taken to be evidence of the loss of the associated consonantal sounds from contemporary pronunciation. Rhythmic poets, however, sometimes react to the presence of potential elisions in performance by trying, if possible, to avoid having such words next to each other at all. The desire to avoid such sequences of final and initial vowel even seems to have increased after the Carolingian reforms of pronunciation. This reluctance is entirely compatible with a wish to make the number of syllables clear, by avoiding giving rise to uncertainties over potential elisions, but is none the less still mildly surprising. In my own study of this I suggested that it may be connected with the fact that rhythmic poems were often intended to be sung, and that in any language it is in the nature of song, especially hymns, to be slower than speech, thereby making elisions seem rather more awkward in hymns than they would otherwise be in speech.[14] Hymns in Modern English are rather more likely to require us to sing "do not" as two syllables than as the contracted monosyllable "don't", for example, even though everybody says "don't" ([dównt]) in real life. The same consideration may also have applied to those words that were in the process of losing internal unstressed high vowels altogether in speech. Song is likely to be a mode which favours the older variant in such cases of ongoing change, for as long as both the newer syncopated and the older syllabic alternatives still co-existed in the vernacular and both were equally intelligible (such as the phonetic forms representable as "*saeculum*" and "*saeclum*").

Stress

Rhythmic verse acquired the label of 'rhythmic' because it was based on patterns of word stress which imitated the quantitative metrics of earlier times. It should, therefore, be possible for us to deduce vernacular word stresses from

---

[14] WRIGHT, *Late Latin*, p. 68.

such rhythmic evidence, particularly since the word stresses of earlier times, unlike their vocabulary, syntax, morphology and spelling, could not have been recovered from a study of ancient texts (and for that reason were not obvious even to Alcuin). Paulo Álvaro gave paroxytone stress to *"celebrat"* and *"tenebras"*,[15] for example, which directly attests the general use of paroxytonic stress in such words (these two give rise to Spanish *"celebra"* and *"tinieblas"*). Norberg's excellent study of this issue gives a number of illuminating examples of further shifts.[16] These include the movement of the stress in words such as *"viola"* from proparoxytone [í] to paroxytone [ó]; Spanish *"vihuela"*, which is still trisyllabic, comes from the paroxytone variant, and we can see evidence of this development in progress in the rhythmic hexameter line written by Paulo Álvaro in the mid-ninth century, *"Et theretes uibrant auro crispose uiole"*.[17] The same applies to Álvaro's use of words such as *fuero*, originally with a stressed [ú], which have since become rising diphthongs in Castilian but which during the ninth century were still in an intermediate stage, as attested in the necessarily trisyllabic and paroxytone example *"(ausus) fuero"* found in Paulo Álvaro's hymn in rhythmic iambics, *"Christus est Virtus Patris Sapientia"*.[18]

Atonic prefixes

Norberg also refers to the Romance tendency not to accentuate prefixes but maintain the stress pattern of the root word.[19] Prefixed verbs such as *"resonat"* were thus paroxytonic in Early Romance, by analogy with *"sonat"*. Álvaro uses this word to end four rhythmic hexameter lines in his *Carmina*:[20] *"Flumina,*

---

[15] Paulo Álvaro, *Carmina*, ed. J. GIL, *Corpus Scriptorum Muzarabicorum* (Madrid, 1973), p. 348, *Carmen* 7, l. 1 and l. 18.

[16] D. NORBERG, *L'accentuation des mots dans le vers latin du Moyen Age* (Stockholm, 1985).

[17] Paulo Álvaro, *Carmen* 6, p. 347, l. 13. The huge manuscript of Álvaro's work is nearly contemporaneous, and GIL, *Corpus*, is meticulous about presenting the manuscripts accurately, so we can trust this to be accurate.

[18] Edited by: C. BLUME, *Analecta Hymnica* XXVII (Leipzig, 1897), pp. 180-183, no. 126; also by: B. THORSBERG, *Études sur l'hymnologie mozarabe* (Stockholm, 1962). NORBERG, *Manuel*, pp. 136-140, with a French translation; partially in: SZÖVERFFY, *A Concise History*, pp. 38-39. This is from line 9. 5. Norberg and Szöverffy accept Thorsberg's attribution of this hymn to Paulo Álvaro, and so do I.

[19] NORBERG, *L'accentuation*, pp. 6-8.

[20] GIL, *Corpus*, pp. 348-354.

nix, glacies, uentus et hunda resonat" (7, l. 10); "*Aggeus hinc clangit, Zacca-rias namque resonat*" (9, 22); "*Dum uentus nubes format, dum unda resonat*" (9, 119); "*Et cinis in cinerem uersus, set lingua resonat*" (9, 151). It is interest-ing to note that this word is also used in Paulo Álvaro's metric verse, and there it is correctly diagnosed as an anapaest; his *Lamentum metricum* (*Carmen* 8) has the two metric hexameter lines "*Et lingua resonans tecum post fata resur-git*" (l. 2) and "*Quem murmur resonat undose margine turgens*" (l. 11), as well as comparable anapaestic uses of "*relegens*" (l. 5), "*relebet*" (l. 15) and "*reco-le*" (l. 24).

Adonic rhythms

As Allen pointed out,[21] though, and as the above lines make clear, the stress patterns of the first four feet of a rhythmic hexameter could vary greatly, so it may only be the adonic rhythm of the last two feet (/../.) which can be taken as certain evidence of spoken stress patterns. This may in practice have been all that the unskilled Latin-speaker was aware of in a hexameter, even in Imperial times. Allen adduces a wonderful example of ten supposed hexameter lines from as early as the first or second century A.D. in which this rhythmic pattern within the last two feet seems to be the only guiding structural principle at all. Its beginning is:

quat ualeas abeas pascas, multos tu habebes amicos.
si haliquit casu alite[r] aduxerit aster,
aut ili Romae frater es aut tu peregre heris
et uocas acliua, quo si tu non nosti amicos,
adcnoscet homines aeg(er) quos no(n) pote sanus.[22]

It is interesting to note that the same reliance on the final adonic is the only apparent constant in the ostensibly hexametric verse of the third-century native Punic-speaker Iasuchthan, recently analysed brilliantly by Adams,[23] although Adams is probably right to attribute the main linguistic peculiarities of this verse to the author's infelicitous second-language-learning experience rather than directly to specific features of Punic. Such adonics also occur in all lines

---

[21] W.S. ALLEN, *Accent and Rhythm* (Cambridge, 1973).

[22] ALLEN, *Accent*, pp. 346-347.

[23] J.N. ADAMS, "The poets of Bu Njem: Language, culture and the centurionate", *The Journal of Roman Studies* 89 (1999), pp. 109-133.

of the ubiquitous Sapphic metre much used in early hymns, regularly appearing before the caesura in the hendecasyllables as well as forming the final line of the strophe, so Sapphics are often good evidence of vernacular stress patterns; and in Romance areas this remains largely true even after the reforms as well, as in the splendid rhythmic Sapphic poem about El Cid, *Carmen Campi Doctoris*, which was composed probably in Catalonia in *c.* 1082.[24]

Ibero-Romance Stress

These tendencies to move the stress were pan-Romance, but it is also possible to find examples of specifically Ibero-Romance phenomena in verse from pre-reform areas of the Iberian Peninsula. One of these concerns the Ibero-Romance movement of the stress of all infinitives to the paroxytone position. Thus Latin *"perdere"* became French *"perdre"* and Italian *"perdere"*, both still rhizotonic, but became paroxytonic Ibero-Romance *"perdere"* [-ére] and hence modern oxytonic Spanish *"perder"* [-ér]. Norberg even indicated a seventh-century example, from the Peninsula, of *"capere"* with paroxytone stress, although in this case the same shift occurred in Italy (to *"capire"*), so we know anyway that it must have occurred early.[25] Since *"capuisse"* is found in the contemporary Visigothic liturgy,[26] this genuinely seems to have involved a whole conjugation shift for the verb (compare: Spanish *caber* < CAPERE, *cupe* < CAPUI). The evidence of the poems seems to suggest, however, that this is a case of the gradual lexical diffusion of a morphological change, since Paulo Alvaro maintained the original accentuation of the Latin verbs in Stanza 9 of his iambic hymn, with the words *"inducere"*, *"ingerere"*, *"gemere"* and *"legere"* being given the same stress pattern as the *"Domine"* of line 5 (despite eventual Castilian oxytones such as *"leer"*). Another example may be the word *"dies"*; the form *"dieï"* is found in an anonymous poem with the stress on the initial syllable as it is in Spanish *"día"*.[27]

Words that had fallen out of vernacular use entirely but still appear in written compositions could form part of the author's active vocabulary only in

---

[24] See: WRIGHT, *Early Ibero-Romance*, chapter 16. A dating to a hundred years later has now been proposed by: A. MONTANER and A. ESCOBAR, *Carmen Campidoctoris o poema latino del Campeador* (Madrid, 2001).

[25] NORBERG, *L'accentuation*, p. 9.

[26] M.C. DÍAZ Y DÍAZ, "El latín de la liturgia hispánica", in: *Estudios sobre la liturgia mozárabe*, ed. J. RIVERA RECIO (Toledo, 1965), pp. 55-87.

[27] NORBERG, *L'accentuation*, p. 22.

the written register, where the original accentuation could only have been achieved by informed guesswork. Errors in stress that exist there without any vernacular counterpart that could have prompted them might be used by linguists as evidence that the word only retained a "crepuscular" existence in the written register of the time.[28]

Prothetic [e-]

One further vocalic phenomenon has become well-known within the rhythmic verse; the "prothetic" [e-] which became attached to the start of words which had originally begun with an [s-] and another consonant. This is in itself a most interesting development to the historical linguist, who is more accustomed to having to account for the loss of original sounds than for the addition of new ones. In this case, Romance seems to have acquired a syllabic constraint which confined preconsonantal [s] to a syllable-final position. A syllable-final position implies the existence of a previous vowel, since all syllables contain a vowel by definition, so a need was felt to add one. This vowel later turned up in Romance as either an [e-], in France and the Iberian Peninsula, or an [i-], in Italy. The requirement for such a vowel is still operative in some varieties of Romance, most remarkably in modern Castilian Spanish, whose speakers are phonologically incapable of pronouncing syllable-initial consonant clusters beginning with [s], whereas modern Italian-speakers have lost this constraint altogether and do this all the time, even extending to non-Latinate initial voiced clusters such as the [zb-] of the word *sbaglio*.

Non-Romance-speaking writers find no problem here. For example, Aldhelm's *Carmen Rhythmicum*, l. 29, consists of the alliterative octosyllable "*Spissa statim spiramina*", and elsewhere in his poem there is no difficulty caused by the words "*sponsam*" (l. 6), "*spumabant*" (l. 104), "*scopulosis*" (l. 114), "*statim*" (l. 131), "*scissa*" (l. 161), "*spectacula*" (l. 166) and "*spiramina*" (l. 179). But some syllable counts in rhythmic verse written by Romance-speakers seem to require the presence of this prothetic vowel in performance, without telling us what the vowel actually is. For example, Paulo Álvaro was in general skilful at limiting the phonetic features required to the high register alternatives appropriate to the hymn-singing performance context. Both the

---

[28] This description of such usages as "crepuscular" comes from: J.N. GREEN, "The collapse and replacement of verbal inflection in Late Latin / Early Romance: How would one know?", in: WRIGHT (ed.), *Latin and the Romance Languages*, pp. 83-99.

unstressed prevocalic [i]s in the word "*sapientia*" of the first line of his iambic hymn, for example, were required to have independent vocalic status in performance. But Blume noticed that seven lines, out of the eighty-five in all, seem to be a syllable light, and that all of these contain a word that begins with an [s] and a following consonant.[29] The words in question were printed by Blume with an initial small superscript letter ᵉ, as "ᵉ*spurcissima*" (l. 3. 2), "ᵉ*stringit*" (l. 4. 2), "ᵉ*studio*" (l. 5. 2), "ᵉ*spiritum*" (l. 6. 2), "ᵉ*splendide*" (l. 12. 3), "ᵉ*stultorum*" (l. 14. 2) and "ᵉ*spatio*" (l. 17. 4). Blume also did this in several other hymns in that volume. There are, however, other words in that hymn, beginning with these same clusters, whose syllable count seems not to imply such a vowel; these are "*spiritali*" (l. 1. 2), "*stipendia*" (l. 3. 5), "*spiritu*" (l. 7. 2) and "*splendor*" (l. 13. 1). None of these four occur in the hymn after a previous word-final vowel, so this absence of the prothetic [e-] cannot be explained by elision. None of the manuscripts include such an initial letter *e*-, superscript or otherwise, but according to Blume's apparatus the Toledo manuscript (referred to by Blume as *MT*, having come to Madrid from Toledo) presents three of these eleven cases with an initial letter *i*-; they are "*ispurcissima*" (l. 3. 2), "*insplendide*" (sic, with *in*-, l. 12. 3), and "*insplendor*" (l. 13. 1). Blume attached a slightly baffling note to the first of these: "(Beleg für vorgeschlagenes e)". How a letter *i* can be seen as direct evidence of a vowel [e] is left unclear, but the point concerning the spoken vowel as inspiring the written letter is sensible enough (and Blume had anyway already mentioned it[30]). Unfortunately, one of these spellings with *i*- in the manuscript is of a word used in a line (l. 13. 1) which does not seem to require the presence of a sung vowel. The written form *in*- cannot be seen as attesting a vernacular prefix in these two cases; the letter *n* here simply attests to the fact that the [n] had long since gone from the [ns] cluster, in such a way that the spelling was known to be 'silent'. But since there seem to exist here eleven words of the type, four of which seem not to require a sung vowel and seven of which do, only three of which are written with an initial letter corresponding to a vowel but one of those three accompanies a word where the vowel is not in fact required in the line concerned, it would seem rash to deduce that the prothetic vowel was always obligatory even in the highest registers of Ibero-Romance vernacular, on the basis of the spellings of the poem. We can perhaps work the other way round, and use our reconstructed knowledge of the vernacular to help understand what is happening in the poem, where the vernacular [e-] seems to be required more

---

[29] BLUME, *Analecta*, pp. 180-183.
[30] In his Introduction: BLUME, *Analecta*, p. 54.

often than not but can be ignored *"rithmi gratia"* if the poet requires. This suggests that we are still in a period of possible linguistic variation. This hymn also requires no vocalic elision, but it does not always avoid the relevant circumstances. This fact also suggests that the sung register was not that of speech. Overall, then, although knowledge of the vernacular of the author can help explain some features of the text, the text itself is not conversely a reliable guide to the pronunciation of the vernacular. For as I have said before, and is still important to appreciate, "the surviving texts are not the records of actual performances".[31]

Conclusions

One conclusion is that editors of these poems should choose one particular manuscript version of each poem and then present it neat, in a version as close to a facsimile as the technology will allow, without any emendations at all; and if there are alternative versions in other manuscripts, those versions should be printed in facsimile fashion as well. We need to forget the mirage of trying to reconstruct a uniquely authoritative but unattested pristine version out of some kind of highest common factor. What linguists need, and philologists need, and students of the educational and social contexts of the authors need, is the existing evidence. We do not need modern editors' interpretations of that evidence, because that is personal and will inevitably become antiquated over time. Norberg and Gil have often pointed this out.[32] It is essential, in any printed version, to give us the evidence as it actually is, not as what the editors would have preferred it to be. Much of the linguistic evidence for these years has been distorted by modern editors' anachronistic ideas of what ought to have been written instead. This editorial tendency is not new, of course. Much of the value of the copious work of Paulo Álvaro's voluble colleague Eulogio de Córdoba, for example, was nullified by the decision of the sixteenth-century editor Ambrosio de Morales to regularize the spellings and the morphology that he found in the manuscripts which have subsequently been lost. This is a very live issue in the editing of early medieval Spanish Romance texts, too. Recent detailed work by Duffell, Martin, Bayo Julve and others has shown how

---

[31] WRIGHT, *Late Latin*, p. 71.

[32] For instance: J. GIL, "Para la edición de los textos visigodos y mozárabes", *Habis* 5 (1973), pp. 189-234.

imperative it is to print the texts as they are,[33] and how obstructive the well-meaning emendations and reorganizations made by earlier editors have been to a proper understanding of the native Ibero-Romance verse forms. It is also advisable for the editors to have at least some general knowledge of Romance and 'Vulgar Latin', and, in the case of later poems, knowledge of geographical variations in Romance as well; so that readers are not misled by ill-advised and unnecessarily over-classicizing 'emendations' of details that in fact accurately reflect the writer's language. But this conclusion is probably unnecessary. I have been much impressed by the seriousness and professionalism of the members of the editorial team involved in the current project to print all the extant rhythmic verses.[34]

---

[33] M. DUFFELL, *Modern Metrical Theory and the Verso de Arte Mayor* (London, 1999). J.C. BAYO JULVE, "Poetic discourse patterning in the *Cantar de Mio Cid*", *Modern Language Review* 96 (2001), pp. 82-91. G. MARTIN, "Gestas de arena", in: *Textos épicos castellanos: problemas de edición y crítica*, ed. D. PATTISON (London, 2000), pp. 23-33.

[34] The European Commission is supporting a digital edition of *Poetry in Early Medieval Europe: Manuscripts, Language and Music of the Latin Rhythmical Texts*, and sponsored the conference in Munich where this study was first delivered.

Section C

The Ninth Century

The ninth century is often seen as a turning point in the development of Romance. Some philologists have described this as the period of the 'emergence' of Romance, having in mind the earliest apparent direct reference to Romance, as "*rustica romana lingua*" (in 813), and the earliest texts that seem to have been deliberately written according to a new system, the Strasbourg Oaths (in 842). This is also the period of the establishment of the Carolingian reforms, which included an attempt to train clerics to use an archaic kind of Latin. There is a connection between the two. This "*renovatio*" created a divide between those who could operate the reformed Medieval Latin and those who could not. One symptom of the divide came to be the simultaneous existence of the two ways of writing which we would now call Latin and Romance.

The key to these developments lies in the work of the Anglo-Saxon scholar Alcuin, who was given the authority by the Emperor Charlemagne to reform clerical education, to prepare a standard text of the Bible, and establish a standard mode of delivery of the Church services. Many kinds of evidence lead to these conclusions. One sign is that Alcuin's treatise *De orthographia* manifests a central concern with reading pronunciation as well as with spelling. It seems to have been aimed at reforming the oral delivery of the sacred texts on the basis of specifying a sound for each letter, probably with a particular eye to those around him at Tours who were native Romance-speakers and had hitherto read the sacred texts with their normal pronunciation. Chapter 9 below looks at this work in detail, and ties it in with the seventeenth Canon of the Council of Tours (813), which was repeated verbatim at the Council of Mainz (847). These required the homilies not to be read in the formal style used elsewhere in the service, because they needed to be intelligible. Since authorized homily texts had been carefully collected by both Alcuin and his pupil Hrabanus Maurus (who was Bishop of Mainz in 847), it seems that that instruction can only primarily refer to oral delivery rather than any desire to change the actual words.

It is not immediately clear whether the conceptual distinction between the two modes, Latin and Romance, precedes or follows the development of the new way of writing ("*scripta*") evidenced by the Strasbourg Oaths of 842. Many scholars have suggested that the conceptual distinction must have been made first, before a new "*scripta*" could be elaborated; others have suggested that the relative chronology is more likely to have been the other way round. Chapter 10 here examines the relevant evidence, and concludes that the development of a new way of writing is best interpreted as having been the main catalyst of the subsequent distinction, rather than the consequence of an already existing one.

There were, of course, many Romance speakers outside the Carolingian area in the ninth century, not directly affected by the Reforms or by the new Latin-Romance distinction. Chapter 11 considers the special case of the Romance-speakers of Moslem Spain, who called their language "*ladino*". Between 830 and 880 there were several voluble Christian writers there, mainly in Córdoba; and yet written "*ladino*" had all but fallen into disuse by the tenth century. The scholars of Córdoba had also made an attempt to return to Classical usage, inspired by a number of works that Eulogio of Córdoba found in the Pyrenees in 848-850. But here the eventual effect was to make the effort of such archaization seem too difficult, and even the Christians, bilingual in speech, came to limit their literacy to Arabic. A combined philological and sociohistorical analysis here explains developments which otherwise have seemed rather mysterious.

There were occasional contacts between Córdoba and the Carolingians in the ninth century. Some of Eulogio's colleagues, for example, apparently travelled as far as Mainz, and were probably there at the time of Hrabanus Maurus' repetition of the edict concerning the performance of the homilies. Chapter 12 attempts to answer the hypothetical, and conceivably actual, question of whether a visitor from Córdoba would have understood the performance of the Strasbourg Oaths. Careful philological analysis, both of the Oaths and of Eulogio's voluminous surviving works, allied to an understanding of the practical circumstances, leads to the conclusion that he probably would. The Romance-speaking world could still be seen as a single speech community in the mid-ninth century, but the elastic was coming nearer to breaking.

Chapter 9

Alcuin's *De Orthographia* and the
Council of Tours (A.D. 813)

The contemporary relationship in the Early Middle Ages between Latin and the Romance Languages is not self-evident. The instinct and practice of most modern scholars who study Medieval Latin has been to regard Latin as Latin whenever it was written, and to view the growth of Romance as being outside their brief. In this book I have been presenting the hypothesis that Medieval Latin, as a recognizably separate entity from the contemporary vernacular of any Romance-speaking community, was an invention of the Carolingian Renaissance. In this chapter the focus will be on Alcuin's *De Orthographia* and the edicts of the Council of Tours (813), both of which can be seen to play an important part in these developments.

As we have seen, for the specific circumstances of reading aloud Church Offices, a pronunciation reform seems to have been instigated which was designed to bring pronunciation into line with traditional spelling, as was already normal in Germanic-speaking areas. Within the Romance-speaking areas, Carolingian Medieval Latin was thus not the mere refurbishing of a system of conservative pronunciation that had miraculously survived the previous millen-

This chapter originally pre-dated *Late Latin and Early Romance*, but the data remain and are valuable as ever. It has been revised and to some extent abbreviated. The original publication is: "Late Latin and Early Romance: Alcuin's *De Orthographia* and the Council of Tours (A.D. 813)", reprinted with publisher's permission from *Papers of the Liverpool Latin Seminar; Third Volume 1981*, ed. F. CAIRNS (Liverpool, Francis Cairns, 1981; *ARCA Classical and Medieval Texts, Papers and Monographs* 7), pp. 343-363. We are grateful to Mrs Sandra Cairns, on behalf of Francis Cairns (Publications) Ltd, for permitting this reprint.

nium unscathed, but a conscious, progressive, revolutionary and demanding innovation. At first the new pronunciation system was probably only meant to apply to reading aloud, as all the Church services were to consist of fixed written texts. It was based on the simple principle of pronouncing one specific sound for each written letter (or recognized digraph); this is what happens universally now in the reading aloud of Latin, as if the traditional orthography were some kind of phonetic script.

Since the reformed mode was intended to apply in the Early Romance-speaking areas as well as in the Germanic, it is worth stressing from the start how very different the result would have been from their normal speech. For those trained in the new method, no longer would written *"virgini"* and *"ferit"* be read in the normal vernacular way as [vjɛrdʒə] and [fjɛrt], but as [virgini] and [ferit]. This skill needed to be taught; it would not have been easy to do, and the resulting readings would have been largely unintelligible to the uninitiated. Were such a reform to be introduced into Modern English, "wright" would have to be read aloud as [wright], "fashion" as [fashion], "gauge" as [gauge], and so on for every single word in the language. At once this would create distinctive pronunciation norms in our previously monolingual community, one of which would be confined to the educated. And yet a reform of this kind is not going to be directly perceptible to scholars of over a millennium later, as they look back at the only surviving evidence, the written texts; for the recommended spelling has not changed.

Recent scholarship has emphasized that the aim of the Carolingian 'Renaissance' was the creation of a reshaped Christian society. Part of this *"renovatio"* involved the standardization of liturgical practice. In 787, Charlemagne decreed that the Roman rite was to be the one performed, and by the middle of the following century this was standard practice. Alcuin of York was given the task of reviewing the liturgy and establishing standard texts. Alcuin retired from the Court to Tours in 796, and in 800 he presented the authorized version of the Vulgate Bible to Charlemagne.

These were four years of intensely focused intellectual activity for Alcuin. The *De Orthographia* is also datable to precisely this period; the earliest manuscript version dates from 799 (in Vienna Nationalbibliothek MS. 795). The standardized performance of the liturgy naturally required a standard spelling for the texts, but also a standardized manner of reading it aloud, and it is this latter aspect of the *De Orthographia* that has usually failed to attract scholarly attention. Only Dag Norberg seems to have noticed the direct causal connection between Alcuin's handbooks and the reforms, although the more general point, that subsequent Latin pronunciation has always been a function of the traditional spelling, was well made by Helmut Lüdtke.[1]

Alcuin's work now known as *De Orthographia* has not been given much attention by modern scholars, probably because it seems at first glance not to be a work of any originality. Marsili's edition (1952) unfortunately accentuated that impression, since his critical study was mainly concerned with documenting its indebtedness to Bede's work which was also given the same title. Bruni's more recent edition (1997) has admirably worked out the manuscript traditions, but still pays almost no attention to the context of the work's composition.[2]

Much of Alcuin's work indeed has Bede as its source, although other details are based on Cassiodorus, Priscian and Isidore. It is not, however, a mere copy. Analysis shows that Alcuin had pronunciation in his sights as much as spelling. Bede's *De Orthographia* had covered much more than orthography. It is probable that the title *De Orthographia* was only given to Alcuin's work after his death in 804, for in the old manuscripts the work is given the heading of an elegiac couplet which (pace Bruni) Alcuin almost certainly placed there himself, whether or not he composed it. There are two alternative versions of this couplet, related by Bruni to the two different manuscript traditions; her group *a* presents:

> Me legat antiquas cupiat qui scire loquelas,
> me spernens loquitur mox sine lege patrum,

which is the one printed by Marsili. The use here of *"loquelas"* ("spoken words") and *"loquitur"* ("speaks") makes it explicit that at least one of the aims of the work is to train people to speak properly, as the *"patres"* used to (in Alcuin's view, at least). The earliest surviving manuscript, however (Vienna 795), has the couplet presented by Bruni as heading her manuscript group *b*:

> Me legat antiquas vult qui proferre loquelas
> me qui non sequitur vult sene lege loqui,

---

[1] D. NORBERG, *Manuel pratique de latin médiéval* (Paris, 1968), pp. 50-53. H. LÜDTKE, "Tesi generali sui rapporti fra i sistemi orale e scritto del linguaggio", in: *XV Congresso Internazionale di Linguistica e Filologia Romanza: Atti*, I (Napoli, 1978), pp. 433-443.

[2] Alcuin, *De Orthographia*, ed. A. MARSILI, *Alcuini Orthographia* (Pisa, 1952); ed. S. BRUNI, *Alcuino "De Orthographia"* (Firenze, 1997). A facsimile of the *De Orthographia* in MS Vienna 795 can be found in: F. UNTERKIRCHER, *Alkuin-Briefe* (Graz, 1969), folios 5r-18v.

which is the one printed by Migne, who corrected "*sene*" to "*sine*",[3] so that the couplet means:

Let the one who wishes to pronounce spoken words as the *antiqui* did, read me;
he who does not follow my precepts is speaking wrongly.

The second heading is also often found, either as a colophon or an introduction, in Carolingian manuscripts of Priscian's *Institutiones*, being particularly current in those from Alcuin's home scriptorium of Tours. The *Institutiones* and Alcuin's *De Orthographia* are thus both seen as part of the new "*lex*". Both headings of the *De Orthographia* make it explicit that pronunciation is part of Alcuin's brief, but most modern scholars have failed to take that literally. Jones, for example, in his edition of Bede's work, merely declared that "Alcuin's *De Orthographia* is little more than a digest of Bede's", apparently being influenced by the similarly dismissive views of William of Malmesbury.[4]

This, at least, is simple to disprove. Under the letter "A", for instance, Bede lists approximately sixty-eight words, but only twenty of these appear in the approximately seventy-one words listed under the letter "A" in Alcuin. These figures are approximate because one heading can cover several words. In Alcuin's text there are forty-six headings under "A", which correspond to sections 2-47 in Bruni's edition, who arranges the text as if it were a numbered sequence of Biblical verses (references here are to Bruni's sections). The extra fifty-one words beginning in "A" in Alcuin are explained for the most part by his use of other sources. Since Alcuin was aiming to recover the past, he did not want to present any data that lacked an authoritative source. But his choice of what to take over is significant. Modern scholars who investigate a work's sources tend to ignore the elements in that source that were not taken by the work in question, but the fact that Alcuin has discarded forty-eight of the items he found in Bede is not insignificant; the point here is that none of the forty-eight comments that Alcuin chose not to take over from Bede's work contain any information which is relevant to pronunciation, whereas most (but not all) of those that are chosen do indeed have such information.

[3] Alcuin, *De Orthographia*, ed. J.P. MIGNE, *Patrologia Latina* 101, cols. 901B-920A, col. 902D.

[4] Bede, *De Orthographia*, ed. C.W. JONES, *Bedae Venerabilis Opera Pars VI: Opera Didascalica* (Turnhout, 1975: *Corpus Christianorum. Series Latina* 123A), pp. 7-57. References are to line numbers in this edition.

Furthermore, Alcuin rarely transcribes Bede verbatim. For example, the entries for *"aula"*, *"apparet"* and *"accedo"* are based on Bede,[5] but are given extra information: respectively, in *"Aula latine domus regia est et per a scribitur"* the *"et per a scribitur"* has been added; in *"Apparet per p quod videtur, adparet per d quod obsequitur"* the *"per p"* and *"per d"*; in *"accedo per duo c"* the *"per duo c"*. Bede considers in detail the semantic distinction between *"ab"* and *"ex"*.[6] Alcuin ignores that in his entry,[7] and considers only the reasons for choosing between *"a"*, *"ab"* or *"abs"*, which mean the same (*"unius significationis sunt"*):

> ab saepissime scribitur, cum sequens verbum a vocali incipit, ne dictio multis consonantibus oneretur, ut ab uno.

This implies that it is the spelling that determines the pronunciation, rather than the other way round; *"ab"* – rather than *"abs"* – "is very often written when the following word begins with a vowel, to stop the spoken form being overburdened with consonants, as in *"ab uno"*. The *ne* clause is taken from Cassiodorus, but Cassiodorus seems to be implying that the written form is based on spoken usage, rather than vice versa (for the [-b] before a vowel was probably still pronounced in the vernacular of sixth-century Italy).[8] Alcuin's entry continues as follows:

> si vero a consonante pars orationis incipit, a solum ponatur, ut a fratre; abs tamen in compositione saepius propter euphoniam integra manet, ut abs te abscondo melius sonat quam ab te vel abcondo, sicut melius sonat ab urbe quam abs urbe.

With reference to *"abscondo"*, Bede had merely mentioned *"absconditus"* as being the correct form rather than *"absconsus"*,[9] a strictly morphological point of no relevance to Alcuin's concerns here, whereas Bede had shown no interest in which "sounded best" out of *"ab"* and *"abs"*.

[5] Alcuin, *De Orthographia*, 44 (*"aula"*), 17 (*"apparet"*) and 3 (*"accedo"*). Bede, *De Orthographia*, l. 30, ll. 118-119 and l. 143 respectively.

[6] Bede, *De Orthographia*, ll. 67-73.

[7] Alcuin, *De Orthographia*, 27.

[8] Cassiodorus's *De Orthographia* can be found in: H. KEIL, *Grammatici Latini*, VII (Leipzig, 1880; reprinted Hildesheim, 1961), pp. 126-210; this passage on: p. 161, l. 35. References are to page and line numbers in this edition. References to Isidore's *Etymologiae* are to J. OROZ RETA (ed.), *San Isidoro de Sevilla: Etimologías*, 2 volumes (Madrid, 1982: *Biblioteca de Autores Cristianos*). References to other works of Isidore and Alcuin, and to those of Hrabanus Maurus, are to: J.P. MIGNE, *Patrologia Latina*.

[9] Bede, *De Orthographia*, l. 109.

"*Alius*" is mentioned by Bede because it is a word with two dative forms, as well as in the prescription that "*alium et dolium per i scribendum*".[10] Alcuin ignores the former comment and takes over the latter, but also includes later a distinction from "*alea*" explicitly directed at how to read it aloud: "*alea si ludum significat per e, si ab alius alia venit per i legitur*".[11] Bede mentions "*alvus*" to distinguish it semantically from "*uterus*" and "*venter*".[12] Alcuin sees it as meaning the same as "*venter*" ("*Alvus cum ventrem significat ...*") and only mentions it to distinguish it from "*albus*".[13] Bede mentions "*aes*" for its plural form "*aera*".[14] Alcuin mentions it in order to discuss whether or not it is a diphthong: "*aer disyllabum est, aes monosyllabum et non habet pluralem numerum nisi aera tantum*".[15] It is true, of course, that some of Alcuin's comments are strictly semantic. "*Albus*" is also mentioned in another entry because "*album natura, candidum cura facit*", for example.[16] The point being made here is the converse, that comments omitted from Bede are not related to pronunciation or spelling.

The letter "A" is not exceptional. Under "B", for example, Bede has eleven words, two of which reappear in Alcuin's nineteen.[17] Under "D", Bede has thirty-six words, of which twelve reappear in Alcuin's twenty-six.[18] Under "G" Bede has eight, of which three occur in Alcuin's twelve, et cetera.[19] The dependence on Bede is thus not that of a mere copyist. As every scholar knows, intelligent use of established research is the basis for intellectual advance. Alcuin had better things to do with his time at Tours than engage in mere hack work. His social context was different from that of Bede. He was reshaping the inherited intellectual and pedagogical tradition for a practical purpose in the renewed educational system, even if, as ever, he preferred to use other scholars' words rather than his own for that purpose.

The deduction that one of Alcuin's aims was to train people to read aloud 'correctly' by basing their reading pronunciation directly on the spelling is supported by several more details of the presentation. He gives, for example,

[10] Bede, *De Orthographia*, ll. 86-89 and ll. 100-101.
[11] Alcuin, *De Orthographia*, 12 and 34.
[12] Bede, *De Orthographia*, ll. 136-137.
[13] Alcuin, *De Orthographia*, 29.
[14] Bede, *De Orthographia*, ll. 61-62.
[15] Alcuin, *De Orthographia*, 8.
[16] Alcuin, *De Orthographia*, 23. This is a summary of: Bede, *De Orthographia*, ll. 133-135.
[17] Sections 48-64 in Bruni's edition.
[18] Alcuin, *De Orthographia*, 95-108.
[19] Alcuin, *De Orthographia*, 161-170.

advice based on *"euphonia"*, a word used by Cassiodorus but not by Bede, in which, unlike Cassiodorus, Alcuin makes it clear that in his view the proper spelling is the element which determines the proper reading pronunciation. A striking example concerns the word *"quantus"*. Alcuin says that *"quantus et tantus per n euphoniae causa, venit enim a quamtus et tamtus"*;[20] that is, that we should write it with an *n* because the resulting pronunciation [kwantus] is aesthetically preferable to [kwamtus]. Bruni correctly refers us in her apparatus to Cassiodorus,[21] without indicating that Cassiodorus had given explicitly contrary advice. Cassiodorus and the monks that he was instructing were Romance-speakers, who automatically said [kwantus], but even so, regardless of the resulting discrepancy between speech and spelling, Cassiodorus wants his monks to transcribe these words with *m* rather than *n*:

> tamtus et quamtus in medio m habere debent. quam enim et tam est, unde quamtitas quamtus tamtus. nec quosdam moveat, si n sonat; iam enim supra docui n sonare debere, tametsi in scriptura m positum sit.

Cassiodorus is probably here giving advice on the practical question of how to resolve the nasal-indicating tilde (˜) when copying manuscripts. Isidore recommended similar orthography, making no reference at all to sounds:

> tamtus, sicut et quamtus, in medio m habebant, quam enim et tam, unde et quamtitas, quamtus, tantus.[22]

Bede only mentions *"quantus"* in order to distinguish it semantically from *"quotus"*: *"quantus quam magnus dicitur, quotus cuius aetatis"*.[23] Alcuin's comment here is an addition.

Alcuin has several other comments on *"euphonia"* which similarly show that the choice of spelling determines the manner of pronunciation when reading aloud, For instance: *"loquor loqueris loquitur per q scribenda sunt; locutus vero euphoniae causa per c et simplex u scribatur"* (218; that is, rather than *"loquutus"*, which would be hard to pronounce); and *"differo diffundo s in f mutata euphoniae causa"* (101, rather than *"disfero"*, *"disfundo"*). This last example shows that ease of reading-pronunciation must be the main criterion

---

[20] Alcuin, *De Orthographia*, 321.

[21] Cassiodorus, *De Orthographia*, p. 152, ll. 3-5.

[22] Isidore, *Etymologiae*, I, 27, 25. The past tense in *"habebant"*, referring to the use of ancient authorities, is mistranslated as a present tense in Oroz's facing translation in Spanish, *"presentan"*.

[23] Bede, *De Orthographia*, ll. 975-979.

here, [ff] being easier than [sf], for it is a decrease in the ease of writing to
have to remember not to write *"disfero"* when *dis-* is such a common prefix.

Occasionally two alternative spellings are declared permissible precisely
because the two alternative ensuing pronunciations are deemed to be acceptable (unlike [disfero]), for instance: *"navita et nauta, utrumque recte dicitur"*
(241; that is *"dicitur"*, not just *"scribitur"*); *"prehendo et prendo, utrumque
dici potest"* (267), repeated within *"dicimus enim prehendo et prendo, vehe-
mens et vemens, nihil nil et nihili"* (395, under the heading of *"traho"*), where
the first-person plural in *"dicimus"* means "those of us who speak the official
way". This certainty contrasts markedly with the comment by Cassiodorus
which underlies Alcuin's example:

> vehemens et vemens apud antiquos et apud Ciceronem lego, aeque prehendo et prendo,
> hercule et hercle, nihil et nil. haec observari eatenus poterunt, consuetudine potius quam
> ratione, in his praecipue verbis quae adspirationem habere debent.[24]

By *"consuetudine"* he means "tradition", and by *"aspirationem"* he means the
letter *h* (not the sound [h]); what Cassiodorus sees as lacking in *"ratio"*, but
nonetheless to be recommended, is to preserve the letter despite the lack of any
corresponding sound in speech (the [h] had ceased to be part of anybody's
vernacular for several centuries). Back in the second century A.D. Velius Longus had had a clear idea of what was happening. He also recommended the
spelling with *h*, but saw it as a 'silent' letter with no counterpart in speech:

> H littera .. inseruit, ut in his, vehemens reprehendit, cum elegantiores vementem dicant et
> reprendit secundum primam positionem: prendo enim dicimus, non prehendo.[25]

By the first person in *"dicimus"* Velius Longus refers to normal good vernacular speakers of his time, who do not pronounce the [h].

Velius Longus had been explicit in his *De Orthographia*: in his view spelling and speech did not need to coincide. Silent letters cause no real problems
to native speakers of the relevant vernacular. But over five hundred years later,
Alcuin, who was planning to base the official reading pronunciation of the
Church on the forms of the traditional orthography, saw silent letters as intrinsically inadmissible. Yet he felt a little unsure in this case: what sound should
the letter *h* actually lead to? Alcuin assumes that it must have some effect upon

---

[24] Cassiodorus, *De Orthographia*, p. 153, ll. 7-10.
[25] KEIL, *Grammatici Latini*, VII, p. 68, ll. 14-17.

the sound, although it is hard to see exactly what he thought he was getting at when he declared:

> H ideo vocalibus extrinsecus ascribitur ut minus sonet, consonantibus autem intrinsecus ut plurimum sonet.[26]

The later attempt at a rule, presented under the letter "R" is linguistically absurd,[27] and must be a garbling of ancient precepts rather than the intuitions of a 'native speaker':

> R sequente, i vocalis semper asspiratur, ut hircus hirquitallus Hirpinus hirsutus hirtus Hirtuleius Hirrus proprium, nisi aut monosyllabum sit, ut ir, aut ex motu verbi, ut eo is irem, ires, iris id est arcus, aut si a post r sequatur: tunc enim non asspiratur, ut ira iratus iracundus irascor et quicquid ab eis fit.[28]

Alcuin occasionally writes *"dicendum"*, *"dici debet"*, or *"debemus dicere"*, and these exhortations are usually his addition to the source. For example, in the following case Cassiodorus, the source, used *"scribere"*: *"ab arcu arcubus, ab arce arcibus dicendum est"*.[29] The following comes directly from Bede but with the addition of *"dici debet"*: *"Belzebub non Belzebul; Belial non Beliar dici debet"*.[30] *"Debemus dicere"* is inserted into Bede's material in *"urgere debemus dicere, non urguere"*.[31] Bede had merely advised *"urgeo, non urgueo"*.[32] Sometimes there is no problem about the spelling at all, and the pronunciation when reading aloud is all that is mentioned; the following is a clear example, using *"proferuntur"* (a traditional term since Quintilian for "utter"):

> manuviae oblivium diluvium suavium lividum Favius Flavius avidus fluvius civitas exuviae: per v consonantem et i brevem proferuntur.[33]

---

[26] Alcuin, *De Orthographia*, 180.

[27] This attempt is based on the list in: Cassiodorus, *De Orthographia*, p. 201, l. 28 - p. 202, l. 4.

[28] Alcuin, *De Orthographia*, 342. 3.

[29] Alcuin, *De Orthographia*, 5. Cassiodorus, *De Orthographia*, p. 156, ll. 16-21.

[30] Alcuin, *De Orthographia*, 54. Bede, *De Orthographia*, l. 145.

[31] Alcuin, *De Orthographia*, 397.

[32] Bede, *De Orthographia*, l. 1241.

[33] Alcuin, *De Orthographia*, 232. Data are taken from Cassiodorus, *De Orthographia*, p. 181, ll. 4-6.

"*Legitur*" also occurs, as in "*si ab alius alia venit per i legitur*" quoted above.[34]

Another feature of the *De Orthographia*, which makes it likely that Alcuin is here presenting an artificial pronunciation system for those who are already used to reading the same words with their usual Early Romance vernacular sounds, is the advice he gives for the distinct realization of some words that have through phonetic evolution become long since indistinguishable in the vernacular. The examples chosen, even if traditional in themselves, are not usually taken from Bede (who was not a Romance vernacular speaker). For example, "*haud*" and "*aut*" had been mentioned by many before.[35] The fact that "*haud*" was almost certainly no longer alive in Romance vernacular vocabulary at Alcuin's time is not relevant, since Alcuin is here concerned with the proper rendering of texts already written in the distant past; prior to his reforms, when a word such as "*haud*" had been met by a "*lector*" in a text, the *h* would have automatically been ignored and the final consonant would have sounded the same as that of "*aut*". Other examples include "*aequus*" and "*equus*",[36] both of which words had dropped from the Northern French vernacular, possibly precisely because of this homonymic clash;[37] "*habeo*" and "*abeo*", "*obnixus*" and "*obnexus*", "*quit*" and "*quid*", "*quot*" and "*quod*", "*vaccas*" and "*baccas*", "*vellus*" and "*bellus*".[38] There is also (in only one of the manuscript traditions) the following attempt, based on Cassiodorus,[39] to unravel the confusion caused by "*vos*", "*vobis*", "*bos*" and "*bovis*":

> vos, si pronomen monosyllabum per v, si disyllabum erit prior syllaba ab v, sequens a b incipit; si animal significat, monosyllabum per b, si disyllabum, prior syllaba a b, sequens ab v incipit, ut bos bovis bovi bovem bos a bove.[40]

Here the instructions are entirely based on phonetics, rather than on the morphological considerations also adduced by Cassiodorus.

These features of the *De Orthographia* are consistent with the theory that Alcuin is here prescribing the proper performance of an artificial system of

---

[34] Alcuin, *De Orthographia*, 34.

[35] Alcuin, *De Orthographia*, 171.

[36] Alcuin, *De Orthographia*, 2.

[37] In the fifth century, the African Grammarian Pompeius could still distinguish the pronunciation of these two words, regarding it as a "*barbarismus ... dicere aequus pro eo quod est equus*" (KEIL, *Grammatici Latini*, V, p. 285, ll. 5-9). In his area "*equus*" survived but the initial vowel diphthongized (as still in the feminine in Spanish "*yegua*", "mare").

[38] Alcuin, *De Orthographia*, respectively 174, 264, 319, 320, 398 and 402.

[39] Cassiodorus, *De Orthographia*, p. 177, l. 6 - p. 178, l. 2.

[40] Alcuin, *De Orthographia*, 405.

reading aloud, in particular for people who would not normally have read aloud heretofore with any pronunciation other than that of their normal Early Romance vernacular. Even though Alcuin used them as sources of information, there seems to have been a change in perspective from Cassiodorus and Isidore, who spoke Early Romance and were writing for speakers of that Romance, to the Germanic-speaking Bede, who in common with other Insular scholars (and his readers) did not have a native knowledge of Early Romance speech. And then again from Bede to Alcuin, who experienced the clash of those two traditions. At Aix and at Tours Alcuin found himself surrounded by people who wrote as he himself had learnt to write, but spoke in a remarkably different way, even when reading the Scriptures. Clearly, if he was to produce a standard performance of the liturgy, a standard pronunciation would be needed, and Alcuin naturally based that on the artificial one he had been taught himself. To the Romance speakers of Tours and Aix and elsewhere, this would have been something new, something difficult, something which needed to be learnt and taught. After a few decades, Romance-speakers who were taught to read aloud would have met this new method from the start, so that if Alcuin's *De Orthographia* was indeed essentially directed to those who had previously learnt to read aloud in the normal and natural vernacular fashion, it would have gradually become less relevant. This is what happened, in any event. It does not seem to have been used much after the mid-ninth century.

Echoes of this concern for standardizing reading-pronunciation appear in edicts concerning ecclesiastical education. It seems possible that this newly recommended system of letter-sound correspondences, in which every letter had to be given a sound, and in which in theory every one of these sounds was specified, was included at the time within the reference of the word "*litterae*".

There had been a general educational directive issued in 789 under the title of *Admonitio Generalis*, to which a supplement accrued, some time in the late 790s, with the title of *De Litteris Colendis*. This concerns literacy rather than literature. It is now generally thought that Alcuin was either sole or part author of this, although it was ostensibly an order from Charlemagne. It is thus roughly contemporary with his *De Orthographia*. The *De Litteris Colendis*, "On the necessity for learning *litterae*", begins as follows:[41]

---

[41] The *De Litteris Colendis* can be found in: ed. A. BORETIUS, *Monumenta Germaniae Historica. Capitularia regum Francorum* I (Hannover, 1883), pp. 78-79 (and in: L. WALLACH, *Alcuin and Charlemagne* (Ithaca, 1959), pp. 202-204). The *Admonitio Generalis* is in: BORETIUS (ed.), *Capitularia regum Francorum* I, pp. 52-62.

... nos una cum fidelibus nostris consideravimus utile esse ut episcopia et monasteria, nobis Christo propitio ad gubernandum commissa, praeter regularis vitae ordinem atque sanctae religionis conversationem etiam in litterarum meditationibus eis qui, donante Domino, discere possunt, secundum unuscuiusque capacitatem docendi studium debeant impendere, qualiter, sicut regularis norma honestatem morum, ita quoque docendi et discendi instantia ordinet et ornet seriem verborum ut, qui Deo placere appetunt recte vivendo, et etiam placere non neglegant recte loquendo...

The requirement to teach and learn *"litterae"* is being set up as a compulsory part of the curriculum in Church education, with the aim of having the priesthood *"recte loquendo"*. This is a phrase taken from the traditional definition of grammar, and is also used by Alcuin in his own definition of *"grammatica"*:

Grammatica est litteralis scientia, et est custos recte loquendi et scribendi.[42]

The purpose of the traditional phrase as used in the *De Litteris Colendis*, however, seems to be to avoid giving offence to God by mispronouncing his liturgy, *"quamobrem hortamur vos litterarum studia .. non neglegere"*. There is a subsequent reference to *"scolasticos bene loquendo .. in legendo seu cantando"*, explicitly stressing the connection between speaking, reading and singing.

Alcuin's brief discussion of *"litterae"* in his own *Grammatica* is largely based on Priscian,[43] and would thus probably have been new in the Carolingian context. He associates letters with sounds, in the traditional phrase *"littera est pars minima vocis articulatae"*.[44] The proposed etymology for *"littera"* however, is similar to that in Isidore's *Etymologiae*, where Isidore had said:

usus litterarum repertus est propter memoriam rerum, nam ne oblivione fugiant, litteris alligantur. in tanta enim rerum varietate nec disci audiendo poterant omnia, nec memoria contineri. litterae autem dicte quasi legiterae, quod iter legentibus praestent, vel quod in legendo iterentur.[45]

Yet Alcuin is not interested in letters as an aid to the memory; all he says is that letters show the way to the reader: *"littera est quasi legitera, quia legentibus iter praebet"*.

The evidence of the *De Litteris Colendis* suggests that Alcuin meant the reformed system to become normal practice, even in ecclesiastical centres outside his own personal area of influence. Even so, the extent to which other

---

[42] Alcuin, *Grammatica*, ed. MIGNE, *Patrilogiae Latina* 101, cols. 847A-902B, col. 857D.

[43] Alcuin, *Grammatica*, ed. MIGNE, *Patrologiae Latina* 101, cols. 854B-856B.

[44] Alcuin, *Grammatica*, col. 855A.

[45] Isidore, *Etymologiae*, I, 3, 2-3. Alcuin, *Grammatica*, col. 855A.

institutions paid any immediate attention to it is indeterminable. In practice, it might have been only Alcuin's immediate circle who at first took this seriously, at Tours and a few other centres. If so, this would shed light on two further aspects of cultural life in these years: the establishment of a standard non-cursive script; and one of the edicts of the Council of Tours in 813, which is not found in the four other Councils of that year held elsewhere.

Pre-Carolingian handwriting was not of a standard type. There were at least a dozen identifiable kinds, many of them cursive, and not all of them immediately legible.[46] In any system of reading aloud which depends on the instant recognition of separate letters to be turned individually into distinct sounds, cursive script is a handicap. The so-called Caroline Minuscule, whose origin pre-dates Charlemagne but which eventually came to be the prescribed standard, had the precise advantage for this purpose of having each letter written separately, with a minimum of contractions and ligatures. It is probable that it was the practical advantage it had for those reading aloud which led to its becoming the standard script. Alcuin did not invent it, but he was influential in establishing it. His Vulgate is seen as an important landmark in the development of the script at Tours, and the scriptorium at Tours became a leading centre of scribal training. The connection between reformed pronunciation and reformed calligraphy is likely to have continued to be close, for such practical reasons; much later they both came into North-Western Spain together, and for the first time, after the initial adoption of the Roman rite there in the late eleventh century.

The Church education system advocated by Charlemagne's advisers was based on the establishment of schools where pupils would learn to read. It should be noted that they were not normally taught to write, but only to read.[47] Reading specifically involved reading aloud, since the programme required the teaching of the psalms, and of chanting, on the basis of properly corrected liturgical texts. As regards the sermons, the requirement in the *Admonitio Generalis* was not that in Church priests should be freely creative and spontaneously fluent, but simply and overtly that they should recite the set texts of the Church services.[48]

---

[46] For a brief survey of scripts, see: L.D. REYNOLDS and N.G. WILSON, *Scribes and Scholars* (Oxford, 1968), pp. 81-83.

[47] See: P. RICHÉ, *La vie quotidienne dans l'empire Carolingien* (Paris, 1973), Part 4, Chapter 2. R. MCKITTERICK, *The Frankish Church and the Carolingian Reforms 789-895* (London, 1977).

[48] *Admonitio Generalis*, c. 78, p. 60.

If carried out conscientiously, this reform had the general effect of making the Church services unintelligible to most of the congregation. No longer, as in the Early Church, could all the congregation join in a collective act of worship: as McKitterick has said, they became spectators at a symbolic spectacle. And yet it was at the same time decreed to be essential for priests to preach.[49] It was forbidden for priests to make up their own sermons:

> ut presbyteros quos mittitis per parrochias vestras ad regendum et ad praedicandum per ecclesias populum Deo servientem, ut recte et honeste praedicent: et non sinatis nove vel non canonica aliquos ex suo sensu et non secundum scripturas sacras fingere et praedicare populo.[50]

They had to preach from a set text, and the set texts were the homiliaries of the Fathers of the Church, in particular the *Forty Homilies on the Gospel* composed by Gregory the Great. One of Alcuin's tasks at Tours was the collection of the authorized homilies into two manuscript volumes; one of the elegiac headings of the *De Orthographia* is directed to those who wish to speak like those "*patres*", who had written the homilies that had to be read aloud. The homily was thus the last and the longest in the series of passages allotted for reading aloud in a service, a passage 'set' in the same way as the prescribed readings from the Bible.

It must therefore have seemed desirable, to supporters of the new standard, to read the Homilies with the same official pronunciation based on giving each letter its specific sound. But that stultified their purpose, for the whole point of the homily was to be of benefit to the listeners, who could not understand it if it was delivered in such a way. It was probably not immediately clear what was to be done about that.

Alcuin died in 804, but his work lived on. In 813 there were five regional Councils, at Arles, Chalon, Mainz, Rheims and Tours, designed to assess the progress made so far in the establishment of a respectable Christian community, and set guidelines for the future. The bishoprics based on these five towns covered most of the Empire. The decisions of these Councils concerned a wide variety of practical matters, one of which was the effectiveness of preaching. The digest of their decrees, subsequently amalgamated, had as its heading XIII "*De officio praedicationis, ut iuxta quod intellegere vulgus possit assiduae*

---

[49] MCKITTERICK, *The Frankish Church*, Chapter 3. P. RICHÉ, *La vie quotidienne*, pp. 238-240.
[50] *Admonitio Generalis*, c. 82, p. 61.

fiat", concerning the need to make preaching generally intelligible.[51] This may be the first time that the "*vulgus*" are specifically contrasted to contemporaries who know Latin (rather than to the "*antiqui*", as in Isidore), a distinction that seems not to have been made before in this way.[52] The wording in this digest seems to have been adapted here from the 25th Canon of the Council of Mainz, "... *qui verbum Dei praedicet iuxta quod intellegere vulgus possit*". This phrasing is mildly ambiguous, for it might just refer to simplicity of reading style, but since the text is fixed in advance and cannot be changed, the manner of pronunciation seems to be the only obvious variable under consideration. The fifteenth canon of the Council held at Rheims similarly said that bishops should take care to preach sermons and homilies from the Holy Fathers in suitable "*lingua*" such that all can follow, using the word *omnes* where the Council of Mainz used "*vulgus*":

> ut episcopi sermones et omelias sanctorum patrum, prout omnes intellegere possent, secundum proprietatem linguae praedicare studeant.

This is ambiguous, although it can be interpreted as advice not to use the reformed pronunciation for this purpose, since that is an inappropriate and not sufficiently intelligible kind of "*lingua*".

Tours, however, where Alcuin's authority lived on even though he had died, produced more specific instructions. The second canon of the Council of Tours runs as follows:

> ut omnes episcopi studiose operam divinae dent lectioni, sanctum evangelium et epistolas beati Pauli apostoli non solum crebro lectitent, sed etiam quantum possint memoriae studeant commendare sanctorumque patrum opuscula super eadem exposita devote frequentent. similiter et de caeteris libris canonicis faciant.

Should the bishops succeed in learning these works, their Latinate pronunciation might well have become fluent. Then the fourth canon reinforces the duty to preach:

> sollicite studeat unusquisque gregem sibi commissum sacra praedicatione, quid agere quidve vitare debeat, informare. et ipse episcopus vita, habitu, forma et conversatione sancta suis

---

[51] The Canons of these Councils can be found in: *Monumenta Germaniae Historica Concilia*, II.

[52] M.C. DÍAZ Y DÍAZ, "Sobre formas calificadas de vulgares o rústicas en glosarios; contribución al estudio de *Vulgo*", *Archivum Latinitatis Medii Aevi (= ALMA)* 22 (1951-1952), pp. 193-216.

subiectis exemplum praebeat, ut iuxta dominicam vocem videant opera eius bona et glorifi-
cant patrem Deum, qui in caelis est.

Canons 5-16 and 18-51 are on other pressing topics, but canon 17 returns to the
question of preaching. After a strikingly emphatic introductory section not
found in any other canon, it specifies not only the content of the essential homilies and their purpose but also the manner in which they are to be delivered:

visum est unanimitati nostrae, ut quilibet episcopus habeat omelias continentes necessarias
ammonitiones, quibus subiecti erudiantur, id est de fide catholica, prout capere possint, de
perpetua retributione bonorum et aeterna damnatione malorum, de resurrectione quoque
futura et ultimo iudicio et quibus operibus possit promereri beata quibusve excludi, et ut
easdem omelias quisque aperte transferre studeat in rusticam Romanam linguam aut thiotiscam, quo facilius cuncti possint intellegere quae dicuntur.

The bishopric of Tours contained few native speakers of German; so the instruction to *"transferre"* the homilies into "Rustic Roman Language or German" will probably, in the immediate context, have been framed with an eye to
the former. We should be grateful, however, to the framers of this canon for
including the word *"thiotiscam"*; this makes it clear that the practice was intended to be standard throughout the Empire, and that something more than
mere simplicity of reading style is at stake.

In the context of the contemporary educational reforms, based on the desire
to train the priesthood in a standard but largely unintelligible new system of
reading aloud, the final sentence of this canon is best interpreted as an instruction not to use that new system in the specific context of the Homilies. The
homilies have to be read verbatim as they were written by the *"Patres"*, without
alteration or innovation, so the word *"transferre"* as applied to the Romance-
speaking areas cannot have been intended as an instruction to change the wording. It can only have been intended to refer to the pronunciation. Thus the word
"transferre" here would be best rendered into English as the vague "transfer"
rather than the more precise "translate": that is, a transference from the official
standard system used throughout the service up to that point into the ordinary
vernacular pronunciation that would have been used anyway in reading other
texts in other contexts, but which had not been used for the previous half hour.
"Rustica" is thus probably used with a lingering geographical sense, to refer to
the local speech habits of the area in question, and *"lingua"* to a variety of
speech deemed appropriate, as it was in Rheims canon 15 (above).

The last part of this canon has, unfortunately, been leapt on by Romance
philologists, who rightly sensed its importance, but took it out of social and
historical context and interpreted it quite inappropriately. It has been reprinted

over and again in philological handbooks by scholars, most of whom seem to feel no embarrassment at their lack of knowledge of the historical circumstances of the decree, as if it were some kind of proof that Latin and Romance had co-existed as separate spoken norms from the end of the Roman Empire onwards; as if it proved that by 813 the natural speech of the priesthood had hardly changed for a millennium and was thus by now so far removed from the speech of the general masses that the priests are consciously having to translate from one whole distinct separate language system into another when they "*transferunt*" the homilies. R.A. Hall Jr., for example, says that "with this edict, official recognition was given to an existing situation in which popular speech had gradually come to be so different from the official language as to be one or more separate varieties".[53] But what "existing situation" can Hall be referring to? No edict of the preceding centuries even mentions this hypothesized "situation", and the reason for that can only be that this problem is something recent and new, having been caused rather than solved by the promulgation of supposedly 'correct' ways of reading the Homilies. Rickard declared that "the existence of a vernacular which was truly different was officially recognized for the first time", as if the (highly improbable) previous survival of Latin pronunciation was the known fact and the existence of the vernacular was in some way debatable.[54] But it should be obvious that vernacular always exists in any community. In this case the artificial 'Latin' pronunciation is the one whose previous existence is what we need to debate. Rickard also shares with many philologists the habit of talking about "the emergent Romance" of the time, a phrase which strikes linguists working in any other field than Romance philology as absurd. Spoken vernacular is a fully functioning entity in any community at any time. The fact that a distinct system of writing this one down in a quasi-phonetic way was not devised until later in the ninth century does not imply that the vernacular was not a completely valid language in previous years. On the contrary, what had just happened "for the first time" was the conscious introduction of an artificial method of reading aloud that was different from anybody's vernacular.

It seems unlikely to me, however, that the idea that Latin and Romance were separate languages was generally held as early as 813. Translation, as the word is usually understood, involves two separate languages. And how we visualize the intention of Canon 17 depends to a large extent on how we interpret the word "*transferre*". Many centuries before, this verb had indeed been occasionally used with the meaning of to "translate from one language to an-

---

[53] R.A. HALL Jr, *External History of the Romance Languages* (New York, 1974), p. 105.
[54] P. RICKARD, *A History of the French Language* (London, 1974), p. 27.

other" (as well as many others), being used by Cicero, Pliny, Quintilian, et cetera. As late as the seventh century, Isidore had used *"transferre"* for translation from Hebrew into Latin, for instance: *"Alleluia autem, sicut et Amen, de Hebraea in Latinam linguam nequaquam transfertur"*;[55] and from Greek into Latin, for instance: *"nam Latinorum interpretum, qui de Graeco in nostrum eloquium transtulerint .. infinitus numerus"*.[56] But these may be among the latest occasions on which *"transferre"* was used with such a sense. Isidore also used *"convertere"* and *"vertere"* for "translate".[57] Romance words for "translate" do not come from *"transferre"*; they all come from *"traducere"*, although *"traducere"* did not have that meaning originally, nor in Medieval Latin: Spanish *"traducir"*, Italian *"tradurre"*, French *"traduire"*, Portuguese *"traduzir"*, Catalan *"traduir"*, Rumanian *"traduce"*. What had happened was that there had occurred a semantic contraction in *"transferre"* to its more central meanings. In Blaise's *Lexicon* the article on *"transferre"* lists three meanings: to transfer a feast, to translate a bishop, and to use a word in a figurative sense, as in *"translato verbo"* (Saint Augustine), originally calqued off Greek μεταφέρω.[58] Most scholars had learnt their grammatical terminology from Donatus, and Donatus used *"transferre"* in the sense of "metaphorical usage", not "translate". This is also the sense that occurs in the *De Clericorum Institutione* of Hrabanus Maurus,[59] entitled *"De translatis ignotis"*, which concerns metaphors that were hard to interpret. *"Translata"* had been previously defined in chapter 8:

> signa ... translata sunt, cum et ipsae res quas propriis verbis significamus, ad aliquid aliud significandum usurpantur, sicut dicimus bovem, et per has duas syllabas intelligimus pecus, quod isto nomine appellari solet; sed rursus per illud pecus intelligimus evangelistam quem significavit Scriptura, interpretante Apostolo et dicente *Bovem triturantem non infrenabis*.[60]

This is significant for our present purpose, because the same chapter goes on to discuss the three Biblical languages with no hint that Hrabanus Maurus might regard the introduction of this topic into a chapter of *"signa propria vel*

---

[55] Isidore, *De Ecclesiasticis Officiis*, ed. J.P. MIGNE, *Patrilogia Latina* 83, col. 750C, I, 13, 2.

[56] Isidore, *De Ecclesiasticis Officiis*, col. 748B, I, 12, 7.

[57] Isidore, *De Ecclesiasticis Officiis*, I, 12, 8 and 6 respectively.

[58] A. BLAISE, *Lexicon Latinitatis Medii Aevi praesertim ad res ecclesiasticas investigandas pertinens* (Turnhout, 1975).

[59] Hrabanus Maurus, *De Clericorum Institutione*, ed. J.P. MIGNE, *Patrologia Latina* 107, col. 386, III, c. 10.

[60] Hrabanus Maurus, *De Clericorum Institutione*, col. 384D, III, c. 8. "Muzzle not the ox that treadeth out the corn", *Deuteronomy*, 25, 4, here quoted from *I Corinthians* 9, 8.

translata" as at all ambiguous. If "*translata*" could have been understood in the
ninth century still to mean "translated", this section would have been at best
confusing. Similarly, Chapter 13 concerns the "*modus inveniendi utrum locutio
propria sit an translata*". There is, in short, no contemporary practice among
the leaders of the Church in using "*transferre*" to mean "translate". Lest it be
thought that Alcuin might have imported a British use to Tours, it is also worth
pointing out that the British *Revised Mediaeval Word List* offers the meanings
of translating bishops, or Saints' relics, alienating possessions, crossing the sea,
and changing University course, but not translating from one language to another. No other dictionary of Medieval Latin alters this picture. Not even the
noun "*translatio*" seems to refer to translation at this time. Since it is impossible to conceive of the framers of the canon as using words with meanings that
would not be appreciated at that time, the conclusion is inescapable that the
word used in the seventeenth canon of the Council of Tours meant "shift" or
"change" rather than explicitly "translate". The fact that transferring to German
would indeed involve translation is not significant; we should not confuse
sense with reference. Translating a bishop would usually have involved his
riding a horse, but horses form no part of the meaning of "*transferre*" either.

The decision of philologists to interpret "*transferre in rusticam romanam
linguam*" as "translate into Old French" rather than "transfer from official Latin
reading pronunciation into that of the ordinary vernacular" is thus merely a
consequence of their pre-existing belief that Latin and Romance were separate
languages at that time, rather than being an argument in support of that theory.
On the contrary, the evidence available is more compatible with the idea that a
clear distinction between Latin and Romance (let alone that between Latin and
French) as being wholly separate languages, rather than variable forms of the
same language, still lay in the future in 813.

This edict is incorporated whole into the second canon of the Council of
Mainz in 847:

> de dogmate ecclesiastico. cum igitur omnia concilia canonum, qui recipiuntur, sint a
> sacerdotibus legenda et intellegenda et per ea sit eis vivendum et predicandum, necessarium
> duximus ut ea, quae ad fidem pertinent et ubi de extirpandis vitiis et plantandis virtutibus
> scribitur, hoc ab eis crebro legatur et bene intellegatur et in populo praedicetur. et quilibet
> episcopus habeat homelias continentes necessarias ammonitiones, quibus subiecti erudian-
> tur, id est de fide catholica, prout capere possint, de perpetua retributione bonorum et aeter-
> na damnatione malorum, de resurrectione quoque futura et ultimo iudicio et quibus operibus
> possit promereri beata quibusve excludi. et ut easdem omelias quisque aperte transferre
> studeat in rusticam Romanam linguam aut in Thiotiscam, quo facilius cuncti possint
> intellegere quae dicuntur.[61]

---

[61] *Monumenta Germaniae Historica. Concilia*, II, p. 176. Michel Banniard has since written

Here again the stress is only on reading aloud written texts. Hrabanus Maurus had recently become Bishop of Mainz. He is unlikely to have authorized edicts whose words meant something different from the meaning he usually gave to them in his own work. The words of the homilies were still fixed; Hrabanus Maurus compiled collections of homilies to be used in Church,[62] and had a practical concern for their effective delivery. These texts were not to be altered by the preacher. There would not have been much point in his making these new authoritative collections if the edict of 847 meant that even in Romance areas priests were expected to change the words into those of a different language when delivering them.

By 847 the Roman rite was effectively the only one used, and the Caroline minuscule had effectively ousted other scripts. The reading-pronunciation reform which Alcuin and his colleagues had worked so hard to establish in the late 790s had by then become standard practice in at least some of the more serious and progressive cultural centres, including Fulda where Hrabanus Maurus had recently been the abbot. Maybe the new pronunciation was already coming to be used in other contexts as well by then. In addition, the established co-existence of two methods of reading aloud was just beginning to give rise to the idea that perhaps those two methods could be individually specified through different orthographies on the written page; that is, that those texts whose words were intended to be read aloud in an ordinary vernacular fashion rather than as the newly reformed Latin, but whose exact wording was important to fix in advance, might be written with a spelling in which the letter-sound correspondences corresponded to ordinary vernacular pronunciations of the words rather than to that of the Church norm. Such cases might, for example, include Oaths whose specific wording had necessarily to be predetermined for legal reasons, but which when sworn had also to be intelligible to unlettered hearers. Suddenly, and for the first time, spelling reform could begin to seem desirable. Hence the invention of what we call 'written Romance', even though all along vernacular Romance had been capable of being written in the quaintly inappropriate orthography established centuries before.

The date of the Strasbourg Oaths is 842.

---

a valuable study of "Rhabanus Maurus and the vernacular languages", in: *Latin and the Romance Languages in the Early Middle Ages*, ed. R. WRIGHT (London, 1991; reprint, Penn State, 1996), pp. 164-174.

[62] Hrabanus Maurus, *Homiliae*, ed. J.P. MIGNE, *Patrologia Latina* 110, cols. 9-468B.

Chapter 10

The Relative Chronology of
New "*scripta*" and New Languages

Michel Banniard has written on many occasions about the "*prise de conscience*" of the new Romance Languages; that is, the way in which Romance-speakers came to think that their own Romance speech and the traditional written forms which they had inherited from the remote past were in practice two different languages. Banniard has also given the impression that the consciousness of such a distinction between two languages must have been in existence before anybody elaborated a new way of writing the contemporary vernacular; that is, a new "*scripta*", as many Romanists say (which uses traditional letters in new combinations, rather than being a new alphabet). This was the natural sequence of events in the history of the Germanic languages, because it was obvious to all that Germanic was a different language from that of the venerable written Latin tradition. But in the case of Early Romance, this was by no means so evident. To quote Banniard: "The three connected problems of the birth of a new language, the realization of the existence of this previously unknown entity, and the consecration of this change via the elaboration of a '*scripta*' that breaks with traditional modes of writing, can be posed in much simpler terms when we consider the Germanic

This chapter is a translated and slightly adapted version of: "La Chronologie relative des nouvelles *scripta* et des nouvelles langues", in: *Langages et peuples d'Europe: cristallisation des identités romanes et germaniques*. ed. M. BANNIARD (Conques, 2002). I have translated it from French myself. We are grateful to Professor Michel Banniard (Toulouse) for permitting this reprint.

languages than when we consider the Romance languages".[1] The same relative chronology is presented in his work on the birth, *"prise de conscience"* and *"scripta"* of Occitan.[2] It is also taken for granted in the heroic five-volume *Inventaire systématique des premiers documents des langues romanes* recently prepared at the University of Freiburg.[3] That is, the authors of these studies seem not even to have considered the possibility that diglossic or bilingual distinctions between Latin and Romance, and geographical distinctions between separate Romance languages, were never made before the ninth century.

Yet it is reasonable to suggest that the relative chronology of these events in the Romance-speaking world was the other way round from the sequence of events in the Germanic-speaking areas. That is, that in the Romance areas they invented a new way of writing their language first, and then only some time afterwards did they begin to think that these two ways of writing, the traditional and the new, were in effect the written representations of two systematically separate languages. This is the view taken by the Swedish Latinist Tore Janson in his consideration of the relationship between linguistic changes and changes in language names. Referring to the Romance context, Janson writes: "It can even be argued that the new written forms appear before the new names. For it seems to be generally true that reasonably standardized ways of writing become established at a time when the name of the language is still not definitely fixed. Thus, for example, in France the term that eventually dominated, *'français'*, for a long time had competition from *'roman'*. In Italy, Dante never used the word *'italiano'* but actually preferred the term *'latino'* for what we call Italian".[4] Janson did not mention the Spanish case, but we see more or less the same happening in the Iberian Peninsula. There is no evidence that the elaborators of the Riojan Glosses, the first scribes to prepare deliberately updated written forms, thought that they were writing a separate language from that represented in the traditional writing system. Instead they almost certainly conceived of their new *"scripta"* as being a different way of

---

[1] M. BANNIARD, "Rhabanus Maurus and the vernacular languages", in: *Latin and the Romance Languages in the Early Middle Ages*, ed. R. WRIGHT (London, 1991: reprint, Penn State, 1996), pp. 164-174. IDEM, "Latin tardif et français prélittéraire: observations de méthode et de chronologie", *Bulletin de la Société de Linguistique de Paris* 88 (1993), pp. 139-162.

[2] M. BANNIARD, "Naissance et conscience de la langue d'oc, VIIIe-IXe siècles", in: *La Catalogne et La France Méridionale autour de l'an mil* (Barcelona, 1991), pp. 351-361.

[3] B. FRANK and J. HARTMANN, *Inventaire systématique des premiers documents des langues romanes* (Tübingen, 1997).

[4] T. JANSON, "Language change and metalinguistic change: Latin to Romance and other cases", in: WRIGHT (ed.), *Latin and the Romance Languages*, pp. 19-28, p. 23.

representing the same language.[5] Only from the early thirteenth century do we see a conscious distinction being explicitly made between Latin and Romance. Gonzalo de Berceo, for example, who wrote at the Monastery of San Millán de la Cogolla between 1230 and 1252, described the language of his own written texts as "*romanz*", and the first Biblical translations into Ibero-Romance, made at the same period, were rendered into "*ladino*", a word whose written form represents the normal pronunciation of the word LATINUM. Only towards the end of the century, at the Court of Alfonso X of Castile, scholars began to refer to their own written Romance forms more specifically as "our Castilian Romance" ("*nuestro romance castellano*").[6]

The Latin-Romance distinction has its origins in the ninth-century Carolingian 'Renaissance'.[7] The word they used themselves was "*renovatio*",[8] because they felt a need to renew intellectual life by getting back to the past. An important aspect of this cultural renovation involved a need for corrected Latin texts, to be read aloud with a standardized pronunciation system. This was based on the one used for such purposes by speakers of Germanic languages, which had been based on the requirement to give every written letter of every word a specified sound when reading aloud. Such a reading technique is very unlikely to have been used previously in any systematic way in the Romance-speaking world, and once this had been prescribed for formal use in the church, the new reading pronunciation of most words would have sounded different, often very different, from the normal pronunciation of the same lexical words in Romance. This is the moment when for the first time two clearly separate phonetic modes were coming to be heard in the same place. And it is likely that the eventual elaboration of a new "*scripta*" for writing Romance is a delayed consequence of these reforms of formal pronunciation.

The envisaged chain of cause and effect runs as follows. Germanic-speakers who did not know normal Romance followed the prescriptions of this 'renewed' Latin when they read a Latin text aloud. But this meant that an

[5] In the words of Blake, the writers were "bigraphic" rather than bilingual: R. BLAKE, "El latín notarial de un escriba bilingüe o 'bígrafo' del XIII", in: *Actas del I Congreso Nacional de Latín Medieval*, ed. M. PÉREZ GONZÁLEZ (León, 1995), pp. 463-468.

[6] The same scholars could also refer to their written Romance as "our Latin" ("*nuestro latín*"). H.-J. NIEDEREHE, *Alfonso X, el Sabio, y la lingüística de su tiempo* (Madrid, 1987), p. 102.

[7] See for instance the articles in: R. MCKITTERICK (ed.), *Carolingian Culture: Emulation and Innovation* (Cambridge, 1994).

[8] J.J. CONTRENI, "The Carolingian Renaissance: education and literary culture", in: *The New Cambridge Medieval History*. II. *c.700 -c.900*, ed. R. MCKITTERICK (Cambridge, 1995), pp. 709-757.

untrained Romance-speaking audience could not understand them at all well. The initial elaboration of a Romance "*scripta*" derived from attempts to solve this problem. When Germanic-speakers needed, for any reason, to read a text aloud in normal intelligible Romance phonetics, rather than in the newly standardized Latin mode, scribes prepared a version for them in which the letters represented vernacular Romance sounds. The letters of this new "*scripta*" were thus chosen according to the recently established correspondences between letter and sound in the newly standardized Latin.

Evidence in support of this hypothesis can be found in the fact that the earliest Romance texts were indeed designed to be read or sung aloud by Germanic-speakers to Romance-speaking listeners in the ninth century. Those who devised the written form of the Romance *Strasbourg Oaths*, the *Cantilène de Sainte Eulalie*, and probably other written texts that have not survived, were in effect performing the same kind of exercise as is carried out in modern times by those who prepare the phonetic forms used in tourist phrasebooks. In both cases the writers have elaborated new written forms, of a language which the modern tourist and the ninth-century German do not know well, on the basis of the sound-letter correspondences used in a different system which the tourist and the Germanic-speaker do know well and are accustomed to reading aloud. In neither case could the new written forms help the already literate native-speaker to read the language so presented.

These developments in the written mode corresponded to no particular linguistic change in speech. The phonetic and morphosyntactic phenomena deliberately attested directly in writing for the first time in the new "*scripta*" were not themselves new. They had been present, if only as variants, for centuries. Sociolinguistic research has shown that internal variation is normal within a language. This perspective has been slow to be generally adopted within historical linguistics, but eventually this will lead to the end of the idea of the co-existence of both an earlier '(Proto-)Romance' language and a completely distinct 'Late Latin' in the pre-Carolingian period.[9] The linguistic features that the Proto-Romance specialists have reconstructed for these centuries existed, but that in itself does not prove that there were two invariant languages co-existing in the communities concerned rather than an unexceptional state of internal monolingual variation. There is no need to hypothesize a whole separate language for each linguistic variant to belong to

---

[9] Such as is still envisaged by: R. DE DARDEL, *A la recherche du protoroman* (Tübingen, 1996).

when we know that variation is the normal unmarked case within a single language anyway.

Monolingualism can be remarkably elastic. I agree with Michel Banniard in seeing the state of the pre-Carolingian Romance-speaking areas as being one of complex monolingualism. Indeed, it seems probable that the initial developments of the Carolingian *"renovatio"* had in part the effect of increasing this sociolinguistic elasticity. The textual evidence supplied by Marc van Uytfanghe, for example, leads to the conclusion that even in the ninth century many writers still made no general intellectual distinction between Latin and Romance as separate languages.[10] And although there can be glimpsed through this period a gradually increasing use of new and experimental *"scripta"*, created for practical purposes, the traditional forms of writing continued in use for a long time yet. Many literate people may have worked with the traditional forms without ever encountering anything written in Old Romance until the twelfth century.

Several different kinds of linguistic variation were accelerated after the events of the ninth century. It seems likely that the definitive conceptual separation of Latin and Romance came to a head in France in the eleventh century, as the use of both *"scripta"*, the traditional Latin and the new Romance one, was being systematically extended. This process was further aided by increasingly professional means of scribal training in France and Provence. This is the time and the context of the promotion of Romance to the status of a language independent of Latin, at least for some purposes. The separate concepts of the different Romance languages developed slightly later, being baptized with names of their geographical origin when the different medieval kingdoms chose to identify separately their own national identity within the larger pan-Romance culture which they inherited. And this process included the elaboration of new national *"scripta"*, in essence one per kingdom. In this way geographical variation came to be privileged.

Romance-speaking kingdoms outside France and Provence gradually came to copy the innovative French idea of elaborating a new writing system to represent their speech, but naturally they did not wish to use exactly the same orthographical forms as the French. They preferred, understandably, to elaborate a separate system within each kingdom (sometimes after a period of variation or confusion), and from the existence of these separate writing

---

[10] M. VAN UYTFANGHE, "The consciousness of a linguistic dichotomy (Latin-Romance) in Carolingian Gaul: the contradictions of the sources and their interpretation", in: WRIGHT (ed.), *Latin and the Romance Languages*, pp. 114-129.

systems there developed the idea that these different *"scripta"* represented different languages, rather than just different diatopic varieties of Romance. To appreciate the process that seems to have taken place between the ninth and thirteenth centuries, we can consider a modern analogy. What would happen in the contemporary Francophone world (*"la francophonie"*) if one small part of that world undertook its own spelling reform? For that could easily seem desirable, given the anisomorphic match in all areas between standard French spelling and any phonetic transcription. But it seems likely that if, for example, a *"scripta"* were for any reason to be elaborated which could approximate to a phonetic transcription of the natural vernacular of speakers in Toulouse, this would not be followed in detail by the inhabitants of, for example, Quebec. But the Quebecois might, even so, think that the basic idea of a spelling reform which approximated a phonetic transcription was a good one, and in that case they would elaborate for their own vernacular habits a different *"scripta"* from that developed in Toulouse. The relationship between symbol and sound could be identical in the two *"scripta"*, but, for that very reason, the geographical variation would mean that many of the spellings newly prescribed for the same individual words in Toulouse and Quebec would differ.

This would be parallel to what happened in the world of Early Romance speech (*"la romanophonie"*, so to speak). As is contemporary French, Early Romance was still monolingual but highly elastic. The first Romance *"scripta"*, initially provoked by problems consequent on the Carolingian reforms (for which as yet there is fortunately no parallel in the modern world) had as its conceptual basis the assumption, probably made explicitly (in the light of what Alcuin's *De Orthographia* had prescribed), that writing ought ideally to be phonographic; that is, that there ought to be a strict correpondence between a single letter and a single sound, as there now was in the reformed Medieval Latin. Regional variation meant that the pronunciations of many words were already different in different places, so this assumption led almost inevitably to the elaboration of different *"scripta"* in different places as well.

What scholars are doing in suggesting analogues between sociolinguistic states of the past and of the present, in the hope that the comparisons can illuminate the past, is what Michel Banniard (and after him also Marc van Uytfanghe) has called *"sociolinguistique rétrospective"*.[11] Specialists who consider these matters need not only to work as linguists and philologists but as social historians too. Following this line of thought leads to the further

---

[11] M. VAN UYTFANGHE, "Mère latin et ses filles", in: *Acta Selecta Octavi Conventus Academiae Latinitati Fovendae*, ed. I. IJSEWIJN and T. SACRÉ (Rome, 1995), pp. 651-681.

conclusion that the conceptual separations caused by the elaboration of different Romance *"scripta"* were on the whole undesirable. The fact that there were different Romance *"scripta"* in operation not only led to the idea that there were different Romance languages in existence, but to the highly dubious belief (or even assumption) that there existed different national identities and cultures, co-terminous with the political units where these newly conceived linguistic entities were so consecrated in written form; and, as Penny has argued, to increasingly evident linguistic frontiers as the standardized form for speakers to styleshift towards came to be different on the two sides of the political boundaries concerned.[12] That is, unnecessary divisions were accentuated in this way. Geographical divisions were created in a cultural space which had otherwise been Pan-Romance, a single culture, versatile, variable, flexible, elastic, certainly, but still a single cultural entity, as the world-wide Francophone culture is today. Toulouse and Quebec (et cetera) are different in many respects, of course, but the differences still fit into the whole. The Francophone world, and the Anglophone and Spanish-speaking worlds too, would run the risk of breaking up into a patchwork quilt of separate and instinctively competing languages and cultures if any of us were to make the mistake of encouraging spelling reforms which only applied to one small part of our whole, as happened to the Romance-speaking cultural world between the tenth and the thirteenth centuries. This may even be happening now in Modern Spain. In the Middle Ages the conceptual invention of Galician and Portuguese as being separate from each other was abetted by the elaboration of different *"scripta"*, since the two belonged to different political units after, but not before, the late eleventh century.[13] And similarly in the present context of the Spanish autonomous regions there are plenty who wish to consecrate their own cultural autonomy with the elaboration of an autonomy-specific *"scripta"* for which there is no other justification than the instinctive assumption that the phonographic method is the ideal.

The feeling that every separately elaborated *"scripta"* represents a separate language seems to be a natural feeling; and it seems to have been a natural feeling in the thirteenth century also, once the orthographical fragmentation had happened. As Tore Janson pointed out, Dante appears to have assumed that there existed as many Romance languages as Romance *"scripta"*. Dante was

---

[12] R. PENNY, *Variation and Change in Spanish* (Cambridge, 2000).

[13] H. MONTEAGUDO, "Aspectos sociolingüísticos do uso escrito do galego, o castelán e o latín na Galicia tardomedieval (SS.XIII-XV)", in: *Estudios Galegos en homenaxe ó Profesor Giuseppe Tavani*, ed. E. FIDALGO and P. LORENZO GRADÍN (Santiago de Compostela, 1994), pp. 169-185.

writing at the end of the great changes in written texts that happened throughout the thirteenth century, which in Banniard's terms led to the general *"prise de conscience"* of several Romance languages and Medieval Latin (*"grammatica"*) as being separate languages. These co-existing languages had thus emerged over the centuries out of the original elastic monolingual ensemble, even though it would have indeed been possible for this monolingual state to have continued if the separate political units had not chosen to institutionalize, and endow with sociolinguistic prestige, different new ways of writing. Another way to look at these developments is to say, as Rebecca Posner does, that the early texts helped to create the new Romance languages.[14] The definitive period of these divergences is thus identifiable as the Twelfth-Century Renaissance, even though they are the long-term consequence of its Carolingian predecessor, and it is thus no coincidence that the first direct textual translations from Latin to Romance are found at that time. The reason why the earliest translations from Latin to Romance are found in the twelfth century and not before, is merely that until that time they were not thought to be the two separate languages needed for 'translation', in its usual definition, to operate. More specifically, texts written in the old *"scripta"* were still generally accessible to native-speakers of Romance when read aloud in the normal unreformed manner. It is only when the reading aloud of texts written in the traditional mode became largely incomprehensible, as a direct result of the Carolingian reforms, that there was any need for such textual translations from the one to the other.

József Herman also lays considerable stress on the question of the comprehensibilty of texts that were read aloud (as all were, with the possible exception of reference books). The view presented above is that the elastic monolingual Romance continuum of styles suffered a shock around 800 A.D., with the elaboration of the reforms of pronunciation, and disappeared for most practical purposes by 1200. In his article entitled "The end of the history of Latin" Herman argued that in Gaul this stage of great elasticity had already come to an end during the eighth century, after weakening for a long time already.[15] Herman sees a directly linguistic reason for this. The loss of unstressed vowels in the final syllable of words in the Northern Gallo-Romance area, which did not happen to anything like the same extent

---

[14] R. POSNER, "Latin or Romance (again!): change or genesis?", in: *Papers from the 10th International Conference on Historical Linguistics*, ed. J. VAN MARLE (Amsterdam, 1993), pp. 265-279.

[15] J. HERMAN, "The end of the history of Latin", *Romance Philology* 49 (1996), pp. 364-382.

elsewhere, can plausibly be dated to the seventh and eighth centuries, and this, in Herman's view, would have made the difference between a text as read aloud and the comprehension of the listening public an unbridgeable gap.[16] There is certainly much truth in this observation with respect to the reading aloud of texts written in the distant past, whose understanding could depend crucially on the recognition of both the form and the function of word-final inflections; such texts could indeed have become harder to follow by the late eighth century. But unlike Herman, I feel that these difficulties were directly related to the age of the works concerned. Those texts represented an older stage of the same language, of the language still in use in the eighth century, rather than being in a different language altogether. We can again illustrate this with an analogy from modern Francophonie. If Modern French audiences have problems in understanding the language of a play by Molière, or English audiences a play by Shakespeare, this is because the texts concerned were written in an earlier stage of French or English, rather than being in a different language altogether. That is, in this case I feel more in sympathy with Michel Banniard than with József Herman, since the writers of the latter half of the eighth century were still able to write new texts in the traditional spelling system – Saints' Lives in particular – without provoking general problems of lack of comprehension when these were read aloud to their audiences. There are difficulties in understanding Molière now, due to the centuries in between, but there is no such problem in understanding Simenon, even though they both, on the whole, wrote French according to the same rules. Both were using the same language, but at different times. From Molière to Simenon there is roughly the same time difference as there was between the Vulgate and the eighth-century hagiographers. The analogy suggests that texts elaborated in the fourth century might have led to some problems of comprehension when they were read aloud in the year 767, but that does not in itself mean that a *Vita* written the year before would offer the same problems. And here too there is no reason not to regard the works concerned as being written in the same language as each other. It took the new "*scripta*", in my view, to catalyse the final conceptual break.

We can come to a similar conclusion concerning the relative chronology of the new "*scripta*" and the new languages in the Iberian Peninsula. It is often said that the first evidence of written Romance in the Peninsula are the glosses

---

[16] A similar suggestion had been made earlier by: M. RICHTER, "A quelle époque a-t-on cessé de parler latin en Gaule? A propos d'une question mal posée", *Annales* 38 (1983), pp. 439-448; reprinted in his: *Studies in Medieval Language and Culture* (Dublin, 1995), chapter 7.

that were written in the eleventh century on two manuscripts, one at San Millán
de la Cogolla and the other at Santo Domingo de Silos. The texts glossed in
this way had first been composed several centuries earlier. Some, though not
all, of the glosses that accompany them, mostly categorizable as 'explanatory',
were written deliberately with a spelling, and on several occasions a
morphology, that is more recent, more evolved than the time of composition of
the text, and which has often been identified as being some kind of Romance.
It is clear that the non-traditional forms of many of these words are quite
deliberate. It is not just a concatenation of crass and catastrophic errors made
by someone aiming for the old ones. António Emiliano describes these forms
as representing an informal register of eleventh-century Ibero-Romance: "*dos
registros del contínuum sociolingüístico y estilístico de la comunidad*",[17] rather
than this being a sign of direct conceptual opposition of the language of the
text and the language of the gloss. This perspective is attractive, and it means
that the elastic and monolingual Ibero-Romance language of the eleventh
century still contained within it the traditional "*scripta*" of the old Roman
Empire, precisely because no other "*scripta*" had yet been elaborated in that
area to replace it. It seems best to refer to it as 'Ibero-Romance' rather than
merely Romance, though, because it is quite likely that there was by then a
general appreciation of the main general differences that existed *grosso modo*
between the Romance spoken on the different sides of the Pyrenees. Aided by
the fact that the Northerners were already using their new "*scripta*" at this
time, if only for relatively unimportant purposes. The upshot is that the
contrasting registers evidenced by these Riojan glosses are reminiscent of the
sociolinguistic versatility which Michel Banniard justifiably envisages as being
within the competence of the hagiographers of eighth-century Gaul, who were
able to write their texts at variable syntactic levels according to the intellectual
level of the intended listening public. There is a closer study of these Glosses
in Chapter 16 below, where the conclusion is that the Romance-speakers of La
Rioja in the eleventh century had not yet come to any general "*prise de
conscience*" of the existence there of two languages, Latin and Romance. That
was going to come later, after the generalization of new "*scripta*" endowed
with some kind of prestige, and not before. Those glosses do not attest the
'birth of Spanish', but they may indeed attest the birth of a new idea, the idea
that their vernacular need not be spelt in the old way and could perhaps be

---

[17] A. EMILIANO, "*Latín y romance* y las glosas de San Millán y de Silos: apuntes para un
plantamiento grafémico", in: R. PENNY (ed.), *Actas del primer congreso Anglo-Hispano*. I.
Lingüística (Madrid, 1993), pp. 235-244, p. 237.

spelt in a new. This idea was very possibly inspired by the realization that in Provence and France some people were doing precisely that, even though the precise Northern spellings of words were not themselves going to be of much help in the Rioja. As we investigate later the intellectual history of the Iberian Peninsula in the following two centuries (through 'retrospective sociolinguistics' allied to philological analysis of the relevant texts) we will see how this idea, which was perhaps even born at the time of these very glosses, came to triumph, but only a long time later. The concepts of new languages came later still.[18]

The conclusion from the present discussion is this: the independent conceptual existence of Latin and Romance arrived not only as a result of the *"prise de conscience"* of the existence of Romance, but also, necessarily, of the *"prise de conscience"* of reformed Medieval Latin (*"grammatica"*) as a separate entity. And we can deduce more than that. It is probable that the idea that *"grammatica"* was a different language from that in normal use had to arrive first, before the *"prise de conscience"* of the existence of Romance could occur. And that the whole process came to fruition only after, rather than before, the rise of two co-existing and recognizably distinct written manifestations of the same lexical items.

[18] See: R. WRIGHT, *Early Ibero-Romance* (Newark, 1995).

Chapter 11

The End of Written *Ladino* in Al-Andalus

M anuel Díaz y Díaz is a Latin specialist, but in practice many of his studies are important also within Romance Philology. Perhaps his most significant publications in this respect are his study of the Latin of the Hispanic liturgy and the lecture he gave in London in 1988 on the Latin of seventh-century Spain, concentrating on the Visigothic slates.[1] In these studies and others he has demonstrated both that the literate of that period used normal vernacular speech, and that the less educated had at the same time greater access to literate culture than they are usually given credit for. Indeed, after the studies of Manuel Díaz and other scholars, we can say that the Iberian Peninsula was in the year 700 (apart from the Basques) a monolingual Romance-speaking community, despite containing a wide range of geographical and stylistic variation. We can call this language 'Early Romance'; but

This chapter is an almost identical reprint of: "The end of written *ladino* in Al-Andalus", in: *The Formation of Al-Andalus*, ed. M. FIERRO and J. SANSÓ (London, Ashgate, Variorum, 1998), pp. 9-17; translated from "La muerte del ladino escrito en Al-Andalús", *Euphrosyne: Revista de Filologia Clássica*, Nova Série, 22 (Lisbon, 1994), pp. 255-268. We are grateful to Sra Maria da Graça Ribeiro Mendes, on behalf of *Euphrosyne* (Lisbon), and Mrs Jacqueline Cox on behalf of Ashgate publishers (Aldershot), for permitting this reprint.

[1] M.C. DÍAZ Y DÍAZ, "El latín de la liturgia hispánica", in: *Estudios sobre la liturgia mozárabe*, ed. J. RIVERA RECIO (Toledo, 1965), pp. 55-87; reprinted in his *Vie Chrétienne et culture dans l'Espagne du VIIe au Xe siècles* (Aldershot, 1992), chapter 2. IDEM, "El latín de España en el siglo VII: lengua y escritura según los textos documentales", in: *Le septième siècle: changements et continuités*, ed. J. FONTAINE and J.N. HILLGARTH (London, 1992), pp. 25-40. The Spanish version of this chapter appeared in a homage volume dedicated to Manuel Díaz y Díaz.

they continued to refer to it themselves with the word written "*latina*" and at that time pronounced [ladína]. To try and avoid confusing their monolingual language either with the Imperial Latin of the remote past or the Romance languages of the remote future, I refer to it here as *ladino*. Despite the variation which undoubtedly existed, it seems clear that they did not themselves draw a sharp dividing line either between educated and popular usages, or between geographically delimited dialects (at least, within the Peninsula). That is, there still existed a stylistic and sociolinguistic continuum, in addition to the geographical continuum, and it would merely confuse matters if our analysis were to erect conceptual frontiers that did not yet exist, between 'Castilian' and - 'Leonese', say, or 'Romance' and 'Latin'. The authoritative studies of Michel Banniard have shown that, within their stylistic continuum, most texts could still be understood when read aloud. Even Isidore of Seville expected that to be the case. This is how Visigothic society managed to function on a basis of written laws and documentation.[2]

The Moslem invasions of the early eighth century brought many novelties, but they did not immediately disrupt this cultural and linguistic continuity. To the north of the new religious frontier both the dialect continuum and the stylistic continuum carried on as they were (and, indeed, to some extent as they still are). In the south, Romance speech did not die out, as has been well known since the studies of Simonet. It seems that within two centuries the majority of the population of Al-Andalus, whatever their religion, were bilingual *ladino* and Arabic speakers.[3] Collins has even suggested that the cultural flowering of Al-Andalus had many of its origins in the high level of cultural life that it inherited from Visigothic Spain.[4] We know that several Christians continued writing their *ladino*, and were taught it with the same pedagogical methods as were used before the Conquest, to achieve the same traditional orthography and written morphology. It may be the case that these Christian writers of eighth and ninth-century Al-Andalus had less direct contact with the Christian north than they had with other Christians within the Moslem world, but even so, when we are able to make deductions about their training, we can see that it

[2] For instance: M. BANNIARD, *Genèse culturelle de l'Europe (V-VIIIe siècle)* (Paris, 1989). IDEM, *Viva Voce: communication écrite et communication orale du IVe au IXe siècle en Occident latin* (Paris, 1992).

[3] See: F.J. SIMONET, *Historia de los mozárabes de España* (Madrid, 1897-1903; reprint Amsterdam, 1967). D.J. WASSERSTEIN, "The language situation in Al-Andalus", in: *Studies on the Muwassah and the Kharja*, ed. A. JONES and R. HITCHCOCK (Oxford, 1991), pp. 1-15. R. WRIGHT, *Early Ibero-Romance* (Newark, 1995), chapter 12.

[4] R. COLLINS, *Early Medieval Spain: Unity in Diversity* (London, 1983).

was still based on the *Ars Minor* of Donatus, as had been the case since the fourth century.

The Christian texts from Al-Andalus have been well edited by Juan Gil.[5] Little survives from the eighth century, but there is a great deal from the ninth. Several texts are of insecure dating, but it is likely that there is no text of any significance in written *ladino* originating from Al-Andalus after 900.[6] Wasserstein concludes that "by the middle of the tenth century ... they had completely ceased to produce writing in Latin".[7] And the question immediately arises: why? In this study I aim to provide a linguistic reason for the Christians' decision to stop writing their language in the old way.

The surviving evidence is somewhat distorted in that almost all of it comes from the city of Córdoba, and the Christians of Córdoba were almost certainly unrepresentative of the Christians in Al-Andalus as a whole. In particular, the martyrs of the 850s are not typical. We should beware of extrapolating from the works of Eulogio, Álvaro and Sansón to draw general conclusions about the whole Christian community there. Despite this necessary *caveat*, however, these three writers are in fact important links in the chain of events that led to the decision to abandon writing their *ladino*. The kind of written Latinity that these Cordobese writers recommended for use was difficult and complicated, and must have seemed impractical and inconvenient to other less determined Christians, with the result that they took the probably conscious decision to keep their *ladino* for oral use alone and write only in Arabic. Since most of them were bilingual in speech, and for social reasons needed to be able to read and even sometimes write Arabic, this seems a sensible and even obvious step for them to have taken. The point is not that they all became Moslems at that point. Even though it seems established that such conversions did indeed increase in the tenth century,[8] there were still Christian communities there at the time of the capture of Toledo in 1085, and the evidence that we have shows that these were literate, if at all, in Arabic.[9] Wasserstein seems less sure of this

---

[5] The texts quoted are taken from: J. GIL (ed.), *Corpus Scriptorum Muzarabicorum*, 2 volumes (Madrid, 1973).

[6] H. FLÓREZ, *España Sagrada*, 23 (Madrid, 1767), pp. 105-131, printed the tale of "*San Pelagio, Mártir*", a Galician prisoner martyred in Córdoba in 962, written by one "Raguel"; the account was probably not written there, and Gil omits it from his *Corpus*.

[7] WASSERSTEIN, "The language situation", p. 13.

[8] R.W. BULLIET, *Conversion to Islam in the Medieval Period* (Harvard, 1989), chapter 10.

[9] In particular: P.S. VAN KONINGSVELD, *The Latin-Arabic Glossary of the Leiden University Library* (Leiden, 1977).

than most Romance linguists are, but there is little doubt that many of them still also spoke Romance.

During these centuries, the Romance speech of the Southern half of the Peninsula is unlikely to have been very different from that of the Northern half. When carpenters and other craftsmen were recruited from Al-Andalus to aid in the Christian repopulation of the largely uninhabited area north of the Duero, they may have come with a recognizably Southern accent, but there is no sign at all in the documentation that the inhabitants of Asturias and León had any problem in understanding them, or that the immigrants had any problem in understanding the Asturians and Leonese. Since several of them were literate, it seems to be the case, as Menéndez Pidal pointed out, that many of the immigrants took on the duties of notary, or at least of the local who could read and write, in their church or village.[10] Asturian-Leonese society, particularly perhaps in the West of the Kingdom, contained a large number of small communities – much of Galicia remains like that – where the presence of someone who could read, and even write if necessary, would have been useful and appreciated; for that society was still based on written documents, such as those concerning the sale of land and property, several of which still survive. Similar transactions would have been carried out in the South in Arabic, but the traditional written *ladino* of the new migrants was enough to enable them to fulfil these tasks in the North. They had to understand what their Asturian-Leonese hosts were saying to them, and their hosts had in turn to be able to understand what the immigrants were saying when they read the documents aloud to them afterwards. Given these circumstances of intelligibility in practice, we can assume that the North-South dialect continuum was still elastic and accommodating.[11] Speakers of the Romance of the time from many areas of the Peninsula also met each other in Almanzor's armies (and probably earlier ones too); merchants, businessmen, masons, painters and others crossed religious and political frontiers in the course of their work. There is, in short, no reason to propose that isoglosses had bundled East-West along the religious frontier in such a way as to disrupt the geographical continuum. This continued to exist in a North-South direction without such a barrier, even in the far West, as Castro has shown.[12] So it is merely anachronistic if we apply now to the language of

[10] R. MENÉNDEZ PIDAL, *Orígenes del Español* (Madrid, 1926; seventh edition, 1972).

[11] M.C. DÍAZ Y DÍAZ, "La circulation des manuscrits dans la Péninsule Ibérique du VIIe au XIe siècles", *Cahiers du Civilisation Médiévale* 12 (1969), pp. 219-241 and pp. 383-392 (= IDEM, *Vie chrétienne*, chapter 12), has shown the strength of the more intellectual contacts there were between North and South.

[12] I. CASTRO, *Curso de História da Língua Portuguesa* (Lisbon, 1991).

the period such geographically-based labels as *"gallego"*, *"leonés"*, *"castel-lano"*, *"mozárabe"*, et cetera, as if they were at the time distinguishable entities.

In the North, the sociolinguistic and stylistic continuum also survived, between all their variations in speech and in writing. If they had had all the modern analytical sociolinguistic techniques it might have been then possible to come up with statistical differences and tendencies, within that continuum, between those who could read and write, those who could read but not write (liturgy, Saints' Lives, Histories, documents, et cetera), the intelligent illiterate, the less talented, et cetera; but there was still a single continuum of registers and styles that united them all within what we can call a complex *ladino* monolingualism.[13] As Alarcos Llorach pointed out, their language served them for practical and social purposes just as well (or as badly) as modern Portuguese and Castilian serve their speakers today.[14] It was, however, different in the South. The pragmatic centre of this continuum was getting squeezed out, leaving an awkward gap between colloquial speech and formal writing, a chasm which was becoming harder to bridge as time went on. For as the decades went by, intellectual speech, dealing with most serious topics other than Christian ones, was being carried on more and more in Arabic. Spoken *ladino* (Romance) was being increasingly confined to the non-intellectual spheres of the market, the household, the tavern. The Arabic-*ladino* bilingualism was thus acquiring some of the characteristics of diglossia, in the whole of Al-Andalus society. We can take Álvaro's famous complaint of 854 as literal truth, that his fellow-Christians were preferring at that time to acquire literacy in Arabic alone (see below). For unless they were dealing with a specifically Christian topic, there was no need to write their *ladino*, whether or not they could still read it. And here in Al-Andalus, as in Asturias and León, written texts would still be generally intelligible when read aloud. It does not look as if notaries who could write *ladino* were much in demand in Al-Andalus. At least, even if some such documents were drawn up, none at all have survived. We cannot be entirely sure, however, that they did not exist in the ninth century, because Álvaro refers to drawing up a deed of sale without specifying the language.[15] Other such linguistic phenomena, that in the North had the important cultural effect of uniting the two ends and reinforcing the centre of the stylistic contin-

---

[13] R. WRIGHT, *Early Ibero-Romance*, chapter 1.

[14] E. ALARCOS LLORACH, *El español, lengua milenaria* (Valladolid, 1982).

[15] Álvaro, *Epistula* IX, 4, ll. 11-12 (*Corpus Scriptorum Muzarabicorum*, p. 212): *"uenditjonem fecimus et per testes firmauimus"*.

uum, were also absent in the South. The reading aloud in public of Homilies and Saints' Lives, for example, which united the literate reader and illiterate listener, was in Al-Andalus at best imprudent, and at times probably even illegal.

Within the Christian community in Córdoba itself, however, texts were indeed read aloud, even those that had been written in distant places and times. In Álvaro's *Vita Eulogii* we read that:

> Ihoanni aepiscopo Iherosolimitano directa epistola legeretur, quam ego cuidam diacono preceperam legere.[16]

> the letter addressed to the Bishop of Jerusalem should be read aloud, which I had told one of the deacons to read.

At the start of his *Memoriale sanctorum* Eulogio seems to expect that this text of his will be read aloud:

> loquar etiam tibi, o uniuersalis ecclesiae sanctae conuentus, ut uerbum ueritatis quod ore nostro edicitur ...[17]

> for I will speak to you, Universal Convent of the Holy Church, such that the words of truth spoken out of my mouth ...

But his style cannot, if so, have made it easy to follow. We cannot imagine that the oral version of the *Documentum martyriale*, dedicated by Eulogio to the martyrs Flora and Maria just before their death in 851, was exactly identical to the written version – or, at least, if it was, we can doubt whether they understood it all. Colbert seems to have thought that they did, however, and even deduces from this evidence that Latin culture was not restricted to an intellectual elite.[18] But it also looks as if Colbert misunderstood the word "*dicavit*" in the initial description of the "*Liber Documentum .. quod in carcere positus uirginibus Florae et Mariae ergastulo mancipatis dicauit*" ("which, when he was in prison, he dedicated to the virgins Flora and María when they had been taken to prison")[19] as if it were "*dixit*", "said", or "*dictavit*", "dictated", rather than "*dicavit*", "dedicated". And in the other direction, we can also be justified

---

[16] Álvaro, *Vita Eulogii*, VII, ll. 7-10 (*Corpus Scriptorum Muzarabicorum*, p. 334).

[17] Álvaro, *Memoriale sanctorum*, I, 4, ll. 8-10 (*Corpus Scriptorum Muzarabicorum*, pp. 371-372).

[18] E.P. COLBERT, *The Martyrs of Córdoba (850-859): a Study of the Sources* (Washington, 1962), p. 228.

[19] Eulogio, *Documentum martyriale*, (*Corpus Scriptorum Muzarabicorum*, p. 461).

in wondering whether the last words of the martyr Digna have indeed been reproduced verbatim in the *Memoriale sanctorum*.[20] Colbert, even so, suggests that the first part of Álvaro's *Indiculus Luminosus* was intended to be read aloud, and even that Álvaro had written it in a colloquial style, but from what we can deduce of the colloquial registers of that time this latter suggestion is quite untenable. Even though some verbs are indeed in the second person form, it is hard to believe that this text was fully intelligible if indeed it was ever read aloud.

Speraindeo had earlier referred disapprovingly, in a letter to Álvaro,[21] to the colloquial usage of those who "... *in locutjonibus uulgalibus malunt inmorari*" ("prefer not to progress beyond colloquial phrasing"). Even so, before 850 the surviving texts are noticeably less complex, more accessible, and more likely to have been understood when read aloud than they became subsequently. The *Acts* of the Church Council of Córdoba of the 20th of February 839 have miraculously survived for us in a contemporary manuscript.[22] The Council seems to have followed the procedures of the seventh-century church. A heresy was condemned there, in a severe and self-confident tone. The bishops came from the same dioceses as had existed in Visigothic Andalucía (and even from Africa). These Acts have, in Gil's phrase, a "barbarous manner of writing" ("*barbara scribendi ratio*"), that is, a style not too far from that of normal speech, which could well have had the consequence of ensuring general understanding when they were read aloud (although this text still needs to be studied more closely than it has been). The text was prepared by the best educated Christians of the time. It contains what look to us like mere errors of spelling, morphology and syntax, such as would infuriate a nineteenth-century public schoolmaster, but which could at times have helped rather than hindered understanding in the immediate ninth-century context. We might be able to conclude from these Acts that it was mostly intelligible, if read aloud sympathetically, and thus that the stylistic continuum was still in existence in 839. But the continuum is being stretched in a dangerous way, given the near total absence of any other register there to fill the gap between the most formal usages of the Christian writers and the most informal usages of the household, and it only needed some inappropriate stimulus to turn up for the continuum to break in two.

---

[20] Álvaro, *Memoriale sanctorum*, III, 8, 3, ll. 12-16 (*Corpus Scriptorum Muzarabicorum*, p. 446).

[21] *Epistula Speraindei Albaro Directa*, VIII, 1, l. 11 (*Corpus Scriptorum Muzarabicorum*, p. 203).

[22] León Cathedral MS 22. See: *Corpus Scriptorum Muzarabicorum*, pp. 135-141.

Is it possible to identify such a stimulus, to the rupture of the stylistic continuum between 839 and 851? Yes, indeed, it certainly is. As has often been pointed out, the voyage that Eulogio made to the Pyrenees in the year 848 (or 850, according to Colbert and Wolf) changed the cultural atmosphere in Córdoba.[23] Most scholars, however, have come to the conclusion that Eulogio's voyage led to a raising of the Latin cultural level there. I have concluded that it led eventually to its demolition, and will explain how in the rest of this study.

In 848 (or 849, or 850) Eulogio returned to Córdoba from the Pyrenees - with a small collection of books hitherto unknown in Córdoba. It may be that Eulogio had been inspired to collect them by being both impressed and alarmed by the Renaissance in Arabic culture that had taken place in Córdoba under Abd-Al-Rahman II (822-852), who had succeeded in bringing in from Baghdad many books of diverse kinds (poetry, astronomy, philosophy, music, astrology, science, et cetera). It is likely that Eulogio was impelled by this to try and import Christian books of similar quality from further north. It is also quite likely, as Colbert suggested, that the Eastern sources for this Arabic cultural Renaissance in Al-Andalus could have included the occasional Christian volume of a semi-mystical nature, which worried Eulogio because of its doubtful orthodoxy.[24] If so, this could well have been another stimulus to his decision that it was worth bringing some Christian books south from more northern Christian lands. Eulogio tells us, for example, that one of his martyrs had arrived in Córdoba from Jerusalem, via Africa, with the intention of going on from there to the land of the Christians (that is, of the Franks). And this man "*uariis linguis peritus existeret, Graeca scilicet Latina atque Arabica*" ("was an expert in several languages, that is, Greek, Latin and Arabic").[25] In any event, it seems likely that Eulogio's importing these books was the result of a previous and conscious intention to do so, although modern scholars tend to present it as the unforeseen and almost capricious consequence of the frustrating of his intention to visit his "brothers" who were visiting Mainz.[26] These "brothers" in Mainz are still mysterious, but their being there in 848 could well be significant. Mainz had seen a new bishop installed in 847, the famous Hrabanus Maurus, pupil of Alcuin, former abbot of Fulda, the centre of a whole web of intellectual contacts, and literate *par excellence*. Did these "brothers" of Eulogio talk to him or his colleagues? (Was that why they went? Had they been in-

---

[23] K.B. WOLF, *Christian Martyrs in Moslem Spain* (Cambridge, 1988).

[24] COLBERT, *The Martyrs*, pp. 114-115.

[25] Eulogio, *Memoriale Sanctorum* II, 23, ll. 29-30 (*Corpus Scriptorum Muzarabicorum*, p. 426).

[26] COLLINS, *Unity*, p. 215.

vited?) They managed to return later to Córdoba. What echoes of the Carolingian Renaissance could have come back with them? We do not know the answers to these questions, but at least we know now that they are worth asking. Perhaps it was just such echoes of Northern Christianity that Eulogio was hoping to cull from his visit north. And once his own proposed visit to Mainz itself turned out to be impractical, he then deliberately chose, from the Pyrenean monasteries that he was able to reach, some books of a kind that he had already intended to look for in the Frankish Empire, so as to return to Córdoba with them. This, at least, is the impression that Álvaro manages to give in his *Vita Eulogii*:

> cotidie enim noua et egregie admiranda quasi a iugeribus et fossis effodiens tesauros elucidabat inuisos.[27]

> for every day he showed us treasures never before seen, new things much to be admired, as if he had dug them up from the ploughed fields and the ditches.

Eulogio's plan was to raise the cultural level of the Christians in Córdoba by rediscovering and studying every forgotten book that he could manage to come across. It was just one aspect of the way he was reacting to the possibility that the Christians of Al-Andalus might lose their cultural identity.[28]

In any event, whatever the reasons for his importing these books, their arrival was going to have far-reaching consequences. Some of these consequences were literary. For example, we know from Álvaro's *Vita Eulogii* that both he and Eulogio were taught the techniques of rhythmic poetry in their youth, in Córdoba.[29] Later both Álvaro and Eulogio destroyed their own early rhythmic compositions in embarrassment at their inadequacy, but there survives, for example, the *Carmen poenitentiale* of Vincentius in octosyllabic hemistichs to attest to the existence of the genre in Córdoba in the 830s.[30] Among the books that came from the Pyrenean monasteries were works, both in prose and in verse, which seemed to Eulogio and Álvaro that it would be

---

[27] Álvaro, *Vita Eulogii*, 8, ll. 12-14 (*Corpus Scriptorum Muzarabicorum*, p. 335).

[28] P. CHALMETA, "Mozarab", in: *Encyclopaedia of Islam*, VII (Leiden and New York, 1993), pp. 246-249.

[29] Álvaro, *Vita Eulogii*, 2, ll. 28-34 (*Corpus Scriptorum Muzarabicorum*, pp. 331-332). Colbert does not accept that these *rithmicis uersibus* were rhythmic; but the Visigothic tradition made a definite distinction between rhythmic and metric compositions, as we can see from Julián de Toledo's Grammar: M.A.H. MAESTRE YENES, *Ars Iuliani Toletani Episcopi. Una gramática latina de la España visigoda* (Toledo, 1973), II, xx, ll. 2-4.

[30] Vincentius, *Carmen poenitentiale* (*Corpus Scriptorum Muzarabicorum*, p. 688).

henceforth essential to try and imitate and emulate in their own compositions. According to Álvaro, Eulogio taught (*"docuit"*) his colleagues the techniques of metric verse,[31] when they were imprisoned in 851, and after. The evidence of the verse that survives from after this date show that not only is this almost certainly true, but that it is quite understandable in those circumstances that their earlier rhythmic verse came to seem unacceptable. Álvaro boasted later of his ability to compose *"metrice"*,[32] even if the result seems awkward and over-blown to our modern taste. The old hymns of a rhythmic nature continued to be sung, and we cannot date with any certainty the time of the last hymn to be composed in Al-Andalus, but the *"Ymnorum catholicorum fulgida carmina"* that came down from the Pyrenees must have had greater prestige as well as increased accessibility.

In the same way, the newly arrived works of Augustine, Vergil, Juvenal and Horace impressed them. Now that they had arrived, it also seemed a good idea to imitate these. According to Álvaro, Eulogio used these books with his own pupils, and Álvaro mentions these books in subsequent letters. The words which he uses to refer to these new books are significant not only for their content, but also for their style:

> Inde secum librum Ciuitatis beatissimi Agustini et Eneidos Uergilii siue Iubenalis metricos itidem libros atque Flacci saturata poemata seu Porfirii depincta opuscula uel Adhelelmi epigramatum opera necnon et Abieni Fabule metrice et Ymnorum catholicorum fulgida carmina cum multa minutissimarum causarum ingenia ex sanctis questionibus congregata non priuatim sibi, sed comuniter studio<si>ssimis inquisitoribus reportauit ...[33]

> From there he brought back with him the *Book of the City* of the Blessed Augustine, and the *Aeneid* of Virgil, and also the metrical poetry of Juvenal, and the full poems of Horace, and the painted works of Optatianus Porphyrius,[34] and the epigrammatic works of Aldhelm, and the metrical *Fables* of Avienus, and the shining songs of the Catholic hymns, with many facets of the most detailed matters brought together concerning Holy questions, not for his own private study, but to satisfy the collective curiosity of interested students ...

The words *"et"*, *"siue"*, *"atque"*, *"seu"* and *"uel"* are used here in sequence to mean simply "and". When he wrote this list, such intentional stylization seemed to him appropriate. These works were being offered as models to admire and even imitate. The compositions which the Córdoba scholars wrote

---

[31] Álvaro, *Vita Eulogii*, 4, 16 (*Corpus Scriptorum Muzarabicorum*, p. 333).

[32] Álvaro, *Carmen* VIII, l. 4 (*Corpus Scriptorum Muzarabicorum*, p. 349).

[33] Álvaro, *Vita Eulogii*, 9, ll. 11-17 (*Corpus Scriptorum Muzarabicorum*, pp. 335-336).

[34] These "painted" geometric poems were so called because they were usually given rubrics in coloured ink.

later attest at times to the anxious desire that their own works should also be sufficiently 'polished'. As Wolf said, an important aspect of their aim to reestablish a distinctively Latin culture lay in their hopes for a Renaissance of Latin erudition.[35]

Michel Banniard made a most interesting analysis of the texts written in the 850s, suggesting that they stretched the monolingual *ladino* continuum to breaking point. It seems, in effect, that rather than raising the level of Latin culture, all that Eulogio and his colleagues achieved was to make themselves so recondite and recherché, in the vocabulary and grammar that they deliberately adopted after 851, that they were largely incomprehensible outside their own immediate circle. Much of what they wrote remains somewhat opaque even to the modern specialist. Banniard points out the important point that Eulogio and Álvaro refer to their own most complex work as being 'polished', 'cultivated'. "*Politus*" is the past participle of "*polire*", and "*cultus*" of "*colere*", and their use implies that someone has indeed 'polished up' the written text in some way. Banniard quotes, for example,[36] Eulogio's *Memoriale sanctorum*:

> ... breuiarium, quod mihi causa expoliendi transmisit, ne incultior sermo fidem rei gestae quibus mittebatur adimeret.[37]

> a breviary which he had sent to me to be polished up, so that an insufficiently cultivated style would not make it seem less trustworthy in content to the people to whom it was sent.

He quotes also the 'topos' at the start of Álvaro's *Epistula* IX:[38]

> Hos inertje mee conticuos apices inculto sermone digestos et inpolito textu confectos uestre decreui presentje destinandos.[39]

> I arranged that these consecutive signs of my lack of skill, distributed in uncultivated style and put together in an unpolished text, should be given to you personally.

He quotes Álvaro's indication that such polishing was done with the aid of Donatus's *Ars Minor*, which would have been particularly useful for polishing inflectional morphology:

[35] WOLF, *Christian Martyrs*, p. 45.

[36] BANNIARD, *Viva Voce*, p. 434.

[37] Eulogio, *Memoriale sanctorum*, II, 10, 24, ll. 2-4 (*Corpus Scriptorum Muzarabicorum*, p. 426).

[38] BANNIARD, *Viva Voce*, p. 437.

[39] Álvaro, *Epistula* IX, 1, ll. 3-5 (*Corpus Scriptorum Muzarabicorum*, p. 211).

Iam te non uerbis deuaccauo, set fustibus, nec sententjis per arte Donati politis, set nudosis arborum troncis.

I will no longer attack you with words but with cudgels, not with comments polished up with the help of the *Ars* of Donatus but with knotty tree trunks.[40]

In practice, the attitude that Álvaro adopts seems at times rather contradictory, as has also often been pointed out, because although he liked to use a complicated style in his own work, he also sent a very long letter to his correspondent John of Sevilla in which he expressed himself opposed to the over-use of grammatical adornments ("*donatistas*") in Christian writings.[41] And this letter can be dated to after Eulogio's return from the Pyrenees, in view of his referring to two of the books concerned.[42] And however 'polished' he liked to appear, his works are not at all of perfect antique Latinity.[43] We can also tell, from the remarks that Ambrosio de Morales made when he edited them, that Eulogio's works were similarly inauthentic, and thus the only version that survives for us of Eulogio's writings is one that was further 'polished' by their Renaissance editor.

What these writers were actually doing was to widen still further the already growing chasm between normal speech registers and high register writing. Since there existed fewer and fewer intervening registers in the *ladino* of Al-Andalus, this led to what Banniard describes acutely as "*la disparition de la collectivité latine*" ("the disappearance of the Latin collectivity"); "*le contraste entre l'ancienne et la nouvelle langue ne pouvait plus, alors, échapper complètement aux locuteurs lettrés*" ("the contrast between the old and the new language could then no longer remain unnoticed by educated speakers").[44] In this comment Banniard is referring to the written form as the "old" language and spoken Romance (our *ladino*) as the "new" language, but in fact the new element after 851 which catalysed the distinction was the suddenly fashionable hyper-archaizing written style, whereas Romance speech was already an old and long-standing phenomenon.

---

[40] Álvaro, *Epistula* II, 1, ll. 8-10 (*Corpus Scriptorum Muzarabicorum*, p. 151); *sic*, "*per arte*"; BANNIARD, *Viva Voce*, p. 438, n. 61, reproduces this incorrectly as "*artem*".

[41] Álvaro, *Epistula* IV (*Corpus Scriptorum Muzarabicorum*, pp. 162-186). See: C. SAGE, *Paul Albar of Córdoba: Studies on his Life and Writings* (Washington, 1943), pp. 43-59.

[42] COLBERT, *The Martyrs*, pp. 154-157.

[43] See: J. GIL, "Apuntes sobre la morfología de Álvaro de Córdoba", *Habis* 2 (1971), pp. 199-206.

[44] BANNIARD, *Viva Voce*, p. 472.

The role of catalyst which was being played at this time in Carolingian France by Germanic Latin, the official use and establishment of which led in due course to a growing conceptual divergence between Latin and Romance as two separate languages, is assigned in Al-Andalus to Eulogio and Álvaro (by Banniard). This is probably right. But I find it impossible to accept the next step in Banniard's argument. In about 864, Sansón, Abbot of Peñamellera, in his *Apologeticus* severely criticizes the written language used in the condemnation of Sansón written by his political enemy Hostegesis, Bishop of Málaga.[45] At the time, Sansón was not in Peñamellera, the Córdoba monastery where three of the martyrs had been illegally buried in 852, but in exile in Martos, a town in the modern province of Jaén. Banniard interprets the usages written by Hostegesis as features of 'Romance'; that is, of a different language supposedly now distinguishable from 'Latin'. The problem with this analysis lies in the fact that although the very few details that Sansón criticises in Hostegesis's text are indeed not acceptable Latin, neither can they have been part of the vernacular of the time. The confusion which there seems to have been in that text between "*contempti*" and "*contenti*" (compared by Sansón to possible confusions between "*oleum*" and "*ordeum*", but that is not a confusion evinced by Hostegesis himself); the use of the nominative case-ending after "*contenti*"; the use of the masculine form "*quidam*" to accompany "*corrupta pestis*"; and the word "*idolatrix*". These are the only usages criticized, but, however we wish to reconstruct it, none of them can be seen as features of ninth-century Ibero-Romance. The word "*pestis*" is as feminine now (Spanish *peste*) as it had been in the Roman Empire, and "*quidam*" cannot be reconstructed to have been a word used colloquially at that time. It is probable that the nominative case-endings, and the nominal word-forms that derived from such original nominatives, did not exist in colloquial usage. We can be sure that they did not use such a word as "*idolatrix*". That is, none of the few features mentioned by Sansón have anything at all to do with vernacular Romance speech habits. The problem with Hostegesis, in Sansón's reiterated opinion, was specifically that he could not write properly. Sansón criticizes details of his spelling and his inability to follow the model of Cicero, Cyprian, Jerome and Augustine.[46] In Sansón's complaint he makes no distinction at all between "*latinus sermo*" and "*romana facundia*"; they are synonymous in "*Si latinus sermo, o baburre, hoc recipere non recusaret, si Romana facundia caperet ...*" ("if Latin speech, you

---

[45] Sansón, *Apologeticus*, II, 1. 7 (*Corpus Scriptorum Muzaraboicorum*, pp. 569-572). M.J. HAGERTY, *Los cuervos de San Vicente* (Madrid, 1978).

[46] Sansón, *Apologeticus*, II, 7, 5, ll. 6-7 (*Corpus Scriptorum Muzarabicorum*, p. 571).

ape, did not refuse to accept this, if Roman eloquence were able to contain it ...".[47] "*Latinitatis facundia*" and "*nitorem Romani sermonis*" are equally synonymous.[48] He describes Hostegesis as "*auctor linguae novellae*" and "*nove Latinitatis inventor*", the creator of his own language, rather than transcribing normal spoken usage.[49] Hostegesis is told:

> Nam crede mihi quia hee ignorantie tenebre abolebuntur quandoque et huc reddetur Hispaniae notitia artis grammatice. Et tunc omnibus apparebit quantis erroribus subiaceas ipse, qui hodie a brutis hominibus putaris litteris nosse.[50]

> For believe me, the shades of this ignorance will be dispersed when the knowledge of the Art of Grammar is brought back here to Spain. And then everybody will realize how many errors you have fallen into, you, the same one who is now thought by the ignorant to be an expert in letters.

Hostegesis, bishop of Málaga, was not part of Eulogio's Córdoba circle, and is being criticized for writing badly. The contrast being presented by Sansón is not, as Banniard describes it, "*opposition entre le registre grammatical et le registre vulgarisant*" ("a contrast between the grammatically correct and the colloquial register"),[51] because Hostegesis's errors are hypercorrections and not 'popularizing' in any way.

Sansón was biliterate, although he only mentions that in passing. He was hired in 863 to translate some important letters from Arabic to Latin "as I used to do before" ("*ut pridem facere consueueram*").[52] So even Sansón himself, an ill-tempered Christian throughly literate in Latin, turns out to have been an expert in Arabic literacy as well. If even he was, nobody can have seen much practical value any more in confining their literacy solely to Latin. Thus the analyses which both Colbert and Banniard make of Sansón strike me as being considerably less convincing than their analyses of Eulogio and Álvaro. Colbert states that the Sansón-Hostegesis argument "attests the vitality of Latin letters in Córdoba".[53] Yet Sansón was not in Córdoba, for he had been sent into exile. This argument was, indeed, the swan song of Córdoba's Latin literacy, because

[47] Sansón, *Apologeticus*, II, 7, 5, ll. 10-11 (*Corpus Scriptorum Muzarabicorum*, p. 571).

[48] Sansón, *Apologeticus*, II, 7, 5, ll. 33-36 (*Corpus Scriptorum Muzarabicorum*, p. 572).

[49] Sansón, *Apologeticus*, II, 7, 5, ll. 5-6 and II, 7, 3, l. 12 respectively (*Corpus Scriptorum Muzarabicorum*, p. 571 and p. 570).

[50] Sansón, *Apologeticus*, II, 7, 5, ll. 26-29 (*Corpus Scriptorum Muzarabicorum*, p. 572).

[51] BANNIARD, *Viva Voce*, p. 477.

[52] Sansón, *Apologeticus*, II, *Praefatio*, 9, ll. 3-4 (*Corpus Scriptorum Muzarabicorum*, p. 554).

[53] COLBERT, *The Martyrs*, chapter 15.

Sansón lost it. The winners were those who wished to make practical compromises between Christians and Moslems. The tenth-century manuscript which preserves Sansón's writings for us has on it glosses in Arabic: Sansón had told Hostegesis that the knowledge of grammar (*"notitia artis grammatice"*) would soon come back to Al-Andalus, but he was wrong. What happened was the exact opposite, quite possibly in part as the direct result of Sansón's extreme rudeness towards those who were deciding Christian policy within Córdoba in the next few years.

In the Carolingian world, the learnèd pressures on the written form increased, and eventually led to the Twelfth-Century Renaissance. Thus in France there eventually came into existence a comparatively clear conceptual distinction between Latin and Romance, a conceptual distinction which was catalysed by the invention in Romance-speaking areas of the new methods of writing which we would now call 'Old French'. But this outcome was hardly a practicable proposition in Al-Andalus. The return of Eulogio with his books from the Pyrenees had the same galvanizing effect as the arrival of Alcuin at Aachen with his books had had a few years earlier, but the social and cultural circumstances were not comparable. In the Romance-speaking areas of the Carolingian Empire, those who wanted to acquire literacy had no option but to set to and learn the complexities of the *Ars grammatica*, right up to the early thirteenth century, which is when the new written Romance became the unmarked written form. But in ninth-century Córdoba almost everyone, of whatever religion, was bilingual to some extent. Eulogio is also likely to have been bilingual: he quotes and translates an Arabic phrase in his *Memoriale sanctorum*.[54] Álvaro could also have been bilingual: he translates three Arabic words in his *Indiculus luminosus*.[55] Eulogio explicitly says in his *Memoriale sanctorum* that one of the martyrs, Aurelio, became literate in Arabic (*"Arabica erudiendus literatura"*) when young.[56] The language which had sociolinguistic prestige, in writing as well as speech, was not *ladino* but Arabic. Social success was allied to literacy there as elsewhere, but this was Arabic literacy. The Moslems had no incentive at all to write the *ladino* which they knew how to speak. Álvaro's famous complaint in his *Indiculus luminosus* of *c*. 854 confirms that,[57] in spite of the best efforts of Eulogio and his colleagues over the last three

---

[54] Eulogio, *Memoriale sanctorum*, II, 1, 3, ll. 11-14 (*Corpus Scriptorum Muzarabicorum*, p. 399).

[55] Álvaro, *Indiculus luminosus*, 23, l. 14; 25, l. 17 and l. 27 (*Corpus Scriptorum Muzarabicorum*, p. 297 and p. 299).

[56] Eulogio, *Memoriale sanctorum*, II, 10, 1, ll. 6-7 (*Corpus Scriptorum Muzarabicorum*, p. 416).

[57] Álvaro, *Indiculus luminosus*, c. 35 (*Corpus Scriptorum Muzarabicorum*, pp. 314-315).

years or so, many Christians, despite being bilingual, were already preferring to become literate in Arabic alone. This is not at all surprising. Even if they had wanted to become literate in the Christian way, Eulogio had made that extremely difficult to achieve. As Colbert says,[58] the reforming Christian writers went out of their way to find the most complicated way to express their ideas in writing. Wasserstein says that "the creation of prestige forms of writing in Latin was ... not only difficult but less likely to provide for feelings of identity or of group solidarity" (than the use of Hebrew by the Jews).[59] Álvaro was probably aware of this reaction, because at the end of the first half of the *Indiculus* he declares, unconvincingly, that he is not using himself an over-ornate style.[60] The conflict between being polished (*"politus"*) and being comprehensible, which Banniard so rightly highlights, was being left by Álvaro almost deliberately unresolved. The style required to write *ladino* was already far from easy, but it had been made far harder by the classical models which Eulogio asked them to imitate, and in the event the end result was not to inspire imitations: it discouraged them.

Most historians do not agree with Hagerty, who says that the tenth-century Christians in Al-Andalus were monolingual Arabic-speakers.[61] On the contrary, they did not stop speaking *ladino*; and as Colbert points out,[62] Aljoxaní seems to refer to some important Christian leaders who only spoke Romance in the caliphate of Abd-al-Rahman III in the tenth century.[63] Most will have been bilingual in the tenth century, and up to the twelfth-century expulsions, only literate in Arabic if literate at all. After the 860s, it looks as if no new generation was taught to write Latin in Al-Andalus (except, as Collins suggests, for the elaboration of epitaphs on tombstones). Most Christians just did not attempt any more to meet the complex requirements of Latin literacy, as they largely turned their back on the ideals of the martyrs and their hagiographers. In this sense we can accept Colbert's comment that it was the hegemony of Arabic and the absence of the Carolingian Renaissance that made the situtaion in Al-Andalus different from that in France.[64]

Christian texts were translated into written Arabic: the psalms at the end of the ninth century, three of the gospels in 946, the Acts of Visigothic Councils,

---

[58] COLBERT, *The Martyrs*, p. 410.
[59] WASSERSTEIN, "The Language Situation", p. 12.
[60] Álvaro, *Indiculus luminosus*, c. 20 (*Corpus Scriptorum Muzarabicorum*, pp. 291-293).
[61] HAGERTY, *Los cuervos*, pp. 275-277.
[62] COLBERT, *The Martyrs*, pp. 124-127.
[63] See the introduction to: J. RIBERA, *Historia de los jueces de Córdoba por Aljoxaní* (Madrid, 1914), although this interpretation of the text is not universally accepted.
[64] COLBERT, *The Martyrs*, p. 104.

and others. When the Asturians came looking for Eulogio's body in 882-884, it looks as if nobody in Córdoba tried to stop them taking it to Oviedo. They allowed the very books that had excited Eulogio so much to leave Córdoba with his body, the books which in practice had finally put an end to any possibility of widespread literacy in Latin in Al-Andalus. If respected bishops such as Hostegesis were going to get nothing other than insults from the hyperliterate writers such as Sansón, there can have seemed little point in continuing that practice. We can see that these cultural migrations northwards coincided with human migrations, and it is quite possible that the emigration of literate Christians was directly connected with the emigration of the books.[65] Notaries, monks and books continued to move north in subsequent years. Emigrants from Toledo built the fortress in Zamora in the 890s. When Cixila moved from Toledo to the monastery of Saints Cosme and Damián at Abellar in León in 927, he brought with him a large collection of Visigothic manuscripts, which implies that they were no longer of much practical use in Toledo. Although there continued to be many Christians in tenth-century Al-Andalus, and there were even a few more martyrs, the end of Latin literacy does not seem to have been regretted by them. Arabic literacy was all they needed. Arabic had within itself all the different sociolinguistic levels that could be required. It would be difficult to prove this, but we can suspect that the famous kharjas are not really bilingual. Even though these contain words of Romance origin, the point was that the very lowest and least prestigious level of colloquial Córdoba Arabic contained within it a large number of words originally taken direct from *ladino*, but by now genuinely Arabic words, and that in the kharja the writers sometimes deliberately used that lowest possible sociolinguistic level of Arabic.

We can answer the initial question: *ladino* literacy died out in Al-Andalus, unlike in Asturias, because there no longer existed there the whole continuum of sociolinguistic registers that sustained it in the north. When Eulogio and his colleagues tried to force the written mode of their language into stylistic models that were even further distant from normal speech, the tenuous link that had hitherto managed to keep the two ends of the continuum connected over the intervening gap became too fragile to hold. The other Christians concluded that this kind of literacy was not only unnecessary, but unattractive and all but impossible to achieve. In this way the phenomenon which Simonet described as the Renaissance of Latin literacy turned out in the event to be the straw that broke the camel's back, and eventually hastened its end.

---

[65] R. COLLINS, "Poetry in ninth-century Spain", *Papers of the Liverpool Latin Seminar* 4 (1983), pp. 181-195. B.F. REILLY, *The Medieval Spains* (Cambridge, 1993), p. 83.

Chapter 12

Early Medieval Pan-Romance
Comprehension

One question that is often asked, but less often answered, is this: how well could speakers of Romance Languages communicate with each other in the Middle Ages? The answer to be found in the specialist philological volumes tends to be pessimistic, implying or even asserting that the Western Romance languages were already in practice significantly different from each other in the Early Middle Ages.[1] I would like to suggest here that that is not true.

This is not an easy subject to discuss, in particular because of the implications of the language names we use. If Latin were still a single language, and still called 'Latin', in the way that Greek is still a single language and still called 'Greek', discussion would be easier. But perhaps the single most remarkable fact about the historical development of the Latin language is not really a linguistic fact at all. It is that what used to be thought of as one language came over time to be thought of as being several different languages, and whereas there is general agreement that the original language of the Roman

This chapter is an almost identical reprint of: "Early Medieval Pan-Romance Comprehension", in: *Word, Image, Number: Communication in the Middle Ages*, ed. John J. CONTRENI and Santa CASCIANI (Firenze, SISMEL – Edizioni del Galluzzo, 2002), pp. 25-42. We are grateful to Professor John Contreni and Sgr Agostino Paravicini Bagliani, on behalf of the SISMEL – Edizioni del Galluzzo, for permitting this reprint.

[1] For instance: R.A. HALL Jr, *External History of the Romance Languages* (New York, 1974). IDEM, *Proto-Romance Phonology* (New York, 1976). IDEM, *Proto-Romance Morphology* (Amsterdam, 1983).

Empire should be called Latin, and that the separate daughter languages used from the later Middle Ages onwards can be given the separate labels Spanish, Portuguese, French, Catalan, Italian, Rumanian (and perhaps more), the way in which we should refer to the speech of the intervening millennium is not immediately obvious, and to a large extent our choice of vocabulary here depends on the prior analysis we have made or assumed of the nature and chronology of the relevant splits. I have been arguing that (perhaps apart from the speech of the ancestors of the modern Rumanians, since we do not really know now where they were then) the conceptual break-up of the single language into many different languages happens right at the end of the intermediate period, that is, in effect, during the thirteenth century. For earlier centuries, to refer to the single language used over most of the former Roman Empire it seems safest to use the label of 'Early Romance' or simply 'Romance'; and perhaps also, from the tenth century or so, we can refer roughly to 'Gallo-Romance', 'Italo-Romance' and 'Ibero-Romance' (or, in Spanish, "*ladino*"). In this way, the geographically-based adjectives such as 'Spanish', 'French', et cetera, can be used with a strictly geographical meaning rather than as metalinguistic labels.

A further complication, after the start of the ninth century, concerns the co-existence with Romance of the artificial entity now known as 'Medieval Latin' (sometimes referred to at the time as "*grammatica*", or "*litterae*", although these terms of course far pre-date the arrival of their special mid-medieval meaning). As we have seen, this was elaborated on the combined basis of Donatus, Priscian and the Anglo-Saxon manner of Latin pronunciation (in which every written letter gave rise to a sound). Since the Latin of the Empire was a natural spoken language, and the Medieval Latin as used by the educated from the Carolingian "*renovatio*" onwards was an artificial construct based on the ancient texts, it can be slightly confusing even to use the word 'Latin' at all for the period between the end of the Empire and the Twelfth-Century Renaissance, which was when the Medieval Latin "*grammatica*" came to be in general educated European use.

In any event, the word 'Romance', used to refer to the language of that monolingual speech community of the Early Middle Ages, is wide-ranging, variable and inclusive. It contained within it an inherited written mode, as used in texts composed at the time, which were on the whole expected to be generally intelligible when read aloud sympathetically. It included within it some ancient linguistic features that were eventually not going to survive in a Romance language. It included some features that had not existed (or, at least, did not exist widely) in the speech of the Empire. It also included many features that have been in use continuously for the last two millennia and more. And it included them all in a conceptual state of monolingualism, by which I mean that it was indeed variable, and likely to have been sociolinguistically complicated, but was still thought of as a single language. The best analogue for the type of Romance speech community envisaged here is probably that of modern English. Both languages belong to a world-wide speech community, still using everywhere their same single written norm, and the presence of wide spoken variation within these communities has not yet led to fragmentation into separate languages. Maybe in the case of English it never will; in the case of Romance it eventually did, but that was not inevitable and was unlikely to have been foreseen during the first millennium.

The foregoing considerations are general. The rest of this study will be specific and even empirical, and try to illuminate the nature of Pan-Romance comprehensibility in the Early Middle Ages by attempting to answer this direct question: would a Romance-speaker from Southern Spain have understood the Strasbourg Oaths of 842, at the furthest northern edge of the Romance-speaking area? This question can only be answered with reference to the practicalities of the society of the day. If Eulogio of Córdoba had decided to travel to Mainz in 848 by jumbo-jet, for example, rather than overland, it is likely that he would have been initially baffled by the Romance speakers of Strasbourg (which was probably a bilingual area, in the diocese of Mainz itself). If a Californian came by jumbo-jet to Liverpool, there might be a similar problem. But that problem did not arise in the 840s. Travel was slow. The Romance-speaker from Spain would take months to arrive, and those months would be spent in traversing the dialect continuum.

The dialect continuum is a wonderful thing. It is the natural result of linguistic evolution if speakers are allowed to develop naturally. That is, without the dead hand of bureaucratic 'language-planning', whose effects are usually catastrophic, and without great movements of whole populations from one place to another, such as occurred during the Christian Reconquest of the southern half of the Iberian Peninsula (which led to the present existence of clear language boundaries in the south, unlike in the north). Languages change naturally over time, and it is also natural for them to change in different ways in different places, since (despite the best endeavours of several historical linguists of the 1960s and 1970s) we know that there is no clear direction for languages to evolve in, and the choices made in different areas, between the same gamut of competing details of pronunciation, grammar or vocabulary, need not be the same. It seems likely that some features which we now think of as being particularly 'Old French', or 'Old Spanish', et cetera, did, in the Romance period, exist in other areas as well as in the one which later gave its geographical name to one of these fragmented 'Romance languages'. In this way it was possible for clear differentiation to arise later than mere variation, and then only because different choices were made from the same lists at the later stage. Thus, the Romance of the ninth century included wide variation even within the same area, and the geographical limits of any one variant (of pronunciation, grammar or vocabulary) did not necessarily, or even often, coincide with those of any other variant. That is, in technical terms, the isoglosses had no reason to bundle; there was no hard and fast frontier that could at that time be drawn on a map between, say, Ibero-Romance and Gallo-Romance in general, even if some of the features involved did indeed have some kind of limit at the Pyrenees. Communication through the north-south Pyrenean passes has always been easier than in an east-west direction, so the isoglosses tend to run north-south in the mountains between the passes, rather than east-west between the political units.

For example, maybe it was true that to express the meaning of "their", speakers in the Iberian Peninsula most commonly used derivatives of Latin SUUS and those to the north and east of the Peninsula used more commonly derivatives of Latin ILLORUM (leading to Italian "*loro*" and French "*leur*"); but "*lur*" was used in Navarra. Rather than a series of clear lines on the ground between competing forms (isoglosses), there was probably in the early Romance period a large series of partially overlapping transition zones, to such an extent that it would not have made much sense to try and decide, on linguistic grounds, exactly where Ibero-Romance ended and Gallo-Romance began.

And the dialect continuum is still essentially there. Naturally, the picture has been muddied everywhere by the language-planners: that is, by the standardization of particular local speech varieties within the political units. From a linguistic point of view, the choice of the speech of Castile, Barcelona, Paris or Florence to be called the 'national standard' was quite arbitrary. The choice was political, based on social factors, rather than on the relative quality of their diphthongs or their suffixes. Yet even now, underneath the distorting effects of the standardizations and centralizing education policies, the continuum is still there. If we draw a line from Galicia, through Asturias, Castilla, Navarra, Aragón, Catalonia, Provence, Liguria, Tuscany, and Rome, down to Sicily, it is still largely true that any averagely-intelligent speaker of the local dialect on that line can fairly easily understand a speaker of another local dialect on that line from within about two hundred miles or so. That is the dialect continuum, and it applied more in the ninth century than it does now. This means that our traveller from Córdoba to Strasbourg, travelling slowly, probably on horseback, would not encounter a serious linguistic barrier between one place and the next. Even if he went at thirty-five miles a day, he would have plenty of days to acclimatize progressively to the linguistic variants he met on the way.

My example of Eulogio of Córdoba, the most intense of all the Christian scholars in Moslem Spain, was not chosen at random. He set out from Córdoba in 848 (probably) to try and find some of his *"fratres"* who had, a few years previously, set off for the Carolingian realms.[2] He never got there himself. Life was too complicated, travel north of the Pyrenees was too dangerous, and he eventually turned back. He had, however, travelled all the long way from Córdoba, across the religious border into Christian Spain and on to the Navarrese Pyrenees, without such difficulties. He spent a considerable time in various monasteries in the Pyrenees, and became a close friend of Wiliesindo, the Bishop of Pamplona. They seem to have discussed many topics when they met, and communicated to each other subsequently in the written mode of their spoken Romance (which looks like traditional Latin to us, since the rules of the written mode had not changed). Their manners of speaking may well have been recognizably different from each other, but none the less it seems that they were mutually intelligible without difficulty, and both their speech styles, their own varieties of Romance, existed within the single monolingual speech community, in addition to their manner of writing. In the same way an inhabitant of modern Glasgow can meet an inhabitant of modern Cornwall, and they can, at least with a little practice, understand each other, and subsequently communicate with each other by writing letters in our normal written form, with all three modes existing inside the one language, English.

We don't know, unfortunately, anything about the previous journey of Eulogio's *"fratres"*. These were probably not actually his brothers but monastic comrades. They seem to have already been away from Moslem Spain for a while by 848, and it is just possible that they could have been present at the scene of the Strasbourg Oaths. If so, the question of comprehension could even have arisen. They probably went via the Pyrenees and then further north overland (rather than by water, as the seas were essentially in Moslem control), and as they travelled they could hear the accents of the southern and then the northern Pyrenees turn within the continuum into those of the Languedoc, and then

---

[2] The works of Eulogio of Córdoba were edited by: J. GIL, *Corpus Scriptorum Muzarabicorum*, 2 volumes (Madrid, 1973), II, pp. 363-503. His letter to Wiliesindo is on pp. 497-503. See also Paulo Álvaro's biography of Eulogio: I, pp. 330-343.

these gradually shifting in space towards those of the Alsatian area. They would have had ample time to get accustomed to the variants of each area they passed through. They eventually went on to Mainz, just north of Strasbourg. Mainz is a German-speaking area now, but may well have had some native Romance-speakers then. It would be fascinating to know what they did there, but we have no idea. The bishop of Mainz from 847 was the famous Hrabanus Maurus, a scholar of linguistic sophistication and centre of a wide range of intellectual contacts. There is, apparently, no sign, in the surviving records from Mainz, of the arrival of these Christian "*fratres*" from the Moslem south, but they were indeed there, for we are later told by Eulogio they had been, and it seems likely that they had discussions with Hrabanus and his colleagues on many interesting topics. They would have learnt about the revival of intellectual life and textual studies; maybe that was even why they were there.

When Eulogio set out he seems not to have heard from his comrades since they left Córdoba, but he told Wiliesindo later that on the way back home he met some merchants at Zaragoza, which was at the northern end of the Moslem-ruled area, who assured him that his "*peregrinos*", the absent brothers, were indeed in Mainz. Eulogio also adds that the brothers had returned by the time of writing (November 851):

> Cumque a vobis egrederer, festinus Caesaraugustam perueni causa fratrum meorum, quos uulgi opinio negotiatorum cohortibus interesse nuper ab ulterioris Francia gremio ibidem descendentibus iactitabat. Deinde urbi appropinquans negotiantes quidem repperi, peregrinos autem meos eorum relatione apud Maguntiam nobilissimam Baioariae ciuitatem exulasse cognoui. Et uerum fuisse hoc negotiatorum nuntium, regredientibus Deo fautore succedenti tempore ab interiori fratribus nostris, didicimus.[3]

> As I was coming back from you, I hurried down to Zaragoza, because I'd heard that there were some merchants recently arrived from the heart of deepest Francia who had news of my *fratres*. Indeed, on the way into the city I met some of these merchants, and was told that my pilgrims had gone to the most noble city of Mainz, in Bavaria. Later we found out that what the merchants said was true, when our *fratres*, by the grace of God, eventually came back safely from the interior.

And yet although Eulogio remained voluble until his martyrdom in 859, he seems never to have referred in writing to these brothers or to their wanderings again.

These "*cohortes*" of conveniently informative merchants are here mentioned with intriguing nonchalance, as if travel between Moslem Zaragoza and

---

[3] Eulogio of Córdoba, *Epistula* 3 (*Corpus Scriptorum Muzarabicorum*, II, pp. 499-500).

Mainz, in the remote Christian interior, was nothing unusual. Maybe it wasn't. Merchants and scholars, and many other people, travelled around more than we sometimes credit them for. The commonest visual image presented in handbooks of the development of the Romance languages is the tree diagram, which suggests that the languages divided and then developed separately, like the branches of a tree, as though the speakers in every area were subsequently isolated from those in every other. This cannot have been the case. Travel was common, at least among certain sectors of society, even if slow. Bishops and other church dignitaries came from wide flung regions to their archiepiscopal councils, such as the Council of Córdoba in 839. Mozarabic exiles – carpenters, farmers, builders, as well as monastic scribes – came in steady trickles to the northern Christian states, particularly to Asturias. Northern royal families sent their ailing relations to doctors in the Moslem south. Sancho the Fat (King Sancho I of León, reigned 956-966) came south for dietary advice, for example. Soldiers were often on the move, and were often settled for long periods away from home, with friends who came from yet other areas. Such armies even at times met and caroused together in multinational forces. And there is never a sign of a need, in the Early Middle Ages, for intra-Romance interpreters. Much later, the distaste for the multilingualism of the Romance-speaking armies, forcefully expressed by the Archbishop of Toledo, Ximénez de Rada, as he prepared the Las Navas de Tolosa campaign in 1212, comes as something rather new.[4] Even those who did not travel far themselves would meet others from elsewhere in the markets, in the churches, on the roads, and be aware of other accents of Romance, of the existence of other lexical items, of other ways of putting things. So they were in practice largely able to understand many Romance usages which they did not use actively themselves. The most travelled routes and itineraries would lead to the presence in the inns of hosts and colleagues who had already met people who spoke like the traveller before. Thus it was a two-way continuum: the traveller gradually met changed versions of Romance each week, but in addition the task of communication was eased because some of the natives he met were already aware of others (such as the merchants Eulogio met in Zaragoza) who spoke as he did. We can conclude, then, that if the *"fratres"* that Eulogio was hoping to find had indeed by some chance been in Strasbourg on St Valentine's Day in 842, they would have been

---

[4] Rodrigo Ximénez de Rada's misgivings about Romance linguistic pluralism are in his: *Historia de Rebus Hispaniae sive Historia Gothica*, ed. J. FERNÁNDEZ VALVERDE (Turnhout, 1987: *Corpus Christianorum, Continuatio Medievalis* 72), VIII, 1. They are commented on pertinently by: F.J. HERNÁNDEZ, "Language and cultural identity: the Mozarabs of Toledo", *Boletín Burriel* 1 (1989), pp. 21-48, p. 40.

of necessity already to some extent acclimatized to the native speech habits even if they had only arrived that very morning.

Once we become accustomed on our travels to the accents, that is, to the phonetic peculiarities and the systematic phonological contrasts of our new local interlocutors, the main possibility of misunderstanding, or of not understanding at all, lies in the vocabulary chosen. The English comparison is helpful here too: even when a Briton is totally attuned to the accent of an American friend, if he doesn't happen to know what a "raincheck" is (a word not used in Britain), he can only guess its meaning when he hears it, and he may perhaps guess wrong. But this possibility, fortunately, can be studied empirically. The details of medieval phonetics are always to some extent a hypothetical matter for us, since the spellings of the time are never phonetic script in the modern sense (not even at Strasbourg, as has been copiously demonstrated) and we need to hypothesize and reconstruct. But the words, the units of vocabulary, are there in the texts, and it is in the event possible to work out whether the visitor from Córdoba would have known the words used in the Oaths.

The two Strasbourg Oaths sworn in Romance and presented in non-traditional spelling (it is best not to beg the question by saying 'in Old French') read as follows, here presented with the original orthography, abbreviations and word-divisions of the sole manuscript (a late tenth-century copy):[5]

1)   Pro dõ amur & pxp̄ian poblo & nrõ cõmun saluament. dist di enauant. inquant dš sauir & podir medunat. sisaluaraieo. cist meon fradre Karlo. & in ad iudha. & in cad huna cosa. sicũ om p dreit son fradra saluar dift. Ino quid il mialtre si faz&. Etabludher nul plaid nũquã prindrai qui meon uol cist meonfradre Karle in damno sit.

---

[5] The Strasbourg Oaths have been much reprinted, with varying degrees of accuracy. The edition and discussion in: W. AYRES-BENNETT, *A History of the French Language through Texts* (London, 1996), pp. 15-30, is admirable for its common sense and concision. See also: J.M.A. BEER, *Early Prose in France* (Kalamazoo, 1992), pp. 15-36. G. HOLTUS, "Rilievi su un'edizione comparatistica dei 'Giuramenti di Strasburgo'", in: *La transizione dal latino alle lingue romanze*, ed. J. HERMAN (Tübingen, 1998), pp. 195-212. None of the many investigators seem to have considered this Pan-Romance perspective, or even at any length the nature of the vocabulary. This version has been checked against the photocopy in: AYRES-BENNETT, *A History*, p. 19. Most of it can also be seen on the front cover of every issue of the journal *Romance Philology* between 1983 and 1998. The manuscript is usually dated to the tenth century, but it has been reallocated to the eleventh by: R. POSNER, *The Romance Languages* (Cambridge, 1996), pp. 177-178, and all analysts accept that the copyist might have changed details from the original. Lexical changes are the most improbable. These Oaths are often said to be the first written attestations of 'Old French', but it would be best to describe them more non-committally as being 'Romance, written in a new way'.

2)   Silodhu uigs sagramento. quesonfradrekarlo iurat conseruat. Et Karlus meossendra desuo part ñ lostanit. si ioreturnar non lintpois. neio neneuls cui eo returnar int pois. in nulla aiu^dha contra lodhu uuig nunli iuer.

These texts are both followed by the Germanic equivalent (*"Teudisca"*), thereby fulfilling in the case of these two oaths, perhaps on purpose, both the conditions stipulated by the Council of Tours canon 17 of 813, and of its recapitulation at Mainz in 847 as soon as Hrabanus Maurus was in post, to *"transferre"* sermons into *"rusticam Romanam linguam aut Thiotiscam"*.

Much of the discussion of the details of the spellings and the phonetics that might lie behind them is not immediately relevant here. For Oaths would have been read aloud fairly carefully and slowly from the pre-established text, and a visiting Romance-speaker from the Peninsula would almost certainly have been able to recognize what the words involved were, if they were words he already knew. The words chosen were not in themselves *recherché*, precisely because their intelligibility was essential, for legal reasons. But this does not mean that they were merely local usages, for neither are they specifically 'Gallo-Romance'; investigation shows that we can call them 'Pan-Romance'.

Fortunately, we are able to check whether the words in the Oaths were also used by Eulogio of Córdoba himself, with the help of the recent monumental concordance of Eulogio's works.[6] The spelling and the morphology of his now lost manuscript texts were unfortunately 'emended' by their sixteenth-century editor, Ambrosio de Morales, so we can deduce nothing with certainty about Eulogio's original spelling or inflections other than that they were less correct than what Ambrosio de Morales allowed his readers to see. But even he seems not to have changed the actual lexical items. With the help of the concordance we can see that, if we disregard the precise spellings, and look for the roots of nominals and verbs rather than tokens with exactly corresponding endings, of the sixty-three lexical items used one or more times in the Oaths, no fewer than fifty-seven of them were also used actively by Eulogio in contemporary Moslem Spain. That is, if Eulogio had been at Strasbourg, and had managed, as he probably would have, to recognize the words he heard, he would have known these words because he used them himself (the details of all the words concerned are in the appendix below). This is a remarkable discovery, and it becomes even more remarkable when we discover that the six words which appear in the Oaths but not (in some shape) in Eulogio's own works would probably have caused him no problem. They are the following:

---

[6] J. MELLADO and M.J. ALDANA, *Concordantia in Eulogium Cordubensem* (Hildesheim, 1993).

1. The proper name *"Ludher"* (*"Lotharius"*); the absence of this name in Eulogio's works is totally unsurprising, and if indeed he had been at Strasbourg he would presumably have already discovered who Lotharius was. On the other hand, the two other personal names, *"Lodhuuigs"* (as *"Hludouicus"*), and *"Karle"* (as *"Carolum"*), are in Eulogio's corpus.

2. The compound form *"cist"*, said by etymologists to be from ECCE ISTE. Both these words exist in Eulogio's corpus separately, and Old Spanish had *"aqueste"* from essentially the same combination (*aqu-* is said to be a variant of ECCE), so the compound form, once recognized, would have been in Eulogio's colloquial repertoire.

3. The word *"cad"*, written as such independently in the manuscript although joined with the following *"huna"* in most modern editions, has an exact equivalent in Old (and Modern) Spanish *"cada"*. It means "each", ultimately from Greek *"κατά"*, and is found in the oldest texts to be called Ibero-Romance by philologists, the famous eleventh-century Riojan glosses.[7] Thus *"cada"* is a neat example of a word which eventually survived in the Iberian Peninsula but not in France, yet existed in France during time of the monolingual Romance continuum (and is thought to have survived in the first syllable of French *"chacun"*).

4. Rather surprisingly, there seems to be no example of the root PRAEHENDERE (PREHENDERE, PRENDERE) in the work of Eulogio; but this too appears in the Riojan glosses, so must have been in the spoken vocabulary. (He did use *"comprehendere"*.)

5. The verb *"iurare"* seems not to be used in writing by Eulogio, though *"ius"* is there as a noun. Yet the verb occurs in the earliest non-Catalan Ibero-Romance literary work, the *Poema de Mio Cid*, so we can probably take it to have existed in the ninth-century vocabulary also.

6. The prefixed verb *"retornare"* is not in Eulogio. Nor is *"tornare"*; the prefix *re-* is ubiquitous. *"Tornare"* too is in the Riojan Glosses, though, so it seems it must have been in the peninsular vocabulary, and recognizing *"retornar"* from its component parts need not have been difficult.

The conclusion is remarkable: Eulogio, born and bred in Córdoba, and probably any other contemporary colleague of his, is likely to have used him-

---

[7] The Ibero-Romance glosses from the monasteries of San Millán (= *Em.*) and Santo Domingo de Silos (= *Sil.*) are still most conveniently available in: R. MENÉNDEZ PIDAL, *Orígenes del español* (Madrid, 1926; seventh edition, 1972), pp. 1-24. The glosses referred to here are: *"quiscataqui"*, a compound including *"cada"* (*Em.* 66 and 128); *"prendet"* (*Sil.* 124), *"presa"* (*Sil.* 162), *"prencat"* (*Sil.* 182); *"tornarat"* (*Em.* 127), *"tornaras"* (*Em.* 143), *"tornato"* (*Em.* 165), *"tornet"* (*Sil.* 42), *"tornare"* (*Sil.* 299), *"tornaren"* (*Sil.* 300).

self every single one of the sixty-three words written down in these Romance Oaths sworn in the far-distant diocese of Mainz except perhaps for the proper name *"Ludher"*. He used almost all of them himself in writing, and we can be sure that the other five were probably in his vocabulary since they were incontrovertibly part of the spoken Romance of at least a large part of the Peninsula. Once he had twigged, probably during the journey, the phonetic correspondences that held between different phonetic forms of the same words, such as the absence in the north of several final vowels which southerners were used to including, and thus usually recognized what the words he heard were, there would not have been a serious bar to comprehension on the lexical level either.

One further point worth stressing here (as Ayres-Bennett does in her excellent critical summary) is that the Oaths include no words of Germanic origin other than the personal names. These were anyway in many cases known in Spain also (not merely *Ludovicus > Luis* and *Carolus > Carlos*). This avoidance of Germanic vocabulary may help to show that our text is actually a high-register legal text that happened to be written in a new way, rather than the low-register text it has at times been assumed to be. Or it may be a coincidence. But whether it is intentional or not, the lack of such words avoided the main potential pitfall within the Gallo-Romance lexicon for a listener from the Iberian Peninsula.

The other possibility for lexico-semantic misunderstanding is serious, but likely to be unnoticed at the time, and rarely studied even now. The vagaries of fragmented semantic changes can mean that an expression exists in two places with different meanings, without speakers from the areas concerned necessarily being aware of the difference. If the visitor did not realize that the verb *"salvar"* here seems to mean "help" rather than "save" (as was the more usual meaning back home), he might have been slightly misled as to the point. If he did not realize that *"frater"* (however pronounced) here means "brother" rather than "comrade in the church", he could have misunderstood. Iberian Romance uses the word written by Eulogio as *germanum* for "blood brother", and the *fratres* in Eulogio are probably all Christian comrades. But in the Strasbourg context the intended meaning of this word would surely have been obvious. And even if he caught the form *"returnar"* he may not have caught the meaning, "turn away from", "dissuade", which is only one of the meanings of Ibero-Romance *"tornar"*. The sum total of possible misunderstandings in this category is small, however, perhaps non-existent in practice and unnoticed even if it existed.

Modern linguists lay great stress on syntax, which is often seen as the central or even the only important branch of linguistics, but in real life syntactic detail is a matter of almost no practical importance. It may be the case that the word order of the Oaths is in some cases slightly different from that of normal Iberian Romance of the time, but these questions are ones of statistics and markedness, which rarely in practice lead to actual incomprehension. Recognizing which noun phrase is the subject and which is the object of the verb is achieved on the basis of many clues, including the context, the valency of the verb, and the inflections of both verbs and nominals, as well as the common sense of the listener, and it is hard to believe that any listener at Strasbourg was misled about who was supposed to be helping who in the first Oath, or who would be dissuading who in the second.[8] And even if they were unsure about this, the local speakers were no less likely to be misled than the visitor, given that word order was probably solidifying more in these border areas of the Romance Far North than elsewhere (Spanish word order has always been freer than French). That is, that the phrase-final verbs that occur commonly in these Oaths may have sounded more odd to the Gallo-Romance listeners than to our visitor, for the southerners were even then more used to deducing subject and object status from clues other than word order. The morphological endings of nouns and verbs had for the most part developed in very similar ways over the Romance world at that time, and little is specifically Gallo-Romance here. The -ai verbal ending is also found in the Riojan Glosses, for example. The main exception to this could have been that the listener did not realize that "*jurat*" is past tense, and could have interpreted it as Ibero-Romance "*jura*" (present tense) rather than the equivalent of "*juró*" (past tense). But in context, this variance in tense does not affect the understanding of the Oath at all.

As regards the different evolution of irregular verbs, the forms of POSSE used in the Oaths might have been slightly surprising; "*podir*" (in which the letter *i* may well have represented an [e] in any case) cannot have misled a Spaniard used to the form of the infinitive pronounced [podére] then (modern "*poder*"). But "*pois*" might have needed time to be recognized as the word usually spelt POSSUM, since it had probably usually been regularized in the Peninsula by then as [pódo], [pwédo] or [pwódo] at the time (modern "*puedo*"); and "*dift*" (intermediate between DEBET and modern French "*doit*")

---

[8] For valency and subject identification, from Latin via the Oaths to Medieval and Modern French, see: L. SCHØSLER, "Permanence et variation de la valence verbale: réflexions sur la construction des verbes en latin, en ancien français, en moyen français et en français moderne", in: *Actes du XXIIe Congrès International de Linguistique et de Philologie Romanes*, 9 volumes, ed. A. ENGLEBERT e.a. (Tübingen, 2000), II, pp. 407-418.

might surprise the southern visitor used to [déße] (modern *"debe"*). But these are very common words, often used and heard, and precisely the sort of feature that the traveller would be likely to have encountered and worked out during the weeks of his northerly voyage.

In short, there was no practical barrier on any linguistic level to prevent a reasonably intelligent visitor from Córdoba understanding the Strasbourg Oaths.

It is worth briefly looking ahead, to see how long this intercomprehensibility could have lasted. Ninth-century Southern Iberian and Alsatian Romance were almost certainly more similar to each other then than they were in the thirteenth century. And it is quite instructive in this context also to look at what a thirteenth-century Iberian transliteration of the Strasbourg Oaths implies (although in this case, of course, the question would not have arisen in practice). The following, in textual order, are, wherever available, cognate Old Castilian equivalents of the words used at Strasbourg, spelt in their normal thirteenth-century Old Spanish spelling:

> Por Dios amor & por cristiano pueblo & nuestro comun salvamiento, deste dia en [adelante], en cuanto Dios saber & poder me dona, assi salvaré yo aqueste mio fraire Carlos & en ayuda & en cada una cosa, assi commo omne por derecho suo fraire salvar deve, en [esto] que el me otrossi faze; & [a] Ludher nullo pleito nunca prendré que mi voluntad aqueste mio fraire Carlos en danno [sea].

> Si Luis sacramento que suo fraire Carlos juró conserva & Carlos mio sennor de sua parte no lo se tiene, si yo tornar no le ende puedo, ni yo ni nullo que yo tornar ende puedo en ninguna ayuda contra Luis no le i [seré].

These versions might be largely intelligible to a Spaniard even now, in fact. The words here presented in square brackets might be exceptions. They are cases where the thirteenth-century Ibero-Romance vocabulary may not have included an exact cognate, but in which there would probably even so have been similarities enough to aid comprehension:

1. There seems not to have been an exact Ibero-Romance cognate of *"avant"* in the thirteenth century, but *"adelante"* is also a compound of Latin *"ante"* (probably in origin AD IN ANTE; Eulogio used *"in ante"*, in the phrase *"id quod in ante est nos"*).

2. The Gallo-Romance *"o"* is from HOC, "this". Ibero-Romance *"esto"* is from ISTUD.

3. The status of the word *"ab"* before *"Ludher"* is controversial, and may be a strange spelling of [a] rather than a form derived from APUD (and thus

preceding later "*avec*"; Eulogio used "*apud*" in his work forty-eight times and would have recognized it). But the Ibero-Romance meaning of "*a*" also makes roughly the same sense here even if the original more accurately meant "with". "*Nullo*" does not occur in Modern Spanish, but is used three times in the *Poema de Mio Cid*.

4. "*Sea*" is from SEDEAT; "*sit*" had probably disappeared from Ibero-Romance speech by this time.

5. "*er*" is the first person singular of the future of "to be" (Latin ERO), a form which does not survive into attested thirteenth-century Spanish, though the second person singular does: "*eres*" < ERIS, now with present tense meaning. Spanish "*seré*" comes from SEDERE HABEO. Maybe the original first person was still surviving in Ibero-Romance in 842, even though Eulogio never used ERO.

6. The strange phrase "*meon uol*" used towards the end of the first of the Oaths seems to be an absolute construction using "*vol*" as a deverbal noun formed off "*volo*". Ibero-Romance "*voluntad*" is thus related. But the phrase is also reminiscent of "*Deo volente*", and a Peninsular visitor might have understood it as an abbreviation instead of the phrase that Eulogio wrote as "*me uolente*" (which may in the event be what "*meon uol*" meant, "with my blessing", though Ayres-Bennett translates it as "to my knowledge").

Otherwise, the words used in the Oaths, as well as being recognizable to a contemporary "*cordobés*", would also have existed in the vocabularies of a visitor from the thirteenth-century Iberian Peninsula, and any grammatical peculiarities (such as the absence of the definite articles which had become more obligatory in those intervening centuries) would merely make it sound a bit strange rather than actually incomprehensible.

We should probably conclude that Pan-Romance comprehension lasted much later than the ninth century. Since it seems anyway that the thirteenth century poets liked using macaronic verse involving several Romance languages, and their audiences appreciated it, the monolingual state may well have been surviving even then, despite the efforts of the early thirteenth-century politicians to codify nationalistic divisions through separate orthographic identities. So it cannot come as a surprise to a cultural historian to be told that a Spaniard probably understood careful Romance spoken in France four centuries earlier. Perhaps it is time for the historical Romance linguists also to accept that the dating of Romance fragmentation should now at last be made at the end of the period concerned. That is, in the thirteenth century, accompanying the first widespread use of different methods of writing Romance in different places. And even after that time, what has been happening since is often better interpreted as a progressive stretching of the dialect continuum, with mutual comprehensibility guaranteed over progressively shorter distances, rather than the establishment of clear boundaries.

Appendix: Lexical comparison of the Strasbourg Oaths with the works of Eulogio de Córdoba

Strasbourg Oaths	*Eulogio de Córdoba* (number of appearances) [*etc.* = other inflected forms of same lexeme]
pro, p̄	pro (118), per (139)
dõ, ds̃	Deo (89), Dei (153), Deus (39), *etc.*
amur	amor, *etc.* (20)
&	et [&] (1482)
xp̃ian	Xpiano, *etc.* (52)
poblo	populo, *etc.* (24)
nrõ	nostro, *etc.* (193)
cõmun	communis, *etc.* (8)
saluament	*Not this lexeme.* salv-: salvus, salvare, salvatio, Salvator (34) -amentum: sacramentum, *etc.* (5) (see below).
d', de	de (214)
ist	iste, *etc.* (35)
di	dies, *etc.* (103)
en, in	in (943)
auant	*Not together* a, ab (308); ante (32), antea (3)
quant	quanto, *etc.* (23)
sauir	*Not as a verb* sapiens, *etc.* (10) [Sp. saber]
podir, pois	*Not* potere; *not* possum posse (16), *etc.* (89) [Sp. poder]
dunat	donat (1), *etc.* (10)
si (< SIC)	sic (72)
saluarai, saluar	salvat, *etc.* (8)
eo, io, me, mi	ego (71), me (109), mihi (50)
cist	*Not together* ecce (20); iste, *etc.* (35) [O.Sp. aqueste]
meon, meos	meum (19), meus (11)
fradre, fradra	frater (16); fratrem, *etc.* (60)

Karlo, Karle	Caroli (1), Carolum (1)
adiudha, aiu^dha	*Not as a noun*; adiuvare (9)
cad	*Not at all* [Sp. cada]
huna	una (19)
cosa	causa, *etc.* (36)
sicũ	sicut (58)
om	homo (3), *etc.* (42)
dreit	directo (2)
son, suo	suum, *etc.* (266)
dift	debet (4), *etc.* (23)
o	hoc (86)
quid, qui, que	quid (34), qui (408), quem (59)
il, l', los	ille, *etc.* (298)
altre	alter, *etc.* (13)
faz&	facit, *etc.* (58)
ab	ab (124) [*or:* apud (48)]
ludher	*Not at all*
nul, neuls, nulla	nullus, *etc.* (91)
plaid	placitum, *etc.* (7)
nũquã	numquam (10)
prindrai	*Not at all* [Sp. prender]
uol	volunt, *etc.* (34); voluntas, *etc.* (10)
damno	damna (1); damnant, *etc.* (7)
sit	sit (42)
si [< SI]	si (130)
lodhuuigs	Hludovicus, *etc.* (4)
sagramento	sacramentum, *etc.* (5)
iurat	*Not as a verb*;
	ius, *etc.* (13) [Sp. jurar]
conseruat	conservare, *etc.* (6)
sendra	Seniorem (1)
part	pars, *etc.* (37)
ñ, non, nun	non (505)
tanit	tenet, *etc.* (15) [*or:* tangentem (1)]
returnar	*Not at all* (*nor:* tornar) [O.Sp. tornar]
int	inde (28)
ne	nec (110)
contra	contra (41)
iu	ibi (29)
er	*Not* ero; eris, *etc.* (30)

Section D

Italy and Spain in the Tenth and Eleventh Centuries

Initially the Carolingian reforms only affected part of the Romance-speaking world. Northern Italy and Catalonia were within their cultural sphere; the rest of the Italian and Iberian peninsulas, as well as the islands, were not, but had come to follow the Carolingian line by the time of the Twelfth-Century Renaissance. During the tenth and eleventh centuries, therefore, it is not immediately obvious whether these areas were affected by the reforms. We need to investigate, in particular, the extent to which Late Latin is still a viable concept in the two peninsulas, or whether here too it was splitting into Medieval Latin and Romance. The chapters in this section suggest that the new metalinguistic conceptions came to Italy rather quicker than they came to the Iberian Peninsula. The problems of what name we should use to refer to the language of the time are addressed in two of these chapters (13 and 16). Three of them (14 to 16) consider in close detail the fascinating but complicated genres of Glosses and Glossaries, concentrating first on the Glossary of San Millán (964), and then on the Glosses of San Millán and Silos (*c.* 1070), which have no obvious connection with any surviving glossaries.

Chapter 13

Periodization and Language Names: Italo-Romance in 1000 A.D.

In this chapter I shall endeavour to decide whether it is possible to fix a date for the development of Romance into several different Romances such as Gallo-Romance, Ibero-Romance and Italo-Romance, so as to decide what we should call the language spoken in Italy in the year 1000. As will be seen, these problems have both a temporal and a geographical dimension; and the main question at issue is not so much that of how and when a language changes, for change is continuous, but of how and when a language changes its name.

There is no particular reason why a language should ever change its name. However much a language changes, all speakers live in a sense of continuity within our own lifetime, and we would not like to think that we are speaking a completely different language at the end of our life from the one which we were speaking at the age of ten. But some linguists of a structural persuasion (including generativists) have assumed that every time there occurs a change in a language, then the whole language changes. David Lightfoot, for example, says this explicitly.[1] But what there is in the real world are people, rather than

This chapter is a translation of: "La periodizzazione del romanzo", in: *Atti del Congresso della Società Italiana di Linguistica 2000*, ed. E. CRESTI e.a. (Firenze, Accademia della Crusca, 2002). The English version is slightly shortened. We are grateful to Sgra Maria Palmerini, on behalf of the Accademia della Crusca (Firenze), for permitting this reprint.

[1] D. LIGHTFOOT, *Principles of Diachronic Syntax* (Cambridge, 1979), pp. 14-16.

handbooks of historical grammar of the nineteenth-century tradition or generative grammars of the twentieth, and the human speakers cannot just be ignored.

According to the normal definition of humanity, human language has existed as long as the human species. This may be because all human languages derive from a single original language, in the same way as all the human race (*homo sapiens*) seems to derive from a single community on the South-East African coasts of two hundred thousand years ago. Or it may be the case that different original languages developed independently in different communities. But in any event, all the languages that are spoken on this Earth today, with the possible exception of genuinely creolized pidgins, have descended directly from languages spoken long ago. Since language change seems to be a constant process in all communities, the languages spoken today are not identical to their ancestors of ten thousand years ago, nor even of two hundred years ago, but in a perfectly intelligent sense it is meaningful to say that modern versions are the same language as the ancestor, only later.

Isolate languages in particular are unlikely to change their name. There are many isolate languages in the world. The history of the last ten thousand years has led to the majority of the languages of the modern world recognizably forming part of a wider family of languages descended from an original ancestor, but – as Johanna Nichols and Larry Trask have pointed out – this was probably not the case before then.[2] Most people lived in small and separately identifiable communities, with their own language which was not necessarily, nor even usually, obviously related to that of their neighbours. New Guinea is just such a place still, as well as some parts of the Americas where several indigenous languages survive. Basque may be the only surviving one in Europe. And since these languages have no known relatives, there is and has never been any reason for them to change their name. An isolate language may, of course, happen to be the only survivor of an otherwise more widespread family, but the speakers of the survivor, and the modern historical linguists, may never know about that.

Several communities are vague about the name of the language they speak. Some aboriginal languages in Australia, for example, have been given, as a name, by outside investigators, the word within that language for "language", since they had no more precise term. It is possible to suspect that they were once asked "what do you speak?" and replied, puzzled, "language", as their

---

[2] J. NICHOLS, *Linguistic Diversity in Space and Time* (Chicago, 1992). R.L. TRASK, "Why should a language have any relatives?", in: *Nostratic: Examining a Linguistic Macrofamily*, ed. C. RENFREW and D. NETTLE (Cambridge, 1999), pp. 157-176.

views on the ignorance of the European anthropologists were once again confirmed. For administrative reasons, however, the modern historical linguist wants each recognizably separate language to have a different name, and this applies to languages of the past as much as, or even more than, to those of the present. And so we give it a name, *a posteriori*, sometimes without too clear a definition of who the speakers were which we have in mind for this language. The specialist, that is, has no qualms about calling a language by a name different from that which the actual speakers gave it. But maybe we should be thinking twice about whether that is a good idea, particularly when referring to speech communities which we know a great deal about.

If we say that a language changes its name, we should not be taken to imply thereby that the actual language is the agent of that change. A decision to change the name of a contemporary language is one made by the speakers. Or, more commonly, by a politically powerful group of the speakers. Or even by just one of them. Maybe it is true, for example, that the decision to call the Ibero-Romance spoken in the kingdom of Castile "*castellano*" was a conscious decision taken by one man, King Alfonso X of Castile (ruler 1252-1282). In any event, such a change tends to be consciously made; and the reason for it is usually based on geography, in an attempt to distinguish the speakers of one geographical area from those of another area who speak with slightly differing habits within the same dialect continuum. Such a change of name is thus particularly liable to happen at times of nationalistic self-assertion. That was the motive of Alfonso X, for example, and it is also the motivation of those in the modern officially monolingual Spanish *autonomía*s who like to claim that they have their own language (just as the Catalans, Basques and Galicians do). They establish the concept and then pin it down with a geographical label that identifies the referent as existing in a particular area ("*aragonés*", "*andaluz*", et cetera). For such reasons many language names are in origin adjectival. They are the nominalizations of what were firstly toponymic adjectives. Sometimes we know what the noun understood to be accompanying the adjective was. For example, before the arrival of "*castellano*" as a noun we find the use of the noun phrase "*romance castellano*", in which the intention to distinguish between the Romance-speakers of one area and another simply according to where they happened to live is made explicit. This identification of political and metalinguistic independence seems to be deep-rooted in the human psyche still. For example, the recent political split between Serbia and Croatia has led to the single language Serbo-Croat being now thought of as being two languages, Serbian and Croatian.

One complication in the modern world is that these geographically based language splits can occur even though the speakers are not only still in regular contact with each other, but are in practice still mutually intelligible. Such is the case of the Galician of Southern Galicia and the Portuguese of Northern Portugal, for example. In such circumstances, a later linguist who did not know about the politics would be unable to see any reason for the metalinguistic split. In earlier times, the situation was often more straightforward than it is now. For example, we can accept that Proto-Indo-European was a single language once, even if we cannot be sure of where or when that single language was spoken, and even if that language contained considerable variation within itself (which we now know is only to be expected anyway). And we can also accept that the reason for the split of this once single language into many languages, and then into groups of languages with separate identities and names, is merely that several groups of speakers of this language separated physically and then lost touch with each other, as they spread over the vast land mass of Europe and west Asia. Having its speakers separated physically in such a way is probably the most straightforward circumstance in which one language can come to be thought of as being two, although even here there is no list of necessary and sufficient conditions which have to be fulfilled in order for us to be sure that we are talking about two languages rather than two variants of the same language. That is why it is so difficult to count the number of languages in the world. The number of languages in the world seems to increase every time a linguistic encyclopedia is published, even though we know that in real life the number of spoken languages is decreasing fast, just because the increasingly sophisticated techniques for deciding what is a separate language and what is not have led people to make more decisions in favour of conceptual separation (splitting) than amalgamation (lumping). So we now have the apparently paradoxical situation in Spain that the number of languages thought to be spoken in the Iberian Peninsula is increasing at the same time as the general range of linguistic diversity over the Peninsula as a whole is in fact decreasing.

It was suggested above that historical linguists need to distinguish between the language names given to their speech by the speakers of the time and those given to their speech by modern specialists. This problem is particularly acute in Romance historical linguistics; and, indeed, as József Herman has shown, it is as much the fault of the subject matter as of the Romanists.[3] As Marc van

---

[3] J. HERMAN, "Spoken and written Latin in the last centuries of the Roman Empire. A contribution to the linguistic history of the Western provinces", in: *Latin and the Romance Languages in the Early Middle Ages*, ed. R. WRIGHT (London, 1991; reprint, Penn State 1996),

Uytfanghe and others have demonstrated, for a long while the words "*Latinus*" and "*Romanus*" (with various inflectional suffixes) could be applied apparently as synonyms, and if to written texts, they were both applied to texts in what looks to us like Latin.[4] But the advent of a choice of writing systems in the ninth century, which we would now identify without hesitation as Latin and Romance, led to a gradual separation of the two words to apply to the two written forms less ambiguously. The name 'Romance' (variously spelt) was, for example, given to the language of some of the earliest texts written in re-formed spelling. Some of the authors of the early Romance texts of the Iberian Peninsula in the thirteenth century are quite explicit about this. Then for a couple of generations the word 'Romance' seems not yet to have acquired its geographical subdivisions, and it could be used indifferently to refer to what seem to us as being different Romance languages; and the distinguishing words, if used, are still geographical adjectives. This habit is comparable to those of the modern English-speaking world. It is, for example, quite common for people to use the noun phrase 'Australian English', but it is still thought of as a bit exaggerated to use the noun-phrase 'Australian' as if it was not a variety within English.

So we can at times note a direct clash between the language names used by the speakers of the time and the language names used by modern specialists. Speakers of the time wanted to use the word 'Romance' as a language name separate from 'Latin' only after the initial development of a separate writing system. This relative chronology is normal, in fact, as Tore Janson showed. Other scholars, including Michel Banniard, have tended to assume that the new language name must be a label for a concept that has already been developed.[5] but this certainly cannot be assumed. Maybe there were initial signs that such a conceptual development was on the way, but in literate communities the advent of a new writing system tends to be the main defining catalyst for the idea that there exist two languages that are actually different from each other. I know of no case in which two languages, generally thought to be separate languages, are written identically. Serbian and Croatian have different alpha-

---

pp. 29-43.

[4] M. VAN UYTFANGHE, "The consciousness of a linguistic dichotomy (Latin-Romance) in Carolingian Gaul: the contradictions of the sources and of their interpretation", in: WRIGHT (ed.), *Latin and the Romance Languages*, pp. 114-129.

[5] T. JANSON, "Language change and metalinguistic change: Latin to Romance and other cases", in: WRIGHT (ed.), *Latin and the Romance Languages*, pp. 19-28. M. BANNIARD, "Rhabanus Maurus and the vernacular languages", in: WRIGHT (ed.), *Latin and the Romance Languages*, pp. 164-174, pp. 164-165.

bets, for example. Those who want to claim that Valencian is not a kind of Catalan try hard to write it in a different way. For many reasons, it seems improbable to me that the speakers of the Early Romance world thought of Latin and Romance as being two separate contemporaneous languages until there was a distinction between two writing systems on which to hang the conceptual split. That split into two writing systems was caused not by the mere fact of language evolution, which is normal, but by the unusual event of the establishment of a separate archaizing pronunciation technique for reading aloud religious texts in the Carolingian Church, at the start of the ninth century.

The common language spoken in the Roman Empire, with its normal written form, was called Latin. The speakers still called it Latin for at least two and probably four centuries after the decline of the Empire itself. The language had changed, but the name did not. And there was no reason why it should. St Isidore of Seville, for example, writing in the first half of the seventh century, could see, as he looked back, four chronological stages of Latin.[6] He knew and could consciously distinguish the usage of the Classical writers from that of his day. To some extent (although much less than we might expect) he was aware of geographical differences within the great continuum. But these were all kinds of Latin to him. Latin was variable, Latin had changed, but it did not occur to him to propose to change the name of the language of his place and time. Modern Romanists feel a bit uneasy about this attitude from the greatest intellectual of the age, since the Latin of Visigothic Spain cannot have been identical to that of the first century A.D.. And of course it wasn't. But that in itself was no reason for them to have invented a new name for it. There is a modern tendency, as Herman has recently observed, to think of languages of the past as if they were actually neatly circumscribed historical grammars,[7] and if we think of Latin as an explicit grammar then seventh-century usage was clearly not the same as that of the fourth. But Isidore did not think this way. And in my view, this is important.

My own initial study of these developments was prepared twenty years ago now, and I have often been asked since if I have changed my mind on anything. The only real regret I have is that in that book I occasionally called the language of these times 'Proto-Romance'.[8] I would not do that now. I feel it is fair

    [6] R. WRIGHT, *Late Latin and Early Romance in Spain and Carolingian France* (Liverpool, 1982), pp. 82-96.

    [7] J. HERMAN, "La teoria del sostrato: un capitolo della storia linguistica – o un metodo euristico della linguistica storica?", in: *Contatti Linguistici e Storia del Latino*, ed. J. HERMAN and L. MONDIN (Tübingen, 2002).

    [8] R. WRIGHT, *Late Latin*.

enough for us to call the language of the speakers of the seventh century 'Early Romance', even though obviously they did not use the phrase themselves, precisely in order to distinguish their speech both from the Latin of Classical times and from the rigidified Medieval Latin of the Carolingian Renaissance that was to follow. But even so I am aware that this phrase 'Early Romance' derives from a modern perspective, and has been forced onto the evidence of the time in order to aid our own thought processes, rather than in order to clarify the metalinguistic world view of the speakers who spoke it.

But 'Proto-Romance' is a different case from 'Early Romance', and it was a mistake for me ever to have used the phrase 'Proto-Romance' to refer to real people. The phrase is not only an invention of the modern era, but a positively harmful one. When Robert Hall and others reconstructed the pronunciation of the Roman Empire, they did us a great favour, for they discovered the pronunciation of Latin.[9] We should be forever grateful to them for this. But they did not know that this is what they had done. They thought they had discovered the pronunciation of a different language altogether, and since their techniques were in theory modelled on those that had been used in the reconstruction of Proto-Indo-European, they called this other language 'Proto-Romance'. In practice, of course, the reconstructionists of PIE were and are pathetically grateful for every new scrap of written evidence they can find, while the more extreme practitioners of Proto-Romance reconstruction disdain all the written evidence provided by those who supposedly spoke their reconstructed language. I never took that view, and indeed the whole thrust of all my research in this field has been what I now call sociophilological. That is, we should accept that reconstruction can be helpful, but in order to understand the linguistic circumstances of the past we also have to look at the texts of that time, and in order to understand the nature of the language of the texts of the time we have to know as much as possible about the sociolinguistics and the language planning of the time. Accordingly, I would not now say that Proto-Romance was the name of an actual language ever spoken by real people, even though the phonetic discoveries of the practitioners of Proto-Romance reconstruction do, in my view and in almost everybody's view now, correspond to aspects of the pronunciation of Latin. Reconstruction does not tell us all we want to know, and in particular it cannot tell us the date when phonetic changes happened. We need careful analysis of other evidence, such as that which has been painstakingly provided over the years by Herman, to tell us that. But to a large ex-

[9] R.A. HALL Jr, *Proto-Romance Phonology* (New York, 1976).

tent we can trust its discoveries, even though necessarily partial and even skeletal on occasion.

Accordingly, to answer the question of when Latin became Romance, there are several ways of proceeding. If we consider the question from the viewpoint of the speakers, and base our chronology on their metalinguistic evidence, this change only happened after the systematic invention of an alternative method of writing, which in turn only happened after, and in my view because of, the Carolingian Renaissance ("*renovatio*"). This change was, though, essentially only orthographical, since evolved syntax, post-Roman vocabulary, and even non-Latin nominal and verbal morphology had been represented within the old spelling for many years already. This was the great discovery of the Italian scholar Francesco Sabatini, which has since been developed by other scholars such as the Portuguese António Emiliano and the American Robert Blake, and even though Professor Sabatini seems strangely reluctant now to accept the importance of his own earlier work, this line of thought is becoming increasingly accepted.[10] There are many documents from before the Reform period, for example, which – if we can ignore the spelling for the moment – seem to attest fairly closely the syntax, morphology and vocabulary of the time in the non-formulaic parts of the documents, what Sabatini himself called their "*parti libere*". This means that the important parts of the texts could be understood even by the unlettered listener if they were read aloud in the normal way, that is, with the reader recognizing the written word as an individual lexical unit and then pronouncing the normal phonetic form associated with that lexical unit in his lexical entry. Therefore, if we accept that a change of language name has been based on the consequences of an orthographic reform, we are in effect identifying a language with the spelling system used to write it.

Which is what happens in real life. Linguists complain, but the normal assumption in most literate human societies, even among the best educated groups, is that a different orthography implies a different language. That is why Anglo-Saxon is widely thought not to be a kind of English, even if the specialists prefer to think of it as 'Old English'. That is why texts written in twelfth-century France, Spain and Italy are said to be in Romance if the orthography has been reformed and in Latin if the orthography has not been reformed, despite the obvious presence of definitively Romance morphosyntactic features

---

[10] F. SABATINI, "Dalla *scripta latina rustica* alle *scriptae* romanze", *Studi Medievali* 9 (1968), pp. 320-358 (and other studies). A. EMILIANO, "Latin or Romance? Graphemic variation and scripto-linguistic change in medieval Spain", in: WRIGHT (ed.), *Latin and the Romance Languages*, pp. 233-247. R. BLAKE, "Syntactic aspects of Latinate texts of the Early Middle Ages", in: WRIGHT (ed.), *Latin and the Romance Languages*, pp. 219-232.

in many of the ostensibly Latin texts and the perhaps less obvious but certainly noticeable presence of definitively Latin morphosyntactic features in many of the ostensibly Romance texts. The spelling has always decided the language which we think a text of these times to be in, even if other levels of language are nothing like as clearly distinguishable as Romance or as Latin.

Historical linguists, however, prefer not to identify languages just on the basis of the way they are written. Most languages of the past have never been written at all, so historical linguists in University general linguistics departments are trained in reconstruction techniques but rarely in any aspect of sociophilology. So we might instead wish to identify what Herman calls the "End of the History of Latin" not on the basis of the orthography but on the basis of a reconstructable internal chronology of changes in phonetics, morphology, syntax, et cetera.[11] But in practice this is difficult, for many reasons. In the first place, a single language is not a single system, however much the elaboration of nineteenth-century Historical Grammars and of twentieth-century Generative Grammars might make it seem to be. A language is a collection of phenomena of differing types, often variable in detail, often changing from place to place, only occasionally having a substructure of some kind available to hold the units together in paradigmatic opposition. A language is not one system in real life, however much the investigator prefers to oversimplify, nor even is a language what some French scholars in desperation call a *"plurisystème"*, in order to preserve a singular word even with a plural semantics.[12] What changes during a language change is not the whole language but a linguistic feature, even though – particularly during phonetic and semantic changes – changes can have direct repercussions on neighbouring units within a substructure. But even that perspective is not clearly enough based on reality. For example, the historical grammar of the old school (or a modern book of outdated perspective, such as Frede Jansen's)[13] will tell us that (for instance) in Spanish [-t-] > [-d-]. The modern scholar who knows even a little about sociolinguistics will be aware that in real life a voiced pronunciation with [d] must have come in hesitantly – this is what the Milroys call the innovation, rather than the change – and gradually spread, leading to a time when both the old and new co-existed, with some words at the head of a lexical diffusion queue preferring the [d], others occurring often in both forms (equally intelligi-

---

[11] J. HERMAN, *Vulgar Latin* (Penn State, 2000), pp. 109-115.

[12] For instance: L. BIEDERMANN-PASQUES, "Le développement de l'écriture du très ancien français à travers les manuscrits (IXe-XIIIe s.)", in: *The Dawn of the Written Vernacular in Western Europe*, ed. M. GOYENS and W. VAN HOECKE (Leuven, 2002).

[13] F. JANSEN, *A Comparative Study of Romance* (New York, 1999).

bly), and yet others resisting the voiced form [d] for reasons that may or may not be clear.[14] Lexical diffusion theory was hardly applied at all to Romance before 1982,[15] but since then Ralph Penny has written a brilliant study in which the process is greatly clarified, using precisely the example of Spanish [t] > [d].[16] The point is that the chronology cannot normally be precise. A state of variation can last for centuries. It might at times lead to the loss of the new variant rather than the old. Or the variation may simplify in favour of the new variant in one place long before it does in another, even if it eventually does simplify out in the same way everywhere (which it needn't; this particular change began when Romance was still one speech community, but intervocalic [-t-] is still unvoiced [-t-] in many words in much of Italy, for example). So to which period should we date the change? To the time of the arrival of the new form? But at that point the older form was still the one used in the great majority of cases. To the arrival of roughly 50%-50% variation? But that offends linguists of many schools, including both the old-fashioned prescriptivist who hates to allow that variation might be a good thing, and prefers to see one variant as right and the other as wrong rather than both as acceptable, and the generativist whose perspective disallows any sociolinguistic phenomena at all. To the loss of all the old forms? But when are these lost? Not many changes affect 100% of the lexical items that might have been thought to qualify for the change, and the continuing presence of a word which for any reason escaped the change would under this definition mean that the change hadn't yet actually happened. There is, in short, usually no obvious precise date which we can pinpoint and say "that is the time of this change". We have instead to adopt a vague dating based on the statistical evidence we can attain, if any, and that is for many purposes good enough. In which case we can say that phonetic developments from what we would like to call 'Latin' to what we would prefer to call 'Romance' pronunciation were continuous, even starting from before the millennium in, for example, the case of the loss of initial [h-], and that on a statistical basis Romance pronunciation existed in the speech of all by the end of the Roman Empire.

But this shows the development of the pronunciation of Latin, not the arrival of a whole different language called 'Romance'. And other levels of language have a contrasting chronological profile.[17] The development of the

---

[14] J. MILROY and L. MILROY, "Linguistic change, social network and speaker innovation", *Journal of Linguistics* 21 (1985), pp. 339-384.

[15] WRIGHT, *Late Latin*, Chapter 1.

[16] R. PENNY, *Variation and Change in Spanish* (Cambridge, 2000).

[17] See now: A. LÓPEZ GARCÍA, *Cómo surgió el español* (Madrid, 2000), pp. 34-39.

morphology is chronologically different from the phonetics. Indeed, it is not internally consistent within itself either. The loss of the neuter gender seems to have come later than the loss of the ablative case, for example, in so far as we can date either development as if it were an 'event'.[18] Nominal morphology changed earlier and quicker than verbal morphology. Much of the verbal morphology of Latin, indeed, has hardly changed at all even now, neither as regards the system or its exponents. It is not feasible, except as a statistical abstraction, to point to an epoch and say that "this is when Latin morphology became Romance morphology". And yet Romance historical linguists often do just that, pointing to the seventh century, and since morphosyntax is often thought to be the most important branch of linguistics, we are often given this as a date for the change of Latin to Romance.

Syntax is even more unhelpful in this dilemma. Many of the syntactic features of Romance which are sometimes indicated as being diagnostics for the identification of Romance syntax and language rather than Latin syntax and language did, in fact, exist in Latin all along, even if only as occasional and unfavoured variants rarely occurring in texts. Plautus, for example, attests features which Romanists want to call late, despite the ostensibly embarrassing fact (even though Romanists don't seem to be embarrassed by it) that Plautus wrote in pre-Classical times. The use of grammatically reflexive "*se*" with inanimate subject and passive meaning, for example, is attested in Plautus, and indeed turns up, unremarked, in some of the Grammarians' own discursive text, without being commented on explicitly. Even the use of "*se*" as a non-agentive passive with an animate human subject, which is often said to be a Romance distinctive feature, and sometimes even said to be a recent development, is there in the *Cena Trimalchionis* of the first Century A.D.. The use of "*quod*" and a finite verb after a verb of saying or perceiving, rather than an accusative and infinitive, is also found in Plautus as an available alternative, probably marked but certainly not peculiar. Conversely, accusatives and infinitives are often used now, particularly after verbs of perception (for example Spanish "*la vi reír*", "I saw her laugh"), even though often with a different unmarked word order from Latin ("*vi reír a la tía*", for example, with the infinitive before its subject). Syntactic change is always slow. It is also incorrect, as Harm Pinkster has pointed out, to say – as Romanists often do – that Latin had SOV word order and Romance has SVO.[19] Other word orders often turn up in

---

[18] See: HERMAN, *Vulgar Latin*, pp. 49-68.

[19] For instance: H. PINKSTER, "Evidence for SVO in Latin?", in: WRIGHT (ed.), *Latin and the Romance Languages*, pp. 69-82.

Latin, and in Spanish, at least, all possible word orders are now acceptable (in varying pragmatic circumstances). In fact, the statistically most usual word order of these three constituents in the *Peregrinatio Aetheriae* is similar to that attested in Ibero-Romance texts of the thirteenth century. In short, the new did not displace the old. The state of co-existence of both the supposedly old and the supposedly new during all the last two thousand years is such that once again statistics might be the only mechanism for deciding when the once un-marked became marked and the once marked became unmarked (which is what tends to happen during a change). But statistics have no more ontological valid-ity than the data they summarize, and we surely cannot say when Latin 'became' Romance on the basis of even the syntactic phenomena that have been used as diagnostics to identify one rather than the other.

Vocabulary is hardly a diagnostic tool at all. New words come into a lan-guage all the time. Words change their meaning, but often both the old mean-ing and the new are around at once (particularly in the Early Middle Ages). Existing suffixes and free morphemes combine intelligibly all the time without it being clear when or if their combination is lexicalized. Even loanwords are not sufficiently diagnostic. It is generally agreed that the huge presence of French loanwords in fifteenth-century English has not prevented that language from being identifiable as English.

There is in short no sensible way, based on purely linguistic data, of dating the start of 'Romance' rather than Latin. To put this in other words, linguistic features are what change, rather than languages, and even then it is rarely obvi-ous how to date a change even if we sometimes can roughly date the innovation that began it. The only time a whole language is thought to change, and thus to deserve to change name, is when the way it is written is changed. A spelling reform, in fact. Which is where we came in. It is not an oversimplification. The native speaker has a point in his instincts. We can cut the Gordian knot and say that the language indeed changes from being a kind of Latin to being a kind of Romance when (and only when) the new written system is introduced. Latin writing continued for centuries after the introduction of Romance writing as an alternative, of course, but the presence of the new written Romance, known to be a closer counterpart to speech, meant that in due course (during the Twelfth-Century Renaissance) Latin became a foreign language for all, even for the Romance speakers.

For the rest of this chapter the discussion will concentrate on Italy. The sociocultural situation in ninth-century Italy was not geographically consistent, of course, any more than Italo-Romance is a linguistically homogeneous concept. Indeed, as Martin Maiden makes clear, "from the point of view of linguistic structure, it is notoriously the case that the so-called Italo-Romance dialects have no single feature which distinguishes all of them from all other Romance dialects".[20] The word 'Italo-Romance' is not being used here with any precision; essentially, it has merely geographical reference.

In the early ninth century, the Northern areas of Italy were to some extent under Carolingian control and influence, but it is not immediately clear how quickly and how seriously the new reformed Latin pronunciation and the new reformed Romance writing that it eventually necessitated were adopted in different Italian cultural centres. There is little such evidence before the tenth century, in the event. Since the peninsula was so politically and culturally diverse, it is likely that some places will have taken to the reformed modes more quickly than others. Rome, and in particular the Papal court, might have been expected to have had a more archaizing kind of Latinity even before the reforms, but the above study (chapter 7) of the meeting of Boniface and Pope Gregory II in 722, as well of the two recensions of the biography of the same Pope in the *Liber Pontificalis*, strongly suggests that there was no pre-Carolingian linguistic reform movement in the Papal court. In the event this is hardly surprising, since until the late eighth century most of the Popes, and their cultural milieu, had been Greek rather than Latin. At the end of the eighth century, the extent to which the mutual admiration between Pope and Emperor, Hadrian and Charles, led to a movement for linguistic renovation at the Papal court has not yet been studied with any clarity. New studies may make this clearer than it is now.

The earliest explicit reference to a conscious difference between Latin and Romance in the Italian peninsula is usually said in the manuals to come in the *Gesta Berengarii*,[21] a poem from the years 915-923 concerning the coronation of King Berengarius at Rome in 915. Here the Senate is said to have spoken "*patrio ore*", and the rest of the community "*nativa voce*", and these two noun phrases are usually taken to mean Latin and Romance respectively. I know of no earlier explicit testimony to this effect. Given that the Papacy and the monks of Monte Cassino were the cultural leaders in the South, it seems reasonable to suppose that both were aware of, and perhaps involved in, the decision to write some legal depositions in reformed orthography. The famous *Placiti Capuani* (or *Cassinesi*, or *Campani*) of 960-963 are four legal documents which contain

---

[20] M. MAIDEN, *A Linguistic History of Italian* (London, 1995), p. 4.
[21] For instance: D. NORBERG, *Manuel pratique de latin médiéval* (Paris, 1968), p. 34.

presumably experimental Romance versions of formulaic depositions which appear in other documents in traditional written form, both earlier (by the same judge) and later.[22] These are not presented in an exact and strict phonetic script. We can deduce that the purpose of the new forms was originally practical, perhaps to inspire a reading aloud that would sound like intelligible Romance rather than formal medieval Latin, rather than to aid the modern dialectologist, and that the brief transcriptions were later incorporated into the longer Latin text, rather as the Strasbourg Oaths were incorporated neat into Nithard's History. As usual in every area, the scribes who wrote the earliest Romance texts were already well practised in writing Latin documents, and what are sometimes called 'Latinisms' in these Romance sentences are more appropriately diagnosed as being the influence of what was the same scribe's normal practice when producing texts in traditional form.

Even though this fashion for writing short documentation in new Romance form apparently disappeared as quickly as it had arrived, the concept of Romance as a separate language from Latin must have been reinforced strongly in the literate circles that decided to use it at all. That is, the Church was becoming bilingual. In Alfredo Schiaffini's words, "*è chiaro che la Chiesa diviene bilingue, e rappresenta a un tempo il latino colto e la lingua popolare romanza*".[23] There is a tenth-century penitential, also from Monte Cassino,[24] which contains the phrase "*fiat confessio peccatorum rusticis verbis*". This suggests that the distinction was generally understood there, at least. This phrase is also of interest for two further reasons. Firstly because it shows that the Carolingian usage of "*rusticus*" to mean "Romance" was in vogue at Monte Cassino at that time, and also because this advice is the opposite of what Banniard suggests that Alcuin had originally wanted at the time of the Carolingian reforms (that confessions should be made in reformed Latin pronunciation).[25] So when we read the elegiac epitaph of Pope Gregory V, datable to the year 999, which mentions his ability not only to speak but also to preach in "*eloquio triplici*" (the complete elegiac couplet is: "*usus francisca, vulgari et voce latina / instituit populos eloquio triplici*"), we can accept that this phrase probably refers to

[22] See: G. SANGA and S. BAGGIO, "Il volgare nei *Placiti Cassinesi*: vecchie questioni e nuove acquisizioni", *Rivista Italiana di Dialettologia* 18 (1994), pp. 7-30.

[23] A. SCHIAFFINI, "Problemi del passaggio dal latino all'italiano (evoluzione, disgregazione, ricostruzione)", in: *Studi in onore di Angelo Monteverdi*, ed. G. GERARDI MARCUZZO, II (Modena, 1959), pp. 691-715, p. 707.

[24] B. MIGLIORINI, *Storia della lingua italiana* (Firenze, 1960), p. 61.

[25] M. BANNIARD, *Viva Voce: communication écrite et communication orale du IVe siècle au IXe siècle en Occident latin* (Paris, 1992), ch. 7.

what we might call Gallo-Romance, Italo-Romance and Medieval Latin. Although Francesco Novati suggested that *"francisca"* could here be being used to refer to Germanic, I agree with Giacomo Devoto and Dag Norberg's view that it refers to Gallo-Romance.[26]

Rome was probably neither ahead of nor behind the game. Even though most of the evidence we have seems to come from the south, Norberg suggests plausibly that the distinction between Latin and Romance was normally made in the northern Italo-Romance area in the tenth century also.[27] The first explicit evidence there has been said, since Novati, to be the comment by Gonzone di Novara, in his *Epistola ad Augienses* of 965, that:

> falso putavit Sancti Galli monachus me remotum a scientia grammaticae artis, licet aliquando retarder usu nostre vulgaris lingue, que Latinitati vicina est.[28]

Latinity is here specifically equated to knowledge of the *Ars grammatica*, which was the basic language text of the Carolingian curriculum, and was in the process of turning Latin into a foreign language even for the Romance-speakers. The date of 965 here is interesting, since it closely follows the date of the *Placiti*. The unusual written form of the latter must have involved some discussion among scribes and linguists, and a grammarian such as Gonzone could well have heard of them and even been involved. The conceptual distinction may not yet have arrived over all the Italo-Romance area by the year 1000, however. Eduardo Blasco Ferrer, for example, implies that it arrived in Sardinia in the eleventh century.[29]

Accordingly, if we ask whether the speakers thought that 'Romance' existed yet in Italy in the year 1000, the answer seems to be generally in the affirmative, although perhaps the situation would have varied from place to place. In those parts of Italy in which a reformed writing system was at least sometimes used, we can probably be sure that a distinction was made between Latin and Romance. Some scholars and others with international contacts seem also to have distinguished further, between Italian and French Romance. In other

---

[26] F. NOVATI, *Storia letteraria d'Italia: le origini* (Milano, 1926), p. 32. G. DEVOTO, *Il linguaggio d'Italia* (Milan, 1974), § 144. NORBERG, *Manuel pratique*, p. 34.

[27] NORBERG, *Manuel pratique*, pp. 33-37.

[28] NOVATI, *Storia*, p. 32. Also now: A. ZAMBONI, *Alle origini dell'italiano* (Rome, 2000), pp. 216-218.

[29] E. BLASCO FERRER, "Les plus anciens monuments de la langue sarde. Histoire, genèse, description typologique et linguistique", in: *Le passage a l'écrit des langues romanes*, ed. M. SELIG e.a. (Tübingen, 1993), pp. 109-148.

places, if in the year 1000 we still just have occasional glimpses of speech peeping through the usual disguise of the old-fashioned writing system, such as Sabatini found from four centuries earlier, then we can suspect that most people in that area may not yet have made any clear distinction, and we can still refer to their language as being 'Late Latin'. Even so, as Norberg pointed out, Romance features in Latin texts of that time written in Italy are often identifiably Italo-Romance, rather than Pan-Romance, so perhaps modern Romanists would be justified in calling their vernacular 'Italo-Romance' at that point, rather than still thinking of it as 'Early Romance'. In the same way, the Romance of the Iberian Peninsula in the year 1000 can legitimately be called 'Ibero-Romance' by the modern analyst, even though they never used the phrase themselves.

The Twelfth-century Renaissance is what brings in the definitive distinction of Latin and Romance, and then also the idea of different Romance languages. Romance was eventually going to be written in different places in different ways, and the thirteenth century was eventually going to bring several different such systems, and thus several different Romance languages in the general view. But in the twelfth century, it looks, from various kinds of evidence, that there may have been a general conceptual distinction sometimes made between French, Italian and Iberian Romance, but probably no more. Charles Burnett's evidence, from the scholars of the age who came from different areas of Europe and met in recently reconquered Toledo, seems to suggest that.[30] It is also the basis for the famous tripartite distinction that Dante was to make a century later. Unlike the distinction between Latin and Romance, which had been made rather unusually on a speech-community-wide orthographical and stylistic basis, these later conceptual splits were geographical in the ordinary way, as explained above. The famous "*descort*" of Raimbaut de Vaqueiras was written in 1199 in five different writing systems, which seem now to be identifiable as French, Italo-Romance, Provenzal, Gascon and Ibero-Romance.[31] Perhaps we have here the basis for the eventual identification of Provençal and Gascon as separate languages. So it seems reasonable to suggest that the concept of Italo-Romance existed at least in some places two hundred years earlier, in the year 1000. But even though Italo-Romance would have

---

[30] C. BURNETT, "The strategy of revision in the Arabic-Latin translations from Toledo: The case of Abu Ma'shar's *On the Great Conjunctions*", in: *Translators at Work: Their Methods and Manuscripts*, ed. J. HAMESSE (Louvain, 2002), pp. 1-62.

[31] See: M. DE RIQUER, *Los trovadores: historias literaria y textos*, 3 volumes (Barcelona, 1975), II, pp. 840-842.

varied noticeably from place to place, we might not be conceptually justified in subdividing further.

Like Martin Maiden, I would not wish to use the phrase 'Old Italian' to refer to the Italo-Romance of a thousand years ago, for several reasons. One is that the use of this phrase seems to imply that they could see into the future, and were all on a road that led to the modern situation. Another is that the phrase indicates a greater homogeneity than is likely, given the probably huge variability of the language of the time. Anthony Lodge is similarly reluctant to use the phrase 'Old French'.[32] A third is that the earliest Romance written forms were new and even revolutionary, rather than 'old'. The word 'Italo-Romance' looks back into the past, but for that very reason it is more justifiable in this context than the phrase 'Old Italian', which looks forward to the future, since the speakers knew to some extent what had happened in the past but had no idea what was going to happen in the future. The later development of Italo-Romance into a state that privileged the dialectal habits of Tuscany cannot have been foreseen in the tenth century, any more than the similar later development of Ibero-Romance into a state that privileged the dialectal habits of Castilian could have been foreseen.[33]

Linguists, looking back, like to periodize. Michel Banniard, who has done so much good to our discipline by showing us how not to overdistinguish diastratically in the Earliest Middle Ages, himself distinguishes diachronically to an amazing extent. He gives us, for example, three successive separate stages of Late Spoken Latin: "*latin parlé tardif 1*", "*latin parlé tardif 2*" and "*protoroman*", in a section rather charmingly labelled "*Prototype de la Métamorphose*".[34] This does little harm provided we realize that it is an administrative fantasy; these are not successive periods of stability which suddenly change in revolutionary mode from one to another. Not even the millennium bug could have changed 'twentieth-century Italian' overnight into a different language to be called 'twenty-first century Italian'. Rolf Eberenz produced an interesting variant on this theme by proposing to establish a 'Middle Spanish' period when inter-related changes occurred.[35] This is the opposite of the usual procedure, as Eberenz is offering us an identifiable period characterized by related changes, rather than one characterized by stability between periods of change. This was an intelligent and interesting suggestion, but it might have

---

[32] R.A. LODGE, *French: from Dialect to Standard* (London, 1993).

[33] R. WRIGHT, *Early Ibero-Romance* (Newark, 1995), Chapter 14.

[34] M. BANNIARD, *Du Latin aux langues romanes* (Paris, 1997), pp. 30-36.

[35] R. EBERENZ, "*Castellano antiguo y español moderno*: reflexiones sobre la periodización en la historia de la lengua", *Revista de Filología Española* 71 (1991), pp. 80-106.

been better if he had not made it, since periodization of this type has now become a fashionable topic for discussion in Ibero-Romance studies just at the
same time as its usefulness is being rightly questioned by those who study the
language often known as 'Middle French'.[36]

Languages usually change name for one of two reasons. Either as a result
of orthographical reform (the Latin-Romance pattern), or on the basis of geographical separation of speakers. Such separation need not have that effect –
separation has not meant that every French-speaking area outside Europe thinks
it does not speak French, for example – and the sea can as often unite as separate emigrants from their original home.[37] Even if separation does have that
effect, it need not be literal and physical; the conceptual split can be the result
of political language planning. The separation of Ibero-Romance, Gallo-Romance, Italo-Romance, and the subdivisions that have come since, owe much
to language planning of the twelfth and thirteenth centuries, and most particularly to the perceived need to write Romance in different ways in different
places (thereby combining with the orthographic principle of identification). In
the year 1000 such planning was not yet in evidence.

There are two types of language naming; that carried out by the actual
speakers, which we need to respect and take seriously, while realizing that it
does not usually depend on the expert analysis of linguistic data; and that made
by modern analysts, which can of course be illuminating – I shall continue to
speak of Early Romance, for example – but which can also introduce needless
complications which we are better off without – such as the names of 'Proto-
Romance' and also, in my view, 'Vulgar Latin', despite my admiration for
József Herman.[38] If it seems after these considerations that not much light has
been shed on what to call the Romance spoken in Italy in the year 1000, then
the argument has been understood. Too much metalinguistic clarity would
misrepresent an essentially variable real life phenomenon.

---

[36] W. AYRES-BENNETT, *A History of the French Language through Texts* (London, 1996).
[37] See several studies in: H. NIELSEN and L. SCHLØSLER (ed.), *The Origins and Development of Emigrant Languages* (Odense, 1996).
[38] HERMAN, *Vulgar Latin*.

Chapter 14

The Glossaries of Tenth-Century Spain: (1) The 1997 edition of *Códice emilianense* 46

This chapter is a review of: Claudio GARCÍA TURZA and Javier GARCÍA TURZA, *Fuentes Españolas Medievales: el códice emilianense 46 de la Real Academia de la Historia, primer diccionario enciclopédico de la Península Ibérica; edición y estudio* (Madrid and Logroño, 1997).

San Millán manuscript *Emilianense* 46, now in the Real Academia de la Historia in Madrid, is for several reasons a jewel of Early Medieval culture. The care and professionalism manifested in its composition attest to the quality of the intellectual life of its time and place, reinforcing the understandable pride that the people of La Rioja feel for their ancient monastery (which has now been designated a World Heritage site). The surprising exactness of its internal dating gives historians a chronological certainty which is rare in studies of tenth-century texts; the manuscript was finished in June of the year 1002 of the Spanish era (that is, 964 A.D.). This pride and confidence need be in no way lessened by the fact that it is a copy made at San Millán of a compilation that had already been elaborated north of the Pyrenees. Specialists in the language of the time know that we should have examined the glossary, which is such a startling sign of the cultural life of those who wrote and used

This chapter is a translation of: Review article: C. GARCÍA TURZA and J. GARCÍA TURZA, *Fuentes españolas medievales: el códice emilianense 46 de la Real Academia de la Historia, primer diccionario enciclopédico de la Península Ibérica: edición y estudio, Lingüística* 10 (1998), pp. 165-176. We are grateful to Professor Humberto López Morales, on behalf of *Lingüística*, for permitting this reprint.

it. The main excuse that we have had for not having done so has hitherto been the lack of a usable edition, although three Glossaries from Santo Domingo de Silos which are now in Paris are closely related to *Em.* 46, and these were published some time ago by Goetz and García de Diego.[1] The excuse of inaccessibility can no longer be made, now that we have this attractive edition prepared by the García Turza brothers.

Manuscripts of this type are of great interest to experts in several fields, both within Spain and elsewhere, so the most important requirement for such an edition is that the published text should resemble the original as closely as possible (given the technology available), with a minimum of intervention from the editors. To some extent, the García Turza brothers have managed to do that in this edition. The manuscript is in Visigothic script. Those of us with a particular interest in spelling can trust this edition on the whole, for with the apparently deliberate exception of the use of capitals, to be considered in detail below, the individual letters are reproduced in this edition professionally and carefully. Where the manuscript has an abbreviation the editors have resolved it sensibly, and indicated the presence of the resolution by italicizing the missing letters. The editors have not thereby indicated what the abbreviation in the manuscript actually is, but a check of the manuscript shows that it agrees almost always with the list of abbreviations presented on pages 135-154 of the Introduction. All the letters *j* of the manuscript are accurately printed as *j*, the capitals *I* as *Í* (with a probably unnecessary accent), the *e* caudatae as *ẹ*, and the superscript ᵛ letters of the manuscript are printed as *v*, but that is not too misleading since the *v* in the edition in fact always represents the superscript letter and never the normal-sized *v*. This unusual exactness is welcome and impressive, and is perhaps due to the fact that the two editors are respectively a linguist and a palaeographer rather than historians.

As regards the transcriptions of the individual words, I have carefully checked the edition with the manuscript between folios 2v and 8v (inclusive), and found only a few errors at the level of the letters. These are: in the edition, entry 2v41 lacks its final word ("*sem*", which is however printed when the same gloss is repeated later, 5r63). In 2v42 the published form "*excelsiis*" should probably be "*excelsus*", although this might be disputed. In 3v8 the edition's "*arma, gladia*" should be the one word, probably "*armagladi*". In 4v55, "*adibet*" should be "*adibe*". In 6r55, "*ocassu*" should be "*occasu*". And in 6v5,

[1] E. GARCÍA DE DIEGO, *Glosarios latinos del monasterio de Silos* (Murcia, 1933). G. GOETZ, *Corpus Glossariorum Latinorum*, 6 volumes (Leipzig, 1888-1923; reprint, Amsterdam, 1965), V, pp. 104-158.

"*fauoris*" should be "*faboris*". On the other hand, it is encouraging to see that several erroneous spellings have been presented in the edition as they are in the manuscript: including "*ubrs*" (3r21), "*accipitrem*" (3v3), "*aeuuum*" (6r41), "*Amalehc*" (8v66), et cetera. This resistance to the temptation to 'emend' is admirable. Many less scrupulous editors would have changed these.

On the level of the punctuation, however, it is less easy to be impressed. The editors have introduced several changes, apparently on purpose, which might well mislead the reader. This volume is intended to be of permanent value, and so it will be for many purposes, but editors cannot always foresee the reasons that future scholars may have for using their edition. One day in the twenty-second century a doctoral student may be going to prepare a valuable thesis on the basis of details that seem of little significance to us now. For example, in the Glossary it is always possible to distinguish clearly between the lemma and the gloss. The hand and the script appear to be the same in both halves of the entry, but there is always a ./ mark between the lemma and the gloss. The editors do not reproduce that mark. They print the lemma in **bold** script (which is a good idea), and the gloss in normal type after it. But several times, and it is not always clear why, the editors have taken no notice of the ./ mark in the manuscript and have moved the border between lemma and gloss to somewhere else in the entry. In this way they move one or more words from the gloss into the lemma, or from the lemma into the gloss. Sometimes this is not too misleading, because they tell us that this is what they have done, and the reader can just move the frontier between lemma and gloss back to its actual position. The first time that this happens is the following (2v21). The manuscript gives us "*aberi et nudius tertjus./ totū tempˢ preteritum. significat*", and the edition gives us instead: "*aberi et nudius tertjus¹ totum tempus preteritum significat*". The ¹ here draws our attention to the note at the foot of the page (p. 227), which reads:

¹   En muchas ocasiones el escribano no separa correctamente la entrada de la explicación. Cuando esto ocurre, se indica el lugar en donde se produce la pausa (*en adelante*, Pausa tras). *Pausa tras* terjius (*sic*, with a misprint; it should be "*tertjus*").

Often the scribe separates the entry from its explanation incorrectly. When this happens, we have indicated the place where the pause is (with the words *pause after*). There is a pause after *tertjus*.

But who are we, scholars of over a thousand years later, to decide whether or not the scribe of the 960s separated them 'correctly'? I would never dare to come to such a conclusion, at least. It seems in fact that these editors often make the decision to criticize the scribe in this way on the basis of what they read in MS Paris *BN* 1296, one of the Silos glossaries edited by García de Diego. Yet it is often possible to conclude that the San Millán scribe distinguished lemma from gloss rather better than the scribe of *BN* 1296 did.

But even if this is not the case, there is no justification for editorial emendations of this sort. For an example, we can consider entry 7r14: in the manuscript we have a gloss written on two different lines, which probably represent two different glosses of the same lemma:

> agita te./ fugam fuge.
> consilium habete.

But in the edition, we read:

> **agitate**[4] **fugam** fuge consilium habete ([4]Pausa tras agitate)

And the potentially interesting use of "*fugam fuge*" has been made to disappear by editorial fiat. And changes of this kind are sometimes not even indicated in a footnote. For example, in the manuscript we can see (5v9 and 5v10):

> Aegreuix./ poene non.
> Aegre uix./ moleste.

And in the edition:

> **aegre** uix,[22] poene, non ([22]Pausa tras uix)
> **aegre** uix, moleste   [that is, without a note].

We can see in this last example the three details in which this edition, quite deliberately, misrepresents the text. That is, the punctuation, the word-separation, and the use of capitals. The manuscript has its own system of punctuation; sometimes there is a full stop between the words in the gloss, and sometimes there is not. The same is true of the edition, although the editors have preferred commas to stops. Yet the presence of the commas in the edition has no connection whatsoever with the stops in the manuscript. It sounds absurd, but the editors have punctuated this text according to modern practice. That is, they seem to have discarded *a priori* the possibility that these signs have a point. Many times the edition omits them when they are there, or includes them where they are not. And even if we think this is of no importance now, the doctoral student of the future who investigates the punctuation of the time will be seriously misled. Sometimes these punctuation mistakes can distort the sense: for example (5v14), the published "***Aegyptus*** *tribulatjo, tenebre*" has a comma where there is nothing at all in the manuscript. Entry 4v27 in the manuscript reads: "*adfiliatjo./ adobtjo pene. nature emitatjo.*" but has been edited as: "***adfiliatjo*** *adobtjo, pene nature emitatjo*".

The edition's word separations can also be misleading. For example, both the lemma and the gloss of 3v54, which are presented in the edition as: "*ac* ***culmini*** *ab alto, a summo*", misrepresent the actual text, which is "*Acculmini./ abalto asummo.*". Clearly, at the start this is not a case of "*ac*", nor even of "*hac*", but of "*a*". Another similar example, which could mislead researchers into morphology as well as syntax, is 5r23, where the manuscript's "*aduliscen-dũ./ addefendendum.*" has been ignored, and the "*ad*" has been presented instead as a separate word rather than a prefix, in: "*ad* ***uliscendum*** *ad defendendum*". It could also be of great interest to these same experts to know that the lemma "*altamente*", which occurs twice (8r60 and 8r63), is written in the manuscript as a single word. But we would never suspect that from this edition, which separates the component morphemes with a space as if we could be sure that there were two free words here. In the cases mentioned the editors' emendations are misguided. But even if they were obviously right, such emendations stultify the point of having an edition at all. This is true of all texts, of course, but exactness is probably more necessary in the edition of a glossary than of any other kind of text, since it will be used by subsequent researchers for its slightest details.

For those who are specifically investigating glossaries, however, more than for the Romanists and Latinists, the problems caused by deliberate and constant editorial changes are likely to be most acute in the case of capital and lower-case letters. This is a highly complicated matter, but it is worth clarifying it here in detail as far as possible. The scribe of this manuscript distinguished fairly clearly between capital and minuscule letters (which was not always the case at this time). The editors also distinguish clearly, but there is almost no correspondence between the capital letters found in the text and those found in the edition (with the already mentioned exception of printing *I* as *Í*). The editors have used capitals in this edition only where a modern Spaniard would use them, and removed them where a modern Spaniard would not. For example, in the edition we see (3r21): "***Acerra*** *ubrs Campanię*", where the manuscript has: "*Acerra./ ubrs cãpanie.*". There is a striking contrast between the admirable exactitude shown in reproducing the form "*ubrs*" correctly, the regrettable and deliberate misrepresentation of the *c*, and the accidental error of *ę* rather than *e* (which is not a common mistake here). But this cavalier attitude towards capital letters leads us to another problem with this edition. The fact that editors tell us so little about the recent copious research that has been undertaken into the Glossary genre.

We can see fairly clearly from the manuscript that by using variable capitalization in the way he does the scribe is representing the consistent and methodical way that the list was compiled in the first place. It is not merely that he used the equivalent of a huge card index in which there was a card for every word, such as St Isidore seems to have used three centuries before (as Díaz y Díaz established).[2] What the scribe had done (or more probably, the previous organizer of his source text) was to compile this huge list from several sources of different kinds, fitting whole sections from each source into the appropriate alphabetical part of the Glossary, and organizing this procedure with reference to the first two or three letters of the lemmata (rarely more than three). Even if our San Millán scribe was merely copying a list from further north neat, without adding anything of his own, he certainly noticed this *modus operandi* in his source text. Modern specialists in the glossaries, unlike Lindsay,[3] realize that it was normal as time went on for glossaries to keep growing in size, right from the origins of the genre in (as it seems) the fourth Century. This means that in the later glossaries – and manuscript *Em.* 46 is a late representative of this genre, in fact, even though it does seem to be the earliest one that has survived directly from the Iberian Peninsula – there are sections from many sources mixed in together. These sources vary chronologically, from lists first drawn up in the distant past which were used to teach apprentice lawyers in pre-Christian contexts, or which were taken from individual glosses added to the margins of Classical texts, through other lists of glosses which had themselves previously been taken from manuscripts of Biblical and Patristic works, or even Grammars, et cetera, up to some entries which had been added comparatively recently. But the sources in question were not always organized with identical alphabetical depth. This means that it is often possible to separate out from a Glossary short sections which have come whole from a previous source, according to the method of alphabetization chosen. These subsections were placed for convenience in the same part of the 'card index' before they became

---

[2] M.C. Díaz y Díaz, "Introducción general", in: *San Isidoro de Sevilla: Etimologías*, ed. J. Oroz Reta, 2 volumes (Madrid, 1982), pp. 1-257.

[3] W.M. Lindsay, *Glossaria Latina* (Paris, 1926-1931; reprint, Hildesheim, 1965).

incorporated as a unit inside the whole final integrated text. We know this above all because of the detailed work of the indefatigable Carlotta Dionisotti.[4]

And we can conclude from the capital letters that are placed in the lemmata of manuscript *Em.* 46, although not from those of the edition, that the scribe in general intended his glossary to be of the ABC type (or even sometimes ABCD). That is, in general the lemmata are organized according to the first three, or sometimes the first four, letters of the initial word. A reader of the actual manuscript can see this quite clearly, because many of the sections that have come from one particular part of the card index are headed by a much larger initial capital letter. This means that readers who are looking for one lemma in particular can find it far more easily in the manuscript than in the edition.

As regards the letter A, this is surprisingly obvious. There is a huge capital A at the very start of the glossary (1v1), which is reproduced photographically twice in the edition, further enlarged in size. The editors have realized, and allow us to realize also, what that is for. Then it seems that the scribe at San Millán had at his disposal seven (or even more, depending on how we classify them) different ways of writing a capital A at the start of a lemma. There are two columns on each page, both in the manuscript and in the edition. And in general each column has the same kind of capital A in all the words in that column. But when we open out each pair of pages we can usually see four different kinds of A corresponding to the four visible columns. That is, for example, there is one kind of A in 2v col. 1, another in 2v col. 2, another in 3r col. 1, and yet another in 3r col. 2. But from time to time in the manuscript we can also see that there is the occasional isolated word in which the A is written differently and larger, often accompanied by an angular mark at the left of the column. And these words correspond in general to the start of a separate alphabetical section (AB or ABC). Thus, for example, from the presence of the extra large A, and the ⌐ that we can see to its left, which begins the lemma of: "*Achate./ genuslapidis.*" (2v48), the user of the Glossary can tell that here is where the section begins of words starting in *Ac-*. The A of "*Aedes*" (5r46) is so large that it also fills the line above it, which would have been totally empty without it (which shows that the large size is completely intentional and foreseen). And that is the start of the section containing words in *Ae-*. In the same way, the large A of "*Aether*" indicates the start of the section including words that begin *Aet-* (6r40). The large A of "*Affauilis*" indicates the start of the sec-

---

[4] A.C. DIONISOTTI, "On the nature and transmission of Latin glossaries", in: *Les manuscrits des lexiques et glossaires de l'antiquité tardive à la fin du Moyen Age*, ed. J. HAMESSE (Louvain-la-Neuve, 1996), pp. 205-252.

tion of words in *Aff-* (6v5). The *A* which indicates the start of the section including words beginning with *As-* (14r26) is so big that it fills the first part of
seven lines. But none of these, so important for the contemporary practical user
of the glossary, so relevant to the modern glossary scholar, can be seen in the
edition. The editors took the decision to correct all the letters according to the
anachronistic prejudices of our times. That is, they just use capitals for proper
names, which the manuscript does not.

The edition as a whole contains 711 pages, with 22 colour plates after the
initial page of each alphabetical section (which have already been reproduced
earlier in black and white). These colour reproductions do not include that of
the letter *O*, already reproduced in black and white on p. 443, because this,
although the editors do not tell us so, is taken not from *Em.* 46 but from folio
136r of the Paris manuscript *BN* 1296 (because some folios are missing here
from *Em.* 46). It would have been a good idea to tell us this.

It is disappointing to see that the lengthy comments made in the edition add
almost nothing to what is already known. Many of the comments just reproduce
parts of the text, or they repeat what previous scholars have said. There is an
index at the end, but this too is a disappointment, for it is an index of the
lemmata, not of the glosses, and is thus presented in almost exactly the same
order as the text is in anyway. The index does not even group together variant
spellings of the same word that happen not to begin with the same letter. For
example, 166r20, printed as "***uox In Rama*** *uox in excelsis siue ciuitas appella-
tur Rama*", and 129v36, presented as "***rama*** *excelsa est, tamem ciuitas Rama
appellatvr*" (*sic*, in the edition: "tame*m*", resolving the abbreviation this way
rather than as "tame*n*") are in separate places in the text, and for the same reason, also in the index. There is not even any indication here when the same
word is spelt differently in different lemmata: 2v41, for example, presented as
"***abrei*** *minati sunt ab qvi pronepus fuit*" in the edition (resolving the abbreviation as "-nep*us*" rather than "-nep*os*") and 5r63, presented as "***aebraei*** *minati
sunt hab Eber, qu*ȩ*prenepus fuit Sem*", are separated for orthographical reasons
in the text and again in this index. Consider how useful in comparison an index
of the glosses would have been, which is what linguists would like, rather than
an index of the already alphabetized lemmata, which is what we are given.

The editors refer, of course, to the brief masterpiece that Díaz y Díaz wrote
concerning glossaries in the Iberian Peninsula.[5] The pages of the introduction
to this edition are longer than Díaz's book, but that does not mean that they are
any more informative concerning what we need to know before undertaking

---

[5] M.C. DÍAZ Y DÍAZ, *Las primeras glosas hispánicas* (Barcelona, 1978).

research into the Early Medieval glossaries. For example, in the first few decades of the twentieth century Goetz and Lindsay between them had established almost everything that was known in this field until comparatively recently. The editors refer in passing to Goetz, without making clear who he was nor what he did, and do not mention Lindsay at all. Even though it is now possible to suspect that several of Lindsay's conjectures were ill-founded, his work should at least be acknowledged. More recent investigations are not mentioned. Perhaps it is worth indicating here that the best place to look for these is among the twenty-two studies gathered together in the Acts of the International Conference dedicated to this topic in 1994.[6] Among other things, it is now known without any room for doubt that glossaries, including those prepared in the Rioja in the tenth century, have ancient and pan-European origins, that they are compilations made from sources of many and varied kinds, that they became more complex over time, and above all that they look to the distant past and not to the future (and hardly even to the present). Neither do they belong to the geographical space occupied by their copyist. Despite this, although there is a brief reference to these matters in seven lines on p. 189, the editors give the impression that what we have here is a kind of encyclopaedic dictionary prepared as if *ex nihilo* in the Iberian context, with the intention of translating Latin into Ibero-Romance and at the same time illuminating the philological enterprises of a thousand years in the future. But a glossary is not like that. It could not have been. Glossaries are fascinating to philologists, of course, but for other reasons than this (and in the next chapter I will explain at length and in detail why these ones cannot really be used as sources of the Ibero-Romance lexicon of the tenth century). The editors give us an excellent and well-commented list (pp. 49-95) of glossary manuscripts, or fragmentary folios, that were found geographically in the Iberian Peninsula, as if Hispanic glossaries were a different genre. They are highly interesting, of course, but not for that reason. There is no problem about the geographical location of any of them, but there did not yet exist a 'Hispanic' culture in the sense intended, separate from the rest of Europe. This is a European genre, which had begun five centuries or more earlier.

What is missing from the edition is a discussion of the genre, an analysis of the antecedents of *Em.* 46, and an explanation of the chronological layers represented in the integrated list. Such research can be undertaken on the basis of the edition, of course, but in such a long introduction these topics could have been at least broached. Rather than this, another topic is addressed, important in

---

[6] HAMESSE (ed.), *Les manuscrits.*

itself but not immediately relevant to the study of the glossary. The question of whether there is a direct relationship between these tenth-century glossaries of San Millán and Silos and the famous glosses of the following century, which were found on manuscripts belonging to precisely these two monasteries. In this section they quote me accurately and courteously. They criticize me for having written that the glossaries were only used very rarely for the purpose of adding glosses to a text unrelated to the base text of its constituent glosses, and they are right about this, for my remarks were unnecessarily definite.[7] This did indeed happen from time to time, mainly with glosses taken ultimately from St Isidore's *Etymologiae*. Yet there is no obvious need to enter into this problem in the introduction to a glossary of a hundred years earlier. For the glossaries and the glosses in question were elaborated in quite separate cultural contexts.

Overall, the introduction to the edition would have been excellent if the glossary had been not a glossary but a Latin-Romance dictionary (which the editors know it was not). The glossary makes no such distinction between Latin and Romance. Among the lemmata, which would be 'Latin' if this were a Latin-Romance Dictionary, there appear words which we would, if we had to classify them as either Latin or Romance, prefer to call 'Romance'. Among the glosses, which would have to be classified as 'Romance' under this perspective, there are often words which we would wish to call 'Latin', if we had to choose one way or the other. Sometimes one entry presents both cases together; as 118r6, for example, which reads "*plorat flet*". The manuals tell us, rightly, that the Latin word FLET was over time replaced by PLORAT and its descendants in the West (Spanish "*llorar*", French "*pleurer*", et cetera).[8] If this glossary really were a Latin-Romance dictionary, then such cases as 118r6 would be back to front. And overall, however we want to define the Latin-Romance distinction, words in each category are to be found in lemmata and glosses alike. We ought not to deduce from this that the compilers and copyists of such lists did not know what they were doing. Of course they knew what they were doing, much better than we do now. What they did not realize, however, was that the philologists of a thousand years in the future were going to presuppose that the conceptual distinction between Latin and Romance was already operative in tenth-century Iberia. This is a distinction which is never mentioned at all in the actual glossaries, which can only be because they did not yet know about it. They had in their repertoire at that time a wide range of lexical items, be-

---

[7] R. WRIGHT, *Late Latin and Early Romance in Spain and Carolingian France* (Liverpool, 1982), pp. 199-200.

[8] J. HERMAN, *Vulgar Latin* (Penn State, 2000), p. 99.

longing to several registers, and with many connotations, but they had not yet separated them out into two separate lexicons belonging to two separate languages. Which is just as well, because if so then a large number of words would have had to appear in both lexicons. This means that many of the comments which the editors have made in their introduction are fair enough in themselves, but the whole conceptual framework in which they operate leads to the discovery of problems that do not really exist, and to the neglect of problems that do. That is, the perspective adopted makes their analysis harder rather than easier.[9]

I do not want this review to seem negative. The ideas expressed are serious, but only partial. And it is good to see that in the edition itself there is none of the journalistic nonsense that accompanied its publication. Headlines such as *"Hallan las primeras palabras en romance en un códice emilianense anterior a las Glosas"* (from *La Rioja*, 3-4-1997, p. 3: "The first Romance words have been found in a manuscript that predates the glosses") merely show how ill-informed journalists are capable of being. The editors do not express themselves that absurd way. They, at least, realize that a scribe who copies a form incorrectly is not thereby creating a whole new language. Nor was anything at all "found". This glossary has been known to scholars, even though unpublished, throughout most of the twentieth century. The national newspaper *El País* was even more confused, referring to this as "... *la aparición del primer escrito romance autóctono de la Península Ibérica*" (4-4-1997, "the first appearance of written native Romance in the Iberian Peninsula"). The only echo that there is in the edition of these misleading descriptions, which are inspired by mere politics, is in the title. It is unfortunate that the title of the edition is as it is. This text is not a *"fuente española"* ("Spanish source"), but belongs to a European genre, which is why many of the glosses have no Ibero-Romance counterpart at all. It is not a *"diccionario"*, not even an *"enciclopédico"* one, however much it looks at first sight like the *Diccionario de Uso* of María Moliner.[10] And several of the glosses, as is usually the case in glossaries, are effectively incomprehensible, uprooted from their original textual context. On the other hand, we should recognize that this attractive and imposing edition has been beautifully produced, and that it will help the genre to come to the attention of those linguists and philologists who have not paid the attention to it that

---

[9] C. PENSADO, "Sobre los límites de la mala ortografía en romance. ¿Por qué el inglés *fish* no se escribe *ghoti* después de todo?", in: *Estudios de grafemática en el dominio hispano*, ed. J.M. BLECUA *e.a.* (Salamanca, 1998), pp. 225-242.

[10] M. MOLINER, *Diccionario de Uso del Español* (Madrid, 1966).

it deserves. There is no study of glossaries or glosses, for example, among the more than one hundred and sixty studies collected in the *Actas* of the first two National Conferences of Medieval Latin.[11] In fact, since *Em.* 46 is so closely related to the Silos Glossaries in Paris (1296 and 1297, edited by García de Diego, and 1298, edited by Goetz), we were probably in greater need of an edition of the other San Millán Glossary, *Em.* 31, which is still unpublished. This latter manuscript, despite not being so old (it is from the eleventh century) is the more interesting, since it seems to be less slavishly derivative of the northern tradition than *Em.* 46 is. Goetz described it as *sui generis*.[12] So it is good to know that the same editors are intending to offer us also an edition of *Em.* 31, and as long as they show a proper respect towards its punctuation, we can look forward to that.

---

[11] M. PÉREZ GONZÁLEZ (ed.), *Actas del I Congreso Nacional de Latín Medieval* (León, 1995). IDEM (ed.), *Actas del II Congreso Hispánico de Latín Medieval*, 2 volumes (León, 1998).
[12] GOETZ, *Corpus*, I, p. 186.

Chapter 15

The Glossaries of Tenth-Century Spain: (2) Romance Vocabulary in the San Millán Glossaries

The two San Millán Glossaries referred to in the title of this chapter are manuscripts *Emilianense* 31 and 46, now in the Real Academia de la Historia in Madrid. The García Turza brothers have published a splendid edition of *Em.* 46 (reviewed in the previous chapter) and are currently editing *Em.* 31. The publicity that surrounded the publication of their edition of *Em.* 46 claimed that this was a dictionary between Latin and Romance, but as we shall see, this description cannot possibly be right.[1]

From a Hispanic perspective, these glossaries, *Em.* 46 and 31, of the tenth and eleventh century respectively, seem early. But from a European perspective, these are in fact two rather late examples of a genre that has much earlier roots. All the glossaries of those centuries have multiple sources, since they reproduce and join together other lists created from glosses added to the margins of previous manuscripts, which could be originally pre-Christian, or Bibli-

This chapter is a translation of: "Léxico romance en los Glosarios de San Millán", in: *Actas del V Congreso Internacional de Historia de la Lengua Española*, ed. María Teresa ECHENIQUE e.a. (Madrid, Gredos, 2002), II, pp. 2421-2426. We are grateful to Professor María Teresa Echenique Elizondo, on behalf of Editorial Gredos (Madrid), for permitting this reprint.

[1] C. GARCÍA TURZA and J. GARCÍA TURZA, *Fuentes españolas altomedievales: el códice emilianense 46 de la Real Academia de la Historia, primer diccionario enciclopédico de la península ibérica* (Madrid and Logroño, 1997). Compare M. CARRERA DE LA RED, "Textos lingüísticos antiguos del romance hispánico", *Epos* 14 (1998), pp. 69-88.

cal, or grammars, or of any other genre. The history of each gloss is still hard
to trace with any exactness, although the work of Carlotta Dionisotti has clarified the general picture.[2] These two manuscripts were copied in San Millán
from others that had been brought there from further north, although it is always possible that the copy was not totally faithful and the scribes might have
changed some of the details in their Riojan scriptorium. Despite their extra-
peninsular origin, though, these texts represent an important facet of the intellectual training of the scribes and scholars of the Peninsula, which means that
it is vital that they should now be investigated closely. For practical reasons,
this present study concentrates on *Em.* 46, with occasional references to *Em.* 31
where appropriate.

In order to decide whether this glossary takes the form of a Latin-Romance
dictionary, we need first to consider the following: whether there is internal
evidence that the scribe or compiler had in mind the two concepts of Romance
and Latin as separate languages. It soon becomes clear that they did not. There
are quite a number of comments of a metalinguistic nature in the explanatory
glosses, but none of them refer to or even presuppose such a distinction. We
find a large number of references to Greek, for example, with the words
"grece", *"greco"*, *"greco sermone"*, *"in Grecam linguam"*, and in this way
Greek usage is often contrasted explicitly with that of Latin. This suggests that
the ultimate origin of the glosses concerned lay in the Eastern Mediterranean,
most probably from the Byzantine area between the fourth and sixth centuries
(where for example Priscian had been explaining Latin to Greek-speakers).
Other Oriental languages are also explicitly mentioned, such as for example
Syriac, with the words *"syriaco sermone"* (98v31), *"sermone syro"* (99v14),
"sirum" (1v3, 26r38); Hebrew, with the words *"aput hebreos"* (88r22, and
"aput ebreos" 136v8), *"ebree"* (88r14), *"ebreo"* (77r5), *"ebreum"* (93v57,
111v47, 136v7), *"in ipso hebreo"* (164v31); there are also references to Phoenician (*"punica lingua"*, 23v39, and *"Fenice"*, 65v8), to Etruscan (*"tusca lingua"*, 91r48), to the speech of the Macedonians (*"lingue macedonum"*, 61r48),
of the city of Tyre (*"Tyrra lingua"*, 52r46), of the Persians (*"lingua persa"*,
69r42, *"lingua persica"*, 154v20, *"lingua persarum"*, 69r44, 137v30, 157r55),
of the Sabines (*"sabinorum lingua"*, 128v44), of the Egyptians (*"lingua
egyptiorum"*, 45r15; *"lingua egyptiaca"*, 144v28-29), of the Chaldeans (*"aput
caldeos"*, 137v29) and of the Assyrians (*"assirii"*, 14r55). That is, there are

---

[2] A.C. DIONISOTTI, "On the nature and transmission of Latin Glossaries", in: *Les manuscrits
des lexiques et glossaires de l'Antiquité tardive à la fin du Moyen Age*, ed. J. HAMESSE (Louvain-
La-Neuve, 1996), pp. 205-252.

explicit references to and distinctions between a large number of languages current further East than the Iberian Peninsula. There is just one reference to the Celtic language of the Gauls (*"lingua gallica"*, 69r11). The word *"latine"* is also used regularly, often contrasted with one or more of these other languages. The compilers have thus quite a sophisticated ability to make distinctions between languages where relevant. But nowhere at all, throughout the whole of the vast Glossary in *Em.* 46, do we find the word *"romanice"*, or any alternative cognate form. No explicit distinction is made at all between Latin and Romance. If this really were a Latin-Romance dictionary, the lack of any such explicit distinctions would be quite astonishing.

The compilers were, on the other hand, quite capable of making sociolinguistic and chronological distinctions within the single vast continuum of Latin. That is, clear and precise distinctions of other kinds are regularly made, most commonly between the Latin of the Ancients and that of the time of the gloss. It is pointed out at times, for example, that the *"antiqui"* used to say things in the past which would not be easy to understand in the contemporary context: for example, the lemma *"falcato curru"* is glossed as *"dextera leuaque rotibus herentis gladii falcatos currus antiqui dicebant, uellabant"* (61v8). Sometimes in these comments the ancients are called the *"ueteres"*, as when the lemma *"esistram"* is glossed as *"quam ueteres nominarunt canapum"* (55r54). In such entries a chronological distinction is explicitly made. There is a striking example of the way in which the *veteres* can be summoned in aid, but relevant information concerning Romance is not, in entry 37v7, where the lemma *"cuium, cuius"* is given the gloss: *"Terentjus 'quid uirgo cuia est', quia ueteres pronominibus uniuersis addebant genus"*. Ibero-Romance also added distinctive gender endings to the originally invariant *"cuyo"* (from CUIUS), to create feminine *"cuya"*, but the glosser does not point this out. Instead he prefers to point the reader to that sentence from the playwright Terence, who had written his plays over a thousand years before the San Millán scribe copied this entry. The name of the great fourth-century grammarian Aelius Donatus is quite often mentioned within the explanatory gloss (entries 22v54, 42r56, 67r20, 69v52, 96r15, 141r3), as well as those of Varro (73r15, 110v10, 123r27, 143r55), Vergil (113r5, 167r30), Quintilian (126r35), Lucan (139r34) and Cicero (132r53), names which would hardly be included in the actual gloss if that gloss were supposed to be representing Romance as opposed to Latin. References are made occasionally to the speech of the *"uulgus"*, but in these entries it seems to be usually the case (perhaps always, since at times it is not clear what the intended point is) that the word of the lemma is the one supposedly of the "*uulgus*" and the explanatory gloss is couched in terms that seem to belong to more straightforward and even respectable Latin. This is exactly the opposite of what we would expect if this were a dictionary which turned Latin lemmata into Romance glosses: for example, the lemma "*coturnix*" is explained as "*quod uulgit[er] quaquilas uocant*" (36r64), and "*desperatus*" as "*uulgo uocatur malus ac perditus ..*" (43v6). And since it seems undeniable that the words "*codorniz*" (< COTURNICEM) and "*desperado*" must have existed in Ibero-Romance, it also seems that the lemmata must be the forms here described as belonging to the "*uulgus*". Overall, there are seventeen entries in which the description as belonging to the "*uulgus*" (or a cognate word) applies to the lemma, and the gloss which accompanies these lemmata seems to involve no reference to sociolinguistic registers. Nor is the word "*rusticus*" used for such a purpose. The "*rustici*" here are explicitly and literally people in the countryside (for example, "*rusticus – rus colens*", 136r13; "*rusticos – illos dicunt qui arant et operant manibus*", 170r16), and when reference is made to the speech of the "*rustici*" this is simply to the way people speak in the country, no more than that. There are just two references made to geographical variation within the Latin-speaking world, in entries 27r31 ("*ciminum – Itali dicunt: cominum galli*") and 61v46 ("*far – genus anone quod Gallie merum dicunt*"), neither of which mention the Peninsula or Ibero-Romance. It is, in short, impossible to believe that the compilers of the glossary had any idea of Romance being a separate language from Latin, nor, if it comes to that, of Latin as being a separate language from Romance, nor of a metalinguistic entity that could be called 'Ibero-Romance'. All of which would seem to be prerequisites for any glossary to be describable as a Latin-Romance dictionary and a "*fuente española medieval*".

If we look closely at the majority of the glosses, which include no such metalinguistic comment of the kind analysed so far, we will come to exactly the same conclusion: these distinctions, which we often make now, were not made then. There are even a number of entries in which the lemma seems to be more characteristic of Romance than the gloss does (if we are going to make the distinction at all). For example, the lemma "*capescere*" is glossed as "*capere*" (22v55; compare Italian "*capisco*"), "*cassulas*" as "*domunculas*" (24r12; compare Romance "*casa*"), "*discitur*" as "*discenditur*" (46v23; compare Old Castilian "*decir*", which meant "descend"), "*hiberno sidere*" as "*hiemis tempore*" (74v46: compare Ibero-Romance "*invierno*"), "*modo*" as "*nunc*" (102v61; compare Old Italo-Romance "*mo*", meaning "now"), "*uetulum*" as "*antiquum*" (162v20; compare Spanish "*viejo*", Italian "*vecchio*", et cetera). If this really were a Latin-Romance dictionary these entries would have been presented in precisely the other order from the one they actually have in *Em.* 46. We can conclude in these cases that what was happening in the context of the original gloss was that the readers had had trouble in understanding the word which we would like to call 'Romance', and needed to be given clarification through a more straightforwardly Latin word.

There is not the space here to consider every gloss from the point of view of its sociolinguistic status as a lexical item. I shall limit myself to mentioning some that are already well-known, and which were used by József Herman as paradigmatic examples of lexical change between Latin and Romance.[3] These are the words that mean "horse", "speak", "fire", "cry" and "eat", plus the curious example of the words for "little".

1. We know that the Romance words for "horse", such as Spanish "*caballo*", French "*cheval*" and Italian "*cavallo*", came to replace the earlier word "*equus*" (although not everywhere in the feminine, as can be seen in the continuing existence of Spanish "*yegua*", "mare"). So it is not surprising to find an entry in the glossary that explains the lemma "*equus*" as "*caballus*" (54v12). And yet there is also one that runs exactly in the reverse direction, in which the lemma "*caballus*" is given the gloss "*cab, equus*" (*sic*, 21v2), in which the chronologically newer word is the one that needs explanation and the chronologically older one is used in the explanatory gloss. There is also an entry in which the lemma "*caballarius*" is glossed as "*alacris*" (21v1) in which the lemma is the etymon of a characteristically Romance word (leading eventually to for instance Spanish "*caballero*") but does not here have the meaning that its Romance derivatives were going to have later. There are also two entries in which the word "*equus*" turns up in both the lemma and the gloss, which implies that the word was not seen as being in any way problematic: "*acri equo*" is glossed as "*uelocia equo*" (3v27, in which the "*acri*" seems to be a copyist's error for "*alacri*"), and "*equus emissarius*" as "*quamdo equam sequitur*" (54v13). Furthermore, there are at least eighteen occasions where the word "*equus*" turns up in the gloss but not in the lemma, implying that the word could be understood without any trouble: examples include "*alipides*" glossed as "*equi ueloces*" (8r40), and "*rugitus*" as "*ferarum mugitus uel equorum ...*" (135v26), in which the lemma, ostensibly needing explanation, is again a word which in fact had a healthy future ahead of it within Romance (leading, for example, to Spanish "*ruido*", the ordinary word for "noise").

---

[3] J. HERMAN, *Vulgar Latin* (Penn State, 2000), pp. 95-107.

2. Another well-known example of lexical replacement concerns the words for "speak". Latin *"loquor"* came to be replaced in the Iberian Peninsula by *"fabulari"* (> Spanish *"hablar"*, et cetera) and in other areas by *"parabolare"* (> Italian *"parlare"*, et cetera). Yet in this glossary some form of *"loquor"* appears in at least thirty-eight of the explanatory glosses. And there is one further entry in which the word appears in both lemma and gloss, when the lemma *"orsa loqui"* is glossed as *"dicta loqui"* (109r2). In addition, morphologically derived forms such as *"adloquor"*, *"loquelle"*, *"eloquens"*, *"loquacitas"* and *"locutio"* are used in the explanatory gloss. *"Parabolare"*, on the other hand, is not used at all. Agentive nouns derived from *"fabulari"* appear twice, in entries where that lexical root appears in both lemma and gloss: the lemma *"fabulo"* is glossed as *"fabulans, conponens"* (60v20), and *"fabulones"* as *"fabularum inventores"* (60v21). In such cases it is impossible to believe that there can have been any metalinguistic distinction made at all between supposedly Latin lemmata and supposedly Romance gloss.

3. Much the same can be said of the words *"ignis"* and *"focus"*, a synonymous pair ("fire") which is another example of lexical change much mentioned in the manuals. *"Ignis"* was eventually lost and replaced by *"focus"*, which survives now as Spanish *"fuego"*, French *"feu"*, Italian *"fuoco"*, et cetera. Even so, although it is true that the word *"focus"* does turn up once in the explanatory gloss, it is there accompanied by *"ignis"* as an alternative: *"pira"* is glossed as *"focus uel ignis"* (117r29). *"Ignis"* can be used in the gloss without apparent embarrassment, as when the lemma *"bona esca"* is glossed as *"qui solbebatur a sole, non ab igne"* (19v55). Here is another case where the lemma would have existed in Ibero-Romance (eventually becoming Spanish *"buena yesca"*) but these are the words apparently needing explanation, being given it with the supposedly outdated word *"ignis"* accompanying a verb of analytical passive morphology (which we would definitely call Latin rather than Romance, if we had to decide one way or the other). That is, again, if there were a distinction between to be made between Latin and Romance in this entry, the lemma is decidely Romance and the gloss decidedly Latin.

4. Spanish *"llorar"* and French *"pleurer"*, et cetera ("cry"), derive historically from *"plorare"*, which replaced *"flere"*. And there is indeed one entry which follows that line, in which the lemma *"flet"* is glossed as *"plorat"* (65v3; this also occurs in the other San Millán glossary, *Em.* 31, where *"flere"* is glossed as *"plorare"*, 31v90). And yet there is also an entry presented in precisely the other order, in which the lemma *"plorat"* is glossed as *"flet"* (118r6). *"Plorare"* is also used with explanatory force in entry 159r46, where the

lemma *"uagit"* is explained as *"plorat"*, and in 164v29, where *"ullulatus"* is explained as *"ploratus"*. But there are other entries in which *"flere"* is used for exactly the same purpose, such as when *"lamentat"* is glossed as *"flet, lacrimat"* (91r28), and *"miserauile"* as *"uulgus dolendo flens"* (102v2). Both words are used in the gloss of entry 159r47, where the lemma *"uagitus"* is explained as *"uoces Infantium, fletus, ploratus, ululatus"*. *"Plangere"*, which is the etymon of Italian *"piangere"*, is used in three of the explanatory glosses (for example when the lemma *"uagiant"* is glossed as *"plangant"*, 159r50), but that lexeme is used in both lemma and gloss of entry 117v18, where *"plangor"* is explained as *"plangentium uox"*. It becomes obvious from the examples that there were many words around in the language to express the meaning of "cry", and that no kind of decision had been taken yet to categorize any of them as being particularly 'Latin' rather than Romance, or 'Romance' rather than Latin.

5. Perhaps the best known example of lexical replacement between Latin and Romance concerns the words for "eat". Latin *"esse"* (with a long [e:]) was replaced by a regularized cognate *"edere"*, but not even that survived into subsequent Romance. In Gaul and Italy they eventually preferred to use *"manducare"* (the etymon of French *"manger"* and Italian *"mangiare"*), whereas in the Iberian Peninsula they eventually preferred to use the prefixed form *"comedere"* (the etymon of Spanish *"comer"*). And indeed in this case, unlike the previous ones, it does indeed seem that the older Latin form appears in the lemmata more than in the explanatory glosses. Even so, there are two examples in the gloss, when *"letosagi"* is explained as *"oblibi edentes"* (93v30) and *"edulia"* as *"ciui que eduntur"* (50v38). And it is also true that the word *"manducare"* never appears in a lemma, while it appears at least twenty times in the gloss, as well as in *Em.* 31, where the lemma *"edet"* is explained as *"manducat"* (17r8). In *Em.* 46, there are four cases when it is used to explain its etymon, the unsuffixed *"mandare"*. For example, the lemma *"mandat"* is explained as *"manducat"* (98v53). It is also true that on four occasions a form in the lemma beginning with *commess-* is explained by a gloss in which the same lexeme has regularized morphology, as when *"commesset"* is glossed as *"comedisset"* (29v29). And apart from these entries, the lexeme *"comedere"* only appears in the gloss, as for example when the lemma *"mandimus"* is glossed as *"commedimus"* (98v59). What we can deduce from all this is that the word *"esse"* (meaning "eat") fell out of general use very early; before, that is, the time of the oldest glosses, perhaps before the third century. Yet even so, we see no trace here of the geographical distinctions which were probably

already operative in tenth-century Romance. Indeed, *"manducare"* is used in these glosses from San Millán more than *"comedere"* is. Sometimes they appear together in the same gloss, as, for example, when the lemma *"edent"* is glossed as *"manducant, comedent"* (50r49), and also in *Em.* 31, where the lemma *"mansu"* is glossed as *"comestu, conmanducatu"* (57r43).

6. The final example to be considered here concerns the words that mean "small". Words such as Spanish *"pequeño"*, French *"petit"*, Italian *"piccolo"*, et cetera, are almost the only Romance words whose etymon really deserves to be printed with the asterisk that indicates an undocumented source.[4] That is, whatever their etymon or etyma may have been, that word has never been found in written Latin form. That is also true in this Glossary, although we can see rather similar forms. The interesting fact, though, is that despite their prototypically 'Romance' nature (if we are going to distinguish between Latin and Romance at all), when these words appear they are usually in the lemma, not in the gloss. This indicates that the words in question were ones which needed explanation, rather than being of use in explaining other words. The word which tends to be used in the explanatory gloss with the meaning of "small" is *"paruus"*. Thus the lemma *"pauxillum"* is glossed as *"paruum"* (112v41). Sometimes the word used in the gloss with this meaning is *"modicus"*, and both appear together when the lemma *"paxillum"* is glossed as *"paruum, modicum, paululum"* (112v46). *"Paruus"* does not survive in Romance. And yet it never appears in these glossaries as a lemma, whereas forms such as *"paxillus"* never appear in the explanatory gloss. Equally surprising is the fact that words endowed with diminutive suffixes, which form the etymon of many Romance words, are hardly used in the explanatory glosses at all, but can be found in several lemmata. At times, in fact, the gloss even points out explicitly that the suffixes are, indeed, diminutives. Thus the lemma *"uirguncula"* is explained as *"uirga modica, minutiue"* (for *"diminutiue"*, presumably: 163v53), and *"uuccula"* as *"uacca diminutiue"* (167r9, for *"uaccula"*). Once again, the phenomena which we would like to call 'Romance' are the ones which need explanation, and they are clarified in the gloss with more traditional Latin words.

The conclusion could hardly be more obvious, and yet it is worth re-emphasizing it here, because it is extremely important that no credence should be given to the notion that these glossaries represent any kind of Latin-Romance dictionary. They were prepared within a speech community which contained a great deal of lexical variability, naturally, but no decision had as yet been taken

---

[4] I have expanded on this point in: R. WRIGHT, *Early Ibero-Romance* (Newark, 1995), p. 50.

concerning which words were going to be classifiable metalinguistically as 'Latin' and which as 'Romance', for the simple reason that nobody as yet made such a distinction. Even if they had, there would have been little point in systematic lexical distinctions, in that most words would have had to belong to both lists at once. The glossary actually makes the point clear and quite explicit: glosses are not translations but "*congregatio sermonum uel interpretatio*" (70v52), and the lemma "*glossema*" is explained as "*interpretatio sermonum*" (70v54). As Rafael Cano has said, referring to glosses in general, "*este procedimiento ... ocurre dentro de una misma lengua, entre sus variedades constitutivas*" ("this process occurs internally within a language, between its constituent variants").[5] Perhaps such a distinction was more likely to be felt in the eleventh century, when *Em.* 31 was written. We will have to wait for the forthcoming edition of this manuscript to be sure, but we can be certain that the tenth-century *Em.* 46 saw no metalinguistic distinction between Latin and Romance.

---

[5] R. CANO AGUILAR, *Análisis filológico de textos* (Madrid: 1991), p. 31.

Chapter 16

In What Language Are the Glosses of San Millán and Silos?

The first attestations of written Spanish Romance are usually said to be the words written in the margins of two manuscripts from the Monasteries of San Millán and Silos, the latter probably written in San Millán, in the Rioja region of North Central Spain, on the southern edge of the Basque Country. The glossed texts, sermons and a penitential respectively, are several centuries old by then. The words used as glosses usually clarify words used in the text, but some of the non-lexical marks and other additions seem to have a grammatical purpose. Two of them are in Basque. Altogether there are some five hundred and thirteen glosses. In the San Millán manuscript they were added subsequently to the text (perhaps in Aragón rather than in San Millán itself), but the Silos copyist has copied text and glosses all together from an already glossed original. The possibility of identifying the language of the glosses as being some kind of Romance arises because several of the words concerned are written with an orthography and a morphology that seem quite deliberately not to be in the traditionally correct form.

This chapter was originally published as: "Las glosas protohispánicas; problemas que suscitan las glosas emilianenses y silenses", in: *Actas del IV Congreso Internacional de Historia de la Lengua Española*, 2 volumes (Logroño, Universidad de La Rioja Servicio de Publicaciones, 1999; ISBN 84-88713-52-5), II, pp. 965-973. The translation is based on a longer unpublished version delivered in English at a conference on "Vulgar Latin" in Cambridge in May 1997. We are grateful to Da. M. Teresa Pinillos Martínez, on behalf of the Universidad de la Rioja, for permitting this reprint.

But the deceptively simple question posed in the title of this chapter raises a number of problems. For these purposes it is probably fair enough to consider the San Millán and Silos glosses together, particularly now that Ruiz Asencio (co-editor of the recent facsimile of the San Millán Glosses) has attributed them all to the same glosser. Although Wolf has severely criticized those of us who have refrained from treating them separately, most researchers do, and in his recent analysis Cano tells us justifiably that "it seems clear that the glosses of both manuscripts belong to the same dialectal type".[1]

1. The Diatopic Problem

A majority of the glosses in question were deliberately written in an incorrect manner, and clearly represent a desire to spell in a way that was not that of the traditional orthographic standard. Modern scholars have often wanted to ascribe these glosses to various dialects with geographical names: many call their language "*castellano*"; or "*riojano*" (Ramón Menéndez Pidal, for example, and the brothers García Turza), or even "*altarriojano*" (García Turza); or "*subriojano*" (Gimeno Menéndez, who has written a thoughtful book on sociolinguistics in mid-Medieval Spain); or "*castellano-riojano*" (Hernández Alonso, who is the other recent co-editor of the San Millán glosses); or "*navarro*" (González Ollé); or "*aragonés*" and even "*navarro-aragonés*" (Coloma Lleal and Heinz-Jurgen Wolf, here following the lead of Rafael Lapesa).[2] Other

---

[1] R. CANO AGUILAR, *Análisis filológico de textos* (Madrid, 1991), p. 31: "*parece evidente que las glosas riojanas de ambos textos corresponden al mismo tipo dialectal*". The glosses are edited at the start of: R. MENÉNDEZ PIDAL, *Orígenes del español* (Madrid, 1926: seventh edition, 1972); and the manuscript in: S. GARCÍA LARRAGUETA, *Las Glosas Emilianenses: Edición y Estudio* (Logroño, 1984). Other references are to: J.M. RUIZ ASENCIO, "Hacia una nueva visión de las Glosas Emilianenses y Silenses", in: *Las Glosas Emilianenses y Silenses. Edición crítica y facsímil*, ed. C. HERNÁNDEZ ALONSO and J.M. RUIZ ASENCIO (Burgos, 1993), pp. 83-118. H.J. WOLF, *Las Glosas Emilianenses* (Hamburg, 1991), referred to here in the Spanish translation by S. RUHSTALLER (Seville, 1996).

[2] MENÉNDEZ PIDAL, *Orígenes*, p. 470. C. GARCÍA TURZA and J. GARCÍA TURZA, "La datación y procedencia de las glosas emilianenses y silenses: anotaciones críticas a los nuevos planteamientos", *Brocar* 19 (1995), pp. 49-64, p. 62. C. GARCÍA TURZA, *Luces y sombras en el estudio de las glosas* (Logroño, 1995). F. GIMENO MENÉNDEZ, *Sociolingüística histórica (Siglos X-XII)* (Alicante, 1995), p. 64. C. HERNÁNDEZ ALONSO, "Las glosas. Interpretación y estudio lingüístico", in: HERNÁNDEZ ALONSO and RUIZ ASENCIO (ed.), *Las Glosas*, pp. 63-82. F. GONZÁLEZ OLLÉ, "El romance navarro", *Revista de Filología Española* 53 (1970), pp. 45-93, p. 55. C. LLEAL, *La formación de las lenguas romances peninsulares* (Barcelona, 1990), p. 173. R. LAPESA, *Historia de la Lengua Española* (eighth edition; Madrid, 1980), p. 164.

scholars, however, have preferred not to use names of such geographical precision. In the title of the Round Table at which the present study was first presented in 1997, these glosses were referred to as being *"protohispánicas"*, which was the label given to them in the previous conference in the same series by Manuel Díaz y Díaz.[3] Just before the Round Table at that Conference, María Teresa Echenique spoke of the glosses as being in the "Romance spoken by the Basques".[4] The late Emilio Alarcos Llorach simply referred to "the protohistoric Romance that would have been spoken in the region", and even more vaguely Micaela Carrera de la Red has referred to "the adoption of a system of writing for their vernacular language, Romance, or where relevant, Basque".[5] Alarcos also referred to them rather neatly as "the oldest written appearance ... of something that is not Latin".[6] I like that.

2. The Chronological Problem and the Historical Context

These glosses were once thought to be of the tenth century. This was Menéndez Pidal's assessment, but most scholars now accept that the most likely date for the glosses is the eleventh century, perhaps about 1070. This is the date implied by the studies by Bézler of the coins mentioned in the Silos text (which is a penitential), and the recent palaeographical and codicological studies by Ruiz Asencio and Hernández Alonso. There is no specifically linguistic argument either way.[7] Even when it was generally accepted, the tenth-century dating always seemed surprising, in that the Riojan scholars of the tenth century, such as Vigila and his colleagues at San Martín de Albelda, were expert Latinists who would neither have needed nor wanted glosses presented in such a shockingly incorrect form.

[3] M.C. DÍAZ Y DÍAZ, "Las glosas protohispánicas", in: *Actas del III Congreso Internacional de Historia de la Lengua Española* (Madrid, 1996), pp. 653-666.

[4] M.T. ECHENIQUE ELIZONDO, "Protohistoria de la lengua española en el primitivo solar castellano", in: *Actas del IV Congreso Internacional de Historia de la Lengua Española* (Logroño, 1998), I, pp. 37-58.

[5] E. ALARCOS LLORACH, *El español, lengua milenaria* (Valladolid, 1982), p. 17: *"el romance protohistórico que se hablaría en la región"*. M. CARRERA DE LA RED, "De nuevo sobre las Glosas Emilianenses", in: *Actas del II Congreso Internacional de Historia de la Lengua Española* (Madrid, 1992), II, pp. 579-595, p. 594: *"la adopción de un sistema de escritura para su lengua vernácula (romance, o en su caso vascuence)"*.

[6] ALARCOS, *El español*, p. 10: *"la más antigua aparición escrita .. de algo que no es latín"*.

[7] F. BEZLER, "De la date des gloses de Silos", *Revista de Filología Española* 71 (1991), pp. 347-354.

The dating to the later eleventh century increases the likelihood that there is some kind of foreign influence or inspiration behind their elaboration. Current scholarship does not agree whether there is or not. Most investigators think there is, to some extent, but Máximo Torreblanca feels sure that the experiment has only a local Hispanic motivation.[8] In the late eleventh century there were French influences of many kinds in that region, from the many Northern visitors who came to Spain during the contemporary process of intellectual and ecclesiastical Europeanization, as well as those who passed through the region on their way to Santiago de Compostela. The American medievalist and musicologist Susan Boynton has studied the Cluniac tradition of glossed hymnals, and pointed out that it was normal at that time for the glossers in the monasteries of different regions to be adapting general traditions to their own localized needs. Thus she relates the presence of glossed manuscripts in Silos, such as the Psalter which is now British Library Additional Manuscript 30851, with the need to give instruction in the new texts and the new liturgical uses of the Roman rite, which was introduced into non-Catalan Spain in the 1070s and 1080s. In a similar way, Birte Stengaard has compared the purpose of the Glosses of San Millán (which were added to sermons) to the famous Jonah sermon fragment of tenth-century France, as attesting a similar intention rather than being any kind of direct textual influence. Ruiz Asencio has seen the influence of French calligraphy in the glosses.[9] Probably the influence was indirect, from contact with French culture in general, rather than specifically from the presence of expert French glossers. For even if there was some kind of direct external inspiration behind this experimental attempt at a new orthography, the fact is that the actual glosses show no trace of being written in any kind of existing French or Provençal orthography, which suggests that the scribes concerned were aware that there were important differences between French and Iberian Romance. It is tempting to be completely indeterminate and just call the language of these glosses 'Romance', but for this reason it seems preferable to refer to them as 'Ibero-Romance'.

---

[8] M. TORREBLANCA, "En torno a las Glosas Emilianenses y las Silenses", in: *Scripta Philologica in Honorem Juan M. Lope Blanch*, ed. E. LUNA TRAILL (Mexico, 1991), pp. 469-479.

[9] S. BOYNTON, "The didactic function and context of Eleventh-Century glossed hymnaries", in: *Der lateinische hymnus im Mittelalter*, ed. A. HAUG (Kassel, 1997). B. STENGAARD, "The combination of glosses in the *Códice emilianense 60* (*Glosas emilianenses*)", in: *Latin and the Romance Languages in the Early Middle Ages*, ed. R. WRIGHT (London, 1991: reprint Penn State, 1996), pp. 177-189.

3. What were the Glosses for?

The new thing about these glosses is not just that they existed. By then there was a long and venerable tradition of glossing texts in Spain.[10] But previously the intention had always been to spell the glosses in the normal way. For example, those added to the magnificent tenth-century codex written by Vigila (now in the Escorial) are no worse orthographically than is the text itself. In the present context, a more useful comparison might be the glosses in traditional Latin form added in Caroline script to the hymnary which was brought in from France to Huesca in Aragón, in order to assist in the change of liturgy.[11] As in the San Millán manuscript, the hymnary also combines non-lexical indications, which we could call grammatical glosses, with the lexico-semantic glosses. Both are together designed to illuminate the meaning of the hymn concerned, but here there is no deliberate attempt to alter the orthographical shape of the words used as glosses, and it is possible to deduce that this is because there was no intention that the gloss should form part of any oral performance of the hymn, since the hymns were supposed to be performed with the precise original wording and grammar. This is significant; the orthography in our Riojan glosses is deliberately different from the inherited standard, unlike all the others of the time that we know of, which is why it has often been suggested that their point lies in prompting a vernacular pronunciation when reading aloud. There can be no direct connection between the hymn glosses and those on our Riojan manuscripts,[12] but the contrast does make clear that the novelty of the Riojan manuscripts lies not in the presence of the glosses but in the fact that many of them are written in a deliberately incorrect form. And the questions that still haunt all investigators in this field are these: why? who could it have helped?

In general, orthographic experimentation of this kind is of no immediate use to the illiterate, because the illiterate could not read anything, whatever the written form. It can only help those who have already learnt to read. In practice, it seems likely that it could only help if the reader is not a native of the area who has to read aloud a text intelligibly to a local audience. More than anything else, the spellings here are reminiscent of the strange systems of de-

---

[10] Studied by: M.C. Díaz y Díaz, *Las primeras glosas hispánicas* (Barcelona, 1978).

[11] Boynton, "The didactic function".

[12] As was established by: J. Villareal, "Las Glosas", in: *Hymnarium Oscense*, ed. A. Durán *e.a.* (Zaragoza, 1987), pp. 125-146. Compare also: C.J. Gutiérrez, "El himnario de Huesca: nueva aproximación", *Anuario Musical* 44 (1989), pp. 24-60.

liberately incorrect forms that we find used in modern tourist phrasebooks, where a language that the visitor does not know is written in the spelling system of a language which the visitor does know. Such incorrect spelling might have been of use in San Millán and Silos in the 1070s if the reader would not have known otherwise how to read aloud comprehensibly to the local community, since he could have a sporting chance of doing so if he treated these spellings as a rough kind of phonetic script. In all other circumstances, anyone who can read a text at all in their own language is much happier to be confronted with a text written in the recognizable traditional orthography that they have learnt, since that will always be easier to recognize, understand and read aloud than any experimental novelty. It is not easy for an English-speaker to read English in phonetic script, nor even for a Spanish-speaker to read Spanish in phonetic script, even though the phonetic forms of the words are closer to the way we are going to read it aloud than the traditional orthography is. But such a text might indeed help a foreign visitor.

Thus it does seem possible to support the most commonly held hypothesis about these glosses, that those in reformed spelling were designed that way in order to help somebody read them aloud, but only if the intended reader was not a native of the area, and thus needed the phrasebook technique.[13] Díaz y Díaz does not accept the theory that the form of the glosses was intended to help oral delivery;[14] neither does Wolf; on the other hand Stengaard's superb study illuminates the presence of the grammatical glosses on the San Millán manuscript through this same hypothesis, that those glosses too were aids to readers.

4. The diastratic question

It has sometimes been suggested that the lexical-semantic glosses involved translation between two different languages. But they could also be categorized as explanatory glosses. As Cano points out: "This kind of glossing can be carried out between different languages, forming part of the process of translation, but it can also be carried out within different varieties of the same language".[15]

---

[13] R. WRIGHT, *Early Ibero-Romance* (Newark, 1995), chapter 15.
[14] DÍAZ Y DÍAZ, *Las primeras glosas*, p. 31.
[15] CANO, *Análisis*, p. 31: "*Este procedimiento puede realizarse entre lenguas distintas, y forma entonces parte del proceso de traducción, pero también ocurre dentro de una misma lengua, entre sus variedades constitutivas*".

The latter view seems preferable here. The majority of the words in the texts are not glossed at all, which suggests that most were probably intelligible. Several of the textual words that seem archaic from the perspective of later Medieval Ibero-Romance could well have still been intelligible in the eleventh century even if they were destined to fall out of use before 1200.[16]

As regards the question of whether we are dealing here with two languages or one, we can once again see a wide range of opinion among contemporary specialists, ranging from visions of clear bilingualism at one end of the scale, through the precise sociolectal distinctions set up by Gimeno Menéndez,[17] to António Emiliano's proposal that both the texts and their glosses, whether correctly or incorrectly written, attest no more than an awareness of two registers of the sociolinguistic and stylistic continuum of the community.[18] To envisage what is at stake in this discussion, it is helpful to consider another modern analogy. The texts in these manuscripts were first composed some four or five centuries before the actual glosses. If a modern Spaniard annotates a Golden Age text with modern Spanish words, however spelt, what he or she is doing is annotating it, not translating it. Glossing it, indeed. Similarly, if modern English-speakers write isolated words in English on the edge of our text of *Macbeth*, we are not translating it. Nor can we say that the glosser(s) chose to gloss those words in the text that they did not understand. That cannot have been the case, for if they did not understand them then they would not have known how to gloss them. What seems to be happening is that they chose words which they understood themselves, because they existed within the Ibero-Romance monastic register, and then added in the margin words which had a greater chance of conveying the intended meaning to a less sophisticated audience, because these were also present in less specialized registers of the same Ibero-Romance language. So this is not a case of translation between two languages, but of a distinction of register or style within the monolingual competence of the glosser.

In this way the glossers' skills at negotiating the contemporary sociolinguistic continuum are reminiscent of the impressive versatility that

[16] See: S.N. DWORKIN, "Latín tardío y romance temprano: implicaciones léxicas de una hipótesis controvertida", in: *Actas del Primer Congreso Nacional de Latín Medieval*, ed. M. PÉREZ GONZÁLEZ (León, 1995), pp. 489-494.

[17] GIMENO, *Sociolingüística*.

[18] A. EMILIANO, "*Latín y romance* en las glosas de San Millán y de Silos: apuntes para un plantamiento grafémico", in: *Actas del I Congreso Anglo-Hispano*, I, *Lingüística*, ed. R. PENNY (Madrid, 1993), pp. 235-244, p. 237: "*dos registros del contínuum sociolingüístico y estilístico de la comunidad*".

Michel Banniard envisages within the competence of the hagiographers of the Merovingian eighth century, who were able to vary the syntax of their own compositions according to whether these were aimed at an audience of laymen or of clerics. Their aim, of ensuring greater intelligibility in oral performance by presenting it in a less forbidding register, is not at all frivolous. This is an entirely serious and practical attitude, and it explains why the decision was taken to copy the penitential into the Silos manuscript with the glosses that had been already added to the model. Penitence was not required only of the literate, and the instructions needed to be understood by all.

The conclusion that the new spellings had a phonetic purpose is not meant to imply that the readers must have been experts in phonetic script. Wolf, however, believes that the Glosses of San Millán were prepared in a rigorous phonetic transcription, which the readers could then follow in detail.[19] Thus traditional spellings imply to Wolf the presence of ancient pronunciations. Wolf takes for granted that the idea of a monolingual community in these monasteries is unsustainable, without even wondering why several specialists wish to sustain it, so he feels the need to make a sharp distinction between Latin words and Romance words. This leads him straight into difficulties when he finds a word among the glosses whose written form happens to contain both traditional and reformed features, for then he does not know which language to ascribe it to. Thus he wonders whether the glosses "*dicet*" (*Em.* 51, present tense) and "*mandaot*" (*Em.* 59) should be included in the list of Latin or of Romance glosses, given the presence of the final letter -*t* (which to Wolf implies the necessary presence of a sound [t]) at the same time as the Romance inflection attested in the preceding vowel (those of "*dice*", "says" and "*mandó*", "sent"). But this is a non-problem. If we do not insist on such a metalinguistic distinction, and allow all forms, spoken and written, to exist together within the ample elastic gamut of eleventh-century Ibero-Romance, then we can avoid tying ourselves into unnecessary knots.

When writing a text of their own, these same scribes went through a procedure which they often called "polishing" ("*polire*"), that is, adding a formalizing disguise, in order to achieve an acceptably correct appearance. One way to look at the glosses in unreformed spelling is to say that the scribe has not bothered to polish them. António Emiliano illuminates the change which the glossers were hereby beginning to institute by referring to the scribe's role here as being one of "scriptolinguistic delatinization". I quote his analysis here because it is so helpful: "The glosses, even if they are an exercise *sui generis*

---

[19] WOLF, *Las Glosas*, especially p. 62.

for their time, are still one link in the continuing chain of *'romanceamiento'* which runs from the earliest medieval documentation through to the wholly Romance texts of the thirteenth century; the Romance glosses are at the same time part of a long tendency of scriptolinguistic change which led in due course to the complete delatinization of the notarial *'scripta'* in the peninsula, and thus to the emergence of autonomous Romance orthographies".[20] The only point of disagreement I have with Emiliano's analysis is that I do not accept, despite parallels that he adduces from *fueros* and other texts, that the errors we find documented elsewhere in the eleventh century were as intentional as the forms of many of these glosses are. So I see something rather more revolutionary in the glosses than Emiliano does.[21]

It is a pleasure to be able to say that no serious scholar talks any more about the glosses attesting the 'birth of the Spanish language'. Writers do not, in fact, give birth to a new language every time they spell incorrectly, however sensible and conscious their purpose in doing so. Even so, Hernández Alonso is happy in his recent edition to talk of "a language in the process of being born",[22] and these glosses do indeed indicate the birth of something: the birth of the idea of the possibility of a spelling reform. Not the birth of a new language, but one of the initial stages in the long period of gestation leading eventually from the conceptually monolingual Ibero-Romance of the Central Middle Ages to the multilingualism of the late thirteenth-century Iberian Peninsula, in which several written Romance language standards co-existed alongside that of Latin.

---

[20] EMILIANO, *"Latín y romance"*, p. 236: *"Las glosas, si son una empresa sui generis para la época en que fueron redactadas, no dejan por eso de ser un lazo más en la cadena ininterrumpida de romanceamiento que va desde los documentos más antiguos hasta los primeros textos verdaderamente romances del siglo XIII: las glosas romances son también parte de una larga tendencia de cambio scripto-lingüístico que resultó en la completa deslatinización de las scriptae notariales hispánicas y en la consecuente emergencia de ortografías romances autónomas"*.

[21] This point could now be studied more closely than before, given the recent collective edition of the *Fuero de Logroño* of 1096: *El Fuero de Logroño y su época* (Logroño, 1996).

[22] HERNÁNDEZ ALONSO, *Las Glosas*, p. 117: *"una lengua en nacimiento"*.

5. Seeing the dialect question in a new light

And so we can return to the original question: what language is being represented in the new spellings of the glosses?

It seems possible that the San Millán glosses were added to their manuscript in Aragón; that they were used and probably read aloud in the Rioja (which was at the time part of Navarra); and that other similar glosses were copied at San Millán to be used for a similar practical purpose in Santo Domingo de Silos, which is in Old Castile.[23] We can deduce from this that there were no dialectal differences of great importance between the three kingdoms of Aragón, Navarra and Castile. Claudio García Turza referred to their language as *"riojano"*, adding that *"'riojano'* is a dialect whose peculiarity lies precisely in the coexistence there of a great variety of component parts, Castilian, Navarrese, Aragonese, Basque, and the specifically Riojan".[24] It is indeed true that the great majority of the linguistic features found in the Rioja are also to be found in other geographical areas, but this just shows how misleading these distinctions made between sub-sections of Ibero-Romance can be. No scholar believes that the isoglosses within a dialect continuum form neat bundles along political frontiers, neither then nor now. Modern sociolinguistics tells us that within a dialect continuum we find clear isoglosses rather less commonly than transition zones of variable width. So it is true that the majority of the features that have been identified as existing in medieval Rioja did indeed exist there, but they also existed elsewhere, even if only as marked variants, and other variants of the same variables would have been found in the Rioja as well.[25]

José Antonio Pascual has established this wider perspective so convincingly that it will be hard to argue against it. Pascual uses the term

---

[23] A. BOYLAN, "The library at Santo Domingo de Silos and its catalogues", *Revue Mabillon* 64 (1992), pp. 59-102, shows that it is unlikely that this manuscript could have been copied at Silos itself. She also mentions the copy of Isidore's *Etymologiae* that was made in San Millán in 1072.

[24] GARCÍA TURZA, *Luces*, p. 63: *"el riojano es un dialecto cuya singularidad radica precisamente en la convivencia de una gran variedad de componentes (castellanos, navarros, aragoneses, vascos, y los específicamente riojanos)"*.

[25] The natural fluidity of the Ibero-Romance dialect continuum was understood by Menéndez Pidal, and well analysed by Máximo Torreblanca and Ralph Penny: MENÉNDEZ PIDAL, *Orígenes*. M. TORREBLANCA, "Isoglosas riojano-castellano-leonesas en la Edad Media", in: *Linguistic Studies in Medieval Spanish*, ed. T.D. CRAVENS and R. HARRIS-NORTHALL (Madison, 1991), pp. 135-147. R. PENNY, "El árbol genealógico: ¿modelo lingüístico desfasado?", in: *Actas del III Congreso Internacional de Historia de la Lengua Española* (Madrid: 1996), pp. 827-839.

"*iberorrománico*" as I use in English 'Ibero-Romance'. He asks us rhetorically, with reference to this period: "can we distinguish '*castellano*' from its wider Ibero-Romance archetype?", inviting a negative answer.[26] Indeed, there is no point in wrenching out individual languages or even dialects from the continuum. The late Emilio Alarcos Llorach, with his usual common sense, commented that "we all know that there are no sharp clear boundaries between neighbouring dialects of common origin, that there is continuity under the variation".[27] We might think that this was obvious, were it not for the fact that so many historical linguists act as if they do not believe it. Hernández Alonso, in his recent commentary, even suggested that the glosser had written specifically Riojan features, in the glosses of the manuscript destined for Silos, with the intention of irritating the monks of Silos by stressing the Rioja's political independence from Castile.[28] This really does not seem very likely, and even if that were the case he could hardly have succeeded in such a purpose, because there did not yet exist such a specifically Castilian standard against which to rebel in such a differentialist and anachronistically autonomous manner.

Such geographical particularism is, I suggest, anachronistic altogether. The conceptually geographical splitting of the Ibero-Romance continuum was not going to happen in earnest until almost two centuries later than this, in the second half of the thirteenth century; in Castile, that means at the court of Alfonso X. We should resist the temptation to apply such dialectal labels before that time. Accordingly, the best answer to our question is this: that these glosses are in an unspecialized informal register of Ibero-Romance.[29]

[26] J.A. PASCUAL, "Del latín a las lenguas romances. La complicada gestión – sobre el papel – del castellano", in: *De Roma al Siglo XX*, ed. A.M. ALDAMA (Madrid, 1996), I, pp. 447-471, p. 462: "*¿Se puede desgajar el castellano de un subarquetipo iberorrománico?*".

[27] ALARCOS, *El español*, p. 29: "*es sabido que no existen límites precisos y tajantes entre dialectos vecinos del mismo origen, que hay una especie de continuidad dentro de la variabilidad*".

[28] HERNÁNDEZ ALONSO, "Las glosas", p. 74.

[29] In the introduction to his edition of the San Millán glosses Wolf criticizes me severely, for four reasons in particular. (1) Because I do not believe that they are written in "*navarro-aragonés*" (p. 110). He is right, I do not. (2) Because I do not wish to make a distinction for that time between Latin and Romance. He is right, I do not (p. 62). (3) Because I do not believe the glosses were written in a strict phonetic script. He is right, I do not (p. 86). And (4) because I believe that the Silos glosses are older than the San Millán ones. He is not right, I do not believe that, nor have I ever said or thought or even hinted as much.

Section E

Twelfth- and Thirteenth-Century Spain

T he Iberian Peninsula in the twelfth century is a specially interesting place for the sociophilologist. We can trace the introduction of Medieval Latin in León-Castile to the decision taken in 1080 to adopt the reformed French liturgy, of which the linguistic changes were probably unintended consequences. Some intellectual centres embraced these reforms almost at once, with varying degress of enthusiasm, while others managed to stick to their inherited Visigothic traditions and resist the tide of Europeanization in general. Sociophilology can aid the historian here, as our analysis of the textual evidence is often sufficient to decide whether the scribes in a particular place still saw their written texts as a polished form of their spoken Ibero-Romance. If they did, we will see, for example, "*illa*" used as a definite article (being the written form of Romance [la]), "*de*" used in preference to genitive cases (except for many Proper Names), "*sedeo*" being used for "to be", and other such examples in which the traditional orthography is applied to twelfth-century Ibero-Romance grammatical and lexical usage. If, on the other hand, the scribal texts from a centre look more recognizably like standard Latin, with, for example, few or no uses of "*illa*" with the function of a definite article, copious genitive cases on ordinary nouns, and the forms of "*esse*" being used for "to be" even in paradigms where the Ibero-Romance has a form derived from "*sedeo*", then we can deduce that the linguistic reforms were known in that place. If we can ally the date of perceptible changes of this kind with that of relevant local events, such as the concomitant appointment of a new bishop, then we may be able provisionally to deduce that that bishop was instrumental in applying these reforms. We can operate the same way with respect to the

Royal Chanceries, where it seems, for example, that the chancellor appointed in Castile in 1192 (Diego García) started by dictating documents to his scribes in the new Medieval Latin pronunciation, but then changed to normal Romance when the scribes found that they could not cope with that. Sometimes the changes can be seen to be coetaneous with a change from Visigothic to Caroline script. The reforms came in everywhere in due course, often closely followed by texts in the new Romance orthographies, which were not needed under the old system. The battle of personalities in the Castilian chancery in the early thirteenth century is reflected in the vagaries of whether texts were prepared in Romance.

These first Romance texts were prepared by scribes whose professional training had been in the old Latinate techniques of adding polish to their Ibero-Romance, and glimpses of their previous training can be seen in a few details. Written Ibero-Romance eventually not only asserted itself as a competitor with Latin for most genres, but became quite dominant during the reign of Alfonso X in Castile. The names of languages were once again a crucial element in these developments, as the word "*latín*" came in with the reforms, borrowed from the French, and since the new "*latín*" was intrinsically and necessarily tied to the reforms in the Christian church, it left the word "*ladino*", which had been used for centuries to refer to the monolingual polymorphic ensemble of pre-reform spoken and written registers, as a word more commonly used by the non-Christian communities in the Peninsula. Thus the Jewish scholars who translated the Old Testament into Romance called it "*ladino*", and this word is often still used to refer to the Ibero-Romance spoken by Jews in Israel.

Chapter 17

Sociophilology and Twelfth-Century Spain

Investigating linguistic states of the past is not easy, and researchers need help from anywhere they can find it. The historical linguist has to understand minute details of both history and linguistics. We also need to take account of the discoveries of sociolinguistics, so that we can place each linguistic development in a plausible context – fortunately the Hispanist now has the excellent book by Ralph Penny to help us here.[1] In addition, when we are investigating a society which is literate, even if only in part, we need to be experts in philological analysis. Textual data are not often direct evidence of speech, however, and we should also investigate the training and intellectual context of the authors and scribes. As we combine philological and sociolinguistic expertise to explain details that might otherwise be unclear, we become sociophilologists.

To make sociophilological progress in a medieval context, we need above all reliable editions of texts. That is, they have to be published without any emendations, so that we can see exactly what there is on the parchment. We never know what might be important to researchers in the future. Doctoral students in the next century might wish to know the precise details of every comma and dot, capital letter, word-separation, and even the most blatant error.

This chapter is a translation of: "La sociolingüística y la sociofilología del siglo XII", in: *VI Congreso Internacional de Historia de la Cultura Escrita*, III, ed. Carlos SÁEZ (Alcalá de Henares, 2002), pp. 7-30. The English version has been somewhat shortened and slightly revised. We are grateful to Dr Carlos Sáez, on behalf of the University of Alcalá de Henares, for permitting this reprint.

[1] R. PENNY, *Variation and Change in Spanish* (Cambridge, 2000).

Manuscripts deserve what António Emiliano (in his study of Late Latin documentation from Portugal) has called "anthropological respect".[2] In the same
way, the discoveries made by Juan Carlos Bayo Julve and Martin Duffell about
indigenous Hispanic metrics could not have been made without the help of
facsimile and diplomatic editions of the texts.[3] Conversely, all editors of St.
Isidore's *Etymologiae* have changed the manuscript evidence to make his language seem more classicizing than it was, which is a main reason why Isidore's
language has not yet been seriously investigated.[4]

The twelfth century in the Iberian Peninsula is of great sociophilological
interest. It is a cliché to say that all linguistic periods are times of transition,
but the twelfth century in the Peninsula was one of the most transitional of all.
The researcher has to try to explain the great change that happened between the
eleventh century, where the Ibero-Romance speech community was essentially
monolingual and with only one written standard, and the thirteenth, in which
we can see several Ibero-Romance languages, geographically distinguished
with some clarity, each written its own way, coexisting with a more archaic
written Latin than hitherto.

As far as possible, we need to keep clear notions of geography and chronology. The sociolinguistic context varies not only from place to place, but
from decade to decade, and even from one year to another, at a different rate in
each intellectual centre. In particular, we need to distinguish between three
basically different types of text:

1. Late Latin texts that were still prepared the same way as before, being
the written mode of Ibero-Romance. Here there are words and morphological
features of Ibero-Romance, lightly disguised, as ever, beneath the veil of the
traditional orthography that the scribes had learnt in their training. The presence of such texts show that the Europeanizing reforms had not yet been systematically introduced into the scriptorium concerned. Even so, since they are
presented in unreformed spelling, however contemporary their morphology,

---

[2] A. EMILIANO, "O mais antigo documento latino-portugués (882 A.D.) – edição e estudo
grafémico", *Verba* 26 (1999), pp. 7-42, p. 9: "*o respeito antropológico pela textualidade
medieval*".

[3] J.C. BAYO JULVE, "Poetic discourse patterning in the *Cantar de Mio Cid*", *Modern
Language Review* 96 (2001), pp. 82-91; M. DUFFELL, *Modern Metrical Theory and the Verso de
Arte Mayor* (London, 1999). G. MARTIN, "Gestas de arena", in: *Textos épicos castellanos:
problemas de edición y crítica*, ed. D. PATTISON (London, 2000), pp. 23-33.

[4] For instance: W.M. LINDSAY (ed.), *Etymologiarum sive Originum Libri XX* (Oxford, 1911;
third edition, 1962). J. OROZ RETA (ed.), *San Isidoro de Sevilla: Etimologías*, (Madrid, 1982:
Biblioteca de Autores Cristianos).

vocabulary or syntax might be, in modern accounts these texts tend to be classified as 'Latin'.

This example comes from the will of Vela, canon of Salamanca cathedral, datable to *c.* 1163:

> De alio meo aver et ganado, vendant totum quantum de meo invenirint et faciant inde illa campana fracta, et complant inde istas mandaciones, et quod remanserit mittant totum in opera Sancte Marie, et si ego usque festivitatem Sancti Iohannis Babtiste obiero, ista sedeat mea mandacion, et si ego potuero vita mea meliorare, mea mandacion sedeat quomodo ego voluero.[5]

If we ignore the spelling, we can see that this text represents the Ibero-Romance of the time: "*sedeat*", for example, represents [séa] (later to be written as *sea*, subjunctive of "to be"), unconnected with the original Latin use of "*sedeat*"; "*illa*" represents Romance [la] (later to be written as "*la*", "the"); "*inde*" represents Romance [end] (later to be written as "*end*", "from there"), et cetera. And we can also note the co-existence in the same text of nounphrases with "*de*" and proper names in the genitive case, as in, for example, "*Sancte Marie*".

2. Medieval Latin Texts written in the Peninsula by foreigners, in particular French writers, who had already learnt how to write, read and even at times speak this archaizing Latin, as a result of their training. This new Latin (and the very word "*latín*") came into the Peninsula as an integral part of the ecclesiastical reforms that began in the late eleventh century. Menéndez Pidal indicated a long time ago how important the arrival of these authors was for the increasingly archaic appearance of their texts.[6] Subsequently these Europeans helped train a new generation of indigenous writers.

This example comes from the *Chronica Adefonsi Imperatoris* II, 55, ll. 1-7, probably written in *c.* 1148 by a bishop trained in Catalonia:

> Deinde ceperunt destruere uineas et arbusta, sed in ciuitate erat imperatrix domna Berengaria cum magna turba militum et ballistorum et peditum, qui sedebant super portas et super turres et super muros ciuitatis et custodiebant eam. Hoc videns imperatrix misit nuntios regibus Moabitarum, qui dixerunt eis: "Hoc dicit uobis imperatrix, uxor imperatoris: nonne uidetis quia contra me pugnatis, que sum femina, et non est uobis in honorem?"[7]

[5] J.L. MARTÍN MARTÍN e.a. (ed.), *Documentos de los archivos catedralicio y diocesano de Salamanca (S.XII-XIII)* (Salamanca, 1977).

[6] R. MENÉNDEZ PIDAL, *Orígenes del español* (Madrid, 1926; seventh edition, 1972). See also: C. LLEAL, *La formación de las lenguas romances peninsulares* (Barcelona, 1990).

[7] E. FALQUE REY, J. GIL and A. MAYA, *Chronica Hispana saeculi XII* (Turnhout, 1990; *Corpus Christianorum. Continuatio Medievalis* 71).

Here we can see genuinely archaic uses of *"sedere"* (in *"sedebant"*) and of *"eam"*, *"eis"* rather than *"illam"*, *"illis"* (which would have represented Romance *"la"*, *"les"*), of genitive cases of ordinary nouns (as in *"militum"*), et cetera.

3. Right at the end of this period we see tentative experiments in writing in a manner deliberately different from that of traditional Latin, following the line already set beyond the Pyrenees (and adumbrated in the Riojan glosses). These texts were prepared in a way that we would call Romance, because of the consciously reformed spelling, however archaic the grammar might be. Yet in spite of their new spelling, these texts are essentially similar to those of the first type. As António Emiliano would say, they have been prepared in a "delatinized" script, rather than being composed in a different language.

This example is taken from the Leonese Chancery version of the *Treaty of Cabreros* of 26th March, 1206 (ll. 7-8 of León Cathedral MS. 27):

> Et aq̃llos q̃ touieren los cast͠llŏs q̃ dichos son de suso. q́ndo los reciberen͞ fagan omenage al Rei de leon. & sean uassallos del͞ por ⁻)plirle el seruicio de t̃ras & de t̃minos & de _ptinenzas daq̃los cast͠llŏs. saquadas las reteñ̃ẽzas dessos cast͠llŏs mesuradas. & esto deuen fer por bona fe͞ senes ẽgano. & si end al fizeren. sean end traidores. Et el Rei de Leon aia hi pedido & comer. & otras derechuras mesurada mentre q̂m̂ en el ot° suo regno. Et si el Rei de leon desmesurada ment̂ los agrauar. aq̃l q̃ el cast͠llŏ touiere en q̃lo fizere͞ bien gelo pueda defender. sin mal estanza de si.[8]

We can note here the use of *"sean"* as subjunctive of "to be", more similar to the use of *"sedeat"* in the first text above than to the *"sedebat"* of the second text; *"los"*, et cetera, more similar to the use of *"illa"* in the first text than to the *"eis"* of the second; *"end"*, more like the *"inde"* of the first text than the *"deinde"* of the second; *"de"* meaning "of"; et cetera.

The reforms were followed with considerable enthusiasm in the late eleventh century, and again from the late twelfth. But during most of the twelfth century the impetus for such renewal was variable, and as a result the geographical effect looks like a mosaic, or patchwork quilt, in which some indigenous centres were more effective in resisting this foreign tide than others. The two written modes, Latin and Romance, were already found co-existing in France and Provence at the start of the twelfth century. But even there, as probably everywhere in the Romance world, we can see that it is only at the start of

---

[8] R. WRIGHT, *El Tratado de Cabreros (1206): estudio sociofilológico de una reforma ortográfica* (London, 2000), p. 45.

the following century that written Romance gained any kind of sociolinguistic prestige. In the Castilian chancery it looks as if this prestige was granted to Romance in 1206, as attested in particular by the decision to write in Romance form the important Treaty of Cabreros (text three above). But even there this decision was revoked in 1208, and the battle took a long time to be resolved.

Thus in principle every archive, every scriptorium, every intellectual and monastic centre of the time needs to have its documentation investigated within a clear sociophilological perspective. And of course, this is what often happens, and we now have good editions of texts from Salamanca, Sahagún, the Chanceries, and several other sources. Legal documents, and most Church documents, have a particular advantage here over the better known literary and historiographical texts, in that they are usually dated and located with some precision. This means that we may be able to follow a chronological sequence of texts from the same place and draw provisional conclusions about how and when the transition was implemented there.

For an example, we can consider Salamanca Cathedral. It seems possible to deduce that the introduction of these reforms into Salamanca cathedral only happened systematically after the arrival there of Bishop Pedro Suárez de Deza in 1166. There are texts from Salamanca in a reformed mode from an earlier date, but there were also still being produced Late Latin texts of our first kind, in which the Latinate appearance is still the written mode of Ibero-Romance. The first text adduced above (Vela's will of *c.* 1163) can only be understood at all if we take it as the written version of a deposition made in Ibero-Romance, rather than as a Medieval Latin text. When the will was read aloud at the time, as we know it was, it would only have been intelligible to the listeners if it had been read in the normal Ibero-Romance pronunciation of the age.[9]

As regards the Castilian Chancery, it seems most likely that Chancellor Diego García (also known as Diego de Campos) was the first chancellor who seriously tried to dictate documents to his notaries using the reformed phonetics of the new Medieval Latin, in which every letter of the written text had to correspond to a spoken sound. We can see from the notes that they added at the end to a few of the documents concerned that the scribes who had been there before Diego's appointment did not like the new system at all, and indeed after a few months they seem to have reverted to the normal mode.[10] And this hap-

---

[9] R. WRIGHT, "Reading a will in Twelfth-Century Salamanca" in: *Latin vulgaire – latin tardif* V, ed. H. PETERSMANN and R. KETTEMANN (Heidelberg, 1999), pp. 505-516. IDEM, *Tratado*, p. 45.

[10] WRIGHT, *Tratado*, pp. 31-32.

pened as late as 1193, more than a century after the initial arrival of the reforms.

It has been suggested that one direct kind of evidence for the progress of
the intellectual changes we are tracing here, of the introduction of the new rite,
and even of the whole Twelfth-Century Renaissance, can be found in the
change of hand. That is, we can see great significance in the date at which each
centre changed from the old Visigothic script to the new Caroline one.[11] This
is certainly a constituent part of the reforms. Even so, it does not seem as
though the change of script was directly involved in the change of rite, since
we can find manuscripts of the new rite prepared in the old script. The French
Cluniac Bernard de Sédirac, for example, was Abbot of Sahagún before his
promotion in 1086 to Archbishop of Toledo, but Visigothic script continued in
normal use at Sahagún until after the Council of Sahagún of 1121, which was
presided over by the reforming Cardinal Boso.[12] Decisions were taken in this
respect in mid-century. The last document in Visigothic script that we know of
from the Leonese Chancery dates from 1158 (almost immediately after the
separation of León and Castile in 1157). The document that Richard Fletcher
found in León, written in Visigothic script but accompanied by a list of
Visigothic-Caroline letter equivalences at the end, was written in 1155.[13] In the
Aragonese Chancery, Caroline script seems not to have been used before 1147,
but we can deduce that the change at that time was a conscious official decision from the fact that the first document we know of in Caroline script was
prepared by a scribe who had previously used the Visigothic. Even so, we find
documents in Visigothic script from there for several more years after that.

So we cannot conclude that the new rite and the inflow of French clerics
made the Caroline script immediately necessary. But we can probably argue in
the other direction, that the new script would not have been used in any centre
that had not accepted the new rite. The historian Lucas of Tuy, at least, who
worked in early thirteenth-century León, saw a direct connection between the
two novelties. He tells us that there was a Council held in León in the year
1090 at which it was decreed, with the authority of the Pope himself, that the
"*Gallica littera*" should be the one used in the Hispanic Church. Ximénez de

[11] R. WRIGHT, *Late Latin and Early Romance in Spain and Carolingian France* (Liverpool,
1982), pp. 233-237.

[12] R. FLETCHER, "El episcopado en el Reino de León, *c.* 1050-1150", in: *El Papado, La
Iglesia Leonesa y la Basílica de Santiago a finales del siglo XI*, ed. F. LÓPEZ ALSINA (ed.)
(Santiago de Compostela, 1999), pp. 27-42.

[13] R. FLETCHER, *The Episcopate in the Kingdom of León in the Twelfth Century* (Oxford,
1978), pp. 115-119.

Rada (historian and Archbishop of Toledo) agrees with his Leonese colleague about this, and the same detail appears in the *Primera Cronica General* (chapter 872) of the late thirteenth century. Whether or not this is true, all these historians thought it perfectly understandable that there should be a direct connection between the change of rite and the change of script. And this is entirely understandable, because the Caroline script, in which it is easier to recognize individual letters one by one, was more appropriate for the reformed kind of reading aloud necessitated in the new rite, in which it was essential to recognize every individual letter in order to give each one its prescribed sound.

By the end of the twelfth century the only place where the old Visigothic script was still in use for new documentation was Toledo, the one area, outside Moslem Spain, at least, in which the old 'Mozarabic' rite was still celebrated (which did not depend on Medieval Latin spelling-pronunciations). Once the main Reconquest was over, after the capture of Sevilla in 1248, we can see the old script fall out of use even in Toledo.

As we have seen, the Ibero-Romance of the eleventh century, for all its variability, was still a single language, as are modern Spanish or English. Linguistic variation can arise for many reasons, but the main one, which is probably appreciated better now than it was before the rise of sociolinguistics as an explanatory force, is that new linguistic features, particularly those of a grammatical and lexical nature, can arrive, spread, and even become generally applicable, without speakers necessarily feeling any need to lose the feature that had carried out the same function in previous years. For example, throughout the first millennium A.D. the use of the preposition "*de*", plus the originally accusative form of the relevant noun, was gradually expanding to fulfil the function of expressing possession. But genitive cases did not disappear from Romance until considerably later, and throughout the Late Latin period we find texts (such as the first one above) in which both prepositional phrases with "*de*" and genitive cases are used. There would not be much point in identifying the latter as exclusively Latin and the former as exclusively Romance, for then we would need to classify all the texts of type 1 as being in a mixture of two languages. The point is simply that both usages coexisted together within the one variable Early Romance monolingual state (what Michel Banniard likes to call "*polymorphisme*").[14] A modern example can make this clearer. In Modern Spanish

---

[14] M. BANNIARD, "Diasystèmes et diachronie langagières du latin parlé tardif au protofrançais", in: *La transizione dal latino alle lingue romanze*, ed. J. HERMAN (Tübingen, 1998), pp. 131-154.

we can hear the notion of the futurity of an action expressed either by a synthetic one-word future (such as *"escribiremos"*, "we'll write") or by an analytic construction involving an auxiliary and an infinitive (such as *"vamos a escribir"*, "we're going to write"). It would be very strange to classify each of these as belonging to different languages (calling one of them 'Archaic Castilian' and the other 'Post-Millennium Castilian', or something), with the result that the Castilian Spanish of the present would have to be seen as a mixture of those two, because obviously the two ways of expressing the future are both integral parts of the contemporary language, regardless of what may be going to happen to these forms in the twenty-third century. And we now know, thanks to sociolinguistic research, that such cases are quite normal. Genitives, and synthetic future and passive forms, led by the twelfth century a life which John Green would describe as 'crepuscular', in which they were still understood when heard in a text read aloud, but were actively used less and less.[15] Even then, we have to grant that the genitive remained a live option, particularly with proper names, in the French Romance of the thirteenth century, and it would be difficult to name the date when these inflections actually died.

All this is of central importance to a historical analysis of eleventh and twelfth-century documents. We cannot simply label a document or a phrase as 'Latin' rather than 'Romance' merely on the grounds that it contains features which would look antiquated from the viewpoint of a Castilian-Romance speaker of 1230. We often know that a document was read aloud in order to be understood by interested parties who were probably illiterate, and sometimes it was necessary, for legal reasons, for the people concerned to confirm at the end of the document that they had indeed heard and understood it. There are a number of consequences that we can draw from this. Firstly, in these cases the reader must have read the text in some style of normal speech, rather than in the new reformed Medieval Latin system, so that the listening public could recognize the words. But we can also conclude that the listeners must have understood the morphology and syntax of the text, at least in those essential sections that concerned them directly, even if the grammar sounded somewhat archaic to them. As Michel Banniard says, reading aloud united an illiterate public with the written text. There is nothing odd about this, for in our own time it is normal for illiterate people, and children, to understand texts read to them by others.

---

[15] J.N. GREEN, "The collapse and replacement of verbal inflection in Late Latin / Early Romance: How would one know?", in: *Latin and the Romance Languages in the Early Middle Ages*, ed. R. WRIGHT (London, 1991; reprint, Penn State, 1996), pp. 83-99.

As for the diatopic perspective, we can be sure that although there were important geographical variations, naturally, there is no need for us to visualize different Romance dialects in the eleventh century. What there was, and still is, was the dialect continuum. Features of speech changed noticeably as travellers went from one area to another, but without their finding geographical barriers to comprehension and communication. That is, the isoglosses still did not usually form bundles. Romance-speakers from different parts of the Peninsula certainly spoke with each other, but we see no reference in texts of the time to any need for translators or interpreters between the Romance of different areas.

Even after the eleventh century, this monolingual dialect continuum ('Ibero-Romance') was still referred to as *"(lingua) latina"* ([ladíno]). This is attested in a surprisingly clear manner within the *Poema de Mio Cid*:[16] when the two Infantes de Carrión were speaking to each other in Romance, thinking that nobody could overhear them, they were nevertheless understood by a *"moro latinado"*.[17] This *"moro latinado"* can only be interpreted as being a Moslem who understood Ibero-Romance, because that is what the Infantes were speaking. Unfortunately, although we can now be sure that the surviving version of the *Poema* dates from 1207, we cannot be sure when this fictitious episode was first elaborated. But it seems that even as late as 1207 it cannot have appeared strange for a Moslem who understood Romance to be described as *"latinado"*. At the end of the thirteenth century, one of the Alfonsine historians included a prosified version of the *Poema* in the so-called *Cronica de Veinte Reyes*, and changed the word *"latinado"* here to *"ladino"*.[18] This was probably because *"latín"* and *"latinado"* by then were understood to mean 'Medieval Latin', but the word *"ladino"* was still used to refer to Romance speech, as [ladíno] had done for centuries, although by the Alfonsine period it was specializing its meaning to refer to the Romance used by non-Christians.

Catalonia is a separate case. In some intellectual centres in Catalonia, the reforms may well have been initiated in the ninth century. Reformed Latin texts, of the second type, were established there by the eleventh. In my edition of the Latin poem about El Cid (the *Carmen Campi Doctoris*) I attributed its origin to the Catalan monastery of Ripoll in 1083. This still seems likely to me, even though the most recent editors, Montaner and Escobar, date it enthusiasti-

---

[16] This is considered further in: R. WRIGHT, *Early Ibero-Romance* (Newark, 1995), chapter 18.

[17] *Poema de Mio Cid*, ed. C. SMITH (Oxford, 1972), p. 82, l. 2667: *"un moro latinado bien gelo entendió"*.

[18] R. MENÉNDEZ PIDAL, *Cantar de Mio Cid*, 3 volumes (Madrid, 1944-1946), III, p. 729.

cally to the Rioja in about 1180.[19] This poem was composed in rhythmic sapphics that depend on the reformed pronunciation. The more purist the Latin that was written in a centre, the more likely they were to feel the need for a new *scripta* to correspond to speech, and it is therefore not surprising to find the Catalans writing a Romance *"scripta"* long before other inhabitants of the Peninsula. Several of them followed the Occitan mode of writing Romance, which had already been worked out in Provence, with the result that their written texts are now called 'Occitan' even if the authors were in fact Catalans.

Further West, the period of linguistic transition probably began *c.* 1070-1080, the years of the arrival of the new rite. This is also the time of the Riojan Glosses, and the sociophilological perspective makes this coincidence understandable. Many other changes were involved in addition, of course.[20] There is a close connection between French influence and Medieval Latin throughout the twelfth century. In the event the Riojan monasteries and Santo Domingo de Silos were not to be among the most *"afrancesado"* centres of the age. They wrote there a fairly traditional Late Latin. The monk Grimaldo of Silos is a good example, who at the very end of the eleventh century wrote the *Vita Dominici Silensis* and the *Miracula Beati Felicis*. In particular, although he used the word *"uulgus"* to refer to a number of linguistic forms, this was not to make a distinction between the speech of the educated and the rest. Grimaldo used *"uulgus"* to refer to everybody, as he still saw his words as fitting within the one polymorphic unit.[21]

Menéndez Pidal was fully aware of the role of the French monks in archaising the language of many Peninsular texts after 1080. Even so, the influence of these monks, and the Gregorian reform in general, on Castilian documentation has never been studied in great detail. The recent investigations of Emiliano, however,[22] have shown in detail the results of the reforms in the documentation of the Cathedral of Braga, in Portugal, between 1050 and 1100. Braga was becoming increasingly prestigious. The cathedral recovered its metropolitan

---

[19] WRIGHT, *Early Ibero-Romance*, chapter 16. A. MONTANER and A. ESCOBAR, *Carmen Campidoctoris, o poema latino del Campeador* (Madrid, 2001). For the important early Catalan Romance text, the *Homilies d'Organyà*, datable to *c.* 1200, see the edition by J. BRUGUERA and J. COROMINES (Barcelona, 1989). For Latin documents in Catalonia at this time, see now: A. KOSTO, *Making Agreements in Medieval Catalonia: Power, Order and the Written Word, 1000 – 1200* (Cambridge, 2001).

[20] See for instance: R. WALKER, *Views of Transition: Liturgy and Illumination in Medieval Spain* (London, 1998).

[21] V. VALCÁRCEL, *La "Vita Dominici Silensis" de Grimaldo* (Logroño, 1982). H. FLÓREZ, *España Sagrada*, 33 (Madrid, 1781). WRIGHT, *Early Ibero-Romance*, pp. 272-276.

[22] A. EMILIANO, *Latim e Romance em Documentação notarial da segunda metade do Século XI*, 2 volumes (doctoral thesis; Braga, 1995).

status in 1099.[23] What we see in the Peninsula during the succeeding years is another variety of linguistic variation: Braga, Santiago de Compostela, Toledo and a few other intellectual centres seem to have welcomed Medieval Latin and the new type of Latin text (type two above), and other places less so. It was too simple to say *tout court*, as I did twenty years ago,[24] that Medieval Latin was introduced into the Peninsula with the Council of Burgos of 1080. As Fletcher has said, in the Kingdom of León continuity and change existed side by side in these years.[25] The linguist and the historian need each other's help here, operating with the most precise chronology possible for every text and the sharpest sociophilological appreciation that we can manage.

Toledo is a special case. Toledo, the old Visigothic state and church capital and by now an important Moslem cultural centre, was recaptured from the Moslems by the Leonese in this same important decade (1085). This reconquest had a whole range of sociophilological consequences, since during the twelfth century there were speakers, readers and writers there of Arabic and Medieval Latin, speakers of several regional versions of Romance (and other European languages), and readers of Hebrew. The presence in Toledo of several translation enterprises, mostly from Arabic into Latin, galvanized linguistic self-consciousness. By the end of the century, it seems that there was a general feeling there that there were three types of Romance spoken, broadly speaking Gallo-Romance, Italo-Romance and Ibero-Romance. But we cannot see a consistent distinction drawn there between Latin and Romance on the part of the native inhabitants, even though there can be no doubt that Medieval Latin was used in Toledo by foreign visitors. There is, for example, the famous case of a "*maestro Pedro de Toledo*" who orally translated a treatise from Arabic into Romance in 1142, but needed a colleague from France to polish it up into written acceptability. This colleague was thus polishing Ibero-Romance into Latin by raising the register, rather than translating from one language to another ("*verba latina impolite vel confuse plerumque ab eo prolata poliens et ordinans*").[26] That is, as late as 1142, written formal Latin was still seen by many people as essentially being a polished register of normal speech rather than a separate language.

And yet half a century before, in 1086, the French Cluniac Bernard de Sédirac had come to the Archbishopric of Toledo, and reformed Latin arrived with him. Ximénez de Rada was to call Bernard "*ab infantia litteratus*",[27] and

---

[23] FLETCHER, "El episcopado", p. 32.

[24] WRIGHT, *Late Latin*, chapter 5.

[25] FLETCHER, "El episcopado", p. 29.

[26] WRIGHT, *Late Latin*, pp. 275-276.

[27] XIMÉNEZ DE RADA, *Historia de Rebus Hispaniae*, VI, 23; edited by: J. FERNÁNDEZ

it is the same historian who has left us the text of the poem that was composed to celebrate the capture of Toledo, the eminently Latin *Oppida capta* which seems to have been written during the ensuing celebrations. There is also the famous *Garcineida*, composed in 1099. These are texts of the second type above, and represent a new genre in the Toledan context. The Christians who lived in Toledo before the Reconquest of 1085 had mostly been bilingual in Arabic and Romance, it seems, but not biliterate. If they could read at all they read Arabic. When Christian texts were brought south to Toledo in the twelfth century, they sometimes therefore received marginal glosses in Arabic.[28] So Medieval Latin had certainly been imported into Toledo, to survive beside the Ibero-Romance spoken by the previous inhabitants of the city (the *"mozá-rabes"*) and by the Leonese and Castilians who came south after 1085. Yet in this case nobody felt the need to invent a new Romance *"scripta"* until the very end of the century.

This lack of written Toledan Romance before the 1190s can be explained by the presence of written Arabic. This continued to be used by the native Christian community in Toledo until that point. Literate Christians did not feel any need to invent a Romance *"scripta"* there so long as they could still operate with written Arabic. The mozarabic population of the city increased after 1086 because of immigration by Christians fleeing before the Almorávide invasion. Thus knowledge of Arabic was being continually reinforced, in the same way as continuous immigration from Mexico is revitalizing the Spanish spoken in Los Angeles. We know, from Ángel González Palencia's collection of documents, that Arabic was used for local documentation up to the 1190s.[29] Immigration from the south was by then no longer as regular as before. From 1196 (if González's documents give an accurate picture) we can see a change. From then on there is a passage at the end of many of the Arabic documents to the effect that the document had been read aloud in Romance so that the interested parties could confirm it. That is to say, that for many Romance-speakers in Toledo Arabic was beginning to have less than even a crepuscular existence at the end of that century. So it is no surprise to note that the start of Romance documentation in the city dates from the same decade. Menéndez Pidal published several Romance texts from Toledo in his *Documentos*, of which the earliest dates from 1191.[30] We also know that the *Auto de los Reyes Magos*, an

VALVERDE (Turnhout, 1987: *Corpus Christianorum. Continuatio Medievalis* 72).

[28] P.S. VAN KONINGSVELD, *The Latin-Arabic Glossary of the Leiden University Library* (Leiden, 1977).

[29] A. GONZÁLEZ PALENCIA, *Los mozárabes de Toledo en los siglos XII y XIII* (Madrid, 1926-1928).

[30] R. MENÉNDEZ PIDAL, *Documentos lingüísticos de España*. I. *Reino de Castilla* (Madrid,

Ibero-Romance liturgical drama, was composed in Toledo in about 1200, and even though we still have no idea who composed it nor who wrote it down on parchment, it is no surprise that French influence has been found in its orthography, given the presence in Toledo of so many foreigners. Nor is it any surprise to discover that it was the Archbishop of Toledo at the time, Martín López de Pisuerga, who most directly promoted the use of written Romance within the Castilian chancery, in which he had great influence before his death in August 1208.[31]

Toledo is in New Castile, and New Castile is also the area of greatest interest as concerns the language of the *fueros* of this century (these are the charters of local government granted to towns newly conquered from the Moslems). It has sometimes been stated that many *fueros* were written in Romance in the twelfth century,[32] but this cannot have been the case. The *fueros* in Romance form are later translations of documents originally redacted in Late Latin form (our first type above). Many of these had been promulgated in the 1100s, and naturally the date of the original grant was maintained in the later Romance translation. These translations were mostly made after 1240, in fact.[33] But the Late Latin *fueros* are still of considerable interest to us. Francisco Gimeno has, for example, used twelfth-century *fueros* of our first textual type to discover important details about Ibero-Romance usage.[34]

A few *fueros*, of no great importance in themselves, were written in Romance form in New Castile between 1206 and 1208. These are precisely the years in which Martín López de Pisuerga, Archbishop of Toledo, was the dominant influence in the Castilian chancery as well as in Toledo. The *Treaty of Cabreros* (our third text above) was written in March 1206. Versions survive from both the Leonese and the Castilian chancery. The meeting in Toledo which is sometimes referred to as the First Cortes of Toledo, held in January 1207, also gave rise to documentation in Romance form.[35] Hernández has also suggested that the surviving version of the *Poema de Mio Cid* was written onto

---

1966).

[31] WRIGHT, *Tratado*, pp. 28-33.

[32] For instance: C. SMITH, "The vernacular", in: *The New Cambridge Medieval History*, V, ed. D. ABULAFIA (Cambridge, 1999), pp. 71-83.

[33] WRIGHT, *Tratado*, pp. 113-116.

[34] F. GIMENO MENÉNDEZ, *Sociolingüística histórica (siglos X-XII)* (Alicante, 1995). R. LAPESA, "El Fuero de Valfermoso de las Monjas", in: *Homenaje a Álvaro Galmés de Fuentes*, I (Oviedo, 1985), pp. 43-98.

[35] F.J. HERNÁNDEZ, "Las Cortes de Toledo de 1207", in: *Las Cortes de Castilla y León en la Edad Media*, I (Valladolid, 1988), pp. 221-263. Also: IDEM, "Historia y epopeya: el *Cantar del Cid* entre 1147 y 1207", in: *Actas del III Congreso de la Asociación Hispánica de Literatura Medieval*, I, ed. M.I. TORO PASCUA (Salamanca, 1994), pp. 453-467.

parchment (whenever it had been composed) for an opening performance in these same Cortes of 1207, a suggestion which remains possible even though the scribes of all four texts (the Leonese and Castilian texts of the Treaty, the *Posturas* of the Cortes, and the *Poema*) seem to have been trained in four different places.

But after Martín's death in 1208, with the arrival of Ximénez de Rada in both the Archbishopric and the Chancery, we see no more such documents. The Castilian Chancery was peripatetic, but had its home base in Palencia, not Toledo. Palencia already had international contacts in the twelfth century, but its years of greatest importance came in the early thirteenth, with the foundation there of the first *Studium Generale* in the Peninsula. During those years this *Studium* came to be a centre of both Latin and Romance writing; as elsewhere, the two grew together. The years 1206-1208 could well have been those of the elaboration of the Ibero-Romance *Libro de Alexandre*, probably composed in Palencia. These are also the years of the so-called *Corónicas Navarras*. If these are not just chronological coincidences, we can glimpse what was happening to official policy. When Ximénez de Rada, educated in Paris in Grammar and Medieval Latin, arrived in the Archbishopric and the Chancery, he did what his masters in Paris would have wanted him to do: both in the Chancery and in the new University he made writers use Latin. This was now, though, the new Medieval Latin (text type 2). Latin grammar had been solidifying considerably throughout the twelfth century, particularly among the scholars at Paris, and the Masters in Paris were not at all sympathetic to new ideas coming from Toledo. Neither was Ximénez de Rada, who preferred to promote the rearguard resistance action in favour of written Latin.[36]

We can also see the transition beginning in the late eleventh century in Santiago de Compostela. The European rite does not seem to have been introduced into Santiago immediately after 1080, but the clerics appear to have been having training in the new Latin during the 1090s. There was a Cluniac bishop, Dalmacio, there briefly (1094-1095), but the name most closely asociated with the arrival of the Twelfth-Century Renaissance in Santiago is that of Diego Gelmírez, bishop from *c.* 1099 and eventually Archbishop. During his time the Santiago Cathedral school gained a reputation for its Latin, which may well be why most of the royal notaries in the Leonese Chancery during the twelfth century seem to have been trained at Santiago. We have already seen that straight after the separation of León from Castile in 1157 the Leonese Chancery

---

[36] This is what Maurilio Pérez González refers to as "the tenacious resistance put up by Latin in the Chancery", in: *El latín de la Cancillería Castellana (1158-1214)* (Salamanca, 1985), p. 37; as if the language put up the resistance rather than the people who used it.

introduced Caroline script. One of the authors of the *Historia Compostellana*, usually dated to *c.* 1137, was "Girardus", master of the Santiago Cathedral school, and from that History we can deduce some details of the transition to the reformed Latin. Between 1137 and the late 1160s we have less explicit written information about Santiago, but we can tell that the reformed Latin continued to be in use. Since it seems likely that the *Chronica Adefonsi Imperatoris* of *c.* 1147 (our second text above) was composed by the Bishop of Astorga, Arnaldo, we have there an impressive witness to the Medieval Latin skills present in the Kingdom of León (even though Arnaldo himself was probably trained in Catalonia). A document of 1169 tells us that Bishop Pedro Gudésteiz was paying for his clerics to learn Latin. Bishop Pedro Suárez de Deza, the one who seems to have introduced reformed Latin into Salamanca after 1166, moved from Salamanca to Santiago in 1173, and thereby reaffirmed its high intellectual level. He even acted as royal Leonese chancellor for a few months in 1183. Thus overall the new Medieval Latin probably took stronger root in the Kingdom of León than it did in Castile. The only Romance documentation from the Leonese chancery before the two kingdoms reunited in 1230 was the *Tratado de Cabreros*, which was organized by Castilian notaries.

Thus the sociolinguistic position in Santiago, as elsewhere, depended crucially on a few strong personalities. It would be possible to sum the transition up as if it were a generalized intellectual movement, but wherever we can see changes taking place they are the result of the work of an energetic individual determined to establish the reformed culture (as, indeed, had been originally the case with Alcuin). It seems safe to deduce this about Pedro Suárez de Deza, even though he, unlike Diego Gelmírez, did not attract the attention of any biographer who could have told us more about his life. Suárez de Deza died in 1202, but the clerics of Santiago and the Chancery officers in León had no intention of yielding ground to the new Romance "*scripta*" at that point, and in 1207 (the year after the *Tratado de Cabreros*) they reaffirmed Pedro Gudésteiz's explicit allegiance to the need for good written Latinity.[37] 1207 was precisely the time when the Castilian Chancery, and quite possibly also the new University of Palencia, were changing their minds and accepting the validity of the new Romance form for official documentation. León was having none of that.

---

[37] V. BELTRÁN DE HEREDIA, "La formación intelectual del clero en España durante los siglos XII, XIII y XIV", *Revista Española de Teología* 6 (1946), pp. 313-357, pp. 321-322. See also: WRIGHT, *Late Latin*, p. 223. For Santiago in the twelfth century, see: M.C. DÍAZ Y DÍAZ, *De Santiago y de los caminos de Santiago* (Santiago de Compostela, 1997).

On the other hand, throughout the century Santiago was attracting more and more foreign visitors and pilgrims from many different lands, including from beyond the Pyrenees, and it is thus not surprising that it is generally believed that the first poems to be written entirely in Ibero-Romance form were from Galicia, even though the oldest Galician-Portuguese poems that we know now are found in manuscripts of a later period. Even as early as 1136 we know that there was a Galician "*juglar*", called Palla, at Alfonso VII's court, although what he actually sang is a matter for conjecture. Galician came eventually to be known as the type of Ibero-Romance most suited to the lyric genre.

So far, I have not mentioned the *Historia Roderici*, the twelfth-century biography of Ruy Díaz, also known as El Cid. Both its date and place of origin are disputed, which makes it hard to use in any investigation that requires secure dates and places. It is a Medieval Latin text (type two), rather than Late Latin. I am one of those who accept a dating from the Eastern part of the Peninsula in the late 1140s, although others prefer a date of 1114, or an origin in Salamanca (neither of which seem likely in view of the type of Latin it is written in), and Montaner and Escobar now prefer Rioja in the 1180s.[38] There is one detail of considerable interest which is worth pointing out here. In the letter which the Count of Barcelona sends to Ruy Díaz (in chapter 38), we read:

> Si autem exieris ad nos in plano et separaberis te a monte tuo, eris ipse Rodericus quem dicunt bellatorem et Campeatorem. Si autem hoc factum nolueris, eris talis, qualem dicunt in vulgo Castellani aleuoso et in uulgo Francorum bauzador et fraudator.[39]

There has been considerable discussion over whether these letters are authentic. They may be, but even if they are not, these phrases are intriguing. The Count of Barcelona, the same Count whose humiliation was celebrated in the *Carmen Campi Doctoris*, knows that Rodrigo was known as "*Campiator*" (the Latinate form for the word later to be written in Romance as "*Campeador*"). The antonym of this epithet seems to the writer to involve three separate words. One of these is "*alevoso*", a word composed of an Arabic root and an Ibero-Romance suffix. The other two are from the Romance of the Franks ("*in uulgo Francorum*"), which might well here mean that of the Catalans: "*bauzator*" and "*fraudator*". All three are Latinate forms of Romance words that mean "deceitful". The Count, or the author of the *Historia*, is making an interesting distinction here between either Gallo-Romance or his own Catalan Romance, the "*uulgus Francorum*", and that of the Castilians, "*qualem dicunt in uulgo Castellani*", with the word "*uulgus*" probably here implying a conscious con-

---

[38] MONTAMER and ESCOBAR, *Carmen*, pp. 117-120.
[39] FALQUE e.a., *Chronica Hispana*, p. 72.

trast with Latin. This is an explicit distinction between kinds of Romance such as we can also find in Toledo. The different kinds of Romance are not here called 'French' (or 'Catalan') and 'Castilian' yet, since such metalinguistic usages of geographical terms still lay in the future.

Right at the end of the century, probably in 1199, Raimbaut de Vaqueiras composed his famous *descort "Eras quan vey verdeyar"*, in five separate *"scripta"*.[40] These five *"scripta"* (which we may or may not wish to see as corresponding to independent languages at this point) can be identified as French, Italo-Romance, Occitan, Gascon and Ibero-Romance. Raimbaut is unlikely to have been making any further distinction between Ibero-Romance dialectal usage. He had never been there. Ramón Menéndez Pidal referred to the language of the Ibero-Romance lines as *"español-aragonés"*, and others, including Mercedes Brea, have baldly referred to its language as *"gallego"*,[41] but this is likely to be anachronistic. At the end of the twelfth century it may have been becoming common to distinguish between Ibero-Romance and other types of Romance spoken further East and North, but not yet to distinguish with any clarity in the Peninsula itself (apart perhaps from the case of Catalan). It would be a mirage, for example, to describe the language of the two Chancery versions of the *Tratado de Cabreros* of 1206 as being Castilian and Leonese respectively in a metalinguistic rather than merely geographical sense. That is, there are differences between the two versions, but these do not on the whole correspond to reconstructable isoglosses between Castile and León.[42] At the turn of the century we are still in only the initial stages of the slow but important sociophilological revolution which would come to its head over the next hundred years. The thirteenth century is the one in which we see the full consequences of the Twelfth-Century Renaissance in the Peninsula, whose protagonists wanted to "separate the clergy from the laity and make them a privileged and disciplined group".[43] One aspect of this attitude was the standardization of reformed Medieval Latin, which eventually led, perhaps inadvertently, to the conceptual invention of separate Romance languages, one for each Kingdom. But the catalysing context for these developments had been gradually establishing itself throughout the twelfth century, as has been shown above.

<hr>

[40] M. DE RIQUER, *Los trovadores: historia literaria y textos*, 3 volumes (Barcelona, 1975), II, pp. 840-842.

[41] R. MENÉNDEZ PIDAL, *Poesía juglaresca y orígenes de las literaturas románicas* (Madrid, 1957), pp. 137-138. M. BREA, "La estrofa V del *descort* plurilingüe de Raimbaut de Vaqueiras", in: *Homenaje a Álvaro Galmés de Fuentes*, II (Oviedo, 1987), pp. 49-64.

[42] WRIGHT, *Tratado*, pp. 78-97.

[43] Quoting: FLETCHER, "El episcopado", p. 36 (in translation).

Chapter 18

The Assertion of Ibero-Romance

The late Yakov Malkiel once wrote an article with the title "Excessive self-assertion in Glottodiachrony: Portuguese *sofrer* and its Latin and Spanish counterparts".[1] He liked the idea of "excessive self-assertion" sufficiently to give a conference lecture shortly afterwards on "New problems in excessive self-assertion versus hypercorrection".[2] The idea surfaced in other papers he gave in that decade, and was usually based on otherwise baffling developments in the history of Portuguese which he explained by suggesting that the Portuguese speakers were deliberately trying to choose alternatives unlike those of Castilian, where there was such a choice of variant forms. Thus the Portuguese, on this view, decided, not necessarily consciously, to adopt the form "*pareço*" as the norm, rather than "*paresco*", in order to be as unlike the Castilian "*parezco*" as could reasonably be achieved. Portuguese "*sofrer*" became unlike Castilian "*sufrir*", and Portuguese "*juiz*" unlike Castilian "*juez*", et cetera, for similar reasons. From the late Middle Ages to the seventeenth century, such a reaction from Portuguese speakers is understandable on political grounds. They wished to differentiate their language from Castilian at a time when they felt in political danger from Castile. In this respect, their moti-

This chapter is a reprint of: "The assertion of Ibero-Romance", *Forum for Modern Language Studies* 36 (2000), pp. 230-240. We are grateful to Ms Fiona Willis, on behalf of the *Forum for Modern Language Studies* and Oxford University Press, for permitting this reprint.

[1] Y. MALKIEL, "Excessive self-assertion in glottodiachrony: Portuguese *sofrer* and its Latin and Spanish counterparts", *Lingua* 65 (1985), pp. 29-50.

[2] Not included in the Acts. It is referred to in: Y. MALKIEL, *A Tentative Autobibliography* (Berkeley, 1988), p. 44 (item 117d).

vation for making the choices they did is seen as political rather than linguistic, and similar to the decisions often made by those who wish to standardize local speeches in modern Spanish *autonomías* in such a way as to stress their individuality. This is the localist instinct sometimes called *"diferencialismo"*. To observers from outside, this often seems absurd; for the speakers of the time and place, it often seems extremely important.

What Malkiel meant by "excessive", though, was not what a modern Castilian would mean in applying the same adjective to the peculiarities of Murcian, Aragonese or Asturian regional speeches and consequently elaborated separatist orthographies. Malkiel was implying no criticism, but merely trying to explain a development that seemed linguistically to go further than necessary. There was no linguistic reason why Portuguese should choose to develop these words or morphemes as radically as they did. The motivation was in essence political. This insight was important, but to some extent has since been overlooked. The present chapter aims to show that this process had distant roots, and was starting to happen in the thirteenth century.

The conceptual fragmentation of Ibero-Romance seems to have followed, although only by a few generations, the emergence into the limelight and into a new written mode of Ibero-Romance itself. The earliest Romance texts are referred to at the time as being *"romanz"* (or *"romance"*) without further explicit geographical marking. The semantic force of this word came from the recent separate emancipation of Latin and Romance into two conceptual entities, each with its own writing system, where previously there had been just the one. Latin had been all-powerful for at least the first millennium of our era. The administrative classes of the later Roman Empire, late Antiquity and the Early Middle Ages all held to the decision that traditional written Latin would be the bureaucratic language of Western Europe, regardless of the fact that it corresponded to speech habits either only in part (in the Romance speaking areas) or not at all (in the Germanic and Celtic speaking areas). Down the centuries, linguistic training in the inherited standard was thus not merely a theoretical desideratum for writers of literature, based on the grammarians, but a practical requirement for the elaboration of all working documentation. And on the whole, it worked far better than might have been expected. Greek took over in the East after the political eclipse of the Empire, but Western European societies continued to be based on written documentation, on laws, deeds of sale, et cetera, drawn up in the ancient forms and styles, which seem for practical purposes to have been assumed to be potentially intelligible to all concerned if they were read aloud. This applied through the Visigothic age and beyond, even into the twelfth century.

As we have seen, it seems likely that there was no strict conceptual divide between 'Latin' and 'Romance' until the period when new ways of writing began to be experimented with, from the ninth century, and that with a little give and take, Early Romance-speakers from different areas could understand each other then in practice at least as well as English-speakers from different areas do now. This implies that the situation of complex monolingualism could continue almost regardless of the fact that the spoken language was changing, and even of the fact that it was to some extent changing in different ways in different places. The advantages of continuing the old methods of writing, even if they now often represented Romance words and grammatical formations (as often happened in the Iberian Peninsula up to the late twelfth century), were as obvious to them at that time as the advantages of maintaining the existing single written English form or the existing single written Castilian form are to most of the users of these languages today.

The earliest texts in written Romance form from the Iberian Peninsula (except Catalonia, where some writers wrote in the Occitan mode rather earlier) date from the very late twelfth century. Texts of any length or sophistication date from the early thirteenth century. By that time, a conscious distinction was beginning to develop in the Peninsula between Latin and Romance, at least in several intellectual centres, a distinction which was catalysed by the introduction of the formal pronunciation used in reading Latin texts in ecclesiastical contexts. These distinctions in modes of writing and reading, which underlie the eventual conceptual distinction between Latin and Romance as entire separate languages, had been inapplicable in the non-Catalan Iberian Peninsula until the French Medieval Latin was introduced late in the eleventh century. It spread through the twelfth century, establishing itself at different times in different centres. Once the new Medieval Latin pronunciation was regularly used, there was an incentive to write texts of other genres in a distinct way, as there had been earlier in France. But they could not just use the French system, which had been adapted specifically for the speech of Northern France, or the system developed for the Occitan of Provence. And although we see here and there attempts to write in a noticeably Provençal manner in some of the earliest Peninsular texts, it must have been clear more or less from the start to all those who wanted to experiment with new writing systems that something more specifically Hispanic was going to be needed.

At first, however, the elaboration of the new methods of writing did not lead immediately to the idea that all the different kingdoms of the Peninsula had their own separate Romance languages. Many Romance philologists of the last two centuries have liked to envisage the different Romance languages of the Modern Age as having already had separable existence in the first millennium A.D., but this is at best a doubtful hypothesis, since those who spoke Romance do not seem to have felt this way at the time. In the thirteenth century, Berceo, and the author of the *Libro de Apolonio*, and other Hispanic writers of texts in Romance, just referred to the language they used as being Romance, without further distinctions (this is not to say that the texts were all written the same way, of course).

Although the phrase "*romance castellano*" appears in the Alfonsine texts of later in that century, the nouns "*castellano*", "*portugués*", et cetera, were not in use until the end of, or in some cases after, the thirteenth century. The idea that the different ways of writing Romance were actually separate languages was deliberately reinforced from the later thirteenth century, as one aspect of the increasingly prevalent idea that the Iberian kingdoms were different countries. Before the 1200s, for example, it would have sounded strange for a Portuguese to refer to Castile as being a foreign country, as being 'abroad'.[3] It probably still sounded a bit strange towards the end of the thirteenth century, but less so than before. Soon after that, the excessive self-assertion of their national identity came to seem more essential than any kind of pan-Romance solidarity (most notably, perhaps, during the campaign of Aljubarrota in the early 1380s), with the linguistic consequences that Malkiel perceived.

However, this fragmentation had to wait its turn. The first half of the thirteenth century was seeing a different struggle altogether, that between the relative official status of Latin and Romance. This struggle seems to have entered a more heightened phase with the unprecedented decision taken in the Chancery to redact the important Treaty of Cabreros in the new Romance style in 1206.[4] This was not just an abstract struggle between social forces or groups; there were indeed a variety of intellectual and social currents competing for attention in this remarkable period, but considerable importance can be attributed to the personalities of some of the leading intellectuals of the age, several of whom are indeed describable as 'excessively self-assertive'.

---

[3] P. LINEHAN, *History and the Historians of Medieval Spain* (Oxford, 1993), p. 310.

[4] The circumstances surrounding this Treaty are considered at length in: R. WRIGHT, *El Tratado de Cabreros (1206): estudio sociofilológico de una reforma ortográfica* (London, 2000).

The outstanding intellectual personality in the Castilian kingdom of the first half of the thirteenth century was Rodrigo Ximénez de Rada. Rodrigo, from Navarra, was educated in Paris in, among many other accomplishments, the proper use of the reformed Medieval Latin. He became Archbishop of Toledo after the unexpected death of the previous incumbent in August 1208, and remained in that post until his death in 1247. He was not only the head of the Church, for as a result of a grant made by Alfonso VIII to the previous Archbishop in July 1206, he was also *ex officio* head of the organization of the Royal Chancery, the office that drew up all the important documentation of the kingdom, despite the simultaneous presence of a Chancellor. In addition, Rodrigo was closely involved in running the first institutions in the kingdom that could now be called 'Universities', in particular at Palencia. Palencia does not have a University now, but it had been an important centre for legal educa-tion in the later twelfth century, and in the early 1200s it was the home of both the Castilian Chancery and the first Castilian University. Rodrigo was also a businessman, landowner, financier, and indeed soldier, being to a large extent responsible for the mobilization that led to the most significant victory of the Castilian Reconquest, at Las Navas de Tolosa in 1212.[5] He wrote a great deal. But few modern Hispanists have studied him, because he wrote in Latin. His contemporary Gonzalo de Berceo, on the other hand, had more modest preten-sions and less importance in his lifetime, but Berceo wrote in Romance, and as a result is far better known now.

Rodrigo Ximénez de Rada wrote in Latin because in his time that was still the serious mode to use. It had had enormous advantages for many centuries, particularly in its international status and its role as the vehicle for the Church of which he was such a distinguished representative. He was naturally not alone, even in thirteenth-century Castile, in assuming the primacy of Latin. His admiring chancellor during the years before 1217, Diego García (Diego de Campos), had also been trained in Paris, and felt this to be the case even more strongly. We can tell from his treatise entitled *Planeta*,[6] written in Latin in 1218, shortly after his leaving the Castilian Chancellorship, that the traditional Latin written forms and spellings held for him an almost mystical significance; the new Romance orthography apparently seemed to him to be bordering on the heretical (as Biblical translations in Romance did in some quarters). Diego García's *Planeta* is one of the most remarkable, and longest, works of the first

---

[5] See: H. GRASSOTTI, "Don Rodrigo Ximénez de Rada, gran señor y hombre de negocios en la Castilla del siglo XIII", *Cuadernos de Historia de España* 75-76 (1972), pp. 1-302.

[6] M. ALONSO (ed.), *Diego García, natural de Campos: Planeta* (Madrid, 1943).

half of the thirteenth century, yet probably even fewer Hispanists have studied Diego García than have studied Rodrigo Ximénez de Rada. By writing in Latin, the two most influential intellectuals in Castile were deliberately, even excessively, asserting the view that Hispanic culture was part still of the old international *Respublica Litterarum*. They followed the line being advocated at their *alma mater*, the University of Paris, whose resident intellectuals were in these same years aiming to resist the theological and other cultural novelties that were being spread from the south, and in particular from Toledo, as a result of what we now refer to as the Twelfth-Century Renaissance. These are also, indeed, the years of the Albigensian crusade against the Occitan culture of Provence, one of whose defining features was the widespread use of written Romance. If this line of thought had eventually won the day, and the internationally-valid Latin writing system had reasserted its old domination and practical value (perhaps with minor updatings), then Rodrigo and Diego would be studied avidly on Hispanic Studies courses of the present. If, conversely, Romance writing had not won the day, Berceo's works would forever have seemed to later Castilians as being as rustic and perversely strange as the written forms of Asturian, Aragonese and Murcian speech appear to many Castilians today. Although the idea behind their elaboration, in each case, is that in this way the writers will assert and enhance the image of their own cultural identity, the effect can in the event be counter-productive.[7] Wiser counsel can then prevail. The orthographical reforms undertaken in Chile in the nineteenth century were sensibly reversed in the 1920s, for example, to maintain a reputation for intellectual seriousness that these reforms had threatened to damage.

It could seem a strange irony that the Archbishop of Toledo should have been resisting some of the intellectual currents that had spread from his own Archbishopric before his arrival (although perhaps this was part of the reasoning behind his appointment in the first place). Toledo had had a different, and in many ways more interesting, intellectual history than anywhere else. Local documentation was mainly prepared in Arabic throughout the twelfth century. But knowledge of Arabic in Toledo was decreasing, and the previous Archbishop, Martín López de Pisuerga, had presided over the gradually increasing use of Romance documentation in Toledo towards the end of the century. Thus the *Auto de los Reyes Magos* was almost certainly written there, although mod-

---

[7] I.M. HASSAN, "Sistemas gráficos del español sefardí", in: *Actas del Primer Congreso Internacional de Historia de la Lengua Española*, ed. M. ARIZA *e.a.* (Madrid, 1988), pp. 127-137, has pointed out that even modern Judeo-Spanish writing systems unfortunately give such an impression to Castilians.

ern philologists still do not agree on where the author and scribe had been trained, and probably performed there too, perhaps in the Cathedral itself. I have shown how the drafting in Romance of the Treaty of Cabreros on Palm Sunday 1206 could well have been the consequence of the wresting of control in the Chancery by Martín López, Archbishop of Toledo, from Diego García, ostensibly Chancellor but increasingly in danger of being kicked upstairs.[8] That Treaty, a document of great political importance, was written in the new style (Romance). So too, nine months later, were the decisions taken at the first Cortes of Toledo in January 1207 (this remains true even though there is some doubt as to whether or not we should accept the description of the meeting as 'Cortes'). Other, shorter, documents survive from between 1206 and mid-1208 to show that the Romance party in the Chancellor's office was asserting itself with increasing success. But then Martín López died in August 1208, the Chancellor had the great satisfaction of seeing the traditionally-minded Rodrigo Ximénez de Rada being appointed in his place, and between them they stopped the advance of written Romance rather than Latin. The Chancery produced no more texts in Romance until the 1220s, after Diego García had been replaced by Juan de Soria. This was not just a matter of the internal organization of one office. Sociolinguistic status depends crucially on what kinds of written and spoken language have prestige, and no documentation had greater prestige than that of the Royal Chancery. Chancery practice would not be expected to be in any way revolutionary, and the change instigated by Archbishop Martín López was probably startling to anyone who saw the Treaty of Cabreros, not just to poor old Diego García. Modern European Union treaties, for example, are unlikely ever to be presented in Phonetic Script.

This conservative reaction after 1208 also seems to apply to the Romance literature being written at or near Palencia. If the dating of the *Libro de Alexandre* to the central years of the first decade of the thirteenth century is accurate, and if the date of 1207 A.D. at the end of the fourteenth-century manuscript of the *Poema de Mio Cid* can be taken seriously, and if the scribe of the 1207 manuscript had been educated at or near Palencia (regardless of whether or not he was the author) – and recent scholarship suggests these to be reasonable hypotheses – then we have in both the written literature and in the Chancery documentation of the time exactly the same chronological pattern: two long texts in mid-decade in Romance, but then from 1208 until the 1220s, well into the reign of Fernando III (1217-1252), there are no more written Romance texts from either the Chancery or the nascent University milieux. Both of these were

[8] WRIGHT, *El Tratado*.

based in Palencia, and it seems for practical reasons natural to visualize the new University and the Royal Chancery as being closely connected. Thus it would be plausible to attribute the anti-Romance assertivity within both genres principally to the influence of Rodrigo Ximénez de Rada himself. That is, here too we are not dealing with social forces, or even social groups, but with the same one influential individual.

Thus it was that in the first half of the thirteenth century those who wished to assert the value of written Romance over the old traditional Latin form had their main fight against the bastions of Latin. They had little time or need for also asserting themselves in this way against each other. But the situation began to change after the Church Council of Valladolid in 1228. Berceo seems to have started writing in Romance in the early 1230s, even though he had apparently been working at the San Millán since at least 1221 (according to the data adduced by the brothers García Turza).[9] In the 1240s, a number of monastic notaries seem to have decided to change, and write predominantly in Romance. Towards the end of that decade, Rodrigo Ximénez de Rada died, and so did the Chancellor who had succeeded Diego García on the accession of Fernando III, Juan Díaz de Soria, who had also composed a History on recent events in Latin. By then the future King Alfonso X and his intellectual advisers were taking a keen interest in establishing a centralised legal system redacted in Romance. Even before Alfonso's accession, they were collecting together *fueros* and, it would seem, translating some of the Latin ones into Romance. This process culminated in the preparation of the *Fuero Real* in 1255 and its promulgation in 1256, which is seen now and was probably seen then as representing the explicit acceptance of the new written system for use in legal documentation.

Rodrigo Ximénez de Rada would not have approved of what happened in the decade after his death. His base at Palencia had been an important centre for the study of international law, necessarily in Latin, since before its designation as *Studium Generale*. It had been explicitly supported by the Papacy in the early 1220s. But now Alfonso X was supporting Salamanca instead, and he was regulating the legal system of Castile through the use of a modern and merely national linguistic modality, rather than the traditional international Latin one. It seems that Ximénez de Rada had countenanced the use of written Romance in his own office only for minor local *fueros* granted to non-Latinate settlers in New Castile, after 1233. Romance writing still seemed at best a minor, slightly

---

[9] C. GARCÍA TURZA and J. GARCÍA TURZA, *Una nueva visión de la lengua de Berceo a la luz de la documentación emilianense del siglo XIII* (Logroño, 1996).

eccentric, genre in the first half of the century in Castile. But suddenly in the 1250s the tables were turned. The new King decided to adopt it and encourage it, essentially for nationalistic reasons. Thus the written Romance mode encouraged by Alfonso was semantically opposed not only to Latin but also to Romance used outside Castile. Castilian Romance became in his eyes a marker of the independent value of Castile, to be nurtured and developed into the main written expression of all the genres that it could take. Latin texts, meanwhile, were backgrounded with remarkable speed. Ximénez de Rada's Latin histories, and others, were used as sources for Alfonso's own histories, and then largely forgotten. In 1250 Guillermo Pérez de la Calzada sent Alfonso a splendid Latin poem about the capture of Seville in 1248, explicitly intended for inclusion in Alfonso's forthcoming historical enterprises; Alfonso ignored it. The Leonese scholar Gil de Zamora, educated abroad, wrote powerful works in Latin in the 1280s, partly modelled on Ximénez de Rada; they have hardly been read since, while the contemporary Alfonsine histories and other works in Romance have excited the imaginations of many. The self-assertion of written Romance against Latin in Castile after the 1240s was so forceful that we could easily feel justified in calling it 'excessive' (and, indeed, in the legal field, the pendulum was to swing back to Latin in the later medieval centuries). In the 1270s, twenty years later than the official assertion of the validity of Castilian, Alfonso helped in the separate establishment of written gallego-portugués as the genre for lyric poetry. It seems that that too briefly acquired the conceptual status of a separate language, before fragmenting in the fourteenth century into Portuguese and Galician.

Conceptual fragmentation of this kind was not inevitable. A Pan-Iberian written Romance form (outside Catalonia) could have come into general use. After all, in modern Latin America the different Spanish-speaking countries have managed to combine national independence with maintaining the international written Spanish standard. They all see it both as 'Spanish' and as their own language. There are no serious movements to invent conceptually separate "*venezolano*", "*chileno*", et cetera, despite the regional variations. In the early thirteenth century, all Romance speakers in the Peninsula (west of Catalonia, at least) seem in a similar way to have thought of their language as Romance without further conceptual divisions, despite the perceptible variability. Ibero-Romance could have stayed that way. But the Alfonsine scholars started to use phrases like "*nuestro romance castellano*". Written standards of a moderately restrictive kind began to operate on a kingdom-wide basis in Castile, in Portugal, and to a much lesser extent in Aragonese, and these standards had the effect of accentuating the differences so that they were felt to operate at a national-language level rather than a regional-dialect one.

This was a political event, but there was in fact a linguistic accident that abetted it. The new Romance spellings used in France were the first, but they could not have been helpful in Castile, Portugal, Catalonia, et cetera, because they were based on Northern French phonology and on the idea (which had come in with the Medieval Latin reforms) that good spelling had to be alphabetic, operating on the basis of the direct transcription of a letter for each speech sound (the phonographic principle). This is anyway a dangerous misconception, as most of the great Oriental cultures demonstrate, and it led almost inevitably to Romance being written down, and then standardized, in different ways in different places.

This kind of differentiation in new writing systems in turn encourages those in public life who have an interest in exaggerating regional or national feelings of cultural inferiority, in claiming wherever remotely plausible to be in some sense oppressed, and in encouraging any other exploitable resentments. Opportunistic (self-assertive) politicians therefore tend to support the use of differential regional writing systems. In this way the process of inventing separate writing modes can reinforce a needlessly rebarbative kind of regional cultural identity, excessively asserting its value in the face of the obvious advantages of tolerant internationalism and human solidarity. Nationalism in Western Europe in the later Middle Ages was thus abetted by the conceptual split of Romance from Latin, and then of Romance into separate Romance languages, a process which began in the later twelfth century and continued throughout the thirteenth. In the Iberian Peninsula it seems fair to characterise this unnecessary fragmentation into separate Ibero-Romance languages as an excessive extension of natural feelings of euphoria, after the long tense struggle between writing in Latin and writing in Romance had definitively turned in favour of Romance. In the late 1240s, one of the teams in this tug of war suddenly collapsed, and at once the victorious team hurtled further away from the centre point than was at all necessary. Ximénez de Rada's history *De Rebus Hispaniae* was even translated into Romance by one of his colleagues soon after his death.[10] It could be said that the team promoting Latin culture never entirely recovered in Castile. It was to remain a minority culture in Castile in a way it was not to be elsewhere (in England, for example, the great majority of printed works in the sixteenth century were in Latin, not English). We could even compare this sequence of action and reaction to the consequences of the

[10] LINEHAN, *History*, p. 468.

death of Franco. In the same way as this led to more linguistic self-assertion against Castilian from the *autonomías* than seems desirable to anyone not involved, we could hypothesise that the personality of Rodrigo Ximénez de Rada was so dominant in his lifetime that the reaction after his death was out of all foreseeable proportion, a linguistic "*destape*", as they no longer had any need to cover their written language up with the traditional Latinate disguise.

It has to be appreciated, however, that the emergence of Romance as a separate written language from Latin is nowhere to be interpreted as a case of the empowerment of a previously marginalized group. Everybody spoke Romance in the Christian Kingdoms, whether or not they could read or write; even if some of the monastic community were also able to speak in a kind of international Latin systematically distinct from their Romance, they were native Romance speakers as much as anyone else and probably more fluent than most. More importantly, perhaps, it is always necessary to remember that the initial written Romance texts were all prepared in educated centres by scribes who knew how to write Latin in the usual way. The Strasbourg Oaths themselves appear, textually unmarked, within a Latin History. The *Cantilena* of Sainte Eulalie accompanies a Latin one on the same topic in the same manuscript. The Provençal *Alba* is a bilingual (or perhaps bi-stylistic) poem. The Treaty of Cabreros between León and Castile was compiled in Romance by two scribes, one from each Chancery, whose names we see at the end of earlier documents redacted in Latin form. It is likely that the *Libro de Alexandre*, probably the earliest "*mester de clerecía*" poem, was composed by a writer already adept in the almost identical Latin metrical form as used in France. Berceo was a monastic notary involved for several years in organizing Latin documents before his Romance-writing career began. Romance writing was thus an alternative mode chosen for a purpose by the same social group as was already working competently with Latin. Anyone who could read and write Romance could already, almost by definition, read and write Latin. In the same way, all those who now write with the separatist Aragonese or Asturian writing systems have already learnt how to write Castilian. What we are witnessing in each case is a change of perspective within the literate members of society, not a victory over them by others. The revolution takes place within the one social group, even during Alfonsine times, though the consequences were eventually to spread more widely. It was only in the following century that the nature of linguistic education changed significantly. Juan Manuel wrote only in Romance, and explicitly proclaimed his insufficiency in Latin without apparent embarrassment, because a reading public had by then come into existence who had been trained to enjoy written works in Romance but had not learnt Latin first.

But this monolingually-Castilian reading group had been created by the Alfonsine reforms. It had not existed before. Before 1200, an Ibero-Romance culture existed, which in many respects could still be envisaged as being part of a wider Pan-Romance culture, presented within its customary international Latinate disguise if it was written at all. The change in writing systems eventually helped break this international culture into smaller parts, as Romance fragmented conceptually into separate Romances. Such fragmentation is a contingential cultural and political invention rather than an inevitable linguistic development. It has been politicians, rather than linguists or normal speakers, who decided in the fourteenth century that Galician and Portuguese were different languages, or in the twentieth century that Valencian is a different language from Catalan.

So perhaps the successful assertion of a single Iberian 'Romance', in semantic opposition to the traditional Latin, as occurred in Berceo's time, was unlikely to last. The tide of release from Latin was such that succeeding generations ran further with his ball than he did himself. This explains why many modern scholars anachronistically refer to Berceo's work as being in 'Castilian' rather than Romance, even though he called it 'romance' himself, and was not Castilian nor even based in Castile. And the pendulum did swing back later within the wider kingdom of Castile, with the extinction of any separate written Leonese after 1300, and the effective smothering of written Galician in the fifteenth century. But the earlier loss of a wider Ibero-Romance cultural unity is worth mourning, and not only because of the nationalisms which the linguistic fragmentations helped create. Ibero-Romance had no future as a single conceptual unit in the event, but it might have had. By not splitting it, the inhabitants of the Peninsula could have combined the advantages of the old traditional Latin with those of the new Romance within a single speech community, similar to the single modern Spanish speech community which currently extends over a far wider geographical area.

Chapter 19

Why Judeo-Spanish Was Called "*Ladino*"

In this book I have been demonstrating that Latin, as we have known it for the last millennium, has not come down to us in an unbroken line of descent from Classical times, but is instead essentially based on the practice of the scholars at the court of Emperor Charlemagne around the year 800 A.D.. At that time the Emperor and his advisers were wishing to establish a revitalized society based on Christian teaching. This plan included the standardization of the Roman liturgy, not only of the precise words of the text, but of the pronunciation to be given to those words in oral delivery. The rules that were taught to Christian priests then and since have been based entirely on the traditional spelling of words. They had to recognize each separate individually written letter, as carefully set down in the Carolingian minuscule script, and know which speech sound correlated with that letter. For this reason, these pronunciation rules were part of the knowledge of "*litterae*", and intrinsically connected to the Christian church.

This was the first time that a distinction had ever been made in a Romance-speaking area between the official Christian mode of reading texts aloud and the usual colloquial vernacular pronunciation of the same words. This difference, in early ninth-century France, could often be quite marked, and had the effect that, for the first time in Romance-speaking areas, a large part of

This chapter is a reprint of: "Early Medieval Spanish, Latin and *ladino*", in: *Circa 1492: Litterae Judaeorum in Terra Hispanica*, ed. Isaac BENABU (Jerusalem, The Hebrew University Press, 1992), pp. 36-45. That paper was delivered in 1984, and has been slightly shortened and revised here. We are grateful to Professor Isaac Benabu, on behalf of the Hebrew University of Jerusalem, for permitting this reprint.

the Church offices became unintelligible to the congregation. The new *"litteratus"* pronunciation, based then, as it still is, on delivering one specified sound for each written letter, was thus initially the preserve of those trained in the Christian church, and it came to be a basic part of Christian ecclesiastical education in subsequent centuries. There seems no reason in the Carolingian period for anyone of another religion to bother to learn the new spoken *"litterae"*, what we now call 'Medieval Latin'.

In previous centuries it seems that education in Romance-speaking areas had not concerned itself with pronunciation at all. The linguistic purpose of specialist training in *"grammatica"* had essentially concerned the ability to write. The grammars used before the Carolingian Renaissance say very little about pronunciation, and what they do say is easier to understand if we accept that the authors, teachers, and recipients of their advice spoke the normal everyday Romance of their area. The eighth-century Romance-speaker in Gaul, saying [vjɛrdʒə] or [vírdʒə], had to be told when to write *"virgen"*, *"virginem"*, *"virgini"* or *"virgine"*, in the same way as twentieth-century French-speaking children have to be taught when to write *"chante"*, *"chantes"* or *"chantent"*, all of which they pronounce [ʃaːt], both when speaking and when reading aloud. If there were to be a Carolingian-type reform of French next week, people would have to read *"chantent"* as [chantent] as suddenly as after 800 some of the Christian clerics were told to read *"virginem"* aloud as [virginem].

The implication is that those of other faiths were unlikely to have occasion to learn to speak the new spoken Medieval Latin until these specifically Christian liturgical bonds were weakened at the time of the Twelfth-Century Renaissance. With the coming of a more secular Medieval Latin culture, non-Christian scholars may then have felt a greater incentive to learn to speak the new Medieval Latin, although in most circumstances there is unlikely to have been any real need for them to do so.

In the Iberian Peninsula, Catalonia was part of the Carolingian Empire, and the distinction between Church Latin pronunciation and everyday Romance vernacular was established in some centres there in the ninth century. But the rest of the Peninsula was in a different category. There the Christians used their traditional Visigothic liturgy, not the Roman liturgy which had been prescribed further north and east. The education system for their priests did not concentrate on a standard manner of spelling-based delivery. None of the monasteries were exclusively Benedictine, nor was there a centralized religious authority over the several kingdoms. The Roman liturgy was introduced into the kingdoms west of Catalonia as a result of papal intervention in the 1070s. It was promulgated for León at the Council of Burgos in 1080. The adoption of the distinctively Latinate reading pronunciation came in at the same time as the Roman liturgy with which it was originally linked. In other words, in non-Catalan Spain, all written texts before 1080 are in the written form of ordinary vernacular Old Romance, 'Late Latin'. The newly introduced language, which we now call 'Medieval Latin', was consciously different from Romance, taught and learnt and indeed spoken as a separate accomplishment. The relationship between the pre-Reform written Late Latin and the Ibero-Romance spoken by those who wrote it is effectively the same as the relationship in modern English or French between written texts and the speech of the writers. Speech styles in modern English or French vary geographically, stylistically and sociolinguistically, and the written form occasionally gives evidence of this variation, but in essence written English and French, particularly as regards spelling, are a single standard used with mutual intelligibility by speakers with varying phonetic habits. Written English is not a different language from spoken English, it is merely the way that we write. Similarly, the tenth-century Ibero-Romance word for "king" was probably [réje], or perhaps [réʒe], and when reading the forms "*rex*", "*regem*", "*regi*" or "*rege*", [réje] or [réʒe] would be the delivered form.[1] Late Latin was merely the way all Romance-speakers wrote, if they wrote at all, before the advent of the Roman liturgy. Accordingly, unlike later Medieval Latin, Late Latin had had no specific religious overtones. Ibero-Romance-speaking Jews who learnt to write learnt the same way as Christians, by following the ancient precepts.

Menéndez Pidal proposed that in León before the eleventh century there was a three-way distinction between Latin, Leonese Vulgar Latin, and Old Leonese.[2] As can be seen from any sociolinguistics textbook, that tripartite distinction is not necessary. All that there was in tenth-century León was Ibero-Romance, spoken in varying styles, and written, if at all, in the old-fashioned way. It was one language, as is Modern French or English. This language was usually called then by the word spelt "*latinus*". Its etymological connection with Latium had long been lost, and this became the usual word used to refer to the one language, whether spoken or written, used in Ibero-Romance communities. Saint Isidore, and other scholars in seventh-century Visigothic Spain,

---

[1] This explains both why REX seems to be thought to be a trochee in a ninth-century poem included in the *Historia Albeldense* ("*Rex quoque clarus omni mundo factus*"), and why the written form "*rege*" is used in subject position in the famous list of cheeses compiled in León in c. 980 ("*quando jlo rege venit ad Rocola*").

[2] R. MENÉNDEZ PIDAL, *Orígenes del español* (Madrid, 1926; seventh edition, 1972).

had used *"latinus"*, *"latine"* and *"latina lingua"* in this sense, specifically contrasting it with other languages entirely, usually with Greek, but occasionally with Semitic languages, including Hebrew. These words are never used to make a contrast between Latin and Romance, because the distinction had not yet been made. The word *"latinus"* was applied then to both the written and the spoken forms of their seventh-century language.

This meaning of the word was also that used in ninth-century Moslem Spain, where literate scholars of indigenous descent were still trained to write as in the old Visigothic tradition. Álvaro's famous lament on the state of literacy in the indigenous community refers to the Christians as *"latini"* (when he complains that *"linguam propriam non avertunt latini"*), and in his own writing the language referred to as *"latinus"* is contrasted only with Arabic. The Arabs also took over the word, using *"al-lathini"* to refer to Ibero-Romance vernacular. The Christian scholars had a taste for archaizing obscurity in both syntax and vocabulary, but there is no sign there of the contemporary reforms which were being applied within the Carolingian Church. They too spoke Early Medieval Ibero-Romance, albeit, perhaps, with an idiosyncratic vocabulary born of *recherché* antiquarianism.

This early medieval Ibero-Romance, spoken by all in the Peninsula except monolingual speakers of Arabic or Basque, had no case-endings on nouns. Ibero-Romance, including in ninth-century Córdoba, had one singular form for each noun, and the name of their language derived from the original accusative form, *"latinum"*, now usable in all syntactic circumstances. The final [-m] had long since ceased to be pronounced, and the short unstressed [u] had developed into an [o]. It used to be thought that the Ibero-Romance of Moslem Spain, unlike Ibero-Romance elsewhere, preserved the unvoiced intervocalic plosives [p], [t] and [k] without voicing them into [b], [d], and [g] respectively, but recent studies (including those of Galmés de Fuentes) have shown that these sounds were voiced in the South as in most of the rest of the Peninsula.[3] Hence both in Córdoba and in León the word spelt *"vita"* was pronounced [bída], the word spelt *"amatos"* was pronounced [amádos], et cetera.

This means that the word spelt *"latinus"* represented a form pronounced by everyone as [ladíno]. This was the normal word used before 1080 by all Romance-speakers of any religious group in non-Catalan Spain to refer to their own language, spoken or written, and it was only contrasted with other languages entirely such as Arabic, Greek or Hebrew. There may have been no alternative at that time. The word *"español"* is an Occitanism of later import.

---

[3] See: A. GALMÉS DE FUENTES, *Dialectología mozárabe* (Madrid, 1983).

The word "*rustica*", used in France to refer to Gallo-Romance language, in Spain still meant "rustic". The word "*romanice*" seems not to have been used. Consciousness of intra-Romance dialectal divisions seems to be a later development, mainly connected with the political desire to establish individually distinguishable written standards after the twelfth century, so we cannot yet visualize them using the words "*castellano*", "*leonés*", et cetera, with a linguistic meaning; [ladíno] seems to have been the word then used by all to refer to their Romance.

What is visualized here can perhaps be made clearer by an analogy with the English spoken in the United States. In the USA, as in England, the word "*latin*" is spelt with the letter *t*. But in this word as in most others, while the English still pronounce an intervocalic unvoiced [-t-], the North Americans usually now give it a voiced sound, phonetically [D]. Thus the second letter *t* in the word spelt "*tomato*" represents [t] in England but [D] in North America, [təméjDə]. In North America there is homonymy between "rider" and "writer", hence also the American pronunciation of [láDn], compared with the English [látɪn]. Similarly, in early medieval Europe, Ibero-Romance experienced a sound change which most of Italo-Romance did not. Those in Visigothic Spain would say [ladíno] but those in Italy [latíno]. The orthographical revolutions of the central Middle Ages made the difference in voicing between Spanish "*ladino*" and Italian "*latino*" explicit and visible for us on paper, but that phonetic difference had been there for centuries.

In the thirteenth and fourteenth centuries, and later, Ibero-Romance "*ladino*" meant "vernacular Romance".[4] Yet this word with that meaning had been in existence for centuries, largely unnoticed by modern scholars because when written it was spelt "*latinus*". Consequently in bilingual communities which also used languages unrelated to Romance, such as, for example, Hebrew, a distinction arose naturally between "*ladinos*", who spoke and wrote Romance, and others who did not.

After the decision taken in 1080 to abandon the old Visigothic Christian liturgy, this situation became confused. The newly prescribed Roman liturgy needed, as the Pope himself insisted, to be pronounced according to the standard European method of "*litterae*", by giving a specific sound to each already written letter. The new liturgy therefore necessitated a reform in the training of the priesthood, a need that can be seen reflected in many developments between 1080 and 1250 in Santiago de Compostela, Toledo, Palencia and else-

---

[4] There are several attestations in: J. COROMINAS and J.A. PASCUAL, *Diccionario Crítico Etimológico Castellano e Hispánico*, 6 volumes (Madrid, 1980-1991).

where. Since the new *"litterae"* were already standard in France, the initial stages of the educational revolution in the Spanish Christian church were overseen by Frenchmen, many of whom became bishops. As well as bringing in this new kind of *"litterae"* (Medieval Latin), the French also brought with them their word *"latin"*, which was in due course borrowed into Ibero-Romance as *"latín"*. Along with it was borrowed its meaning, which depends on the erection of a semantic conceptual boundary between this Medieval Latin and Romance vernacular. In the twelfth century there were thus two words with opposed meanings in Spanish vernacular, [latín] and [ladíno] (or [laδíno]), both of which would be spelt the same way in writing, as *"latinus"*. So there must have been some confusion, when reading, over whether the written form *"latinus"* represented [latín], 'Latin', or [ladíno], 'Ibero-Romance'. It may be for this reason that those that used the new Christian Latin pronunciation stopped using that written form with the meaning of 'Romance', and kept to that of 'Latin', and thus eventually preferred in speech to use a word other than [ladíno] to refer to Romance vernacular. This ambiguity of the written form *"latinus"* could only have arisen in progressive Christian centres during the twelfth century, since Medieval Latin, as a separate spoken entity from Romance, only existed in such places. Meanwhile, Romance-speaking Jews in the Peninsula continued as before to think of their own language as *"ladino"*, unaware, perhaps, of the distinctions newly brought into the Christian community. The same probably applied to Romance-speaking Moslems as well.

We can feel sure that the word *"latín"* was a twelfth-century Gallicism, although discussion of the history of the word *"latín"* in Spanish vernacular is hampered by the fact that the words *"latín"* and *"latino"* are not included in Corominas and Pascual's *Diccionario etimológico* (because they are proper names). The Ibero-Romance word *"latín"* is used, for example, in the Castilian version of the Canons of the 1228 Council of Valladolid, which was summoned to encourage the spread of the Reforms decreed in the Lateran Council of 1215. The third ordinance decreed at Valladolid concerns the teaching of clergy who had never learnt *"litterae"*:

DE BENEFICIATIS ILLITERATIS: Stablecemos, que todos Beneficiados que non saben fablar latin, sacados los viejos, que sean constreñidos que aprendan, et que non les den los Beneficios fasta que sepan fablar latin.[5]

[5] J. TEJADA Y RAMIRO (ed.), *Colección de Canones de la Iglesia española*, 7 volumes (Madrid, 1849-1862), III, p. 325: "Concerning priests without '*litterae*': we decree that all priests who do not know how to speak Latin, apart from the old, should be forced to learn how to do so, and that they should not be given their benefices until they do know how to speak Latin". The

That is, not only *"latín"*, but the ability to deliver it orally, *"fablar latín"*, was seen as one area of specifically Christian practice in need of encouragement by this reforming Church Council. The exclusively Christian function of the new spoken Medieval Latin implies that Spanish Jews did not normally have a reason to learn to speak it. Since they were still able to learn the traditional way of writing their Romance in the twelfth century, as they had been in the tenth (that is, as Late Latin), such an absence of *"litterae"* would not have harmed their ability, for example, to act as intermediaries in the translation enterprises at Toledo. On the other hand, there is no reason why some of them should not have learnt it for other practical purposes, such as the desire to converse with North European scholars in Toledo who knew no Romance.

By the time we reach the age of King Alfonso el Sabio in the second half of the thirteenth century, Latin and Romance have become conceptually distinct languages throughout the Kingdom of Castile. The new *"litterae"* pronunciation plus the old traditional way of writing were considered together to be one language, Latin, and the old ordinary pronunciation plus the newly-elaborated methods of writing Castilian Romance were considered together to be another, by now called *"romance castellano"*. Dialectal divisions had become psychologically and politically salient during the thirteenth century, so its general 'Romance' meaning made the word *"ladino"* no longer suitable.

Jewish communities, however, still used the word *"ladino"* for their own Romance speech. They too had learned by then how to represent that speech on paper in the new Romance spelling, as in their extensive translations from the Old Testament. They naturally applied the word *"ladino"* to the written language of these texts, endowed with a semantic contrast with Hebrew. Probably they used the word *"ladino"* for this purpose without any self-consciousness, perhaps unaware that the word was gradually ceasing to be used by those of the Christian faith to describe written language at all. It is, therefore, an irony of history that many modern scholars of Judeo-Spanish, for perfectly sensible reasons, consciously prefer to call spoken Judeo-Spanish *"judezmo"* and "use the term *'ladino'* exclusively to designate the unspoken liturgical language used mainly for translating Hebrew religious texts".[6]

The conclusion that can be drawn, then, is that *"ladino"* was the ordinary word for both the written and the spoken Ibero-Romance of everyone through-

original Latin *acta* are lost. This is a fifteenth-century vernacular version. These edicts are discussed further in: R. WRIGHT, *Late Latin and Early Romance in Spain and Carolingian France* (Liverpool, 1982), pp. 254-257.

[6] P. WEXLER, "Marrano Ibero-Romance: classification and research tasks", *Zeitschrift für romanische Philologie*, 98 (1982), pp. 59-108, p. 60.

out the early Middle Ages. Internal reforms in the Spanish Christian church which began in 1080 and became general after 1228 led to the word's not being used in the Christian community for written language, and decreasingly to be available to refer to Romance speech either. This explains how the word *"ladino"* came to be restricted semantically to refer to the Romance of non-Christians alone.[7]

---

[7] The later history of *"ladino"* is considered in: R. WRIGHT, *Early Ibero-Romance* (Newark, 1995), chapter 17.

Chapter 20

A Sociophilological Approach to the Earliest Romance Texts: [-t], -/t/ and -*t* in Castile (1206-1208)

T he topic of "L'Essor des Langues Vernaculaires Écrites" (the title of the conference where this chapter was first presented) is more complicated than it might seem at first sight. It is understandable metaphorical short-hand to refer to the "Dawning of the Written Vernaculars" as if the languages existed independently of their users, but we cannot really envisage the agents of this 'dawning' as being the languages themselves. The agents of the emergence of the first texts in a form other than the traditional Latin were individual writers, who were working in their own particular social context. All linguistic data are produced by human beings, and in the case of written texts the ideas, experience and attitudes of the human beings who wrote them decided the nature of the evidence available for subsequent investigators. This is a necessary consequence of the fact that speech is instinctive, but writing has to be taught, a fact which implies that the sudden emergence of texts in a new coherent reformed orthography must be the result of deliberate decisions taken in advance, since a detailed knowledge of the techniques of phonetic script cannot seriously be seen as innate in human competence. Furthermore, all the earliest Romance vernacular texts were prepared in cultural centres of expert Latinity,

This chapter is a reprint of: "A sociophilological approach to the earliest Romance texts: [-t], -/t/ and -*t* in Castile (1206-08)", in: *The Dawn of the Written Vernacular in Western Europe*, ed. Michèle GOYENS and Werner VERBEKE (Leuven, University Press, 2002), pp. 201-214. We are grateful to Dr Michèle Goyens, on behalf of the University of Leuven, for permitting this reprint.

which in turn implies that the scribes who wrote them must inevitably first have been trained to use the traditional Latin written norms. So it is not the case, as is occasionally implied even now, that these scribes of the first Romance documents could not cope with writing Latin. For indeed they could, and often did.

This suggests that some details present in the new orthographic forms may have been consequences of aspects of the scribe's original training, rather than directly corresponding to any aspect of the vernacular itself. Accordingly, during our analyses of the few Romance texts produced by ninth-century Carolingians, or of the first vernacular texts produced in Castile, León and Portugal in the early thirteenth century, *et cetera*, it is essential to investigate as far as we can the writers' educational background, and their linguistic experience and assumptions. Given that the scribes in question had all been already trained in the writing of Latin, the early Romance texts present a further problem, peculiar to Romance, which is not always recognized by modern analysts. Germanic and Celtic languages were clearly separate languages from Latin, but "Romance" as a conceptual entity distinct from "Latin" was still in the process of being definitively invented at the time of the earliest Romance documents. Indeed, it seems reasonable to argue that the formulation of these new Romance writing systems was the catalyst which finally precipitated the conceptual split between Latin and Romance, as being two separate languages rather than remaining (as hitherto) one single complex language of great variability. So to some extent the scribes of these earliest documents were inventing Romance as much as representing it. Modern Romanists need, therefore, to augment the straightforward philological analysis of these texts with an understanding of their writers' educational and social context, and of why they wrote in a new non-standard way at all when we know that they were already capable of getting written texts right according to the traditional norms.

One of the main problems in the analysis of texts of these times concerns the extent to which we are entitled to deduce phonetic details from the new orthographies. It is tempting, for example, to assume that the spelling of the very earliest Ibero-Romance texts was decided on a purely alphabetical basis, as if it were essentially a phonetic transcription. And indeed, on the whole this is more true of the Iberian Peninsula at that time than at any other time before or since. But within the study of the spelling there are also practical questions that we need to be aware of, related to the education and attitudes of the scribes who wrote these documents in the strange new form (we may call it "Old Spanish", but it was of course new to them.) The years 1206 to 1208 in Castile have a special place within these sociophilological analyses, because in this short period there was a window of opportunity for written Romance to establish itself there in official circles, under the aegis of the Archbishop of Toledo (Martín López de Pisuerga). Martín López was also in charge of the Royal Castilian chancery, as a result of a decision made by Alfonso VIII on 1 July 1206, despite the simultaneous existence of a Royal Chancellor in the shape of the steel-jawed Diego García. When Martín López died in August 1208, he was succeeded by the most famous Archbishop of Toledo of them all, Rodrigo Ximénez de Rada, a comparatively conservative northerner, who tended to the view that writing in Romance was largely undesirable and even perhaps inherently heretical. He seems to have changed the policy, and from 1208 this window of opportunity closed again. But in the meanwhile a small corpus of substantial texts had been written in the new Romance form, which repay careful investigation.[1]

These texts include what was almost certainly the first written version of the *Poema de Mio Cid*, which in its surviving form we can now accept was written down in 1207 (not necessarily for the first time) – regardless of when it was actually composed – and of which the sole surviving version, in a fourteenth-century manuscript, is by common scholarly consent generally believed to have been intended to be faithful to the original. The Romance texts of these years also include the two versions of the Treaty of Cabreros and the decisions of the Cortes of Toledo of January 1207, which were printed by Hernández under the title of *Posturas*. There are also three Romance documents from Toledo written during these years in Menéndez Pidal's *Documentos Lingüísticos*.[2] We could probably also include in this list the original written version of the Ibero-Romance *Libro de Alexandre*, whose provisional though still controversial dating to the central part of the first decade of the thirteenth century seems acceptable. But the surviving manuscripts are later and have been rather renovated in detail, which is why I am leaving the *Libro de Alexandre* out of the present investigation.

The one linguistic feature to be examined here in detail concerns word-final *-t*. Orthographically, this letter occurs word-finally on three hundred and forty-four occasions in the *Poema de Mio Cid*, involving seventy-three separate word-forms; the details are all in the appendix below. The statistics presented here are slightly different from those in Menéndez Pidal, because his are based

---

[1] Many further details are to be found in: R. WRIGHT, *El Tratado de Cabreros (1206): estudio sociofilológico de una reforma ortográfica* (London, 2000).

[2] WRIGHT, *Tratado*. F.J. HERNÁNDEZ, "Las Cortes de Toledo de 1207", in: *Las Cortes de Castilla y León en la Edad Media*, I (Valladolid, 1988), pp. 221-263. R. MENÉNDEZ PIDAL, *Documentos Lingüísticos de España. I. Reino de Castilla* (Madrid, 1966), docs. 265-267.

on his own edited text, and mine are based on the manuscript facsimile, with help from Waltman's Concordance and the CD-Rom *Admyte* (accessed with valuable assistance from Dr Joel Rini).[3] Very nearly all these final letters in the written forms correspond to a final unvoiced dental consonant in speech, and thus seem to be inspired by a direct desire for isomorphism.[4]

In many words this final -*t* represented a [-t] which had only recently become final as the result of the recent dropping of a final [-e]. These are the forms in section 1 of the appendix. Those in sections 1a, 1b and 1c involve word-forms which after this loss of final [-e] ended in two consonants, and were for this phonotactic reason destined to reacquire the same final sound [-e] (and letter -*e*) in the moderately near future. Such forms include "*adelant*" and "*orient*" (now "*adelante*" and "*oriente*"), and second person singular past tense verb-forms such as "*fizist*" and "*resuçitest*" (now "*hiciste*" and "*resucitaste*"). In section 2a, we see some clitic forms that had even lost a previous final -*o* (such as "*sant*" and "*q̨nt*"). The final cluster in these words was equally destined not to last, but being clitics these words were destined to shorten further by losing the [t] altogether (to become "*San*", as it is already on twenty occasions in the *Poema*, and "*cuan*").

The nine cases in section 1d involve an object pronoun "*te*" that has become attached enclitically to the previous word and then lost its final [-e]. Such forms include "*mandot*" (for "*mando te*") and "*metistet*" (for "*metiste te*"). Such forms would not appear after the forthcoming loss of enclisis as an option for the pronouns. The words in section 1e had once ended in -*de*, such as "*grant*" (for "*grande*"). Variants with a letter -*d* are usually found in these cases as well, which suggests that there may have been phonetic variability here (or that voicing in word-final dentals was becoming neutralized). These all have a final syllable [-de] now, if they survive, except for the clitic "*gran*". The words in section 1f are similar: in these words a Latin intervocalic [-t-] had voiced to [-d-] in the ordinary way, but they also seem, on the evidence of these and other spellings of this century, to have had unvoiced variants once the following final [-e] dropped (as in second person plural imperatives such as "*sabet*" – with "*sabed*" found as well – or "*dexat*"; these are voiced now: "*sabed*", "*dejad*", *et cetera*). The Graecism "*abbat*" is unusual. This word always has at least one diacritic above it in the manuscript, as if it was known

---

[3] R. MENÉNDEZ PIDAL, *Cantar de Mio Cid*, 3 volumes (Madrid, 1944-1946), pp. 193-196. *Poema de Mio Cid; edición facsímil* (Burgos, 1988). F.M. WALTMAN, *Concordance to Poema de Mio Cid* (Penn State, 1972).

[4] None of the words concerned would still have a final phonetic [-t] by the time of the Renaissance.

to be an abbreviation. It never ends in the letter -*d* in the Poem, and perhaps may only have voiced later than this time anyway.[5]

The original non-apocopated forms of section 2b even ended in -*do*, in the proper names "*Remont*" and "*fagunt*". The latter is a form midway between "*Facundo*" and the latter part of this Saint's toponym "*Sahagún*" (< SAN FACUNDUM, the headquarters of the Cluniacs). No form of the word "*según*" appears in the Poem, but this too had a similar written variant in the thirteenth-century form "*segunt*", probably inspired by a final [-t] during its development from SECUNDUM to "*según*" in proclitic positions.

In section 3 there are three Arabic proper names, whose phonetics may not have had an obvious transcription in the Roman alphabet: these are "*mafomat*" himself, and the placenames "*calatayut*" (which is spelt in five different ways on its eight appearances, and is now "*Calatayud*") and "*alucāt*" (spelt three different ways). The three forms in section 4 are probably only explicable as mistakes, either made by the scribe in 1207 or the copyist in the fourteenth century.

This leaves the forms of section 5 in need of further consideration, since unlike all the others they concern words which probably did not contain a final dental consonant at the time. The words concerned appear in the following lines:

i). *Poema de Mio Cid*, l. 1754: "*Rogand al čador q̃ uos biua algunt año*".

El Cid is here talking to his wife. This line is translated by Hamilton and Perry as "Praying God to spare my life a few years longer",[6] as if "*algunt*" were plural – which does indeed seem to be the sense, as it is elsewhere in the Poem, for example l. 2372: "*por sabor q̃ avia de algun moro matar*".

ii). *Poema de Mio Cid*, l. 610: "*Myo çid gaño a alcoçer sabent por esta māna*".

Most editors unnecessarily take the form "*sabent*" here to be a scribal error for "*sabet*", "you know" (addressed to the audience). It is probably more likely to represent [sáben], elsewhere spelt "*saben*", "they know". The subject is then the Cid's troops, who were the subject of the plural verb "*llegavan*" in the previous line, "*luego legauan los sos ca fecha es el arrancada*". With "*saben*", the two lines would thus mean "then his men arrived, for their skirmish was

---

[5] This word has a written *t*, always intervocalic, in all the tenth-century cases from Galicia studied in: R. WRIGHT, *Early Ibero-Romance* (Newark, 1995), pp. 192-193.

[6] I. MICHAEL (ed.), *The Poem of the Cid*, with English translation by: R. HAMILTON and J. PERRY (Manchester, 1975), p. 115.

over; they know that El Cid had won Alcoçer by these tactics". There is nothing remarkable about the switch of tenses, which happens all the time. The form "*saben*", without the letter *-t*, occurs in a similar context just before the same battle, in l. 549: "*non lo saben los moros el ardiment q̃ an*" ("the Moors don't know what plans they have"). It seems an unlikely copyist's error to write "*sabent*" for "*sabet*", and an understandable scribal error to write "*sabent*" for "*saben*". But the word is clear in the manuscript, and should certainly be printed by modern editors as "*sabent*", whatever we think the form's motivation might be. Linguists are legitimately angry when confronted by editors who refuse to print what is in the manuscript and prefer to print what they presumptuously think ought to have been there instead. This is why researching linguists are best advised only to use the excellent facsimile of the *Poema de Mio Cid* published in Burgos in 1988 rather than even the most prestigious edition. Menéndez Pidal, for example, was a genius, working brilliantly within the restrictions of his own context, when he published the first modern edition a hundred years ago. But we know things now that he did not know then, so his reconstructed edition, considerably different from the text in the manuscript, has become unusable for serious research. That is, Menéndez Pidal's editions and ideas also need now to be approached sociophilologically (as they are, for example, by Del Valle).[7]

iii) *Poema de Mio Cid*, l. 1174: "*Mal se aq̃xan los de valencia q̃ ño sabẽt q̃s far*".

The meaning of this line is uncontroversial; translated by Hamilton and Perry as "The Valencians lamented loudly, for they were at their wits' end".[8] Inconsistently, editors have not wished to changed this form to "*sabet*" in the way that they have tended to do in l. 610. Here, "*sabẽt*" has been allowed to remain what it is, a third person verb form, and this is obviously right. As it is in the similar l. 1155, only just earlier: "*Miedo han en valençia q̃ non saben q̃se far*", with the form written "*saben*".

Despite the fact that all other cases of final *-t* correspond to [-t], these three seem genuinely to be 'silent'. Spanish "*algún*" comes from Latin ALICUNUM, and we cannot envisage any phonetic cause for the introduction of a variant with [t]. Even so, the "silent" *-t* at the end of "*algunt*" in line 1754 is strangely

---

[7] J. DEL VALLE, "Lenguas imaginadas; Menéndez Pidal, la lingüística hispánica y la configuración del estándar", *Bulletin of Hispanic Studies* 76 (1999), pp. 215-233.

[8] MICHAEL (ed.), *Poema*, p. 85.

described by Menéndez Pidal with the single word "admisible". He also cross-refers to the equally strange form "*ningūd*" ("none", usually written "*ningún*" < NEC UNUM), found in one manuscript of Juan Ruiz's *Libro de Buen Amor*, line 1366d (fourteenth century)[9] – which is clearly some kind of error, since it fails to rhyme with the three other rhyme words of the stanza. The best explanation that can be suggested for this final *-t* may be the orthographical influence of the only other words ending in *-gun*, "*Sahagún*" and "*según*", both of which varied orthographically with a form in *-gunt* during the development from *-UNDUM* to [-un].

The other two forms in section 5, "*sabent*" and "*sabēt*", are third person plural verb forms. There are, of course, very many third person forms in the Poem without this final letter, including six cases of this lexical item as "*saben*". Specialists in Ibero-Romance would be reluctant to see these two written forms as evidence of the existence of a phonetic variant [sábent] with a final [-t]. Historical linguists would prefer to think that no third person inflections in the Peninsula had had a variant with a final [-t], nor even the final phoneme /t/, for quite a while by now, particularly after [n], where the *-t* is sometimes even missing in the eleventh-century Riojan glosses (even though it was still to be heard in Northern France). Such a [t] certainly did not survive in Castilian verb inflections in the following century, and the continued presence of these two written forms in the fourteenth-century manuscript is just one of the many reasons for believing that that copyist was actually a very good one, who did not change the original text (except occasionally by mistake). No copyist would have added a *-t*, of course, so this must have been there in the 1207 version.

But then the next question has to be this: why is the letter *t* there in these two representations of [sáben] in the *Poema de Mio Cid*? And sociophilology can give us a simple answer. The point is that all the scribes who were working in Castile in the year 1207 were Romance-speakers, without a final [-t] in these verb forms in their own speech. And over the years they had become very used to representing their [t]-less third person Romance verb inflections with a silent final written letter *-t* when preparing formal texts in the normal traditional Latinate way. They added such a letter *t* on hundreds of occasions every working day, since all other texts were still at that time being prepared in the unreformed mode, by these same scribes. Thus the techniques they had learnt in their training had always involved endowing third person verb inflections with a silent final letter *-t* (much as nowadays French children learning to write have

---

[9] MENÉNDEZ PIDAL, *Cantar*, p. 456 and p. 193; "*algunt*" is also found elsewhere in the thirteenth century.

to be taught to include the *-t* of *-ait, et cetera*). A few decades later than this there were going to be texts written by scribes who did not spend all the rest of their time trying to get the ancient spellings correct, so such phenomena all but disappear. Nor do the earliest Romance written texts from Portugal contain such written inflections with *t*.

This analysis implies that the other longish Romance texts from Castile mentioned above, written in the years 1206 to 1208, the immediately pre-Ximénez de Rada years, ought to show such occasional features too. They do. Indeed, the mathematics are exactly the same. The *Poema de Mio Cid* has these two third person verb inflections ending in the letter *-t*, and each of these three other long texts dating from 1206 to 1208 also has precisely two verb forms with such a silent *-t* added (a statistic that is at once breathtakingly improbable and totally insignificant).

The two forms with *-t* in each of the two texts of the Treaty of Cabreros of 1206 are not the same forms in each text. Those in the Leonese version of the Treaty are *"aiudent"* (l. 57) and *"serant"* (l. 63). They are the only cases with inflection-final *-t* appearing in the text (before the final witness formula in Latin form), out of a large number of third person verb forms, and the corresponding words in the Castilian version both lack the final written letter *-t*: *"aiuden"* (l. 58) and *"seran"* (l. 63). This difference in itself strongly suggests that these two cases of written final *-t* corresponded to no sound, since it seems likely that the two texts were taken down from the same dictation, probably by the Castilian chancery's chief notary, Domingo.

The contexts of the forms in question are:

> ambos los Rees cũ todos los otros fieles **aiudent** se (León)
> ambos los Rees cõ todos los otros fieles **aiuden** se (Castile)
>
> estonz q̃ los castⁱlõs **serant** q̀tos desta fieldad (León)
> estonz q̃˜los castllos **seran** q̀tos desta fieldad (Castile)

The forms with *-t* in the Castilian version of the Treaty are *"teñẽt"* (l. 2) and *"p̣dat"* (in a section written later, but by the same scribe, above l. 25). Again the corresponding forms in the other version lack the final *-t*, being *"tenen"* (l. 2) and *"pierda"* (l. 24):

> & solta aq̃llos q̃ **teñẽt** las arras. (Castile)
> & suelta   q̃ **tenen** las arras. (Léon)[10]

---

[10] The Leonese version has a manuscript gap corresponding to *"aq̃llos"*.

& nolo emēdare fasta sex meses. **p̱dat** de istos q̇nq. (Castile)
& no lo emendare fasta sex meses pierda destos q̇nq; (Léon)

The two forms in the documentation from the Cortes of Toledo of January 1207, as printed by Hernández under the title of *Posturas*, are "*saluet*" and "*dent*". The latter in context can only be the present subjunctive of *dar* rather than an apocopated form of "*dende*" (this verb form also appears many times in the written form "*den*"):

e el otro **saluet** se por so cabeza (l. 33)
et los alcaldes **dent** le end la quinta part dello (l. 58).

It might be worth considering if there could be special conditioning factors at play here to explain a [-t], but there are not. Six of the eight inflected verb forms with -*t* in these texts are plural and two are singular. Four are subjunctive and four are indicative. There are no past tenses, a fact which may conceivably be significant. Otherwise, there seem to be no obvious morphological conditioning factors in play which could explain the existence of a [-t]. The inflections include both [e] and [a] vowels, of which one [e] and one [a] are stressed and the others unstressed. All the forms are followed in context by a word beginning with a consonant, almost certainly within the same breathgroup except for *Poema de Mio Cid*, l. 610. So there are no obvious phonetic conditioning factors in play either which could explain a [t]. The eight forms involve seven separate lexical items. The form "*saluet*" also appears in the phrase "*quem Deus saluet e onret*" included in one of the Romance Toledo documents of 1206, referring to Archbishop Martín López himself,[11] so perhaps the scribe of the *Posturas*, also working and probably trained in Toledo, was used to this form as a logographic whole. This possibility seems improbable in the other cases. There is thus no apparent lexical or logographic conditioning factor in play to explain a [t].

Despite the fact that in his edition of the *Poema* Montaner Frutos calls the form "*sabēt*" a "*grafía latinizante de 'saben'*",[12] this spelling cannot seriously be called "Latinizing", since the written Latin form of this word was in fact "*sapiunt*". "Latinism" could perhaps be invoked as regards both the forms in the *Posturas*, since in those cases the correct Latin form was in fact the same as the one that happened to be written ("*saluet*" and "*dent*"). This also potentially applies to "*p̱dat*", Latin PERDAT, and to "*teñēt*", Latin TENENT, in the

---

[11] MENÉNDEZ PIDAL, *Documentos Lingüísticos*, doc. 266, l. 5.
[12] A. MONTANER FRUTOS, *Cantar de Mio Cid* (Barcelona, 1993), p. 173.

Castilian Chancery's version of the Treaty. But there is absolutely no reason why a deliberate Latinism should have been included in any of these sentences, so it is hardly satisfactory as an explanation. And it cannot apply at all to the others. Not only had the lexical etymon for *"sabent"* been *"sapiunt"*, the lexical items concerned in the Leonese version of the Treaty did not exist at all in Latin. Spanish *"ayudar"* ("help") comes not from *"iuvare"* but reconstructably from *"adiutare"*, created off the supine *"iutum"* with a prefix *"ad"* (which would have thus had a correct written subjunctive form *"adiutent"*, not *"aiudent"*). *"Serant"* ("they will be") had as a reconstructable etymon *"sedere habent"*, which would not have been the correct Latin form here (*"erunt"* being the Classical future). In any case, both the lexical roots of *"serant"* and *"sabent"* no longer meant in Ibero-Romance the same as their etymon had (respectively "sit" and "taste"). "Latinism" cannot therefore be a sensible way for us to describe these cases of -*t*.

What we have here is evidence of a practical trick regularly used already by scribes before 1206 in the preparation of documents in the traditional Latin form. It was a trick which we can describe as morphographic, since it involved forming the spelling by adding a silent letter -*t* specifically to vernacular third person verb forms. The trick would have been used regularly by these same scribes in the preparation of documents in normal unreformed spelling in order to make words such as our eight examples, pronounced in their normal Ibero-Romance as [dén], [sáben], [serán], [sálβe], [ajúden], [tjénen] and [pjérða], look traditionally correct on paper. It can only have been a morphographic trick, applied to recognizable cases of verb inflection. It cannot have been inspired by any logographic habit, since, as we saw, many of the eight resulting whole forms were not correct Latin and thus cannot have been taught to the scribes as whole units. We can tell they knew how to apply the trick to words in deliberately unreformed spelling, since both the Chancery scribes of the Treaty correctly put a letter -*t* at the end of the word pronounced normally as [fwéron] in the introduction to the list of witnesses at the end of the Treaty text, writing *"fuerunt"*.

It cannot have been easy for these scribes, suddenly being told in 1206 to approximate a phonetic transcription and leave all their familiar techniques behind. They would always have been severely criticized hitherto, prior to March 1206, if they had tried coming up with incorrect phonetically-inspired spellings in a serious document (for instance writing *"tienen"* rather than *"tenent"*), and here we have a glimpse of long ingrained techniques which they inadvertently did not always manage to abandon. Writing phonetic script is difficult, much harder than reproducing forms we have been taught. Even if English-speakers were all now told that henceforth they had to write Modern English words like "night" ([nájt]) as "nite", written forms in "night" might well slip onto the page unintended.

We know in any event that such tricks were used by the Ibero-Romance scribe trying to write an acceptable document in traditional orthography.[13] Some tricks were simply phonographic, regardless of the morpheme. For example, even within these same words, the letters *e* in the first syllable of both "*teñēt*" and "*pdat*" in the Castilian version of the Treaty – where the underlined *p* is as always an unambiguous abbreviation for "*per*" (and not for "*pier*") – are evidence of another such normal scribal trick, that of writing a letter *e* for the sound [jé], a trick which usually worked well when traditional orthography was required (that is, in Latin documents) but is inappropriate here. There can be no doubt that both vowels were diphthongized within the dictation of the Treaty, in [tjénen] and [pjérða]. I have examined several other such cases found in the two texts of this Treaty, which include morphographical decisions apparently taken in advance even with reference to some of the new Romance forms.[14] Most noticeably the written form of the future subjunctive, where there seem to have been different decisions taken in the two chanceries.

Thus a look at the data from a sociophilological perspective helps to clarify details that a philologist unaware of the social circumstances might find needlessly baffling or inappropriately exciting. I am thinking, for example, of some of the remarks on the language of the poem made by Montaner Frutos in his edition of the *Poema de Mio Cid* (an excellent edition, except for textual details and some of the linguistic comments). One relevant example of such inappropriateness would be Montaner's description of the form "*puedent*" in l. 555: "*Acerca corre Salon agua nol puedent vedar*" – which in context can only be a written variant of "*puede ende*" (it means "The River Jalón runs nearby, he cannot cut off the water from there") – as being "*ortografía latinizante*". A Latinizing orthography would have been "*potest inde*", not "*puedent*", although since Montaner wrongly renders this in his gloss as the plural verb-form "*pueden*", it is easy to suspect that the Latin form he actually has in mind here is present plural, which would in fact have been written in Latin orthography as "*possunt*". A more problematic example is his description of the written form

---

[13] R. PENNY, "La grafía de los textos notariales castellanos de la Alta Edad Media: ¿sistema logográfico o fonológico?", in: *Estudios de grafemática en el dominio hispano*, ed. J.M. BLECUA *e.a.* (Salamanca, 1998), pp. 211-223.

[14] WRIGHT, *Tratado*, pp. 78-88.

"*p̄ndēd*" in l. 656 as being "*forma arcaizante, seguramente sólo gráfica, de 'prenden'*". The relevant Latin form would in fact have been "*praehendunt*", although maybe by "archaizing" Montaner means something else. If anything, this form seems in the event to be a mistake in the application of the morphographic trick, at a time when some words other than verbs seem to have alternated written -*nt* with -*nd* (and not only for forms with original [d], as in section 1e of the appendix; compare the form "*p̄send*", l. 1649).

Overall, we can conclude that despite the usual existence of a [-t] to correspond with a -*t* in texts from Castile in these years, they are indeed silent letters -*t* in the two written forms of [sáben] found in the *Poema*. So we need not adjust our chronology for the sound-change in this inflection on the basis of these two scribal vagaries, for they are easily explicable from a sociophilological perspective.

Appendix: *Poema de Mio Cid word-forms with a final -t.*

1) Those where [-t] was word-final because of apocopated [-e]:

1a) Originally the second consonant in an [-nt-] cluster:
adelant 27 times (*adelante* 2), *adellant* 1; *cabadelant* 1; *delant* 29 (*delante* 4, *delantel* 1, *deland* 1), *dellant* 1; *aorient* 1, *orient* 1; *ardiment* 1; *fuent* 1; *mont* 7 (*monte* 3); *pueent* 1, *puent* 1 (never **puente*).

1b) Originally the second consonant in an [-st-] cluster:
apareçist 1; *est* 2 (*este* 18); *fezist* 4, *fizist* 1; *fust* 1 (*fuste* 3); *mintist* 1; *pedist* 1; *prisist* 1; *resuçitest* 2; *saluest* 3; *uenist* 1; *uist* 1 (*uiste* 1).

1c) Originally the second consonant in an [-rt-] cluster:
apart 2 (*aparte* 4); *art* 2, *hart* 4 (no *arte*); *cort* 54 (never **corte*; *corth* 1); *fuert* 3 (*fuerte* 10); *muert* 6 (never **muerte*); *part* 25 (*parte* 12; 2 of these are verbs).

1d) Where the -*t* is the enclitic and apocopated pronoun *te*:
diot 1; *estot* 1; *mandot* 1; *metistet* 3; *miembrat* 1; *riebtot* 1; *ueot* 1.

1e) Originally a [d], second consonant in an [-nd-] cluster:
agrant 3 (*agrand* 2); *alent* 2 (*alen* 2), *dalent* 2, *dallent* 1; *daq̃nt* 2 (*Daq̃nd* 1); *dent* 10; *dont* 1 (*dond* 1); *grant* 43 (*grand* 58, *grande* 4); *puedent* (1, = *puede end*; *end* 1, *ende* 2).

1f) Originally intervocalic [-t-]:
abб̃at 15 times (never **abbad; Graecism); *dat* 3; *dexat* 1; *fet* 1 (*fazed* 3, *fed* 1); *prendet* 5; *sabet* 21 (*sabed* 9); *uerdat* 1 (*uerdad* 14); *uanidat* 1; *uenit* 2 (*uenid* 3).

2) Those where [-t] was word-final because of apocopated [-o]:

2a) Where [t] was the second part of a consonant cluster:
Çient 1 (*çiento* 15, *ciento* 1); *q̃nt* 2 (*quanto* 42); *sant* 6 (*santo* 3, *san* 20), *asant* 1. NB: *cosiment* 1 (*cosimente* 1) is a Provençalism, borrowed from a form with no final vowel.

2b) Where [t] was originally [d], second part of a cluster:
fagunt 2; *Remont* 10 (*Remond* 6, never **-*o*).

3) Arabic Proper Names:
alucāt 1, *alucat* 1, (*alucad* 1); *calatayut* 2 (*calatauth* 1, *calatayuch* 2, *calata-yuh* 1, *calatayuth* 2); *mafomat* 1.

4) Not very explicable mistakes, but definitely not silent:
delent 1 (probably error for *deleite*); *lidit* 1 (error for *lid*, 13); *Pelayet* 1 (probably an error, for *Peláez*).

5) Apparently 'silent':
algunt 1; *sabent* 1, *sabẽt* 1 (*saben* 6).

Section F

Sociophilology and Historical Linguistics

Historical linguistics, as a branch of linguistics, developed almost independently of traditional philology. This was partly because the main brief of historical linguistics was felt to be the study of communities with no tradition of writing. Thus historical linguistic techniques could be applied to the prehistory of subsequently literate communities, but tended to be ignored when studying texts from literate communities of the past. This was not a very satisfactory state of affairs, and in practice much of the recent research effort within historical linguistics has involved the study of literate European languages. For example, these form the object of study in the majority of the papers in the recent conferences of the International Society of Historical Linguistics.

Sociophilology can help the historical linguist, and historical linguistics can help the sociophilologist. Two branches of study which are in principle common to both disciplines are sociolinguistics and graphemics (the relation between writing and speech). Several sociolinguists have been exploring the way that language changes can spread through a society, which needs to be investigated in the light of the fact that changes cannot be instantaneous. Specialists in many areas, including psycholinguistics and primary education, have been investigating the differences between how we write and how we read, with important consequences for our study of texts.

The four chapters in this section explore these themes. The first (21) examines how sociolinguistics has gradually been coming to the fore in historical Romance linguistics. The second (22) shows how the relationship between speech and writing can be very different in different historical circumstances.

The third (23) considers the relationship between changes in a language and changes in the textual evidence, which is not straightforward. The final one (24) considers what we actually mean when we refer to a 'sound change', a development with important sociolinguistic aspects.

Chapter 21

Comparative, Structural and Sociolinguistic Analyses of the History of the Romance Languages

Historical Linguistics and Historical Reality

The historical-comparative method of reconstructing pre-literate languages proved so valuable that scholars in more recent areas of historical
linguistics were tempted to use it too. But this has led to problems. Even
in the original field of application it has to be admitted that the value of the
method lay essentially in the lack of any competition. Linguists, as linguists,
could do nothing else but extrapolate backwards from later attested and potentially cognate languages. When the linguists in the tradition have been moved
to speculate on the identity and whereabouts of the real people who spoke these
reconstructed forms, however, they bump into the fields of expertise inhabited
by archaeologists, and increasingly by such unforeseen collaborators as geneti-
cists, and the results are not always such as to confirm the tentative conclusions
reached on the basis of comparative historical linguistics alone. Thus even in
these rarified realms, historical fact, however established, needs to be taken
into account when we study historical linguistics. But whereas historical linguistics has for many years been taken to be part of linguistics, needing to take

This chapter is a reprint of: "Comparative, structural and sociolinguistic analyses of the history
of the Romance languages", in: *The Emergence of the Language Sciences: Studies in Honour of
E.F.K. Koerner.* II *Methodological perspectives and applications*, ed. S. EMBLETON, J. JOSEPH
and H.-J. NIEDEREHE (Amsterdam and Philadelphia, John Benjamins, 1999), pp. 175-188. We
are grateful to Professor John Joseph and Ms Anke de Looper, on behalf of John Benjamins
(Amsterdam and Philadelphia), for permitting the reprint.

into account the advances and hypotheses made by linguistics in general, it has proved harder to establish the fact that it is also part of the study of history. And in one particular field, the study of the Early Romance (Late Latin) spoken before the separate emergence of different Romance languages in different written forms, it seems that the historical-comparative method has outlived its usefulness.

Structuralism, however, the fashion that immediately followed the historical-comparative, and which was exploited to help understand the data that the earlier method had discovered, deliberately ignores historical realities to an even greater extent. Indeed, it cannot be used to find out what happened, only (at best) to explain it once we know. Synchronic linguistic reality is there perceived to lie solely in internal structural oppositions. In synchronic phonetics, for example, even if a bilingual speaker pronounces the [ð] of English "lather" and Spanish "*lado*" identically (giving rise to identical acoustic spectrograms), the structuralist is forced to override this reality and claim they are not the same, since in English [ð] and [d] represent contrasting phonemes (as in "lather" versus "ladder") but in Spanish they are allophones of the same phoneme in complementary distribution ([lado] is impossible). In synchronic semantics, two British English-speakers who refer to an identical vehicle with the word "bike" will be said by the structuralist to mean different things if one sees "bike" as incompatible with "motorbike" and the other sees it as superordinate to both "motorbike" and "pushbike".

The point is that in this way neither the tradition of comparative reconstruction nor that of structuralism have seen the relationship between language and the real world as being essential primary data, which is probably why history itself was edged out of so much historical linguistics. Both the reconstruction of "Proto"-Romance, as exemplified for present purposes by the work of Robert Hall Jr. and Robert de Dardel,[1] and the present widespread delight in structural explanations of linguistic changes in Romance, seem to have been at least partly inspired by dissatisfaction with traditional, amateurish, explanations of change in terms either of historical events or of bilingualism and influences from other languages. And, indeed, both have clearly helped to raise the level of the discussion. In the first category, nobody would now seriously claim, as they used to be tempted to, that the development of the Romance languages was directly caused by the fragmentation of the Roman Empire, or that the change in the French accentual system was related to the Black Death.

---

[1] R.A. HALL Jr, *Proto-Romance Phonology* (New York, 1976). R. DE DARDEL, *A la recherche du protoroman* (Tübingen, 1996).

Or even that the specific developments of (for instance) French were caused by (for instance) the Germanic spoken by the Franks. Substratum and adstratum languages can provide vocabulary, although even this is not in itself predictable, for neologisms are as often coined through derivational morphology and semantic change as through inter-lingual borrowing. But on other linguistic levels it is now no longer tenable, for example, to attribute to Oscan the developments that happened later in the area where Oscan was once spoken, and still less those that occurred in the Aragonese town of Huesca (< OSCA), as was once seriously suggested. The influence of Basque on Ibero-Romance is now agreed by all serious commentators (such as Echenique and Trask) to have been small, for the languages are still, as they always have been, very different.[2] The influence of Arabic on the development of Spanish, although it seems chill and unromantic to say so, is almost equally undetectable. Thus it was that explanations in terms of external historical events fell into disrepute, and explanations in terms of phonetic laws, structural pressures, typological drift, syntactic reanalyses and abductions, et cetera, largely came to take their place.

The Value of Historical Sociolinguistics

But this decontextualized scenario has also slowly come in turn to seem partial, and the pendulum is swinging back, not to the ingenuous explanations favoured in the past, but to the more sophisticated versions of historical sociolinguistics that have been growing up in the last few years, apparently to the surprise of some of our structuralist colleagues. The key development here has been the distinction made by James Milroy between innovation and change.[3] An initial linguistic innovation may well have structural motivation, but the spread of that innovation throughout a community, which is what leads to a 'change', needs to be seen in historical and sociolinguistic terms. The sociolinguistics of bilingualism may have been deservedly relegated as an explanatory force in itself, but monolingual sociolinguistics remains more important than the structural tradition wants to give it credit for. And it is worth noting that bilingualism can still be used seriously to explain a change, even if it can no longer explain the original innovation. For example, it is no

---

[2] M.T. ECHENIQUE ELIZONDO, *Historia Lingüística Vasco-Románica* (second edition; Madrid, 1987). R.L. TRASK, *The History of Basque* (London, 1997).

[3] J. MILROY, *Linguistic Variation and Change: on the Historical Sociolinguistics of English* (Oxford, 1992).

longer possible, for various reasons, to claim that Basque directly caused the Castilian development of initial [f-] to [h-] in words such as Latin FACERE > Old Castilian [hadzer] (spelt *"fazer"*), which has since become Modern Castilian [aθer] (spelt *"hacer"*). On the other hand, all attempts at a solely structural or other internal explanation are going to fail to deal with the question of why this development happened in some geographical areas but not in others. The present state of play in this case (well expressed by Lloyd)[4] is to accept that there was pre-existing linguistic variation among the allophones of Latin /f/, two of which were probably [f] and [ɸ], and that Basque-Latin bilinguals had a greater than average tendency, attributable to phonotactic features of their native Basque, to choose the more aspirated (less occluded) variants, but that this skewing of the allophone statistics could not have happened without the pre-existing allophony. In the absence of such already current variation within Latin for Basque to influence statistically, many other remarkable features of Basque have failed to leave any echo in the Romance of the bilingual areas. Thus the initial innovation of allophonic variation for /f/ in Latin needs an internal explanation – if it was internally inexplicable, it would not have happened at all – and the satisfactory explanation of the subsequent spread needs knowledge of the world on the part of the historical linguist, that is, in this case, that the phenomenon happened particularly in the mouths of native speakers in the area of the Iberian Peninsula which provided the speech varieties that – for historical reasons alone – came to be treated as 'standard' Spanish. A particularly interesting aspect of the sociolinguistic effects of bilingualism on language change in the modern world is unearthed in the painstaking analyses by Silva Corvalán of the Spanish of Los Angeles.[5] Developments within angeleno Spanish can be attributed to the nature of local Spanish-English bilingualism without particularly being attributable to English itself.

Another aspect of Romance development which has been greatly illuminated by historically-inclined sociolinguists in the recent past concerns the formation of what Trudgill calls an "interdialect", and Romance specialists have tended to call a *"koiné"*, out of cohabiting mutually comprehensible dialects.[6] This perspective has proved most useful so far in increasing our understanding of what happened to Spanish in the Americas. For many years it was normal to claim that Latin American Spanish descended from the speech of

[4] P.M. LLOYD, *From Latin to Spanish*, I (Philadelphia, 1987), pp. 267-273.

[5] C. SILVA CORVALÁN, *Language Contact and Change: Spanish in Los Angeles* (Oxford, 1994).

[6] P. TRUDGILL, *Dialects in Contact* (Oxford, 1986).

Andalucía, and as a generalization this was not unreasonable, since Latin-American Spanish is more like that of Andalucía than that of any other separate region of the Iberian Peninsula. But there are features of andaluz that have not travelled to the New World: most obviously "*ceceo*", in which standard /s/ and standard /θ/ are both [θ], and which in fact covers a greater extension of Andalusian geography than the "*seseo*" which is normal in America, in which both are [s].[7] And there are also features of other areas that have indeed crossed the ocean, such as the Asturian initial [ɲ-] found in parts of Argentina and elsewhere. The establishment of the American Spanish *koiné* has recently been traced by many experts on both sides of the ocean,[8] and is now largely understood, at least in broad outlines. They seem not to realize it, but this is essentially parallel to the work carried out by Trudgill on the English of the southern hemisphere. In each case the resulting speech, developed out of the separate but mutually intelligible dialects that contributed to its formation, particularly in colonial settlements and imperial armies, is a distinctive and essentially simplified combination of the highest common factors of the features of the contributory dialects. Ralph Penny has illuminated the reasons for the changes in the internal history of Castilian between the ninth and sixteenth centuries along these lines,[9] and I have pointed out that the development of Early Romance outside Italy during the Roman Empire can also be largely explained in terms of the formation of an interdialect of this type among the areas outside the Italian Peninsula, a *koiné* that eventually came to be influential in Italy itself also,[10] and this helps to explain why the history of the later developments of the Roman Empire seem to imply that, as well as being a time of considerable linguistic evolution, it was a time of convergence rather than divergence.

Unfortunate Romance Corollaries of the Comparative Method

At this point the application of modern language-internal sociolinguistics, employed to explain the sociohistorical trajectories of successful innovations and the formation of *koinés*, crashes head on into one of the central beliefs of the comparative method as applied to Romance, the belief, enshrined in the

---

[7] A. NARBONA JIMÉNEZ and R. MORILLO-VELARDE PÉREZ, *Las hablas andaluzas* (Córdoba, 1987), p. 60.

[8] For instance: J. LÜDTKE (ed.), *El español de América en el siglo XVI* (Frankfurt, 1994).

[9] R. PENNY, *Patterns of Language Change in Spain* (London, 1987).

[10] Compare chapters 1 and 2 above.

image of the tree diagram as a model for the evolution of separate languages from a common source, that fragmentation is both geographically discrete and historically linear. The specialists in Proto-Romance reconstruction have modelled their theoretical activity on Proto-Indo-European. In the P.I.E. field it makes some sense to provide tree diagrams of divergence, both because the time scale is enormous and because the speakers of Proto-Indo-European can legitimately be seen to have spread out as distinct communities, often separated from each other by considerable distances in the sparsely inhabited world of the prehistoric centuries, and lacking any kind of unifying force in a common written standard. None of this applies in the Early Romance world, within which there was continuous travel and intercommunication, and a unifying standard conveniently available in written form to act as a centripetal magnet for all styleshifting. But the force of the analogy has proved so strong that the language-internal variation which is known to be an inevitable feature of all wide speech communities has been completely ignored within this tradition (or at best dismissed as a 'kitchen-sink' theory), and there has instead arisen a tendency for every conceivable reconstructed variant to be allotted to a discrete language variety localized on the soil on which the historical descendants of the variant concerned are known to survive in the attested medieval languages or in the present day. Thus it is that a very early separation from 'Proto'-Romance in general for '(Proto)-Sardinian', dated – if at all – to three centuries before Christ, is seen as gospel in this tradition, and the main bifurcations between geographically separable Romances are dated to well before the end of the Roman Empire. The only evidence for this is the analogy with P.I.E., and a feeling that it must be so. Historical evidence, on the other hand, overwhelmingly suggests that there was a monolingual (if variable and complex) community for almost a millennium after that.

I have examined elsewhere another baleful consequence of the analogy with P.I.E.;[11] there are probably others unrecognized: the inappropriate use of the asterisk. The asterisk is a device used sensibly within the reconstruction of P.I.E. (popularized by Schleicher, although, as Koerner has shown, not invented by him)[12] to indicate the reconstructed existence of a word, presented in its hypothesized phonetic form. In discussing a pre-literate age, this device makes sense. Within Romance historical linguistics, however, it has become normal to use the asterisk with unattested forms of otherwise well attested lexical items (for example *COMPERARE, between Latin *"comparare"* and Italian

[11] R. WRIGHT, *Early Ibero-Romance* (Newark, 1995), chapter 5.
[12] K. KOERNER, *Practicing Linguistic Historiography* (Amsterdam, 1989).

"*comprare*"). In such a case what has been reconstructed is a pronunciation, but what is unattested is a written form that would be isomorphic with that reconstructed pronunciation if Latin spelling were a phonetic script. But of course Latin spelling was not a phonetic script, and the lexical item concerned is indeed often copiously attested. Over 90% of the asterisks used (in the twenty-three studies investigated in that study) turn out to be in this category, added to an unattested written form of a lexical item which is attested in some other written form. This approach is by definition not applicable to the P.I.E. centuries, in which the question of what a word's written form would have been if the speakers had been literate is irrelevant in the extreme. The practice of adding asterisks to 'Proto'-Romance forms presented in putatively isomorphic orthography has often led to confusion between a lexical item (as a vocabulary unit), its orthographical shape (on papyrus or parchment), its phonological shape (in the mind) and its phonetic shape (vibrations in the air), and thus to many inconsequential and dangerously misleading arguments that would never have arisen without the unfortunate overapplication of this aspect of the comparative method to a literate community.

The Discovery of Latin Pronunciation

The origins of the comparative reconstruction of Proto-Romance are entirely honourable. They lay originally in the recognition of the fact that traditional Latin orthography was not a phonetic transcription of its writers' vernacular. This fact is still occasionally capable of eluding Latinists even to this day, as when they, for example, describe the orthography of a Late Latin text under the heading of 'Phonetics'. Robert Hall Jr., in particular, realized, correctly, that the texts of the first millennium A.D. could be no reliable guide as to the vernacular pronunciation of the period. So he and his colleagues used the attested facts of mid-medieval Romance languages, on the partly-justifiable assumption that at least in the twelfth and thirteenth centuries these were fairly close to being a phonetic transcription of the habits of their scribes, as the prime data for reconstructing backwards and establishing the nature of the common phonetics (or phonology) of the language from which all the Romance languages had sprung. This was valuable and important, and Robert Hall's great achievement. What he and his colleagues had done was to discover the pronunciation of Latin, and for this they ought to deserve eternal gratitude. But the problem was that they did not know that this was what they had done. Instead they said they had discovered the phonetics (or phonology) of 'Proto-Romance', conceived of as being a different language from the Latin of the Empire. For they assumed, without argument or even consideration, that the Latin of the Empire was at that time pronounced in the manner of later medieval Latin (that is, a specified sound per written letter, as Latin is indeed now pronounced, but as has almost certainly only been the case since the invention of medieval Latin as a separate entity in the early ninth century A.D.).[13]

The Myth of a Proto-Romance 'System'

Following this line of thought, the reconstructors of Proto-Romance deduced that since all texts were Latin, and thus in a different language, texts were therefore irrelevant to the study of Proto-Romance. De Dardel, in his 1996 book, took this conclusion to remarkable lengths. For De Dardel, texts of the time are "*parole*", whereas he is interested in the Proto-Romance "*langue*". This attitude is to some extent acceptable if we are studying phonetics and phonology alone, for traditional orthography was the only one taught (and probably often taught logographically, one word – or abbreviation – at a time), although even then it is advisable to have our proposed chronology of phonetic developments in rough alliance with the order and existence of attested orthographical peculiarities in the texts. It is partly acceptable in the study of nominal morphology, for we know from the surviving manuals on *Orthographia* that the inflections of nouns and adjectives were taught during the process of learning to write. But such deliberate evasion of the textual evidence is not acceptable if we are studying verbal morphology, syntax, semantics or even vocabulary, which were less open to conscious pedagogical control than the orthography and much of the nominal morphology were. It is the function of the grammarian down the ages to confuse the evidence, certainly, but writers are not going to change features of their own speech of which they are not even aware, such as the semantic changes that might have occurred recently in the words they are using, or the pragmatic value of the different available methods of expressing passive meaning. An appropriate appreciation of the relationship between speech and writing is a central crucial aspect of all historical analysis

---

[13] This assumption is still not dead, see for example: N. CULL, "Reconstruction of the Proto-Romance Syllable", in: *Historical Linguistics 1993: Selected Papers from the 11th International Conference on Historical Linguistics*, ed. H. ANDERSEN (Amsterdam, 1995), pp. 117-132 (and see chapter 13 above).

of literate languages, for the relationship can vary greatly between different social and historical contexts, and the analyst needs to be aware of the relationship in the historical context of the language being analysed. This has indeed been studied for the Early Romance-speaking world (by Banniard, Herman, Varvaro, myself, and several others),[14] but is discarded as irrelevant within the Romance comparative tradition. De Dardel, indeed, invents his own examples to exemplify the syntactic features he claims to have "reconstructed". In particular, he claimed (in an earlier article)[15] to have reconstructed four separate changes of basic word order in Romance between the third century B.C. and the sixth century A.D., including one which is not otherwise attested in Europe (he regards this not as a drawback of the theory but as its crowning achievement). Actual texts do not attest these developments, but that is seen as neither here nor there, even though it is exceptionally difficult for writers to vary their natural word order in their own compositions, at least in the absence of explicit pedagogical instruction (and the idea that Latin should have verbs at the end of their sentences, for example, is not one which is stressed in the pedagogical grammars of this age, which largely refrain from mentioning syntax at all). As Bob Blake has shown on several occasions, ostensibly Latin (or "Latinate") texts of central medieval Spain, in the period preceding the orthographical reforms, show Romance word order patterns.[16]

The structuralist idea that each language is a 'system' seems to be to blame for all this unnecessary confusion. Languages are in reality mostly composed of accidental conglomerations of contingentially concomitant details, only some of which are at times organized architecturally into inter-relating partial substructures – indeed, it may be debatable whether any language other than a genuine isolate is in reality an isolatable entity at all – but an intellectual obsession with finding intrinsic language-wide systematicity can obscure this unwelcome fact. In this case, the one simple mistaken idea, that the reconstruction of 'Proto'-Romance phonology was that of a separate language different from Latin (rather than just being what it was, the pronunciation of Latin), is a mis-

---

[14] M. BANNIARD, *Viva Voce: communication écrite et communication orale du IVe au IXe siècle en Occident latin* (Paris, 1992). J. HERMAN, *Du latin aux langues romanes: études de linguistique historique*, (Tübingen, 1990). A. VARVARO, "Latin and Romance: fragmentation or restructuring?", in: *Latin and the Romance Languages in the Early Middle Ages*, ed. R. WRIGHT (London, 1991: reprint, Penn State, 1996), pp. 44-51.

[15] R. DE DARDEL, "L'hypothèse d'une base OVS en protoroman", *Probus* 1 (1989), pp. 121-143.

[16] For instance: R. BLAKE, "Syntactic aspects of Latinate texts of the Early Middle Ages", in: WRIGHT (ed.), *Latin and the Romance Languages*, pp. 219-232.

apprehension easy to dispel with a simple knowledge of basic historical and social facts about the late Empire and the early Middle Ages (which are not at all 'Dark' Ages: we actually know a surprising amount about this period, each century of which saw the writing of more texts than survive from each century of the Empire). Even so, it seems to have been what led to the further idea that there were two whole distinct languages during the Roman Empire, not just the two hypothesized separate phonologies. Therefore, in the inexorable logic of De Dardel, there must have been a separate syntax too, since all autonomous languages are said in the structuralist approach to be complete language systems, with their own separate syntactic structure; and since, in his view, by definition Proto-Romance was not Latin, therefore the syntax shown in texts cannot by definition have been the same as that of speech, and therefore improbable conjectures, justified by the use of rigorous comparative procedures alone, have greater validity than the direct textual evidence which was so thoughtfully provided for us by those who supposedly spoke in this reconstructed manner. This is all achieved in the name of the dignity of comparative method. Yet let us look at the method as employed elsewhere: comparative historical linguistics in other fields has achieved wonderful progress, of course, but not by refusing to consider the available textual evidence. New data that turn up in the sands of Turkey are avidly examined and exhaustively analysed, not ignored. Specialists in Proto-Bantu would love to have a seventh-century text. Specialists in Proto-Romance reconstruction have available for study a large number of seventh-century texts, particularly from the Iberian Peninsula, and prefer to ignore them.

Why Romance Fragmentation happened when it did

For these reasons it seems fair to conclude that historical comparative method in the Romance languages has probably achieved all that it ever will. We should, of course, forever honour the discovery of Latin pronunciation, and of otherwise unattested vocabulary and derivational morphology. The Romance languages and structural linguistics can still co-exist: for they provide a wonderful testing ground for all the potentially explanatory internal structural proposals that come to be made within historical linguistics as a whole, although it is still the case that Spanish and Italian, in particular, tend to be used in the most patronizing and even insulting manner as 'test cases' for improbable theories developed on the basis of English. But if we first look at the Romance historical data pre-theoretically, we are likely to conclude that the most interesting feature of the development of Romance is probably not internal at all, and thus intrinsically not amenable to a merely structural explanation. For contrary to an apparently widespread assumption made by historical comparativists, language splits are not inevitable. And yet – at a much later date than that usually proposed, but still undeniably occurring – we have here a well documented real-life scenario in which what was originally one language has come to be thought of as being several different languages, even in an area which – unlike the vast geographical extension of the original Indo-European languages – continued to be literate, and whose communities continued to be in direct personal contact throughout (with the conceivable exception of Early Rumanian-Romance speakers, since we do not really know where they were). It now seems reasonable to claim that the fragmentation can only be explained through a knowledge of history allied to a knowledge of what is plausible in sociolinguistic terms. The reconstruction theory can offer branching trees, but no convincing dating for the branches (and glottochronology and lexicostatistics are at best unconvincing). The theory is effectively unable to help with the time dimension. Structuralism, on the other hand, is also stumped by geography. Structural analyses are often able to explain the initial rise of an innovation, but not why it should have been adopted in some places but not in others, a variability in practice which is the defining characteristic of the fragmentation at the focus of our lens. Typological analyses are especially impotent in such cases, since if typological explanations of change, even when vaguely rephrased as examples of 'drift', are taken to be predictive, then there is no way to explain the undoubted fact that the Romance languages are not all the same as each other (nor are all the Germanic languages; nor all the Indo-European languages, for that matter).

In the particular case of the conceptual separation of the Romance languages from Latin and from each other, a knowledge of external history, including conscious language planning, leads us to a scenario which is more straightforward and likely. More, that is, than either the quasi-mystical belief in perpetual bilingualism (sometimes rephrased as diglossia) and very early geographical fragmentation proposed by the application of historical comparative method, or the reliance on decontextualized typological or other forces proposed within the structural tradition. The Late Latin-speaking world, which can also be conceived of as the Early Romance world, continued for many centuries to develop, quite rapidly on phonetic, morphological and lexical levels, quite slowly on a syntactic level – as is usual – but until at least the sixth century A.D. there were centripetal cultural forces leading to convergence which could counteract any evolutionary potential for divergence. This chronology in itself lessens the possibility of substratum influence. There may well still have been features attributable to Iberian in the Latin of the third-century Peninsula, or features attributable to Phoenician in the remarkable third-century data that has been recently emerging from Bu Njem in Tunisia,[17] but these would be far less likely to have been still present five centuries later (as Arabic influence was much more apparent in thirteenth century Spanish than in that of the eighteenth century). This monolingual Early Romance world, containing variation of a wide but normal language-internal kind such as happens in any large community, probably continued at least to the end of the eighth century, with contemporary written texts still largely intelligible when read aloud (even if older ones may not have been).[18] The subsequent separation of Latin from Romance is due to a historically contingent occurrence: that is, it was a consequence of the establishment of the artificially normativized Latin established in Charlemagne's Empire. In due course, and once again for contextually explicable reasons that can be historically traced, different Romance-speaking areas began to write their vernaculars in different ways. Eventually, for political reasons connected with growing mid-medieval nationalism, every Romance kingdom, around the year 1200, seems to have wanted to establish its own written form as a symbol of national identity and pride. The point being made here is that all these developments were, from a solely linguistic point of view, quite unnecessary and in any sense unpredictable. The English, French and Chinese experiences show that it is possible for a conceptually monolingual state of affairs to continue despite huge linguistic variability, perhaps even indefinitely, for the variations that can be held within such elastic monolingualism can be enormous, both socially and geographically, without such conceptual fragmentation necessarily occurring. The Romance developments are easy to explain if we can see the historical background, and hard or even impossible to understand if we cannot.

---

[17] J. ADAMS, "Latin and Punic in contact? The case of the Bu Njem Ostraca", *Journal of Roman Studies* 84 (1994), pp. 87-112.

[18] J. HERMAN, *Vulgar Latin* (Penn State, 2000), chapter 8.

Why This Conclusion is Significant

We can say that historical comparative method has achieved valuable results in the Romance field, but there is no need to push the method further any
more; that structural and typological approaches have obvious value in synchronic analyses, and in several Pan-Romance diachronic developments, but
their over-determining nature means that they are at a loss to explain one of the
most salient features of Romance development, which is the mid-medieval
conceptual fragmentation; and that it is time now for all workers in this field to
accept that sympathetic analyses of the texts and their writers, of sociolinguistics, and indeed of simple linguistic history, all have an important role to play
in our understanding of the evolution of Romance languages. That these external details happen to be available to the Romance specialist to a greater extent
than to students of any other linguistic family is not something for which the
Romance specialists need to apologize. We just need to exploit it in a sensible
way, and help specialists in other families to accept that the particularities of
a long-past historical context might, if only they knew what it was, have explained developments that seem inexplicable on comparativist and structural
grounds alone.

Chapter 22

Writing: Photo or Disguise?

All the direct evidence we have for linguistic states before the twentieth century is written. It is tempting to carry out research as if this evidence was a more or less photographic representation of the speech of the authors. But before we can feel confident about doing that, we need to find out how the writers of the time in question viewed the connection between their speech and the writing system that they used.

Sociolinguistic research has shown that there are always differences between these two modalities, of many kinds. Whatever language is involved, writing needs greater preparation, gives more scope for self-correction, and tends to use more complex morphology and syntax, whereas speech tends to be more complex as regards contextual and sociolinguistic interactions, in, for example, the use of deictics and elliptical expressions, and to include more variation and flexibility.[1] But the differences are greater in some places and at some times than others, and the historical linguist has to appreciate the role played by literacy and written texts in the society concerned before we can even begin to deduce linguistic details concerning the speech of those who wrote the texts being studied.

This chapter is a slightly abbreviated translation of: "La escritura, ¿foto o disfraz?", in: *Actas del Primer Congreso Anglo-Hispano*. I. *Lingüística*, ed. Ralph PENNY (Madrid, Castalia, 1993), pp. 225-234. We are grateful to Professor Ralph Penny and Dr David Pattison, on behalf of the Association of Hispanists of Great Britain and Ireland, for permitting the reprint.

[1] F. KLEIN ANDREU, "Speech priorities", in: *The Pragmatics of Style*, ed. L. HICKEY (London, 1989), pp. 73-86.

Graphemics, the study of written language, is thus a central part of historical Romance linguistics, unless we rely exclusively on reconstructions (as
some do). Spoken morphology and syntax can be represented on paper exactly
if we want it to, but this only happens rarely, and it is worth emphasizing the
fact that no writing system has ever been invented which represents phonetics
exactly, without omission or ambiguity. Even when modern sociolinguists and
phoneticians try with total seriousness to transcribe on paper all the details of
the recorded conversations that they use as their corpus, they have never been
able to represent exactly through the written units every phenomenon of tone,
suprasegmental intonation, acoustic frequencies, relative speed, rhythm,
sandhi, et cetera, that are to be found whenever anybody talks at all. It would
be possible, of course, to print acoustic spectrograms, which represent graphi-
cally all the acoustic elements of sound waves, but then we would meet another
problem at once, the fact that these spectrograms communicate nothing at all
to their readers, not even to specialists in acoustic phonetics. Such an exact
representation of the sounds themselves has never in effect been the aim of
those who have invented writing systems, nor of those who teach them to the
apprentice scribes, because in practice what the readers require most of all is
not, or not necessarily, the phonetic details, but clear indications of what the
words and morphemes are, however they may be pronounced. For writing is
not, and is not intended to be, a photographic representation of phonetics. Its
practical point lies in the ability to transmit meanings, and this is only going to
be successful if the readers manage to recognize the lexical items. And the
practical point of reading is to be able to recognize these items, whatever the
graphemic symbols involved and their relationship to the phonemes.

Specialists in teaching the reading and writing of modern languages often
emphasize the fact that we read with our eyes even if, so to speak, we write to
some extent with our ears.[2] This means that for the reader to know what the
words involved are, there is no necessary need for the phonetic details to be
represented exactly in the written form. Many languages indicate the lexical
items in other ways. As is probably generally realized, there are two main kinds
of writing system: the logographic, which is based on a desire to indicate morphemes directly, without any phonetic analysis, and the phonographic, which
is based on a desire to indicate sounds (or phonemes). Logographic systems,
such as that of Chinese, tend to be easier to read – a fact which usually comes
a surprise to Europeans, but which seems to be true – while phonographic
systems tend to be easier to write, at least in the initial stages (although cursive

[2] U. FRITH (ed.), *Cognitive Processes in Spelling* (London, 1980).

Chinese can also be written with great fluency). So we should not be tempted to conclude that one system is intrinsically better than the other.[3] In practice, many of the systems in use operate on both levels at once to some extent, both the lexical-semantic and the phonetic. The Chinese system itself, in fact, has acquired a number of details based on phonetics. Conversely, initially phono-graphic systems tend over time to acquire logographic symptoms; that is, the writer and the reader both operate on the lexical level as well as the phonetic. This is what has happened to our own 'Roman' alphabet, used to represent many modern European languages, including Spanish, French and English, in which phonetic changes over the years have led to the traditional orthography of many words being rather different from their phonetic transcription. This is why the unit that is taught to the child at a British primary school tends to be the whole word. That is, the total orthography of whole words is taught, as well as generalizations about letter-sound correspondences. It seems likely that something similar happened in the early Middle Ages in Romance areas, before the Twelfth-Century 'Renaissance', when the literate used words with both evolved phonetics and old-fashioned orthography. For, as Sampson pointed out, the fact that the separate Roman letters of the alphabet were originally intended to correspond directly with separate phonemes was not in itself any bar to using them within more logographic systems.[4] Obviously, both now and in the tenth century it was necessary for a reader to be able to recognize the separate letters, in order to identify the right word, but reading is best achieved without any intermediate stage of allotting individual sounds to each of the letters used. What happens when we read aloud is that as soon as we recognize the word involved, we go straight to the lexical entry and pronounce it in the ordinary way as indicated there. In the English, French or Spanish of this or any previous age, it would just be an unnecessary obstacle to have to allot a sound to every individual letter and then go through laborious rules of deleting those that happened not to apply to the lexical item in question. The unit we work with when reading is lexical, not phonological.

The officially correct orthography used in the Late Latin area before the end of the twelfth century had been elaborated for the most part in the second century B.C. Those who initially devised the Roman system had largely worked by adapting that of the Greeks, fitting the letters to the sounds of their own speech. For this historical reason we tend to assume that the oldest Latin texts were written in a spelling that corresponded more or less isomorphically

---

[3] F. COULMAS, *The Writing Systems of the World* (Oxford, 1989).

[4] G. SAMPSON, *Writing Systems: A Linguistic Introduction* (London, 1985), p. 203.

with their phonology. But even if we are right in this, we cannot assume that the letters they used had exactly the same representative value then as they have now, in any modern language; nor even in the phonetic alphabet; nor in Medieval Latin. Which means, for example, that if we want to reconstruct an ancient Latin phonology that had no labiodental consonants, the fact they used the letter *F* is not in itself an argument against such a hypothesis. And then the Latin of the Roman Empire changed over time, inevitably, until the original isomorphism between letters and sounds came to be considerably diluted. In the fourth century, Saint Augustine still took the view that letters represented sounds,[5] but later, in the seventh century, Saint Isidore of Seville considered that letters were images without sound which represented words and even things themselves:

> Litterae autem sunt indices rerum, signa verborum, quibus tanta vis est ut nobis dicta absentium sine voce loquantur. Verba enim per oculos non per aures introducunt.[6]

Isidore understood about reading with the eye rather than the ear.

This means that the relative closeness between an apparently phonographic text and the speech of its author depends more than anything else on chronology. If they were written immediately after reforms based on the phonographic principle, we will give texts more evidential value than we will to those written at other times. It looks on the surface as if texts from the second century B.C. were using the same orthographic system as those of the seventh century A.D., but it was only the older ones that were representing at all closely their writers' phonetic habits. The newer ones are evidence instead of the writers' ability to achieve traditional orthographic correctness, a tradition which was established in a fixed form towards the end of the Empire, and which, by the time we reach the seventh century, had in effect the role of disguising the author's phonetic habits rather than representing them.

The texts written in the Iberian Peninsula during the following centuries, from the eighth to the twelfth, the period which Menéndez Pidal labelled as that of the "Origins of Spanish",[7] can often leave the modern scholar feeling somewhat perplexed. We need to decide whether the scribes of that age were wishing to represent their own phonetic habits directly and in detail, or whether

---

[5] Augustine, *De Trinitate libri XV*, ed. W.J. MOUNTAIN and F. GLORIE (Turnhout, 1968: *Corpus Christianorum. Series Latina* 50), 10, c. 19.

[6] Isidore of Sevilla, *Etymologiae*, ed. J. OROZ RETA, *San Isidoro de Sevilla: Etimologías* (Madrid, 1982), I, 3, 1.

[7] R. MENÉNDEZ PIDAL, *Orígenes del español* (Madrid, 1926; seventh edition, 1972).

they were still wishing to achieve traditional correctness, as the Visigothic scholars did. The problem is that the evidence seems to point both these ways at once. In the event, the scribes seem to have been wanting for the most part to follow correct orthographic tradition rather than offering a photographic representation of their own phonetics. But often they were unable to achieve this, particularly as regards the antiquated nominal morphology which they had been supposedly taught in their training (they had much greater success on the whole with traditional verbal morphology, probably because there was more of it left in speech).[8] It seems quite likely that the correct spelling of many words would have been taught to the apprentice scribes of the tenth century in the Peninsula with the essentially logographic methods used nowadays in the Anglo-Saxon world, that is, as whole units, without much phonetic analysis.[9] Even so, in order to write other less immediately accessible word forms, which they had not learnt whole in their training, they needed some rough rules of thumb concerning correspondences between letters and sounds (which obviously would not have coincided with our own correspondences). This is roughly the conclusion which Carmen Pensado came to in her own important study of these questions.[10] She points out, for example, that the written form "*eglesia*" was so common in documents from León that the scribes may well have been taught to write "*ecclesia*" that way, even if that was technically incorrect. Pádraig Breatnach has similarly pointed out that in ninth-century Ireland this word must have been taught in the written form "*aecclesia*".[11]

During this period, even if they were trying to write the old-fashioned correct way, the scribes often came across words, particularly the names of places or people, that did not possess a correct written form at all. In these cases they tended to invent a written form which approximated phonetics more closely than elsewhere. The initial role played by toponyms within the elaboration of new "*scripta*" has been noticed in many different cultures, and Menéndez Pidal naturally noticed it in the Peninsula. Subsequently, the ideas that we see attested in the new toponymic forms of the tenth century can be seen to spread gradually to other areas of the lexicon in the eleventh and twelfth centu-

---

[8] J.N. GREEN, "The collapse and replacement of verbal inflection in Late Latin / Early Romance: How would one know?", in: *Latin and the Romance Languages in the Early Middle Ages*, ed. R. WRIGHT (London, 1991; reprint, Penn State, 1996), pp. 83-99.

[9] R. WRIGHT, *Early Ibero-Romance* (Newark, 1995), chapter 13.

[10] C. PENSADO, "How was Leonese Vulgar Latin read?", in: WRIGHT (ed.), *Latin and the Romance Languages*, pp. 190-204.

[11] P.A. BREATNACH, "The pronunciation of Latin in Early Medieval Ireland", in: *Scire Litteras*, ed. S. KRAMER and M. BERNHARD (Munich, 1988), pp. 59-72.

ries, as, in some places, registers and genres, the traditional Latinate disguise was applied with less intensity. This means that we can use some non-traditional orthographic details as evidence for evolved phonetic details, if we operate with great care, but on the other hand there is no reason to attribute traditional spellings to archaic pronunciations. The decision taken by some notaries to write documents with less of the Latinizing disguise (or 'polish', as they sometimes referred to it themselves), to become thereby less logographic and more phonographic in their operating procedures, was only taken gradually.[12] Within other genres and registers the transition was made far more abruptly, around the turn of the thirteenth century.[13] Thus there is continuity, both cultural and linguistic, between the Ibero-Romance vernacular of the eleventh century, which had been written in more or less traditional ways, and that of the later thirteenth century, written in a way that looks startlingly novel to us. In Castile the writing system of the later thirteenth century was based once again on speech, for the first time in fourteen centuries. The Leonese were still having to impose a disguise, but for other reasons. They had to write the Castilian way now, rather than the Roman. The intentionally isomorphic standardizations of Ibero-Romance writing in the thirteenth century, those which we now call Old Castilian, Old Catalan and Old Portuguese, encourage historical linguists to believe once again that we can treat many of the orthographic details as if they were direct photographic evidence of phonetics. But even here we need to work with care. As Ralph Penny has shown,[14] we cannot assume that the correspondences that they operated with, between letter and sound, were the same as those of any modern language, or of any phonetic alphabet. In Castile the sound [h] was then written with the letter *f*, for example, and the sound [ʒ] with the letter *y*.

The last part of the Middle Ages did not experience the same kind of intense pedagogical neurosis over correct spelling as we can glimpse among some seventh-century Visigoths, or nineteenth-century schoolteachers, which means that we can continue to deduce some phonetic details from spellings in

---

[12] See: A. EMILIANO, "Latin or Romance? Graphemic variation and scripto-linguistic change in medieval Spain", in: WRIGHT (ed.), *Latin and the Romance Languages*, pp. 233-247.

[13] See: R. WRIGHT, *El Tratado de Cabreros (1206): estudio sociofilológico de una reforma ortográfica* (London, 2000).

[14] R. PENNY, "The Old Spanish graphs 'i', 'j', 'g' and 'y' and the development of Latin G^{e,i} and J-", *Bulletin of Hispanic Studies* 65 (1988), pp. 337-354. IDEM, "Labiodental /f/, aspiration and /h/-dropping in Spanish: the evolving phonemic value of the graphs *f* and *h*", in: *Cultures in Contact in Medieval Spain: Historical and Literary Essays Presented to L.P. Harvey*, ed. D. HOOK and B. TAYLOR (London, 1990), pp. 157-182.

texts of the fourteenth and fifteenth centuries (as in the speech of the fictitious *"serranas"* in Juan Ruiz's *Libro de Buen Amor*, for example), although such an argument can rarely be regarded as conclusive. In the sixteenth and seventeenth centuries there were different attitudes in evidence to this question among the many Golden-Age grammarians. It is also in these centuries that we find for the first time explicit observations from Spanish linguists, some of which can help us.[15] In modern times, we can usually trust the careful transcriptions of phoneticians, and as regards the syntax of speech, those of the sociolinguists.[16] Sometimes even the works of dramatists or novelists who are aiming to reproduce natural speech can give us useful data, although in practice the misguided ideas that some of them have about language can mislead rather than illuminate.

Thus the great majority of the texts written in Ibero-Romance languages were not prepared at a time when the spelling was being reformed on a phonographic basis. This means that almost all the writers were consciously trying to achieve written correctness. This was usually based on the speech habits of a bygone age, and writers often felt that it was their moral duty to disguise their phonetics if this happened not to coincide with the written forms known to be 'correct'. Furthermore, although it seems instinctively obvious to such would-be reformers as Jesús Mosterín that writing ought to be directly phonographic,[17] there have at times been reforms specifically designed to make the written forms less like a transcription of speech, rather than more. Standardized Medieval Latin was based on just such an intention. Some of the decisions about spelling taken by the newly established *Real Academia de la Lengua* in the eighteenth century also had this effect. During the preceding two centuries there had been considerable discussion, often quite heated, between those who preferred an etymological orthography, in which written words resembled their Latin etymon, and those who thought it should be based on contemporary phonetics.[18] The *Academia* came down on the etymological side, preferring *"digno"* to *"dino"*, *"haber"* to *"aber"*, *"aceptar"* to *"acetar"*, et cetera (where the letters *g*, *h* and *p* corresponded to no sound). This choice was made for the

---

[15] See now: K. ANIPA, *A Critical Examination of Linguistic Variation in Golden-Age Spanish* (New York, 2001).

[16] As in: KLEIN ANDREU, "Speech priorities". C. SILVA CORVALAN, *Sociolingüística: teoría y análisis* (Madrid, 1988).

[17] J. MOSTERÍN, *La ortografía fonémica del español* (Madrid, 1981).

[18] See for instance: A. SALVADOR PLANS, "La adecuación entre grafía y fonema en los ortógrafos del Siglo de Oro", *Anuario de Estudios Filológicos* 3 (1980), pp. 215-227. My views on the effect of the Academy's reforms have been developed since by: L. WILLIAMS, "The act of reading: how straightforward is it?", *Bulletin of Hispanic Studies* 74 (1997), pp. 265-274.

logographic convenience of readers, which the *Academia* thought to be more important than the phonographic convenience of those learning to write. The purpose of this reform was precisely to make writing less directly isomorphic with speech, which had the inevitable consequence of making the orthographic system more logographic in the way it indicated the right word to the reader. If we see the unit written as *"haber"* we automatically read it aloud as [aβer], without worrying about the ostensibly anomalous fact that this *h* corresponds to no sound. In practice, strictly phonographic writing only helps those who do not know the language well, or native speakers who do not know that word. This means that words that are mispronounced because a reader has produced a sound for a normally 'silent' letter are symptoms of incompetence, or at the least of inexperience; if, for example, we read *"haber"* with [h].

Unfortunately, many specialists in Romance philology have not understood this, and keep telling their students that such errors, when found in the history of Romance languages, are symptoms of learned and erudite influence (they are called in Spanish *"cultismos"*, and in French *"mots savants"*), rather than of the incompetence which they actually attest.

The conclusion is straightforward. We need to know how reading and writing were taught and practised within any particular community before we can deduce details about speech on the basis of texts. This seems obvious, and yet many Romanists seem not to accept it, particularly when dealing with the early Middle Ages in Spain (the so-called *"Época de Orígenes"*). Often, of course, we have very little direct knowledge of the relevant details. But that in turn means that it is worth trying to deduce such details from the internal evidence of the texts themselves, comparing genuinely reconstructable pronunciations with the unemended written forms, to see if this helps us understand the reasoning behind the spellings they used.[19] The sociophilologists of the year 3000 will need to do something similar when they study our own written texts, because the moral panic about correct spelling is as prevalent now as it ever was, and considerably more than it was a thousand years ago.

[19] See: WRIGHT, *Early Ibero-Romance*, chapters 11 and 14.

Chapter 23

Textual Evidence for Language Change

It seems to be an inevitable fact that all spoken languages change. This can be attested for the twentieth century through tape recordings, newsreels, et cetera, and the repetition of research in communities already studied. But for language states before the twentieth century, all the direct evidence is written. For several languages, it is possible to see the way in which their written attestation has changed, and come to conclusions concerning the way the language thus transcribed might also have changed. The procedure is not simple, because the relationship between speech and writing varies widely in different communities. Even so, there are some general considerations that apply.

Writing and Speech

It is tempting for a historical linguist to act as if a written text was a direct representation of speech. Very occasionally it is; modern specialists in phonetics and in sociolinguistics often take considerable care in transcribing tape-recorded data. The fact that the resulting written versions often look unfamiliar and even startling serves to show that writing is not usually a direct transcription of spontaneous speech, even in the work of supposedly realist dramatists and novelists. Many of the differences apply to any literate commu-

This chapter is a slightly abbreviated reprint of: "Language change: textual evidence", in: *Encyclopaedia of Language and Linguistics*, 9 volumes, ed. R.E. ASHER (Oxford, 1994), IV, pp. 1947-1952. We are grateful to Mrs Frances Rothwell, on behalf of Elsevier Science, for permitting the reprint.

nity. Writing requires more preparation and self-monitoring, and tends to use both more complicated and more explicit syntax (such as nominalizations and subordinate clauses) and longer words more often than speech, whereas speech is more varied and versatile in the nature of sociolinguistic interactions between participants, reflected, for example, in a higher incidence of deixis, first and second person morphology, redundancy, and elliptical expressions. Writing inevitably reflects and helps to create a prestige norm (or norms, since different written genres exhibit different features). Historically, written texts in many European languages were influenced by their authors' expertise in Latin. Yet the grammatical and lexical differences between writing and speech are merely statistical, for spoken language can be transcribed verbatim and written language can be read aloud, and the features that predominate in one are rarely barred from the other (except in some extreme cases such as Arabic, where it might be argued that the written form is no longer the same language as the spoken). An allied question concerns the extent to which the written language itself affects speech. At a vague level, the presence of writing in a society alters the oral practice even of the illiterate (as Goody has established), and writing is often thought to change irreversibly the nature of the human mind. More precisely it is reasonable to hypothesize, for example, that the development of subordination in writing to replace the contextually disambiguated juxtapositions of spoken parataxis might in itself lead to a higher incidence of subordinate clauses being used in speech. Very literate people can, in some moods, even be heard speaking essentially the written form of the language. At the other extreme, phonetic changes due to spelling pronunciations are mostly the end result of widespread incompetence (such as pronouncing [h] for the originally silent *h* in English "humble"). The idea, widely held, that writing puts a brake on linguistic change, refers to the temporal prolongation of obsolescent features rather than the erection of any serious barrier against innovation.

Texts and Reconstructions

Graphemics – the study of writing – is therefore an essential part of historical linguistic study, unless the analyst relies exclusively on reconstructions. Reconstruction theory was developed, naturally, in an attempt to discover the nature of languages at a time before they came to be documented, usually on the basis of comparing subsequently attested languages which are believed to be related. Thus knowledge of Proto-Iroquois, Proto-Bantu, et cetera, is merely the best that can be done on the basis of informed extrapolation from the present. Proto-Indo-European has been reconstructed by working backwards from the oldest written documentation of its descendant languages. In general it is assumed that reconstruction is not widely necessary if texts exist from the time whose language one is attempting to recreate, but in one case, 'Proto-Romance', the reconstruction techniques have been extensively applied to invent a common 'Proto-Romance' base for all the subsequently attested Romance languages which in fact developed from Latin. Since there are copious texts written in Latin by speakers of this supposed reconstructed language, the differences between the texts and the reconstructions are particularly instructive to the general consideration of whether texts reflect speech and how far textual change is evidence of language change. The reconstructors of 'Proto-Romance' tend to act as if the texts were irrelevant, in effect adopting the cliché used by historians in other fields that history is just "prehistory confused by documents". But this intentional refusal to consider the textual evidence has not proved convincing, and it is impossible in practice to avoid conceding that in the late Roman Empire and early Middle Ages people were speaking approximately as the reconstructions suggest while still writing in the traditional way. The conclusion to be drawn is disturbing both ways: reconstruction is clearly partial at best, but textual evidence is also partial and often even misleading. Since this Proto-Romance case is the most remarkable example, most of the data adduced here will come from that. In a thousand years' time Modern English may well seem similar. If reconstruction then suggests that Britons now pronounce the word written "station" as [stéjʃən], or often say "no way" but rarely write it, reconstruction will be a surer guide to speech and language change than the surviving texts are.

Phonetic Change: phonographic and logographic scripts

The relationship between textual and spoken developments is most complicated in the realm of phonetic change. It is at least physically possible to reproduce on paper the morphology, syntax. and vocabulary of speech exactly as it is heard by the tape recorder of a phonetician or a realist novelist. But no writing system has been devised which can capture all the phonetic details. Suprasegmental intonation, acoustic frequencies, sandhi, relative speed, pitch and rhythm, for example, are not normally indicated at all, but might have had a crucial role to play in sound changes. If all writers wished to do was reproduce the speech sounds, then they could in theory just print a sequence of spectrograms, but these would convey no meaning at all to a reader (even an expert in acoustics). Written texts are only very rarely intended to be mere recordings of a section of speech; they are usually intended to convey meaning to a reader. When we read a text we do so in order to find its meaning, regardless of the original phonetics, and we do that by recognizing the words and morphemes, however transcribed. As the specialists say, we "read by eye" even if in part we "write by ear".[1] Thus phonetic transcriptions are in practice a hindrance to most readers, even if in theory they might be easier to learn to write. Since nobody learns to read without at the same time being taught the usual spellings of at least the commoner words, it is easier for a modern English reader to recognize and understand the written form "oranges" than [ɔ́ɹɪndʒɪz] (or even "orindjiz"), for a French reader to read "*heureuses*" than [œrǿːz] (or even "*oeroeuz*"), for a tenth-century Spaniard to read the traditional form "*folia*" than the then unfamiliar "*hojas*" (for spoken [hóʒas]), et cetera, even though in each case the latter is a closer analogue of the sounds produced, both by the writer and any contemporary reader aloud. Readers, once they recognize a word, read it with their ordinary pronunciation of that word, regardless of how close to being a transcription of that pronunciation the spelling is. It is only words which they do not recognize that are given some kind of phonographic rendering – that is, based on learnt correspondences between each written letter and a sound.

Indeed, it seems to be generally agreed that essentially logographic scripts (such as Chinese), which allot a particular written symbol to a whole word rather than to a sound, are, once learnt, easier to read than the originally phonographic scripts such as the Greek and Roman alphabets (probably using the right half of the brain rather than the left). As time goes on, scripts that were originally elaborated on a phonographic principle come, as a result of inevitable sound change, to indicate pronunciations less isomorphically, but this does not matter greatly, for readers are usually taught to recognize the written language word by word in an essentially logographic manner, and continue to be taught that the old written form is the correct one. Similarly, in Ancient Egypt, instruction seems to have been based on copying, and perhaps reciting, units larger than the hieroglyphic sign. All kinds of script can be mastered logographically; that is how the deaf learn to read and write. Furthermore, old texts are often subsequently distorted (or 'emended') specifically in order to

---

[1] J.F. KAVANAGH and I.G. MATTINGLY, *Language by Ear and by Eye* (Cambridge, Mass., 1972).

reflect their author's speech less directly, and often only such emended copies survive for investigation by linguists. For several reasons, then, sound change need not necessarily be reflected at all in writing.

Interpreting Spelling Mistakes

Nevertheless, phonetic change can often in practice be illuminated by textual analysis. Within the present case, the study of spoken Late Latin (Early Romance), if probable pronunciations are reconstructed on the basis of later developments, these sometimes help to explain mis-spellings. Sometimes one can only conclude that an ostensibly incorrect written form was so common that it must have been taught as such. For example, the form *"eglesia"* in tenth-century northern Iberia is much commoner than the officially correct *"ecclesia"* ("church"). Yet *"eglesia"* is not itself a direct transcription of reconstructable old Ibero-Romance phonetics, because Castilian Spanish *"iglesia"* and Portuguese *"igreja"* suggest that there was then indeed a [g] but also probably an initial [i]. Americans sometimes write "nite" on purpose for "night" ([najt]), but not because they pronounce it [nite]. Sometimes spelling mistakes happen in the absence of any phonetic change, and it is possible to hypothesize that writers know rough phonographic rules of thumb for how to spell words whose whole form they cannot remember or have never been told. In tenth-century north-western Spain, the word *"sobrinus"* (originally "cousin", but by then "nephew") appears far more often with a letter *u* in the first syllable than a letter *o*, and significantly more often with a *p* than a *b* (the commonest written form of the stem being *"suprin-"*), even though there had been reconstructably no phonological sound change at all in the first two syllables. Deriving from *"sobrinus"*, it was probably still pronounced [sobri-] (or perhaps [soβri-]; the modern Galician is [soβriɲo], *"sobriño"*). This textual change thus occurred in the absence of any language change. The explanation seems to be that more often than not the letter *u* was then the right one to represent [o] with (as in countless nouns in [-o], written *-um*) and *p* to represent [b]/[β] with (since [-p-] > [-b-] > [-β-] was a common development). Maybe the writers had worked out this trick of the phonographic trade, which was in this case neither traditionally correct nor an indication of a language change. Mis-spelling "sporadic" as "sporatic" in American English is a symptom of a similar combination of lack of phonetic change and statistical intuition (since there [-d-] is often spelt *-t-*). However, words sometimes need to be written for which there is no correct form: most commonly, names of places and people, particularly foreigners. The only fairly reliable, though rare, occasions when innovations in Chinese script illuminate pronunciation occur when a foreign word is adapted and spelt with graphs that already approximate the pronunciation of that word's successive syllables. The analyst has to know a great deal about both languages in order to make deductions. The Russian name spelt "Kruschev" in English was spelt with an initial *J-* in Spanish, a comparison which could be as helpful to a philologist in the thirtieth century as Anglo-Saxon names in Latin chronicles are now. Occasionally, texts of an already literate language are written in unaccustomed alphabets: Latin in the Greek alphabet in seventh-century Ravenna, Arabic in the Hebrew alphabet in Moslem Spain, Hittite (originally written in Sumerian cuneiform) in hieroglyphics, et cetera. This evidence is often the best there is.

The Effects of Spelling Reforms

Individual writers occasionally devise systematic new spellings on a phonographic basis, as the earliest writers of Anglo-Saxon in the Roman alphabet seem to have done, and as Orm did for his twelfth-century English *Ormulum*, and general spelling reforms are sometimes undertaken on the conscious basis of allotting a letter (or digraph such as *th*) to each sound. The initial elaboration of syllabic and alphabetic scripts for almost all languages, often adapting systems borrowed from elsewhere, is usually presumed to have been organized on that principle. If a language has undergone two such developments (as with Old Latin and Old French, for example), differences of detail can usually be taken as evidence of change. "*Canem*" probably represented [kanem] ("dog") in the second century B.C. and its derivative "*chien*" [tʃjen] (also "dog") in eleventh-century northern France, for example, whatever pronunciations are reconstructed for the intervening centuries. Even in these cases, though, the stability of correspondence cannot be guaranteed; for example, perhaps *f* did not represent the same sound for each set of standardizers. In addition, periods when spelling reforms are instigated are not immune from geographical and diastratic variation, so most written standards represent either one dialect chosen from several spoken by the standard's users (as Modern Basque) or compromises between them (as Modern Galician). Spoken variants thought now to be non-standard are not necessarily new. They may always have existed, unrecorded. Even so, progress is possible. Dees's careful statisti-

cal analyses of the spellings of thirteenth-century French charters have revolu-
tionized historical linguistic analysis, showing that documents from a single
province have more regularity when considered collectively and may at that
time have been more phonographically prepared than they are usually given
credit for. Toon's work on Early Old English "structured heterogeneity" has
also shown that ostensibly random data need not preclude illuminating analysis. Significantly, both Dees and Toon accept lexical diffusion theory.[2]

Spelling reforms are not necessarily designed to reach a closer match between symbol and sound. The prevailing mood in the seventeenth and eighteenth centuries, for example, was more in line with etymological rather than
phonetic spelling. Thus, since the eighteenth century, Spanish texts usually
attest [aβer] ("have") written with *h-* ("*haber*"), whereas previously there was
often no such *h-*. But that letter is as silent now as it ever was, and [h-] is as
absent as in cognate French "*avoir*" and Italian "*avere*". A decision was taken
consciously to imitate the Latin spelling ("*habere*") in Spain, but not in France
or Italy. If one did not know about the Spanish Academy's deliberations, one
could be easily misled into envisaging a sound change here. French spelling is
now notoriously a mix of etymological reminiscence and phonetic approxima-
tion, but as usual this worries foreign learners and apprentice native writers
rather than native readers, and given the agonizingly sluggish pace of French
spelling reform, their traditional spellings could continue to disguise language
change for centuries yet.

Writing systems themselves can be intentionally developed to reflect pre-
existing but untranscribed features. The formation of semantic-phonetic compound characters in Chinese; the decision to represent vowels, and to standardize the eighth-century diacritics, in Semitic script; the invention of Han'gul
script in Korea based on distinctive features; the decision to write Japanese
horizontally rather than vertically, et cetera. All fail to coincide with any related developments in the language itself. The invention of printing led initially
to clumsy inconsistencies. In English the digraph *ea* is common in manuscripts
of 1450 and books of 1550 but hardly appears at all in intervening incunabula,
and the orthographic tastes of several printers could vary even within the same
book. Subsequent standardizations can also mislead: "flower" and "flour"

---

[2] A. DEES, *Atlas des formes et des constructions des chartes françaises du 13e siècle*
(Tübingen, 1980). T.E. TOON, *The Politics of Early Old English Sound Change* (New York,
1983). Also: D.G. SCRAGG, *A History of English Spelling* (Manchester, 1974). On writing
systems in general, see: F. COULMAS, *The Writing Systems of the World* (Oxford, 1989). G.
SAMPSON, *Writing Systems: A Linguistic Introduction* (London, 1985). J. GOODY, *The Interface
between the Written and the Oral* (Cambridge, 1987).

represent the same sound now, "person" and "parson" (also from a single etymon) do not. There are often political motivations for orthographic distinctiveness. Webster encouraged several non-standard British forms as standard American English for essentially the same reason (political feelings of independence) that non-Castilian Spaniards are now preferring non-Castilian spellings, even (in each case) for words identically pronounced in all regions.[3]

Morphological Change

There is more chance that texts can be trusted to reflect language change in the fields of morphology, syntax, and vocabulary, where differences between speech and writing usually lie in the different statistical distribution of variants. In modern English writing as a whole, the proportion of "I've gone" relative to "I've went" is higher than in speech. Some sportsmen tend to say "we played brilliant" but write "we played brilliantly". The relationship is thus different in kind from that at the phonology-orthography interface, for there are indeed some people who exclusively say "we've gone", and many who may use both forms on different occasions, but everyone will understand either (whereas nobody at all says [orange] for "orange", and they would not be understood if they did). Morphological change often involves the reallocation of existing forms to other functions, rather than the invention of new morphemes. The occasional use of "bringed" for "brought" involves two existing and recognizable morphemes, "bring" and "-ed". The loss of the Latin synthetic passive forms (such as "*dicitur*") was compensated in speech both by reallocating the tenses of existing analytic forms ("*est dictus*", "was said" > French "*est dit*", Spanish "*es dicho*", Italian "*è detto*", "is said") and by expanding the use of grammatically reflexive forms. These already existed (for instance Italian "*si dice*" < Latin "*se dicit*") and were indeed already intelligible if used with passive meaning (a use to which modern English reflexives are also adapting themselves). The fact that the form with the new spoken meaning already exists, inhibits at first written use with the newer meaning, for the reader is more likely to interpret the text as having the old meaning until the new one is unmistakably the commoner one; that is, it might mislead your public to write "*est dictus*" with specifically present-tense meaning until the chances of that combination of words conveying the original past reference have declined considerably. In practice, it tends to be assumed that textual examples of

---

[3] N. WEBSTER, *A Dictionary of the English Language* (London, 1852).

reconstructably outdated morphology are as misleading for the modern analyst as is anisomorphic phonographic-based script, but in this case such dismissal of the textual evidence as having no direct value seems less convincing than an alternative view: that outdated morphology lingers on in a kind of twilight existence for a long time, understood by readers (and listeners to texts read aloud) even if very rarely or never found in speech. *"Thou doest"*, *"he did go"*, for example, are not normal spoken Modern English morphology, effectively ousted now by *"you do"*, *"he went"*, but survive intelligibly in, for example, folk songs. The advent of the new need not imply the complete loss of the old, and if, as often happens, the old variant is the one preferred by pedagogues it will remain half-alive until pedagogic practice changes and the support-machine is thereby switched off.[4]

Some deductions can still be made from texts on a relative statistical basis. Many Late Latin texts from Romance areas exhibit generally correct, and even hyperstylized, verbal morphology but case inflections allotted to nominals almost at random, a combination which suggests that the original verbal suffixes were still not dead, and in general had a longer life than the nominal ones. In the allied field of Latin epigraphy, where texts have the advantage (for us) of being unemendable, Herman's work has established that relative statistics for correct and incorrect forms might merely reveal educational levels, whereas comparing these relative correct-incorrect proportions for different linguistic features may indeed indicate that some reconstructable changes are under way earlier than others.[5] Lexical diffusion of some changes makes generalizations inconclusive, however. Regularization of irregular verb forms, for example, is diffused through the vocabulary verb by verb. In English and Romance several verbs that once had irregular pasts now have regular analogically created ones, and others are changing now (*"leapt"* giving way slowly to *"leaped"*, for example), but within each of these changes both forms can remain viable for centuries, and textual statistics may or may not correlate with the spoken proportions. This, however, is an empirical issue. Further statistical research into modern spoken and written distributions of such pairs may prove illuminating, although uncertainty will usually remain as to when the regularized form was first used in speech.

---

[4] See: J.N. GREEN, "The collapse and replacement of verbal inflection in Late Latin/Early Romance: How would one know?", in: *Latin and the Romance Languages in the Early Middle Ages*, ed. R. WRIGHT (London, 1991; reprint Penn State, 1996), pp. 83-99.

[5] J. HERMAN, *Du latin aux langues romanes* (Tübingen, 1990).

Syntactic Change

Within syntactic change distributional statistics in diverse texts are the main investigative weapon, and may even give a rough reflection of spoken reality. Syntax has only recently come to be the central obsession of linguists, for ancient grammarians rarely mentioned it at length. Thus writers were correspondingly less likely to be deflected from isomorphism by prescriptive echoes of their training. Perhaps the greatest advance in Latin linguistics since Priscian (in sixth-century Byzantium) came in Panhuis's analysis (in 1982) of Latin word-order from pragmatic viewpoints that the old grammarians had no inkling of.[6] Some of the results are surprising, in that (for example) the statistics of orders of subject, verb, and object are not all that different in the unstylized texts of the fifth century from those of written Romance languages of the thirteenth. This textual evidence of comparative lack of change in a linguistic aspect beyond the reach of didactic neurosis is a boost to the reconstructionist procedural assumption that, at other levels too, medieval written Romance is a better guide to most features of earlier speech than are most written Latin texts.

In other cases of syntactic change, such as the replacement of one type of construction by another, notions of correctness have distorted the vision of subsequent analysts more than that of the original writer. For example, the use of Latin "*quod*" plus indicative to replace the accusative plus infinitive construction for indirect statements has been shown to have started as a useful pragmatic alternative, in which available variation embodies a principled distinction, rather than a mere symptom of linguistic 'barbarism'.[7] Tracing the course of such a change usually becomes an exercise in the statistics of relative distribution in different lexical, semantic, situational, geographical, and stylistic contexts; what has been called the development of 'quantity into quality'. Here, as with the morphological and much of the orthographical evidence, the textual representation of a new phenomenon at least attests its existence, and the analytical problem essentially is to determine the rate of spread of the new usage and the timing of the loss of the old one which it seems in retrospect to have neatly replaced. In the case of a simple syntactic change, such as that in twentieth-century English from "different from" to "different to", textual distri-

---

[6] D. PANHUIS, *The Communicative Perspective in the Sentence: A Study of Latin Word Order* (Amsterdam, 1982).

[7] J. HERMAN, "Accusativus cum infinitivo et subordonnée à *quod, quia* en latin tardif – nouvelles remarques sur un vieux problème", in: *Subordination and Other Topics in Latin*, ed. G. CALBOLI (Amsterdam, 1989), pp. 133-152.

butional statistics may lag only a decade or so behind the proportions in speech.

Lexical Change

Lexical change is different again. The two ways in which a new word gets absorbed into a language are by piecing together existing morphemes (derivational morphology) and borrowing from another language. In this case, unlike the others, textual evidence can actually precede the change. If an author wrote the form "evolvement" (rather than "evolution"), either by mistake or design, in such a context that its meaning was obvious, communication would be successful (by analogy with such words as "involvement"), but that unit might never appear in a written text again. Rudyard Kipling liked to incorporate words of Indian origin into his English books, some of which are now intelligible and others not, but for words in both categories that attestation is not necessarily evidence of the word's existence in the language. Lexical invention is sometimes a kind of necessary national sport (as in Hebrew in the twentieth century), but the inventions are not always adopted generally. When a neologism is domesticated into a general lexical acquisition, printers are less likely to underline it or enclose it in inverted commas, which is often acceptable evidence that speakers no longer see the word as strange. Forms created by derivational morphology often have an uncertain lexical status anyway. Lexicographers can vary widely over which forms to include. Dictionaries are not exhaustive, and sometimes copy errors from other dictionaries, so are not necessarily trustworthy inventories.

Lexical loss is very hard to assess. If the words are accessible in texts that are still read, they cannot be regarded as totally dead unless their meaning is completely opaque. Yet they may hardly ever be spoken. Writers in some societies (and essay-writing students) have often felt it to be their duty to use in writing words (or, indeed, whole sentences) found in older, authoritative sources, whether they understand them or not. Conversely, words can exist even in literate societies without being written at all, usually for sociolinguistic reasons, although in the reconstruction of Proto-Romance the trend to multiplying hypothetical proto-forms currently remains fashionable only within the field of derivational morphology, where it is still acceptable to postulate unattested combinations of separately attested morphemes.

Semantic Change

A surprisingly large number of words derive from etyma with a different meaning. Each word has its own history, but there are universal semantic processes too, as when a prototypical meaning shifts reference slightly, or a superordinate is progressively used only with the narrower meaning originally allotted to a subsequently obsolescent hyponym. Sensitive analysis of textual evidence is absolutely essential in every case of a word that has changed meaning, for the few scholars in the field have sometimes been tempted to create elaborate structural hypotheses that have no reflection in the contemporary texts. In such cases the textual evidence should have precedence over the reconstruction, for writers do not write words with intended meanings that the words do not then possess. Historians tend to be unaware that words can change meaning at all, so their interpretations of a particular attestation of a word suspected of partaking in a semantic change are often in need of linguistic support, rather than providing the linguist with data. Yet if independent external evidence provides assurance that a word makes better sense with its evolved meaning, that interpretation of the textual evidence can be solid. Latin *"populare"*, for example, meant "devastate"; Spanish *"poblar"* means "settle", "colonize". Ninth-century chronicles use the word in ostensibly ambiguous sentences to describe events that external evidence suggests can only have been colonization rather than devastation, which in turn implies that the semantic change was by then over, for any lingering ambiguity would probably have inhibited this choice of word. Similar considerations can also conversely suggest that a change had not yet started by the time of a textual attestation. For example, in the seventh-century Visigothic prayer-book one finds the request that people be placed by God's right hand, phrased with the word *"conlocemur"*. *"Conlocare"* ("place") became Spanish *"colgar"* ("hang"), but this development cannot yet have begun, for the resulting undesirable ambiguity would have led the liturgists to prefer a different phrasing.[8] In this case, the reader's deduction reinforces the reconstructionists' perspective, for the same word became French *"coucher"* ("put to bed"), and the semantic divergence in Spain and France suggests that in that Early Romance period the superordinate meaning was still general and the specializations happened later. Analyzing the textual attestations of words involved in semantic change is thus possible, but requires genuine painstaking old-fashioned philological expertise.

[8] R. WRIGHT, *Early Ibero-Romance* (Newark, 1995), chapter 5.

Conclusion

There is no default procedure. It is inappropriate either to assume that textual evidence is likely to be direct *prima facie* evidence of speech or to assume that texts are so artificial that they cannot override the extrapolations of reconstruction. Texts cannot be ignored, but evidence from other directions, including reconstructions, should be sought whenever available. Changes in textual evidence are primary indications of lexical, semantic, and types of syntactic change which involve constructions rarely mentioned in the old grammatical tradition. If used with care they refine understanding even of phonetic, morphological, and other types of syntactic change. There are a few general principles, based on the likelihood that the past will be understood better in the light of well-understood analogical situations in the present, but even then there is no advantage to be gained in disregarding old-fashioned philological analysis. The role of historical linguistics in the enterprise is to make the philological analysis of texts better informed and less prone to come up with unconvincing explanations.

Chapter 24

What Actually Changes During a 'Sound Change'?

hen linguists refer to a 'sound change', what is it that we think has changed? This question has been much discussed in recent years, both in general and within Romance historical linguistics,[1] and there seem to be so many possible answers that it would be worth disentangling the various strands of argument. This chapter considers sound changes, but the problem is not confined to this level, and the example to be considered in detail is that of LUPUM > *"lobo"* (from Latin to Spanish), referring to other cases where relevant.

Is This a Lexical Change?

One possible way to look at this is that the two are different words, that the change is a lexical change. Let us grant for the moment that Latin LUPUM and Castilian *"lobo"* ([lóβo]) are semantically equivalent, that is, that the semantic

This chapter is a translation of: "¿Qué cambia?", in: *Historia lingüística es historia de variedades. Acerca de la historiografía y de la sociolingüística diacrónica de las lenguas románicas en homenaje a Jens Lüdtke por su 60° aniversario*, ed. Rolf KAILUWEIT e.a. (Tübingen, Stauffenburg, 2001). We are grateful to Professor Andreas Wesch, on behalf of Stauffenburg Publishers (Tübingen), for permitting the reprint.

[1] R.L. TRASK, *The Dictionary of Comparative and Historical Linguistics* (Edinburgh, 2000), p. 201 (under the heading "Locus of diachronic process"). J. HERMAN (ed.), *La transizione dal latino alle lingue romanze* (Tübingen, 1998), in particular the "Discussione generale", pp. 237-260.

content of the two forms has been more or less identical, even though the Hispano-Romans had greater personal experience of wolves than modern Castilians. This semantic equivalence is what is expressed in the conventional formula, "LUPUM > *lobo*".

But this just reformulates the question rather than answering it. For there are at least four phonetic differences between the two. We do not wish to give the impression that the entire speech community went to bed one night saying [lúpum] and woke up the next day saying [lóβo]. We can be sure that these changes did not happen all at the same time, nor even all within the same century, whether or not we prefer to think that the voicing of the original [p], the opening of the two vowels [u] and the loss of the [m] happened gradually or abruptly. However the word may have been pronounced at any given time, the identity of the lexical word must have remained intact throughout, and this presupposition has to underlie all possible research into the question. This must be more than a simple lexical substitution. If not, the formula "LUPUM > *lobo*" would be no more valid than "LUPUM > *can*" (which developed from CANEM).

Is This a Change of Sound?

Another possible way of looking at this is to say that the sounds have changed. One of the greatest advances in the history of philology occurred when the specialists realized that the same sound, within the same phonetic context, tended to evolve the same way even in different words. This discovery came to be known as the "Neogrammarian" principle. According to this, we can rephrase the nature of the change in order to specify that what has changed are the separate sounds, rather than the word as a whole unit, specifying the phonetic context if necessary but without mentioning any particular lexical item. Thus, with reference to the intervocalic consonant in the middle of the word that means "wolf", we could rephrase the developments as follows: "[-p-] > [-b-] > [-β-]", or, if we prefer, as "[-p-] > [-b-]" and separately "[-b-] > [-β-]", if we would rather think that the voicing and the fricativization are not intrinsically related. If we see this as a 'drag-chain', then they are indeed connected. If not, probably not. This could then be seen as one or more 'sound changes'.

This is a highly respected and venerable way of presenting the facts, but that does not stop it being an exceedingly strange one. By definition, the sound [p] is always the sound [p]. It is not the case that [p] became [b]. Before, during and after these developments, [p] is [p] and [b] is [b], whether intervocalic or not. The acoustic formants and articulatory characteristics of [p] are always the same, however a language evolves. That is, after all, what the International Phonetic Alphabet is for, to ensure that the same written symbols necessarily always refer to the same sound.

In this case, all we want to indicate, through our formula, is that some lexical entries which previously included an intervocalic /-p-/ came later to have a /-b-/. The intervocalic conditioning factor is important, of course, but even so it is not the case that after these developments Ibero-Romance had no intervocalic sound [-p-]. They have [-p-] from Latin geminates, as in CUPPAM > "*copa*", or when a Latin [p] preceded a semivowel that came to be promoted to the preceding syllable, as in SAPUIT > "*supo*" and CAPIAT > "*quepa*". So we cannot even rephrase this development as the loss of [-p-] accompanied by the arrival of [-b-], given that the [-p-] did not disappear from several words. Besides, the sound [-b-] is not new either; it was there at the start (for instance in BIBERE).

There is a further complication, which has sometimes been overlooked.[2] If we refer to [-p-], distinguishing it in this way from word-initial [p-], we are already taking for granted a knowledge of where the word boundary is. Because even when it is intervocalic the normal thing is for word-initial [p-] not to voice. We can hypothesize that it did indeed voice sometimes, in some words and the mouths of some speakers. It is possible that occasionally in some words this might have happened sufficiently often for it to have affected the lexical entry. The late Harri Meier used to like to postulate such effects of sandhi (or "syntactic phonetics") in order to clarify the etymon of a number of Spanish words that now begin with [b-],[3] and he was particularly fond of suggesting a Latin etymon with the prefix PER- for words that begin in Spanish with [br-], such as "*bramar*" ("bellow"), derived according to Corominas from a hypothetical Gothic word *BRAMON, but according to Meier derived from Latin "*peramare*". If Meier is right about this, the lexical entry will have

---

[2] But see: T.D. CRAVENS, "Phonology, phonetics and orthography in Late Latin and Romance: the evidence for early intervocalic sonorization", in: *Latin and the Romance Languages in the Early Middle Ages*, ed. R. WRIGHT (London, 1991; reprint, Penn State, 1996), pp. 52-68. K. WIREBACK, "The relationship between lenition, the strong word boundary, and sonorant strengthening in Ibero-Romance", in: *Essays in Hispanic Linguistics dedicated to Paul M. Lloyd*, ed. R. BLAKE *e.a.* (Newark, 1999), pp. 155-172.

[3] H. MEIER, "Sobre la historicidad del lenguaje", in: *Actas del coloquio hispano-alemán Ramón Menéndez Pidal*, ed. W. HEMPEL and D. BRIESEMEISTER (Tübingen, 1982), pp. 181-207. IDEM, *Notas críticas al DECH de Corominas/Pascual* (Santiago de Compostela, 1984).

changed permanently even though the initial consonant is often not intervocalic at all (as in *"mientras bramaba"*, say). I am not here pronouncing on the validity of such etymologies, but pointing out a problem. Whether or not these reconstructions are right, we need to be able to indicate through our formulas the presence and absence of word boundaries before we can say whether [-p-] > [-b-] operated or not. It seems probable, for example, that *"que poner"* has never been said as [kebo-], for all that the labial consonant is there intervocalic. That is, the ability to recognize individual words remains important even if we are trying to limit our analysis strictly to the phonetics.

Is This a Change of Phoneme?

A third possible way of looking at this is to say that the phonemes have changed in the relevant lexical entries in the brain. Under this perspective, we are not investigating the change of [-p-] to [-b-] but of /-p-/ to /-b-/. And many relevant lexical items have indeed changed their constituent phonemes. What has changed, then, is a large number of similar entries. In this case, we are not investigating [lúpum] > [lóbo] but /lúpum/ > /lóbo/. This is more satisfactory, for since phonemes can be represented by different allophones, and there is no *a priori* reason why a given sound should be an allophone of one phoneme rather than another, it is at least possible that the seat ("locus" in Trask's terms) of the change should lie here. This would mean that a so-called 'sound change' happens in the brain rather than the mouth, even if the motivation for changes of an allophonic nature could well have been initially phonetic and even essentially articulatory. This is how lexical diffusion of changes is possible. Lexical diffusion annoys those of neogrammarian instincts in that it points out the undoubted fact that not all words change at the same time. But if we are concluding that the seat of each change happens in the brain, it would be miraculous if all relevant words and all speakers changed at once. And since lexical diffusion is not only possible but normal, it is as well to operate with a theory that does not deny its validity. It may be rather late for us to suggest that we should not refer any longer to phonetic changes, and get used instead to referring to changes in individual lexical entries, but we do need to bear in mind continually that although [b] could well have been a frequent allophone of /p/ in intervocalic position, as well as of /b/ in other positions (and of /m/ for those with a head cold), [b] has always been [b].

Of course, /lúpum/ > /lóbo/ cannot have happened all at once, any more than [lúpum] > [lóbo], for two reasons: neither all the phonemes nor all the speakers could have evolved at precisely the same rate. As regards the sounds and phonemes, it seems reasonable in this case to suggest that the first development was the loss of the final nasal; that then the final unstressed vowel evolved before the stressed one; and that the voicing of [-p-] happened even later than that. If this indeed happened as clearly as this sequence suggests, we could thus have a series of lexical formulas as follows: /lúpum/ > /lúpu/ > /lúpo/ > /lópo/ > /lóbo/ (and later > /lóβo/). Generativist phonologists work with such chains, which at least have the merit of clarity.[4] Such a chain implies, however, that one change must have finished before the next one started, which is not always plausible, particularly given lexical diffusion (which can often be very slow). This means that we are often dealing with what Wang called "competing changes",[5] changes which coincide chronologically at least in part without it necessarily being obvious which should have affected a given word first.

If phoneme theory has any validity at all (and I think it does), it works at the level of the individual lexicon. Lexical entries have to contain explicit phonemes. The central consonant in this case must have been either /p/ or /b/, however great the allophonic variation even in the mouth of a single individual, and even if there was no clear way of deciding which phoneme underlay usage at any particular time. And for a long time, perhaps more than a century, the two lexical entries could have co-existed together within the speech community. Within the speech community, we all speak the same language, but we do not all have the same brain, and it would be highly unlikely for everyone to have changed from /lópo/ to /lóbo/ at the same time, even if we could have found out which was in each person's head.

Is This a Change of Language?

We might wish to locate the change in the language itself. That is, when /lópo/ changed to /lóbo/, what changed was the whole language. It sounds unlikely, but this idea has in fact been seriously suggested and is widely held.[6]

---

[4] For instance: C. PENSADO, *Cronología relativa del castellano* (Salamanca, 1984).

[5] W.S.-Y. WANG, "Competing changes as a cause of residue", *Language* 45 (1969), pp. 9-25.

[6] For example by: D. LIGHTFOOT, *Principles of Diachronic Syntax* (Cambridge, 1979). R. LASS, *Historical Linguistics and Language Change* (Cambridge, 1997).

If that were the case, we would be speaking a different language every week. There is a basic confusion here, which can be easily resolved with the help of James Milroy's most helpful distinction between an innovation and a change.[7] For every change that leads to the existence of something that did not exist before, there must have been a first time. Somebody somewhere must have been the first to pronounce /lúpum/ with a [b], probably much earlier than most Romanists would suggest.[8] Then somebody, perhaps somebody else, must have been the first to do this consistently rather than as an occasional whim. Here we indeed have an innovation, but as yet shared with very few speakers (or none), and it would be an exaggeration to refer to this as a linguistic change. But it has begun. If the innovation does not just disappear, which is possible, then it is going to initiate a period in which both the old pronunciation and the new one can be heard, and both can be understood by all, whatever the listeners' own allophonic preference. Those who regularly voiced this consonant intervocalically had [b] as an allophone of /p/. Those who did not, did not. But such differences would never have disturbed intercomprehensibility. What happens after this stage (if it does) is the change, rather than the innovation, to be precise, a change in the statistics of the relative distribution of the variants that are now in competition with each other.

Is This a Social Change?

Following this train of thought, we can say that a linguistic change, as opposed to the initial innovation, is located in society. Such a change is effected through sociolinguistic variation, and the variation can be found between different people who may themselves never have actually changed anything in their own linguistic competence. This is possible because changes can occur through generational variation. That is, it is quite conceivable that no actual individual may ever have changed from having the entry /lópo/ to having the entry /lóbo/. What could have happened is simply that all those who ever had /lópo/ stuck with that throughout their lives, while younger people in the same society always had, right from the start of their speaking career, the entry /lóbo/ without ever having had /lópo/. This fits well within Henning Ander-

---

[7] J. MILROY, *Linguistic Variation and Change: on the Historical Sociolinguistics of English* (Oxford, 1992).

[8] Except: CRAVENS, "Phonology".

sen's "abduction" hypothesis, in particular.[9] It might seem that it should be easy to work out if an individual has actually changed a lexical entry during - their lifetime, but it is not, even in these days of magnetic tape.

If this scenario is right, then the change progresses through the gradual death of the older generation involved. The statistical distribution of the old and new variants changes just because those that have /lópo/ leave the stage and all the new entrants have /lóbo/. This is hardly even a sociolinguistic change, more a demographic one. At a phonetic level, however, people can indeed vary with themselves. After the sociolinguistic discoveries of William Labov, specialists in historical linguistics need to consider the likelihood that in this case some speakers at some times might well have pronounced this word with a [b] in some registers, or when drunk, or in other less formal circumstances, and [p] in some others, whatever their lexical entry might have contained. Such variation is not allophonic, but sociolinguistic.

The Chronological Problem

Given all these uncertainties, it is worth wondering whether it makes sense any more to try to date a change, as if it were a discrete event. We had a generativist's precision in the five-part formula above, but real life may well not have been so neat. It is quite possible that some speakers had an opened final vowel before losing the nasal: /lúpom/; or, later, that some speakers voiced the intervocalic consonant before opening the initial vowel: /lúbo/. And even if we limit ourselves to considering just the central consonant, rather than the whole word, we cannot offer more than a highly approximate dating. We cannot date the change to the first appearance of the innovation, [b], nor even to the first occurrence of the phoneme /b/ in this word, because at that time the majority of the speakers still did not speak that way, and the change (which, as we have seen, is a sociolinguistic phenomenon) had not yet taken place. After several decades, perhaps a majority of speakers in the Ibero-Romance area had /b/ in their lexical entry for this word, but even so, /p/ (and possibly also [p]) would have been current in several places and in the brains and mouths of the oldest speakers.

From this perspective, the sociolinguistic change operates through periods of variation between different allophonic realizations.[10] Yet we can hardly wait

---

[9] H. ANDERSEN, "Abductive and deductive change", *Language* 49 (1973), pp. 765-793.
[10] R. PENNY, *Variation and Change in Spanish* (Cambridge, 2000).

until [p] is never heard at all in this word before calling this a change. And as regards the general change of [-p-] to [-b-], the nature of the lexical diffusion of phonetic changes means that we would often not feel sure of whether a change had been established or not. There could well have been a time when some of the words in question regularly contained the phoneme /b/, others were still in complete variation, and others usually had /p/ in their lexical entry. In such circumstances, how would we know whether the words in the last category were going to voice eventually or not? Many general changes have exceptions, but maybe they are just words at the end of the diffusion queue, for reasons that may or may not be explicable. Even if Meier was wrong, and there are no cases of word-initial /p-/ > /b-/ in Castilian, the similar change of word-initial /k-/ > /g-/ is quite common and undeniable (CATTUM > "*gato*" is not the only case). And we would not wish to conclude that the change from intervocalic [-k-] to [-g-] has not yet become established, and still less that it has not happened at all, from the fact that "*can*" < CANEM is still showing no signs of changing to **[gan] when it follows a vowel.

This phonetic contrast between "*gato*" and "*can*" suggests that there can be no conditioning factor involved here of a semantic nature, particularly when we see that French "*chien*" and "*chat*" have the same initial consonant. It is just that some changes, perhaps the majority, have not yet affected 100% of the words that seem to qualify for them, which would be strictly impossible in the neogrammarian view.

Yet changes can stop. We do not always have to consider the possibility that the exceptions are at the end of the queue and are thus bound to be affected eventually. We can be sure that the voicing of /-p-/ to /-b-/, /-t-/ to /-d-/ and /-k-/ to /-g-/ is now over. We know this because modern words with unvoiced intervocalic consonants are never affected this way, whatever their previous history. The initial consonant of Latin "*cattum*" voiced many centuries ago. Its intervocalic geminate [-tt-] simplified but did not subsequently voice, for as far as I know, nowhere does anybody say [gádo] for "cat". Neither did "*boca*" (from "*buccam*") voice to [bóga], nor "*copa*" (from "*cuppam*") to [kóba]. This means that the change is indeed over. Maybe its completion date could even be established. And if one day those communities in Alto Aragón that still have /p/ in their word for "wolf" change that to /lóbo/, that will be the result of Castilian influence rather than an internal change in altoaragonés.

The Geographical Problem

The same sound change can be 'regular' in one place but not in another, and we need not assume *a priori* that the change has to operate in the whole of a speech community. In view of the nature of the dialect continuum, in which there is no necessity for isoglosses to coincide, we could not even indicate in advance that the speakers in one particular place will change their lexical entry, while these others in another place will feel no such temptation. Thus the word-initial change of /ka-/ to /ʃ-/ can be called 'regular' in Northern France, but would seem strange and eccentric in Iberia. These geographical differences present a problem for the neogrammarian perspective which has not always been noticed. Under the present perspective, there is no problem at all. The locus of the change is in the brains of speakers, not in geographical areas.

Even so, the whole approach presented here, that the changes are lexical-phonological in nature and spread during a period of possibly prolonged sociolinguistic variation, is in turn an over-simplification when there have been great population movements from one area to another. The clarity of such a summarized formula as "/lópo/ > /lóbo/" depends crucially on speakers staying where they are. Such formulae can be inappropriate, for example, with reference to the Canary Islands, or Spanish America.[11] When speakers of mutually comprehensible dialects from within the same continuum move to live in the same place, such direct lines and arrows (">") can hardly be used. The formation of a *koiné* or interdialect implies that later generations have created their lexical entries from several different sources. Perhaps the most appropriate image for this would indeed be a tree diagram rather than an arrow, but of an inverted tree.

Is this a spelling change?

For many years I found it hard to understand why phonetic changes were not represented on paper, in traditional Romance philology handbooks, with phonetic symbols. That is, these books offer us "LUPUM > *lobo*" rather than "[lúpum] > [lóβo]", as if the change were essentially an orthographic one. But there was a spelling change, of course. That cannot be denied. In the first part of the thirteenth century, Ibero-Romance scribes progressively stopped writing forms such as "*lupum*" and began to write forms such as "*lobo*" instead, along

---

[11] See: J. LÜDTKE (ed.), *El español de América en el siglo XVI* (Frankfurt, 1994), particularly Lüdtke's own chapter on the Canaries, pp. 39-56.

with many other similar forms ("*saber*", "*ciudad*", "*luego*", et cetera). This general change was the result of deliberate and official reforms in the practice and the training of the scribes, and can be dated to the early thirteenth century. This can be stated with some certainty even though we can see from the famous eleventh-century glosses, and occasional experiments in the twelfth century, that most of the forms which would later belong to the new standard were already being experimented with earlier from time to time. And after these reforms it still seems that the scribes learnt to write several Ibero-Romance words in a logographic fashion. That is, they would learn the written form of the Romance words whole.[12] This means that the traditional manner of representing the change through written forms, such as "LUPUM > *lobo*", does indeed reflect a real change, of a sociophilological nature.

All the philologists knew, of course, that the changes happened in speech long before they were reflected in writing, but the written forms seemed the most convenient way of presenting as a whole everything that had happened to the word by the thirteenth century. So it was taken for granted that the writing systems must have been more or less phonographic, both in the Latin of the Empire and the Romance of the thirteenth century, and maybe they were right for these times if not for the intervening period. This also means that in the absence of relevant later orthographic reforms, the subsequent change from [lóbo] to [lóβo] (or even also /lóβo/) cannot be presented in terms of orthographic forms, since both pronunciations are represented on paper as "*lobo*".

What, Then, Changes?

Lexical entries change. Probably through a sociolinguistic mechanism, in that gradually the younger generations use a different form from the older, although it is probably also possible for individuals to change. It cannot be called a lexical change, though, since it continues to be the same word with the same meaning; nor a phonetic change, since the sounds are in themselves always the same sounds; nor a phonological change, since (in this case, at least) the phoneme inventory is the same; nor a change in the whole language (or we would speak a different language every week). We probably need a concept of 'social change of the phonemes in the lexical entry' rather than 'phonetic change'. And I have only recently come to realize that this is in effect how I

---

[12] R. WRIGHT, *El Tratado de Cabreros (1206): estudio sociofilológico de una reforma ortográfica* (London, 2000).

have always visualized sound changes. This is the perspective that underlies the first chapter of my *Late Latin and Early Romance* of 1982.

Chapter 25

Conclusion

The Roman Empire in the West ended politically in the fifth century A.D.. It continued in the East, but there it became gradually mainly Greek-speaking rather than Latin-speaking. The western inhabitants largely remained where they were, however, and spoken Latin (Early Romance) continued in most of that area. By the end of the thirteenth century, several written Romance systems existed, standardized to a greater or lesser extent, represented on paper or parchment in different ways in different places. These were probably widely thought of even then as being conceptually separate languages, but there does still seem also to be a feeling, for example in the mind of Dante, that Latin and the Romance languages form a single cultural unit. The way in which the one language developed over time to be thought of as several different languages has long occupied my attention. With hindsight it may seem an inevitable or even obvious thing to have happened, but we can doubt whether it felt that way at the time. The broad view offered in this book, concerning the intervening processes, sees a crucial and complicated role played by the standardization of several, geographically based, distinct written systems in the conceptual separations both between Latin and Romance and between what we now think of as different Romance languages.[1]

This chapter is a slightly revised version of an article which first appeared in 1997, summarizing the conclusions that my research had led me to as regards the Iberian Peninsula, first published as: "Linguistic standardization in the Middle Ages in the Iberian Peninsula: advantages and disadvantages", in: *De Mot en Mot: Aspects of Medieval Linguistics; Essays in Honour of William Rothwell*, ed. Stuart GREGORY and David A. TROTTER (Cardiff, University of Wales Press, 1997), pp. 261-275.

[1] This paper first appeared in a volume presented in homage to Bill Rothwell, whose

It has come to seem justified to envisage the existence of an essentially monolingual Early Romance (Late Latin) speech community until at least the ninth century. Since they themselves do not seem to have made any systematic distinctions between the speech habits either of different areas or of different social groups, we may well be confusing the issue if we make such distinctions ourselves for that period now. There were, of course, social and geographic variations, as is only to be expected, but they were perceived and felt to be language- internal and particular, rather than symptoms of complete and separate whole linguistic systems. There is no theoretical problem here, because sociolinguists expect all single languages, indeed, all individual human beings, to manifest linguistic variation, without the variants being necessarily geographically based in different places.

The above considerations, however, apply to speech. Early Medieval Europe was not a pre-literate society. There were many texts written and read then, only a very few of which survive now. Most texts were carefully prepared according to the established standards of written grammar, rather than being the phonetic transcriptions of vernacular colloquial morphology, syntax and vocabulary. That is the case in every literate community, where speech and writing involve different and variable points in a continuum of variation in registers and modes of communication.

The nature of linguistic standardization becomes immediately relevant here, with its apparently intrinsic and essential connection to literacy and writing. Linguistic standardization, like all other kinds of standardization, is, of course, an artificial phenomenon. Languages only acquire 'standards' if someone in a position of authority has consciously decided which forms belong to the standard canon, and (as the Milroys and others have established) that usually involves a prescription of which words and morphemes can 'correctly' appear in written texts, and in what orthographical shape. Standardized writing in early Medieval Latin Europe was based on the grammar (known as the *Ars Minor*) of the fourth-century writer Aelius Donatus and his subsequent commentators. Grammars were at that time only concerned with writing, and so took the form, as they usually do, of a limitation, in writing, of the many linguistic options available in speech. Standardization's "chief characteristic ... is intolerance of optional variability in language".[2] In particular, Donatus and his commentators concentrated on the nominal paradigms, and learning the correct

expertise in these areas I am delighted to be able to acknowledge here.

² J. MILROY and L. MILROY, *Authority in Language: investigating language prescription and standardization* (London, 1985), p. 26.

inflections of nouns and adjectives seems to have come to be thought of as a branch of orthography as much as of syntax.

In the early Middle Ages this still remains the essential panorama: wide spoken variation, allied to a single written standard inherited from half a millennium earlier. Banniard has established that writers in Latin Europe (including the great St. Isidore himself, in seventh-century Spain) expected their texts to be intelligible to the general public when read aloud, up until the eighth century. In early Medieval Europe there was a wide range of intelligent people who were unable to read but were none the less able to participate in the culture of their age by understanding texts read aloud, at least as much as the general public do nowadays. So in Romance Europe there was no need yet to invent any other written standard. The existing one worked well for both local and international communication. In the ninth century, they might not have understood Cicero, but then that question never arose.[3]

The linguistic consequences of this kind of sociolinguistic reconstruction are as follows: that in the early Middle Ages everyone in a particular area used more or less the same phonetic system as each other, along the same scale of patterned sociolinguistic variation, such that listeners to texts could recognize the words from the pronunciations of the readers. And also that the old morphology and syntax still posed no serious hindrance to intelligibility. Vocabulary items that were no longer within even the listeners' passive competence would have the potential to cause confusion. This could well be the main reason why a number of manuscripts have glosses of individual lexical items added, so that the reader-aloud could add the gloss if he felt that it was in context appropriate, or even substitute it for the textual item, believing that the whole would thereby as a result be largely intelligible. They did not yet want wholesale reform of the standard, because having their existing traditional international standard had enormous advantages. It could be read, written, taught and understood anywhere in Europe. Its 'Grammar' was known, there was a solid educational tradition, the language had all necessary registers from the legal and ecclesiastical to the everyday. And given Banniard's scenario, the illiterate could follow texts when they were read aloud. Eventually these formidable advantages were going to be thrown away for an initially uneasy and awkward series of local experimentations, largely based on a newly fashionable but essentially fallacious view of the connection between writing and speech.

---

[3] Especially: M. BANNIARD, *Viva Voce: communication écrite et communication orale du IVe au IXe siècle en Occident latin* (Paris, 1992).

In the central Middle Ages (from the ninth to the thirteenth century) different geographical areas saw different developments. In Moslem Spain, the situation seems not to have changed at all, and Romance speakers produced long
texts intended to achieve the standard written form, but from the late ninth
century the Christians, probably all of them Arabic-Romance bilinguals in
speech, seem to have confined their literacy to Arabic, which was already standardized. Thus the Romance speech of Southern Spain never acquired a separate written standard of its own, and if occasional words did happen to get
transcribed in a different way from their traditional written shape, that was
because they appeared in the Arabic or Hebrew alphabets. Further north, however, in the areas of the Iberian Peninsula to the west of Catalonia, there was no
such alternative ready-made standard as Arabic in their communities, and, as
time went on, polishing their texts to conform to the ancient traditions of the
standard Donatus tradition became increasingly arduous. Several versions survive of the so-called *Chronicle of Alfonso III* of the very late ninth century, for
example, of which the earliest are the least polished and the closest to unvarnished vernacular, and the later ones see incrementally more passive verbs and
other antiquarian symptoms of written 'correctness'.[4]

Practical literacy, however, had no time for such complications. The lawyers who drew up bills of sale and other working documents in tenth and early
eleventh-century Galicia, León and Castile, for example, had less leisure time
in their offices, and the surviving texts are correspondingly in a less polished
form. But their non-standard morphology, syntax and orthography is not merely
random and whimsical. There could well have existed some kind of unofficial
standard, or several unofficial localized standards, in operation there, taught
and learnt as working methodologies.[5] We can catch occasional glimpses of
such pragmatic accommodations according to a less rigid kind of standard,
where vernacular verb and noun morphology is not barred from written texts,
and several orthographic approximations occur:

1. Of a logographic nature for some whole words. That is, where the spelling of the word was learnt whole, as in modern British English.
2. Of a morphographic nature for some morphemes. That is, where the
spelling of some inflections was learnt whole.

---

[4] P. LINEHAN, *History and the Historians of Medieval Spain* (Oxford, 1993), pp. 76-78, does
not share this view of the chronology of the manuscripts. Compare: R. WRIGHT, *Early Ibero-
Romance* (Newark, 1995), chapter 11.

[5] Studied for Galicia in: WRIGHT, *Early Ibero-Romance*, chapter 14.

3. Of a phonographic nature. That is, where corresponding letters are learnt for some syllables and individual sounds.

Correspondences of all three types seem to have been operated in a sufficiently regular way to be interpretable (by us) as having been conscious patterns, even if other words, morphemes and sounds had no such written equivalent instilled in the writers' training. This conclusion developed from the fact that some words and morphemes, in the data from Galicia being considered, were almost always spelt 'correctly' – probably because their correct form had been learnt whole, logographically – while other phonetically similar ones could have wide orthographic variation, probably because in contrast they had not been learnt logographically.

The Peninsular documents of these central Medieval times are not easy to study. Menéndez Pidal's pioneering analysis implied in many cases that the scribes operated directly with a phonetic script on their own speech, but the existence of such partial alternative localized unofficial standards seems a more plausible explanation for several details, and understanding the nature of their logographic practice helps us to explain many textual features of the period preceding the Twelfth-Century Renaissance.[6]

Then, once the Twelfth-Century Renaissance is under way, the situation becomes quite different again. In order to explain why, we need to turn to Carolingian France. In the central medieval centuries, Northern France saw a completely different scenario from that of the Iberian Peninsula. Eventually the essentials of the French situation came to the Peninsula as well. Germanic scholars established, in the Carolingian realms, for the first time in any Romance-speaking area, an official spoken standard, in addition to the old written one, a standard spoken form for use originally when reading aloud in Church contexts, in which the ancient morpho-syntax prescribed by Donatus and standardized in the subsequent tradition was newly allied to the artificial spelling-pronunciation techniques already used as standard by native speakers of Anglo-Saxon and other forms of Germanic. In this new reading standard every written letter of a word was given a specified sound (which is how we all still read Latin aloud today, that is, on the phonographic assumption, that every written letter of the standard spelling should be given a regular sound). Many words thus sounded in this system quite different from their normal vernacular pronunciation, so this reform meant that texts, read aloud with the newly stan-

---

[6] R. MENÉNDEZ PIDAL, *Orígenes del español* (Madrid, 1926; seventh edition, 1972). Also see: WRIGHT, *Early Ibero-Romance*, chapter 13.

dardized and artificial spelling-pronunciation, came for the first time to be largely unintelligible to the uninitiated Romance-speaker. Outside the church context, and until the Twelfth-Century Renaissance, it seems probable that most, or even all, texts were still read aloud in normal vernacular phonetics as before, as McKitterick, Guerreau-Jalabert and others, have either argued explicitly or implied.[7] In the clerical world, the Carolingian higher education system adopted (for the first time in Western Europe) Priscian's serious and intelligent *Institutiones Grammaticae*, written in Constantinople in the early sixth century, and between them Donatus, as the initial writing manual, Priscian, as a higher-level Linguistics text, and the new standard pronunciation, established – in due course for the whole of Romance Europe – the nature of standard late Medieval *Grammatica* (what we would now call 'Medieval Latin'). This thus became a whole separate systematic language of its own, freshly standardized in that way so as to be clearly distinct from everyone's normal speech, and itself usable in speech as well as writing on an international scale. The process of deciding which linguistic details were to be deemed to belong to the new formal Medieval Latin, and which phenomena belonged to local Romance vernacular, cannot have been simple, and took a long time to be generally intuited, but it had its roots in these early ninth-century reforms.

In due course, the existence of this newly standardized Medieval Latin language gave rise to the very occasional need for a different written orthographical technique for a text that was desired to be read aloud intelligibly to a non-clerical audience, that is, in effect, it inspired the oldest texts in what we now think of as being written Romance, which – all over the Romance world – all came from highly literate centres of expert Latinity. This cannot be stressed too often. The earliest texts in new, Romance, spelling were prepared by scribes who were already competent in the traditional methods of writing, and prepared for a conscious purpose, consequential on the nature of the new Medieval Latin standard with its phonographic assumptions. The collection of studies on this topic by Selig and her colleagues at Freiburg is worryingly old-fashioned in a number of respects, but they grasp this essential point.[8] Written Romance was developed by skilled Latinists and not, as handbooks still tend to imply, by people who could not cope with traditional written forms. Another point that needs continual stressing is that even in France, until the thirteenth

---

[7] R. McKitterick, *The Carolingians and the Written Word* (Cambridge, 1989). A. Guerreau-Jalabert, "La 'Renaissance Carolingienne': modèles culturels, usages linguistiques et structures sociales", *Bibliothèque de l'École des Chartes* 139 (1981), pp. 5-35.

[8] M. Selig *e.a.* (ed.), *Le passage à l'écrit des langues romanes* (Tübingen, 1993).

century, large numbers of texts of all kinds continued to be written according to the old standard, and were still widely accessible to interested parties when read aloud. These texts do not deserve to be as invisible as is implied in the strange title given to her book by Jeanette Beer, *Early Prose in France*, apparently implying that texts not in French were not in France.[9] For all the period under discussion here, until well into the thirteenth century, standard written Latin is still the standard, and even when rival Romance standards came to be elaborated they contained considerably more variability and less dogma than the Latin one did. This was indeed an advantage, in practice. Joseph sensibly asserts that "to call Old French 'standard' is metaphorical, and potentially misleading".[10]

The earliest written Romance texts in the Peninsula followed the same intrinsically phonographic principle worked out in France. That is, vernacular morphology, syntax and vocabulary could be represented in writing with an orthography that used the already established letter-sound correspondences inherent in the new Medieval Latin pronunciations, but used them in reverse, in order to produce new word spellings that were different from the existing Latin standard forms of the same lexical items. Thus usually the particular letter-sound correspondences of written Romance were not in fact new, although as a consequence the spellings of the same lexical item often were. In due course, because the whole vocabulary had potentially, for these reasons, two alternative written forms and two alternative spoken forms in use in the same place, one of each for formal usage in the international Christian standard and one for informal local usage, the whole came to be perceived eventually as comprising two languages in the same place rather than one. The subsequent spread and elaboration of written French norms has been widely studied and is not examined further in this book.[11]

One consequence of the elaboration of the new standards was the promulgation of the fallacious idea that spellings ought to be both phonographic and alphabetic, that is, containing regular letter-sound correspondences only, rather than also including the word-level logographic correspondences that had been normal in tenth-century Spain and are normal in modern Britain (where school-children learn lists of words to spell whole). Under that assumption, traditional orthography indeed presented an awkward problem, needing new standardiza-

---

[9] J.M.A. BEER, *Early Prose in France* (Kalamazoo, 1992).

[10] J. JOSEPH, *Eloquence and Power: the Rise of Language Standards and Standard Languages* (London, 1987), p. 132.

[11] For instance by: A. DEES, *Atlas des formes et constructions des chartes françaises du 13e siècle* (Tübingen, 1980). R.A. LODGE, *French: from Dialect to Standard* (London, 1993).

tion for those wishing to write in a new way. But the spelling was the only problem that required the elaboration of new written systems, since the representation of vernacular morphology and syntax required no such thought, for that was already there in their minds, and all of the details of normal word-order and syntactic construction could, if desired, be transcribed more or less direct in whatever orthographic form was deemed to be required. In general, standardization applies to spelling more than any to other linguistic level. The consequence of this is that standardizations do not and did not seriously affect speech habits, where spelling is usually irrelevant. Besides, as all investigators know from medieval manuscripts, Romance standards were never as rigid in the late medieval centuries, even in spelling, as standardized Latin or Arabic were, including at the Alfonsine court, despite the valiant studies aimed in that direction by Harris-Northall.[12]

Variations of all kinds, including of whole literary texts, were normal and tolerated, and need to be respected by modern editors more than they usually are. Thus Cerquiglini's "praise of the variant" is a very welcome development.[13] Indeed, from the geographical point of view we could see the rise of medieval Romance writing as a kind of de-standardization, being an officially acceptable increase in diversity. (There were no attempts to standardize syntax in written Ibero-Romance before Nebrija, and even he was not particularly authoritarian.)

From the ninth century onwards we can watch the new French-based assumptions spread out geographically over what was still in essence a monolingual international culture of Early Romance speakers. The new perception of a Latin-Romance bilingualism, which had been established, and to a large extent caused, by the ninth-century reforms in France, was gradually extended to the rest of the Romance-speaking world (other than Rumania). Northern Italy, Provence and Catalonia were all in the Carolingian realms anyway, and began to acquire the new Medieval Latin standards during the ninth century. In Provence, it seems that written local Occitan norms were elaborated early and were used from the eleventh century even in some legal documents, unlike elsewhere, as well as in verse by Catalans and some Italian writers. The legacy of Carolingian culture expanded in the early part of the Twelfth-Century Re-

---

[12] For example: R. HARRIS-NORTHALL, "Algunos aspectos de la variación ortográfica en los textos alfonsíes", in: *Actas del Primer Congreso Anglo-Hispano. I. Lingüística*, ed. R. PENNY (Madrid, 1993), pp. 181-192.

[13] For instance: B. CERQUIGLINI, "La paraphrase essentielle de la culture scribale", *Cahiers de Linguistique Hispanique Médiévale* 14 (1989), pp. 9-16.

naissance to reach the rest of the Iberian Peninsula, Sardinia,[14] and, so far as we can interpret the evidence, the Papacy and the rest of Southern Italy. Spoken as well as written Medieval Latin thus became in due course an international standard used all over Europe. In its pronunciation it had naturally acquired variations in detail from place to place, based on differences within Romance phonologies, but the basic phonographic principle, of a sound for each written letter of the standard spelling, survived.

The particularities of the new experimental Old French orthographies were already solidifying into some kind of alternative standard by the turn of the millennium, probably largely under the aegis of the monks of Cluny. The spellings of individual words in that system were only directly useful for those who had the phonology used in Northern France (including England) in their own mental lexical entries. So the orthographical forms to be standardized elsewhere would clearly need to be different in detail from the forms elaborated and taught in the Northern French areas. In the same way, if there were to be established a reformed vernacular spelling in England corresponding to a phonetic transcription of standard educated English pronunciation (or any other variety), the newly elaborated written forms of words would be of little assistance to English-speakers in Chicago, Alabama, Jamaica, Pakistan, Australia and so on. The phonographic principles underlying such an English experiment could well, however, act as a stimulus and a model for the elaboration of different new written forms in each of those areas and more. There is still now a wide cultural similarity, but the conditions that led to the break-up of general Early Romance culture into separately parochial geographical units are coming ominously closer in the modern English-speaking world too.

In the Iberian Peninsula, techniques using roughly the same orthographic principles as had already been used in France were elaborated experimentally, probably first in the mid-eleventh century. The earliest glimpses we now have of such enterprise, of scribes attempting, with partial success, to write words with a new spelling worked out by applying the sound-letter correspondences to local Iberian sounds, can be found in several of the famous glosses appended in the eleventh century to two manuscripts from the Rioja area. Despite this, though, it looks as if in the twelfth century most centres continued the previous method of partially regularized local techniques of polishing up words, morphemes and sounds, for legal texts in particular. Different centres were still experimenting along different lines around the turn of the thirteenth century.

---

[14] E. BLASCO FERRER, "Les plus anciens monuments de la langue sarde. Histoire, genèse, description typologique et linguistique", in: SELIG *e.a.* (ed.), *Le passage*, pp. 109-148.

But the documents need more sympathetic investigation than they have some-times had hitherto before we can say with any certainty how far these local unofficial orthographies were systematically regularized and intentional, rather than representing random failures to achieve the ancient norm.

It was suggested above that the process sometimes called the rise of the standard Romance languages is in practice as much a question of de-standard-ization. For in due course, in the Peninsula, different political units tended to want to establish different new standard written systems as symbols of their own separately affirmed national identities, following the same train of thought as that of those modern Spanish autonomous regions who feel a need for their own separate distinctive written norm, for political reasons. Language-planning is always (alas) directed by politicians rather than by linguists, and that was probably as true of the thirteenth century as it is now. As a result, it seems to me that the process has often hitherto been presented in a somewhat over-ideal-ized light.

The development of the several Romance standards is usually seen nowa-days as a good thing. Perhaps in the long run it has been, but it had genuine drawbacks at the time. It led to the increasing professionalization of serious culture, as the general population lost contact with work still in the traditional form, and partitions came to be erected, or reinforced, along social and educa-tional lines. It led to the loss of valuable international cultural relations, as the general Early Romance traditions, in literature as well as in other aspects of life, saw unnecessary partitions erected along geographical lines. It led to the need for an educational revolution that took a long time to become generally effective. It reinforced divisive nationalistic distinctions that they all might well have been better off without. It is known now that it is only the existence of different prestige norms in different places that can lead eventually to the later existence of genuine isoglosses along political frontiers within a continuum such as the Early Romance one. It distorted linguistic instincts by establishing the 'alphabetical fallacy', that is, the assumption that phonographic writing, as used in standard Medieval Latin, was intrinsically superior to logographic writing, as widely used in pre-Reform times. This misapprehension can affect European academic assessments even today, for there are still scholars who see alphabetical writing as intrinsically superior to that used with total success in Japan, a largely syllabic script, or Chinese, a basically logographic script, et cetera. It seems an enormous pity that the wide monolingual Romance contin-uum, that had existed well into the Twelfth-Century Renaissance, was then in its last stages. It was not standardized except in the old writing techniques, it was certainly diffused, variable, versatile, and tolerant, but these are good attributes rather than necessarily disadvantages, and they supported an extensive international oral culture, literature and legendary stock. It could probably have continued, as in practice the conceptually monolingual Chinese continuum has to this day, but the poison of nationalism was invading perceptions of language, as different sociopolitical units wanted to focus their own individual status more distinctively, and at that time a separate orthography of their own, even for pan-Romance lexical items, seemed an essential part of their national and social identity. This is not an original observation of mine, of course.[15] What needs to be stressed here is how unnecessary the process was. It erected needless barriers.

Imagine how much would be lost if twenty different written languages turned up in the next century to replace the present continuum of English, or, indeed, of Spanish. Lapesa is not alone in hoping for the continuation of Spanish as a conceptually monolingual international language.[16] A thousand years ago, this was the stage that Romance had reached. Eight hundred years ago, the uniting links were being deliberately weakened. It may be best to see these separate Romance standardizations as a regrettable and avoidable political phenomenon, rather than an inevitable linguistic one.[17]

It looks as if the Catalans only decided that they wanted their own systematized writing standard, rather than continuing to write in the Occitan manner as they had done successfully for well over a century, after the decisive break between Catalonia and Provence that followed the battle of Muret in 1213. There was linguistic variation there already, naturally, but the way people spoke in the two areas was similar then as now, and if the Catalans had managed to prevent the French from taking over their possessions in Provence, they could all well have happily continued using the Occitan orthography, even perhaps right up to the present day.

---

[15] It can be found, for example, on the first page of: R. PENNY, *A History of the Spanish Language* (Cambridge, 1991).

[16] R. LAPESA, "Nuestra lengua en España y en América", *Revista de Filología Española* 72 (1992), pp. 269-282.

[17] I prepared the initial draft of this section on the poison of nationalism immediately before Michael Portillo delivered his unpleasant speech to the Conservative Party conference (1994) on the "poison of internationalism" (which helps prove my point). Compare several comments in: W. ROTHWELL, "Adding insult to injury: the English who curse in borrowed French", in: *The Origins and Development of Emigrant Languages*, ed. H. NIELSEN and L. SCHØSLER (Odense, 1996), pp. 41-54.

Similarly, the establishment of Galician and Portuguese as separate languages, needing separate written standards, only came to be thought desirable after the areas were definitively understood to be separate political units. Separate norms for written Galician and Portuguese have never really been necessary from a linguistic perspective, even now. One of the suggestions made during the discussions about the new norms for written Galician in 1982 was simply that they could follow the Portuguese norms. For understandable political reasons, rather than linguistic ones, this suggestion did not succeed. For political inspiration in the thirteenth-century detail, we can watch the Portuguese standardizers at work. They, in particular King Afonso III in the late thirteenth century, seem to have wanted consciously and deliberately to make their new standard correspondences distinctive from the recently established Castilian ones (which were also used in Galicia), even in cases where cognate words had identical phonetics, and they accentuated their individuality with respect to the Castilians and Galicians (and perhaps in addition their political sympathy for Occitan-speakers) by choosing some of the Occitan letter-sound correspondences rather than the ones used in the Kingdom of Castile. The Portuguese and Occitan letters *nh* and the Castilian and Galician *ñ* represent the same sound, for example, [ɲ]. From a linguistic viewpoint, this is an absurdly unnecessary complication. Once again, the thought process is that of some modern Spanish autonomous regions, who like to think that they have their own separate linguistic as well as social identity, and thus might choose (as Judeo-Spanish has) to advocate to spell the sound [k] with a letter *k* rather than the letter *c* or *qu* as in Castilian, in words such as *"kanta"* / *"canta"*, despite the phonetics being exactly the same. In a similar way, the differences that there are between standard American and standard British spellings of the same words, usually in words that are more or less identically pronounced in the two areas, can be traced back to Webster's Dictionary, when Webster, consciously inspired by feelings of political independence, affirming the separate political identity of the United States of America, deliberately chose to standardize some forms that were not those of the British standard in cases where there happened to be an available alternative. Fortunately, the English-speaking world has resisted following this road further so far, and the language remains an international continuum.

We can see the exact reverse of the Catalan-Occitan and Galician-Portuguese splits in León and Castile. Castile was originally part of the Kingdom of León, but then "the creation of the Kingdom of Castile in 1035 no doubt sharpened awareness of the separate identity of Castilian speech".[18] In the late twelfth century, when León and Castile were once again independent political units, their professional scribes were gradually elaborating different new orthographies for a number of words and morphemes, as we can tell, *inter alia*, by comparing the two Royal Chanceries' versions of the Treaty of Cabreros between the two kingdoms, drawn up on Palm Sunday 1206.[19]

But Castile was the dominant partner after – indeed, because of – that treaty. León was politically subsumed by Castile from 1230, and although for a few decades more we can trace a separately developing standard (or conglomeration of local standards) in Western León, emancipating itself with painful slowness from the former Latin one – as explained in the analyses of Emiliano and Morala[20] – any prospect of a general and separate Leonese standard was in effect stillborn with the decay of independent political aspirations for León itself in the late thirteenth century. And they will not get a separate spelling until the *autonomía* of Castilla-León splits. This loss of a separate written form did not occur because all the Leonese started then speaking like Castilians, but because the combined kingdom of Castilla and León was centrally administered from Castile and only needed one written standard, and the Castilian-based one chosen was close enough to Leonese speech habits to be in practice employable easily in León as well (under some degree of compulsion, of course).

Within Castile and León we can see a variety of locally available partly regularized norms in the first half of the thirteenth century. When these have been fully investigated, we might even be able to locate the provenance of manuscripts from their spelling, which is as yet a somewhat optimistic practice, given the tendency of editors to change the spellings of the texts.[21] Later the Court of King Alfonso X (1252-1282) saw a largely successful attempt to work out a kingdom-wide norm for many features of written Castilian, probably on a conscious basis, as used in the later Alfonsine chronicles. This norm became 'supraregional' in that it seems to have been based on a selection of features

---

[18] PENNY, *A History*, p. 14.

[19] R. WRIGHT, *El Tratado de Cabreros (1206): estudio sociofilológico de una reforma ortográfica* (London, 2000).

[20] For instance: A. EMILIANO, "Latin or Romance? Graphemic variation and scripto-linguistic change in medieval Spain", in: *Latin and the Romance Languages in the Early Middle Ages*, ed. R. WRIGHT (London, 1991; reprint, Penn State, 1996), pp. 233-247. J.R. MORALA RODRÍGUEZ, "Norma gráfica y variedades orales en el leonés medieval", in: *Estudios de grafemática en el dominio hispano*, ed. J.M. BLECUA *e.a.* (Salamanca, 1998), pp. 169-188.

[21] For English, see: M. BENSKIN, "Local archives and Middle English dialects", *Journal of the Society of Archivists* 5 (1977), pp. 500-514.

from different areas (as has happened in the recent elaboration of a standard written Galician) rather than by choosing one particular local dialect to be the standard (as has happened to some extent in the elaboration of a standard written modern Basque, "*batua*"). Although New Castile provided probably a majority of the details, a fact which has not prevented some areas of Old Castile claiming subsequently that their native vernacular is in fact the same as the standard.

One by-product of the process was the introduction of the general idea that there was a 'correct' and 'incorrect' way of vernacular writing. As in some of the modern *autonomías*, this would have had the unfortunate consequence of giving many speakers two inferiority complexes at once, thinking they were prone to be 'incorrect' in both applicable standards, old and new. The centralized normativization process in Castile probably preceded the similar process in France, for the impressively well-documented studies of Dees have shown local unofficial norms of writing in northern France persisting throughout the thirteenth century, and the Paris-based scripta only really becoming a wider norm in the fourteenth century.[22]

Elsewhere in the Iberian Peninsula, Basque was not standardized in this period, being never written. Aragonese presents an instructive contrast. It seems to have remained at the stage of containing several different localized standards, without these ever being consolidated into a centralized norm as happened in Castile, probably largely because it was not the main official chancery language of the state of Aragón. That was the function of Catalan or Latin, and although there are chancery documents in Aragonese, nobody seems to have suggested that all texts in Aragonese should follow their detailed practice (or, at least, if they did, they did not tell Heredia and his fourteenth-century colleagues). Yet unlike written Leonese, which fades away, written Aragonese survived the Middle Ages, precisely because the Corona de Aragón was not a centrally administered state in the same sense as late medieval Castile was. They had Catalan as their main language and culture, and there was no comparable need to focus Aragonese into one written standard. So written Aragonese survived but remained in comparison diffuse, and nobody seems to have minded that. The term 'diffuse' here is used as a technical term, meaning lacking a standardized and focused identity. The terminology of 'diffuse' and 'focused' languages is the one used by Le Page and Tabouret-Keller, and in the Iberian Peninsula, the change from the ninth to the fourteenth century is largely

---

[22] Dees and his colleagues have computerized the data from a huge number of documents from France.

a change from diffuseness to focus.[23] But, in fact, even Castilian was not at all rigidly focused, or dogmatically standardized, until the founding of the Royal Academy of the Spanish Language in 1713, and even then standardization has had little effect on speech. Medieval standardization only really affected Latin and Arabic, and where relevant Hebrew. Even the French were quite tolerant of diversity in those days, and indeed it may have been this fact that led to the general but erroneous view that vernacular languages had no grammar. Even the advent of printing in Spain led to as much chaos as to general uniformity (unlike in England). Between Alfonso x and the Academy, despite the existence of many intelligent linguists in Golden Age Spain, there were fewer of the centralized language-planning instincts that lead to updated standardizations.

Improbable Conclusion

In the end, I still cannot help feeling that on the whole things would have gone better in Medieval Europe if the Carolingian reforms had never happened, and the whole Romance-speaking world had still preserved, even perhaps until the present day, only the old international written standard spellings of words, with all the attendant advantages, Late Latin, in short. If they had continued to spell words as they had been spelt in the Roman Empire, they could still have been taught and learnt whole as logographic units, as in Early Medieval Spain, as in Modern Britain, with different pronunciations in different places, obviously, but one internationally recognizable written form. There would have been no problem in representing on paper their natural contemporary syntax and word order, as happened anyway in the eleventh century. No reforms are ever needed as regards the representation of syntax on paper, and any outdated recommendations made by Priscian could have been, tacitly or explicitly, ignored. The system could quite easily have been updated by discarding the ancient morphology where it was unused in the current vernacular, and just keeping, for example, one form for the singular and one for the plural of nouns. This idea would have needed no specific reform, and in any event several studies in the present book have shown that this was in the event already happening in texts. This updating, rather than wholesale reform, is also roughly what has happened in the English-speaking world, where reading is actually facilitated by the direct access to lexical items enabled by our logographic script. The

---

[23] R. LE PAGE and A. TABOURET-KELLER, *Acts of Identity* (Cambridge, 1985).

many advantages of keeping the old system had been sufficiently obvious to maintain it for general purposes well into the twelfth century, even in France, where it is only really literary texts for oral performance that were written, in that century, in what we now call Old French. It may not have been at all clear which phenomena of the existing register continuum belonged on which side of the new artificial Latin-Romance divide, or which phenomena in the existing geographical continuum belonged on which side of the many new Romance-Romance divides. This implies that words in thirteenth-century texts identified (by us) as Latinisms or as the result of regional influence are not actually evidence of such influence at all, but of insufficient delatinization in the first case and internal variation in the second. The Latin and separate Romance standardizations made the situation less linguistically flexible, rather than more, as writers in the new Latin now had no obvious colloquial registers (at least until the so-called Goliardic literature became widely known) and writers in Romance had no obvious technical registers until the massive relexifications of the Alfonsine period. In sum, they drove dangerous wedges of class distinctions and nationalistic prejudice between people that largely otherwise had a common culture. That was not only unnecessary, it was unfortunate.

National divisions are not really caused by such phenomena as palatal digraphs, of course, and it has to be conceded that the modern concept of nationalism is not entirely applicable to thirteenth-century Europe. But the modern disease of nationalism is predicated on the ridiculous and dangerous assumption that everyone who happens to live in one state has a homogeneous nature clearly different from the nature of those people, however similar, who live just over an artificial political boundary, and that attitude was given a huge boost in the thirteenth century by the new and fallacious idea that the language used in each state is intrinsically separate from the cognate language(s) spoken beyond its political borders. That assumption would never have arisen with any clarity if there had not been standardized different writing systems for use on the different sides of such political borders. This process had in turn been inspired by the misconception that there was a need to have a new and completely different writing system for every different kingdom. This idea was itself fuelled intellectually by the phonographic principle inherent in the reformed standard of 'Medieval Latin', but which had been largely inoperative in the Late Latin centuries before the arrival of those reforms. A shared logographic script does and did not stop people fighting each other, of course, neither in tenth-century Spain nor in modern China. The point being made is that the psychological balance, between regarding your neighbours as intrinsically different or feeling that you have more things in common with them than separate you, is often a fine balance that can be tipped either way by ostensibly minor considerations. It is possible, for example, that the present bitterness between Serb and Croat, who use essentially the same language but write it in different alphabets, could have been lessened if they were prepared to acknowledge that they do indeed share a common language. The conceptual differences that turn up between the ninth and thirteenth centuries in the Romance-speaking world, where what was in the ninth century still thought of as one language came to be thought of as being several different ones, seem to have helped to tip this balance in a disastrous direction. The Kingdoms of the Iberian Peninsula fought each other quite enough anyway, and the continuing use of re-formed written Latin still helped unite the small but influential group able to operate with it (the abandonment of reformed Latin much later as the usual international language was also a shame). But the thirteenth-century consequences of the eighth-century Anglo-Saxons' inability to avoid succumbing to the alphabetical fallacy form just one of the reasons why I have been slowly coming to this conclusion, that it would have been better if Late Latin had continued and the Carolingian linguistic reforms had not happened at all.

Bibliography

ADAMS, J.N., "The vocabulary of the *Annales Regni Francorum*", *Glotta* 55 (1977), pp. 257-282.

ADAMS, J.N., review of: WRIGHT, *Late Latin*, in: *Liverpool Classical Monthly* 14 (1989), pp. 14-16 and pp. 34-48.

ADAMS, J.N., "Some neglected evidence for Latin *habeo* with infinitive: the order of the constituents", *Transactions of the Philological Society* 89 (1991), pp. 131-196.

ADAMS, J.N., "Latin and Punic in contact? The case of the Bu Njem ostraca", *Journal of Roman Studies* 84 (1994), pp. 87-112.

ADAMS, J.N., "The poets of Bu Njem: Language, culture and the centurionate", *The Journal of Roman Studies* 89 (1999), pp. 109-133.

ALARCOS LLORACH, E., *El español, lengua milenaria* (Valladolid, 1982).

ALLEN, W.S., *Vox Latina* (second edition; Cambridge, 1970).

ALLEN, W.S., *Accent and Rhythm* (Cambridge, 1973).

ALONSO, M., *Diego García, natural de Campos: Planeta* (Madrid, 1943).

ANDERSEN, H., "Abductive and deductive change", *Language* 49 (1973), pp. 765-793.

ANDERSON, J.M., *Ancient Languages of the Hispanic Peninsula* (Lanham, 1988).

ANDERSON, J.M., "Structural elements of Ancient Iberian", *Hispanic Linguistics* 2 (1989), pp. 179-190.

ANIPA, K., *A Critical Examination of Linguistic Variation in Golden-Age Spanish* (New York, 2001).

ATSMA, H., and J. VÉZIN, *Chartae Latinae Antiquiores*, XIII (Zürich, 1981).

AVALLE, D'A.S., *Latino "circa romançum" e "rustica romana lingua"* (Padua, 1965).

AYRES-BENNETT, W., *A History of the French Language through Texts* (London, 1996).

BALSDON, J.P.V.D., *Romans and Aliens* (London, 1979).

BALLAIRA, G., *Prisciano e i suoi amici* (Turin, 1989).

BANNIARD, M., "Vox agrestis", *Trames* (1985), pp. 195-208.

BANNIARD, M., *Genèse culturelle de l'Europe (Ve-VIIIe siècle)* (Paris, 1989).

BANNIARD, M., "Rhabanus Maurus and the vernacular languages", in: WRIGHT (ed.), *Latin and the Romance Languages*, pp. 164-174.

BANNIARD, M., "La voix et l'écriture: émergences médiévales", *Médiévales* 25 (1991), pp. 5-16.

BANNIARD, M., *Viva Voce: communication écrite et communication orale du IVe au IXe siècle en Occident latin* (Paris, 1992).

BANNIARD, M., "Naissance et conscience de la langue d'oc, VIIIe-IXe siècles", in: *La Catalogne et La France Méridionale autour de l'an mil* (Barcelona, 1991), pp. 351-361.

BANNIARD, M., "Latin tardif et français prélittéraire: observations de méthode et de chronologie", *Bulletin de la Société de Linguistique de Paris* 88 (1993), pp. 139-162.

BANNIARD, M., *Du Latin aux langues romanes* (Paris, 1997).

BANNIARD, M., "Diasystèmes et diachronie langagières du latin parlé tardif au proto-français", in: *La transizione dal latino alle lingue romanze*, ed. J. HERMAN (Tübingen, 1998), pp. 131-154.

BARATIN, M., *La naissance de la syntaxe à Rome* (Paris, 1989).

BAUER, B., *Du latin au français: Le passage d'une langue SOV à une langue SVO* (Nijmegen, 1992).

BAYO JULVE, J.C., "Poetic discourse patterning in the *Cantar de Mio Cid*", *Modern Language Review* 96 (2001), pp. 82-91.

BECKMANN, G., *Die Nachfolgekonstruktionen des instrumentalen Ablativs im Spätlatein und im Französischen* (Tübingen, 1963).

BEER, J.M.A., *Early Prose in France* (Kalamazoo, 1992).

BELTRÁN DE HEREDIA, V., "La formación intelectual del clero en España durante los siglos XII, XIII y XIV", *Revista Española de Teología* 6 (1946), pp. 313-357.

BENSKIN, M., "Local archives and Middle English dialects", *Journal of the Society of Archivists* 5 (1977), pp. 500-514.

BERSCHIN, H., *Greek Letters and the Latin Middle Ages* (Washington, 1988).

BEZLER, F., "De la date des gloses de Silos", *Revista de Filología Española* 71 (1991), pp. 347-354.

BIEDERMANN-PASQUES, L., "Le développement de l'écriture du très ancien français à travers les manuscrits (IXe-XIIIe s.)", in: *The Dawn of the Written Vernacular in Western Europe*, ed. M. GOYENS and W. VAN HOECKE (Leuven, 2002).

BIVILLE, F., "Tradition grecque et actualité latine chez les grammairiens latins: l'approche phonique de la langue", *Ktéma* 13 (1988), pp. 155-166.

BIVILLE, F., "Réflexions sur la notion d'interférence et ses realisations: le cas du grec et du latin", in: *Contatti linguistici e storia del latino*, ed. J. HERMAN and L. MONDIN (Tübingen, 2002).

BLAISE, A., *Lexicon Latinitatis Medii Aevi praesertim ad res ecclesiasticas investigandas pertinens* (Turnhout, 1975).

BLAKE, R., "Syntactic aspects of Latinate texts of the Early Middle Ages", in: WRIGHT (ed.), *Latin and the Romance Languages*, pp. 219-232.

BLAKE, R., "Squeezing the Spanish turnip dry: Latinate documents from the Early Middle Ages", in: *Linguistic Studies in Medieval Spanish*, ed. R. HARRIS-NORTHALL and T.D. CRAVENS (Madison, 1991), pp. 1-14.

BLAKE, R., "El latín notarial de un escriba bilingüe o 'bígrafo' del XIII", in: *Actas del I Congreso Nacional de Latín Medieval*, ed. M. PÉREZ GONZÁLEZ (León, 1995), pp. 463-468.

BLASCO FERRER, E., "Les plus anciens monuments de la langue sarde. Histoire, genèse, description typologique et linguistique", in: *Le passage à l'écrit des langues romanes*, ed. M. SELIG *e.a.* (Tübingen, 1993), pp. 109-148.

BLUME, C., *Analecta Hymnica*, XXVII (Leipzig, 1897).

BORETIUS, A. (ed.), *Monumenta Germaniae Historica. Capitularia regum Francorum* I (Hannover, 1883).

BOYLAN, A., "The library at Santo Domingo de Silos and its catalogues", *Revue Mabillon* 64 (1992), pp. 59-102.

BOYNTON, S., "The didactic function and context of Eleventh-Century glossed hymnaries", in: *Der lateinische hymnus im Mittelalter*, ed. A. HAUG (Kassel, 1997).

BREA, M., "La estrofa V del *descort* plurilingüe de Raimbaut de Vaqueiras", in: *Homenaje a Álvaro Galmés de Fuentes*, II (Oviedo, 1987), pp. 49-64.

BREATNACH, P.A., "The pronunciation of Latin in Early Medieval Ireland", in: *Scire Litteras*, ed. S. KRAMER and M. BERNHARD (Munich, 1988), pp. 59-72.

BRUGUERA, J., and J. COROMINES (ed.), *Homilies d'Organyà* (Barcelona, 1989).

BRUNI, S., *Alcuino "De Orthographia"* (Firenze, 1997).

BRUNOT, F., *Histoire de la langue française* (second edition; Paris, 1966).

BULLIET, R.W., *Conversion to Islam in the Medieval Period* (Harvard, 1989).

BURNETT, C., "The strategy of revision in the Arabic-Latin translations from Toledo: The case of Abu Ma'shar's *On the Great Conjunctions*", in: *Translators at Work: Their Methods and Manuscripts*, ed. J. HAMESSE (Louvain, 2002), pp. 1-62.

CALBOLI, G. (ed.), *Subordination and other topics in Latin* (Amsterdam, 1989).

CANO AGUILAR, R., *Análisis filológico de textos* (Madrid, 1991).

CARNOY, A.J., *Le Latin d'Espagne d'après les inscriptions: étude linguistique* (Brussels, 1906).

CARRERA DE LA RED, M., "De nuevo sobre las Glosas Emilianenses", in: *Actas del II Congreso Internacional de Historia de la Lengua Española* (Madrid, 1992), II, pp. 579-595.

CARRERA DE LA RED, M., "Textos lingüísticos antiguos del romance hispánico", *Epos* 14 (1998), pp. 69-88.

CASTAÑER, R.M., *Estudio del léxico de la casa en Aragón, Navarra y Rioja* (Zaragoza, 1990).

CASTRO, I., *Curso de História da Língua Portuguesa* (Lisbon, 1991).

CASTRO Y CASTRO, M., *Fray Juan Gil de Zamora: De Preconiis Hispanie* (Madrid, 1955).

CENNAMO, M., "The loss of the voice dimension between Late Latin and Early Romance", in: *Historical Linguistics 1997*, ed. D. STEIN *e.a.* (Amsterdam, 1999), pp. 77-100.

CERQUIGLINI, B., "La paraphrase essentielle de la culture scribale", *Cahiers de Linguistique Hispanique Médiévale* 14 (1989), pp. 9-16.

CHALMETA, P., "Mozarab", in: *Encyclopaedia of Islam*, VII (Leiden and New York, 1993), pp. 246-249.

COLBERT, E.P., *The Martyrs of Córdoba (850-859): a Study of the Sources* (Washington, 1962).

COLEMAN, R., "Vulgar Latin and the Diversity of Christian Latin", in: *Latin vulgaire - Latin tardif*, ed. J. HERMAN (Tübingen, 1987), pp. 37-52.

COLLINS, R., *Early Medieval Spain: Unity in Diversity* (London, 1983).

COLLINS, R., "Poetry in Ninth-Century Spain", *Papers of the Liverpool Latin Seminar* 4 (1983), pp. 181-195.

COLLINS, R., *The Basques* (second edition; Oxford, 1990).

CONTRENI, J.J., "The Carolingian Renaissance: education and literary culture", in: *The New Cambridge Medieval History*. II. *c.700-c.900*, ed. R. MCKITTERICK (Cambridge, 1995), pp. 709-757.

COROMINAS, J., and J.A. PASCUAL, *Diccionario Crítico Etimológico Castellano e Hispánico*, 6 volumes (Madrid, 1980-1991).

COULMAS, F., *The Writing Systems of the World* (Oxford, 1989).

CRAVENS, T.D., "Phonology, phonetics and orthography in Late Latin and Romance: the evidence for early intervocalic sonorization", in: WRIGHT (ed.), *Latin and the Romance Languages*, pp. 52-68.

CULL, N., "Reconstruction of the Proto-Romance Syllable", in: *Historical Linguistics 1993: Selected Papers from the 11th International Conference on Historical Linguistics*, ed. H. ANDERSEN (Amsterdam, 1995), pp. 117-132.

CURCHIN, L.A., *Roman Spain: Conquest and Assimilation* (London, 1991).

DAVIS, R., *The Lives of the Eighth-Century Popes* (Liverpool, 1992).

DE DARDEL, R., *Esquisse structurale des subordonnants conjonctionnels en roman commun* (Geneva, 1983).

DE DARDEL, R., "L'hypothèse d'une base OVS en protoroman", *Probus* 1 (1989), pp. 121-143.

DE DARDEL, R., *A la recherche du protoroman* (Tübingen, 1996).

DE DARDEL, R., and J. WÜEST, "Les systèmes casuels du protorroman: les deux cycles de simplification", *Vox Romanica* 52 (1993), pp. 25-65.

DEES, A., *Atlas des formes et des constructions des chartes françaises du 13e siècle* (Tübingen, 1980).

DE LA CHAUSSÉE, F., *Noms demi-savants (issue de proparoxytons) en ancien français* (Toulouse, 1987).

DEL VALLE, J., "Lenguas imaginadas; Menéndez Pidal, la lingüística hispánica y la configuración del estándar", *Bulletin of Hispanic Studies* 76 (1999), pp. 215-233.

DEMYTTENAERE, A., "Qu'une femme ne peut être appelée homme. Questions de langue et d'anthropologie autour du concile de Mâcon (585)", in: *Spoken and Written Language. Relations between Latin and the Vernaculars*, ed. M. MOSTERT (Utrecht, 2002: *Utrecht Studies in Medieval Literacy* 4).

DE VOGÜE, A. (ed.), *Grégoire le Grand: Dialogues*, 3 volumes (Paris, 1978-1980: *Sources chrétiennes* 259, 260 and 265).

DEVOTO, G., *Il linguaggio d'Italia* (Milan, 1974).

DÍAZ Y DÍAZ, M.C., "Sobre formas calificadas de vulgares o rústicas en glosarios; contribución al estudio de *Vulgo*", *Archivum Latinitatis Medii Aevi* (= *ALMA*) 22 (1951-52), pp. 193-216.

DÍAZ Y DÍAZ, M.C., "El latín de la liturgia hispánica", in: *Estudios sobre la liturgia mozárabe*, ed. J. RIVERA RECIO (Toledo, 1965), pp. 55-87; reprinted in: IDEM, *Vie chrétienne et culture dans l'Espagne du VIIe au Xe siècles* (Aldershot, 1992), chapter 2.

DÍAZ Y DÍAZ, M.C., "La circulation des manuscrits dans la Péninsule Ibérique du VIIe au XIe siècles", *Cahiers du Civilisation Médiévale* 12 (1969), pp. 219-241 and pp. 383-392 (= IDEM, *Vie chrétienne*, chapter 12).

DÍAZ Y DÍAZ, M.C., *Las primeras glosas hispánicas* (Barcelona, 1978).

DÍAZ Y DÍAZ, M.C., "Introducción General", in: *San Isidoro de Sevilla: Etimologías*, ed. J. OROZ RETA, 2 volumes (Madrid, 1982: *Biblioteca de Autores Cristianos*), pp. 1-257.

DÍAZ Y DÍAZ, M.C., "El latín de España en el siglo VII: lengua y escritura según los textos documentales", in: *Le septième siècle: changements et continuités*, ed. J. FONTAINE and J.N. HILLGARTH (London, 1992), pp. 25-40.

DÍAZ Y DÍAZ, M.C., "Las glosas protohispánicas", in: *Actas del III Congreso Internacional de Historia de la Lengua Española* (Madrid, 1996), pp. 653-666.

DÍAZ Y DÍAZ, M.C., *De Santiago y de los caminos de Santiago* (Santiago de Compostela, 1997).

DIONISOTTI, A.C., "On Bede, grammars and Greek", *Revue Bénédictine* 92 (1982), pp. 111-141.

DIONISOTTI, A.C., "From Ausonius' schooldays? A schoolbook and its relatives", *Journal of Roman Studies* 72 (1982), pp. 83-125.

DIONISOTTI, A.C., "Latin grammar for Greeks and Goths", *Journal of Roman Studies* 74 (1984), pp. 202-208.

DIONISOTTI, A.C., "Greek grammars and dictionaries in Carolingian Europe", in: *The Sacred Nectar of the Greeks: The Study of Greek in the West in the Early Middle Ages*, ed. M. HERREN (London, 1988), pp. 1-56.

DIONISOTTI, A.C., "On the nature and transmission of Latin glossaries", in: *Les manuscrits des lexiques et glossaires de l'Antiquité tardive à la fin du Moyen Age*, ed. J. HAMESSE (Louvain-la-Neuve, 1996), pp. 205-252.

DU CANGE, C., *Glossarium Mediae et Infimae Latinis* (Paris, 1884-1887).

DUCHESNE, L., *Le Liber Pontificalis* (Paris, 1886-1892; reprint, 1955).

DUFFELL, M., *Modern Metrical Theory and the* **Verso de Arte Mayor** (London, 1999).

DÜMMLER, E., *Epistolae Merowingici et Karolini Aevi* (Berlin, 1892).

DUTTON, B. (ed.), *Gonzalo de Berceo, Obras Completas*, 5 volumes (London, 1967-1981).

DWORKIN, S., "Studies in lexical loss: the fate of the Old Spanish post-adjectival abstracts in *-dad, -dumbre, -eza* and *-ura*", *Bulletin of Hispanic Studies* 66 (1989), pp. 335-342.

DWORKIN, S.N., "Latín tardío y romance temprano: implicaciones léxicas de una hipótesis controvertida", in: *Actas del Primer Congreso Nacional de Latín Medieval*, ed. M. PÉREZ GONZÁLEZ (León, 1995), pp. 489-494.

EBERENZ, R., "*Castellano antiguo y español moderno*: reflexiones sobre la periodización en la historia de la lengua", *Revista de Filología Española* 71 (1991), pp. 80-106.

ECHENIQUE ELIZONDO, M.T., *Historia Lingüística Vasco-Románica* (second edition; Madrid, 1987).

ECHENIQUE ELIZONDO, M.T., "Protohistoria de la lengua española en el primitivo solar castellano", in: *Actas del IV Congreso Internacional de Historia de la Lengua Española* (Logroño, 1998), I, pp. 37-58.

ELERICK, C., "Italic bilingualism and the history of Spanish", in: *Spanish and Portuguese in Social Context*, ed. J. BERGEN and G.D. BILLS (Georgetown, 1983), pp. 1-11.

EMERTON, E., *The Letters of Saint Boniface* (New York, 1940: reprint 1973).

EMILIANO, A., "Latin or Romance? Graphemic variation and scripto-linguistic change in medieval Spain", in: WRIGHT (ed.), *Latin and the Romance Languages*, pp. 233-247.

EMILIANO, A., "*Latín y romance* y las glosas de San Millán y de Silos: apuntes para un plantamiento grafémico", in: *Actas del I Congreso Anglo-Hispano. I. Lingüística*, ed. R. PENNY (Madrid, 1993), pp. 235-244.

EMILIANO, A., *Latim e Romance em Documentação notarial da segunda metade do Século XI*, 2 volumes (doctoral thesis; Braga, 1995).

EMILIANO, A., "O mais antigo documento latino-portugués (882 A.D.) – edição e estudo grafémico", *Verba* 26 (1999), pp. 7-42.

FALQUE REY, E., J. GIL and A. MAYA, *Chronica Hispana saeculi XII* (Turnhout, 1990: *Corpus Christianorum. Continuatio Medievalis* 71).

FERNÁNDEZ VALVERDE, J. (ed.), *Historia de Rebus Hispaniae sive Historia Gothica* (Turnhout, 1987: *Corpus Christianorum, Continuatio Medievalis* 72).

FISHER, E.A., "Greek translations of Latin literature in the fourth century A.D.", *Yale Classical Studies* 27 (1982), pp. 173-215.

FLETCHER, R., *The Episcopate in the Kingdom of León in the Twelfth Century* (Oxford, 1978).

FLETCHER, R., "El episcopado en el Reino de León, *c.* 1050-1150", in: *El Papado, La Iglesia Leonesa y la Basílica de Santiago a finales del siglo XI*, ed. F. LÓPEZ ALSINA (Santiago de Compostela, 1999), pp. 27-42.

FLOBERT, P., *Les verbes déponents latins des origines à Charlemagne* (Paris, 1975).

FLOBERT, P., "Les graffites de la Graufesenque: un témoignage sur le Gallo-Latin sous Néron", in: *Latin vulgaire – latin tardif* III, ed. M. ILIESCU and W. MARXGUT (Niemeyer, 1992), pp. 103-114.

FLÓREZ, H., *España Sagrada*, 23 (Madrid, 1767).

FLÓREZ, H., *España Sagrada*, 33 (Madrid, 1781).

FONTAINE, J., *Isidore de Séville et la culture classique dans l'Espagne wisigothique* (second edition; Paris, 1983).

FONTAINE, J., "Allocution d'ouverture", in: *L'Europe héritière de l'Espagne Wisigothique*, ed. J. FONTAINE and C. PELLISTRANDI (Madrid, 1992), pp. 5-7.

FONTAINE, J., and J.N. HILLGARTH (ed.), *Le septième siècle: changements et continuités* (London, 1992).

FONTANELLA DE WEINBERG, M.B., *El español de América* (Madrid, 1992).

FRANK, B., and J. HARTMANN, *Inventaire systématique des premiers documents des langues romanes* (Tübingen, 1997).

FRITH, U. (ed.), *Cognitive Processes in Spelling* (London, 1980).

El Fuero de Logroño y su época (Logroño, 1996).

GAENG, P.A., "La morphologie nominale des inscriptions chrétiennes de l'Afrique", in: *Latin vulgaire – latin tardif* III, ed., M. ILIESCU and W. MARXGUT (Tübingen, 1992), pp. 115-132.

GALMÉS DE FUENTES, A., *Dialectología mozárabe* (Madrid, 1983)..

GARCÍA DE DIEGO, E., *Glosarios latinos del monasterio de Silos* (Murcia, 1933).

GARCÍA LARRAGUETA, S., *Las Glosas Emilianenses: Edición y Estudio* (Logroño, 1984).

GARCÍA TURZA, C., *Luces y sombras en el estudio de las glosas* (Logroño, 1995).

GARCÍA TURZA, C. and J. GARCÍA TURZA, "La datación y procedencia de las glosas emilianenses y silenses: anotaciones críticas a los nuevos planteamientos", *Brocar* 19 (1995), pp. 49-64.

GARCÍA TURZA, C. and J. GARCÍA TURZA, *Una nueva visión de la lengua de Berceo a la luz de la documentación emilianense del siglo XIII* (Logroño, 1996).

GARCÍA TURZA, C. and J. GARCÍA TURZA, *Fuentes españolas altomedievales: el códice emilianense 46 de la Real Academia de la Historia, primer diccionario enciclopédico de la península ibérica* (Madrid and Logroño, 1997).

GARCÍA Y BELLIDO, A., "La latinización de España", *Archivo Español de Arqueología* 40 (1967), pp. 3-29.

GEBAUER, G.J., and B. LÖFSTEDT (ed.), *Bonifatii (Vynfreth) Ars Grammatica* (Turnhout, 1980: *Corpus Christianorum. Continuatio Medievalis* 133B).

GIBSON, M., "Milestones in the study of Priscian, circa 800 – circa 1200", *Viator* 23 (1992), pp. 17-33.

GIL, J., "Apuntes sobre la morfología de Álvaro de Córdoba", *Habis* 2 (1971), pp. 199-206.

GIL, J., "Para la edición de los textos visigodos y mozárabes", *Habis* 5 (1973), pp. 189-234.

GIL, J. (ed.), *Corpus Scriptorum Muzarabicorum*, 2 volumes (Madrid, 1973).

GIMENO MENÉNDEZ, F., *Sociolingüística histórica (siglos X-XII)* (Alicante, 1995).

GOETZ, G., *Corpus Glossariorum Latinorum*, 6 volumes (Leipzig, 1888-1923; reprint, Amsterdam, 1965).

GÓMEZ MORENO, M., "La escritura ibérica", *Boletín de la Real Academia de la Historia* 112 (1943), pp. 257-281.

GONZÁLEZ OLLÉ, F., "El romance navarro", *Revista de Filología Española* 53 (1970), 45-93.

GONZÁLEZ PALENCIA, A., *Los mozárabes de Toledo en los siglos XII y XIII* (Madrid, 1926-1928).

GOODY, J., *The Interface between the Written and the Oral* (Cambridge, 1987).

GRASSOTTI, H., "Don Rodrigo Ximénez de Rada, gran señor y hombre de negocios en la Castilla del siglo XIII", *Cuadernos de Historia de España* 75-76 (1972), pp. 1-302.

GREEN, J.N., "The collapse and replacement of verbal inflection in Late Latin / Early Romance: How would one know?", in: WRIGHT (ed.), *Latin and the Romance Languages*, pp. 83-99.

GRUNDMANN, H., "Litteratus – illiteratus," *Archiv für Kulturgeschichte* 40 (1958), pp. 1-65.

GUERREAU-JALABERT, A., "La 'Renaissance Carolingienne': modèles culturels, usages linguistiques et structures sociales", *Bibliothèque de l'École des Chartes* 139 (1981), pp. 5-35.

GUERREAU-JALABERT, A. (ed.), *Abbo Floriacensis: Quaestiones Grammaticales* (Paris, 1982).

GUTIÉRREZ, C.J., "El himnario de Huesca: nueva aproximación", *Anuario Musical* 44 (1989), pp. 24-60.

HAGERTY, M.J., *Los cuervos de San Vicente* (Madrid, 1978).

HALL Jr, R.A., *External History of the Romance Languages* (New York, 1974).

HALL Jr, R.A., *Proto-Romance Phonology* (New York, 1976).

HALL Jr, R.A., *Proto-Romance Morphology* (Amsterdam, 1983).

HALM, K., *Rhetores Latini minores ex codicibus maximam partem primum adhibitis* (Leipzig, 1863).

HAMESSE, J. (ed.), *Les manuscrits des lexiques et glossaires de l'Antiquité tardive à la fin du Moyen Age* (Louvain-la-Neuve, 1996).

HARRIS, R., review of: AVALLE, *Latino*, in: *Medium Aevum* 36 (1967), pp. 52-54.

HARRIS-NORTHALL, R., *Weakening Processes in the History of Spanish Consonants* (London, 1990).

HARRIS-NORTHALL, R., "Algunos aspectos de la variación ortográfica en los textos alfonsíes", in: *Actas del Primer Congreso Anglo-Hispano*. I. *Lingüística*, ed. R. PENNY (Madrid, 1993), pp. 181-192.

HARRISON, R.J., *Spain at the Dawn of History* (London, 1988).

HARVEY, A., "Latin, literacy and the Celtic vernaculars around the year A.D. 500", in: *Celtic Languages and Celtic Peoples*, ed. C.J. BYRNE *e.a.* (Halifax, 1992), pp. 11-26.

HASPELMATH, M., *Transitivity Alternations of the Anticausative Type* (Cologne, 1987).

HASSAN, I.M., "Sistemas gráficos del español sefardí", in: *Actas del Primer Congreso Internacional de Historia de la Lengua Española*, ed. M. ARIZA *e.a.* (Madrid, 1988), pp. 127-137.

HATCHER, A.G., *Reflexive Verbs: Latin, Old French, Modern French* (Baltimore, 1942).

HERMAN, J., "La situation linguistique en Italie au VIe siècle", *Revue de linguistique romane* 52 (1988), pp. 55-67.

HERMAN, J., "Accusativus cum infinitivo et subordonnée à *quod, quia* en latin tardif – nouvelles remarques sur un vieux problème", in: *Subordination and Other Topics in Latin*, ed. G. CALBOLI (Amsterdam, 1989), pp. 133-152.

HERMAN, J., *Du latin aux langues romanes: études de linguistique historique* (Tübingen, 1990).

HERMAN, J., "Sur quelques aspects du latin mérovingien: langue écrite et langue parlée", in: *Latin vulgaire – latin tardif* III, ed. M. ILIESCU and W. MARXGUT (Tübingen, 1992), pp. 173-186.

HERMAN, J., "Spoken and written Latin in the last centuries of the Roman Empire. A contribution to the linguistic history of the Western provinces", in: WRIGHT (ed.), *Latin and the Romance Languages*, pp. 29-43.

HERMAN, J., "The end of the history of Latin", *Romance Philology* 49 (1996), pp. 364-382.

HERMAN, J. (ed.), *La transizione dal latino alle lingue romanze* (Tübingen, 1998).

HERMAN, J., *Vulgar Latin* (Penn State, 2000).

HERMAN, J., "La teoria del sostrato: un capitolo della storia linguistica – o un metodo euristico della linguistica storica?", in: *Contatti Linguistici e Storia del Latino*, ed. J. HERMAN and L. MONDIN (Tübingen, 2002).

HERMAN, J. and J. WÜEST (ed.), "La fragmentation linguistique de la Romania", in: *Actes du XXe Congrès International de Linguistique et Philologie Romanes*, II (Tübingen, 1993), pp. 335-698.

HERNÁNDEZ, F.J., "Las Cortes de Toledo de 1207", in: *Las Cortes de Castilla y León en la Edad Media*, I (Valladolid, 1988), pp. 221-263.

HERNÁNDEZ, F.J., "Language and cultural identity: the Mozarabs of Toledo", *Boletín Burriel* 1 (1989), pp. 21-48.

HERNÁNDEZ, F.J., "Historia y epopeya: el *Cantar del Cid* entre 1147 y 1207", in: *Actas del III Congreso de la Asociación Hispánica de Literatura Medieval*, I, ed. M.I. TORO PASCUA (Salamanca, 1994), pp. 453-467.

HERNÁNDEZ ALONSO, C., "Las glosas. Interpretación y estudio lingüístico", in: *Las Glosas Emilianenses y Silenses. Edición crítica y facsímil*, ed. C. HERNÁNDEZ ALONSO and J.M. RUIZ ASENCIO (Burgos, 1993), pp. 63-82.

HERREN, M.W., "Hiberno-Latin philology: the state of the question", in: *Insular Latin Studies*, ed. M.W. HERREN (Toronto, 1981), pp. 1-22.

HOFMAN, R., "Glosses in a ninth-century Priscian MS probably attributable to Heiric of Auxerre († *ca.*876) and their connections", *Studi Medievali* 29 (1988), pp. 805-839.

HOLTUS, G., "Rilievi su un'edizione comparatistica dei 'Giuramenti di Strasburgo'", in: *La transizione dal latino alle lingue romanze*, ed. J. HERMAN (Tübingen, 1998), pp. 195-212.

HOLTZ, L., *Donat et la tradition de l'enseignement grammatical: étude sur l'Ars Donati et sa diffusion (IVe-IXe siècle) et édition critique* (Paris, 1981).

HOWLETT, D., "Aldhelmi Carmen Rhythmicum", *Archivum Latinitatis Medii Aevi (= ALMA)* 53 (1995), pp. 119-140.

IRVINE, M., *The Making of Textual Culture: "Grammatica" and Literary Theory, 350-1100* (Cambridge, 1994).

ITKONEN, E., "Un conflit entre facteurs phonétiques et facteurs fonctionnels dans un texte en latin mérovingien", *Neuphilologische Mitteilungen* 70 (1969), pp. 471-484.

IZZO, H., "Pre-latin languages and sound-change in Romance: the case of Old Spanish /h-/", in: *Studies in Romance Linguistics*, ed. M.P. HAGIWARA (Rowley, 1977), pp. 227-253.

IZZO, H., "Andalusia and America: the regional origins of New World Spanish", in: *Studies in Romance Linguistics*, ed. E. PULGRAM (Michigan, 1984), pp. 109-131.

JACKSON, K., *Language and History in Early Britain* (Edinburgh, 1953).

JANSEN, F., *A Comparative Study of Romance* (New York, 1999).

JANSON, T., "Language change and metalinguistic change: Latin to Romance and other cases", in: WRIGHT (ed.), *Latin and the Romance Languages*, pp. 19-28.

JONES, C.W. (ed.), *Bedae Venerabilis Opera Pars VI: Opera Didascalica* (Turnhout, 1975: *Corpus Christianorum. Series Latina* 123A).

JOSEPH, J., *Eloquence and Power: the Rise of Language Standards and Standard Languages* (London, 1987).

KASTER, R., *Guardians of Language: the Grammarian and Society in Late Antiquity* (Berkeley, 1988).

KAVANAGH, J.F., and I.G. MATTINGLY, *Language by Ear and by Eye* (Cambridge, Mass., 1972).

KEIL, H., *Grammatici Latini*, 7 volumes (Leipzig, 1855-1880; reprint Hildesheim, 1961).

KENNEDY, G.A., "Rhetoric", in: *The Legacy of Rome: A New Appraisal*, ed. R. JENKYNS (Oxford, 1992), pp. 269-294.

KISS, S., "'Solutions parallèles' dans l'histoire des langues romanes et interprétation des textes tardifs", in: HERMAN and WÜEST (ed.), "La fragmentation", pp. 651-655.

KLEIN ANDREU, F., "Speech priorities", in: *The Pragmatics of Style*, ed. L. HICKEY (London, 1989), pp. 73-86.

KNAPP, R.C., *Aspects of the Roman Experience in Iberia, 206-100 B.C.* (Alava, 1977).

KOCH, M., "Observaciones sobre la permanencia del sustrato púnico en la Península Ibérica", in: *Actas del I Coloquio sobre lenguas y culturas prerromanas de la Península Ibérica*, ed. F. JORDA *e.a.* (Salamanca, 1976), pp. 191-199.

KOCH, P., "Pour une typologie conceptionnelle et médiale des plus anciens documents/monuments des langues romanes", in: *Le passage à l'écrit des langues romanes*, ed. M. SELIG *e.a.* (Tübingen, 1993), 39-81.

KOERNER, K., *Practicing Linguistic Historiography* (Amsterdam, 1989).

KOSTO, A., *Making Agreements in Medieval Catalonia; Power, Order and the Written Word, 1000 – 1200* (Cambridge, 2001).

KRUSCH, B., and W. LEVISON (ed.)

LANCHETAS, R., *Gramática y vocabulario de las obras de Gonzalo de Berceo* (Madrid, 1900).

LAPESA, R., *Historia de la Lengua Española* (eighth edition; Madrid, 1980).

LAPESA, R., "El Fuero de Valfermoso de las Monjas", in: *Homenaje a Álvaro Galmés de Fuentes*, I (Oviedo, 1985), pp. 43-98.

LAPESA, R., "Nuestra lengua en España y en América", *Revista de Filología Española* 72 (1992), pp. 269-282.

LASS, R., *Historical Linguistics and Language Change* (Cambridge, 1997).

LAW, V., *The Insular Latin Grammarians* (Woodbridge, 1982).

LAW, V. (ed.), *History of Linguistic Thought in the Early Middle Ages* (Amsterdam, 1993).

LAW, V., *Grammar and Grammarians in the Early Middle Ages* (London, 1997).

LE PAGE, R., and A. TABOURET-KELLER, *Acts of Identity* (Cambridge, 1985).

LEVISON, W. (ed.), *Vitae Sancti Bonifatii archiepiscopi Moguntini* (Hannover and Leipzig, 1905: *Monumenta Germaniae Historica. Scriptores rerum Germanicarum in usum scholarum*).

LEVISON, W., *England and the Continent in the Eighth Century* (Oxford, 1946).

LEWIS, C.T., and C. SHORT, *A Latin Dictionary* (Oxford, 1879).

LIGHTFOOT, D., *Principles of Diachronic Syntax* (Cambridge, 1979).

LINDSAY, W.M., *Glossaria Latina* (Paris, 1926-1931; reprint, Hildesheim, 1965).

LINDSAY, W.M. (ed.), *Etymologiarum sive Originum Libri XX* (Oxford, 1911; third edition, 1962).

LINEHAN, P., *History and the Historians of Medieval Spain* (Oxford, 1993).

LIPSKI, J., *Latin American Spanish* (London, 1994).

LLEAL, C., *La formación de las lenguas romances peninsulares* (Barcelona, 1990).

LLOYD, P.M., *From Latin to Spanish*, I (Philadelphia, 1987).

LLOYD, P.M., "On the naming of languages (and other things)", in: WRIGHT (ed.), *Latin and the Romance Languages*, pp. 9-18.

LODGE, R.A., *French: from Dialect to Standard* (London, 1993).

LÓPEZ GARCÍA, A., "Algunas concordancias gramaticales entre el castellano y el euskera", in: *Philologica Hispaniensia in Honorem M. Alvar*, II (Madrid, 1985), pp. 391-405.

LÓPEZ GARCÍA, A., *El rumor de los desarraigados: conflicto de lenguas en la Península Ibérica* (Barcelona, 1985).

LÓPEZ GARCÍA, A., "Respuestas a algunas preguntas no formuladas a propósito del 'vascorrománico'", *Verba* 15 (1988), pp. 375-383.

LÓPEZ GARCÍA, A., *Cómo surgió el español* (Madrid, 2000).

LOT, F., "A quelle époque a-t-on cessé de parler latin?", *Archivum latinitas medii aevi* (= *ALMA*) 6 (1931), pp. 97-159.

LÜDTKE, H., *Geschichte des romanischen Wortschatzes* (Freiburg, 1968).

LÜDTKE, H., "Tesi generali sui rapporti fra i sistemi orale e scritto del linguaggio", in: XV *Congresso Internazionale di Linguistica e Filologia Romanza: Atti*, I (Napoli, 1978), pp. 433-443.

LÜDTKE, J. (ed.), *El español de América en el siglo* XVI (Frankfurt, 1994).

LUHTALA, A., "Syntax and dialectic in Carolingian commentaries on Priscian's *Institutiones Grammaticae*", in: *History of Linguistic Thought in the Early Middle Ages*, ed. V. LAW (Amsterdam, 1993), pp. 145-191.

LURAGHI, S., "The relationship between prepositions and cases within Latin prepositional phrases", in: G. CALBOLI (ed), *Subordination and other topics in Latin* (Amsterdam, 1989), pp. 253-272.

LYONS, C., "On the origin of the Old French strong-weak possessive distinction", *Transactions of the Philological Society* (1986), pp. 1-41.

MAESTRE YENES, M.A.H., *Ars Iuliani Toletani Episcopi. Una gramática latina de la España visigoda* (Toledo, 1973).

MAIDEN, M., *A Linguistic History of Italian* (London, 1995).

MALKIEL, Y., "Excessive self-assertion in glottodiachrony: Portuguese *sofrer* and its Latin and Spanish counterparts", *Lingua* 65 (1985), pp. 29-50.

MALKIEL, Y., *A Tentative Autobibliography* (Berkeley, 1988).

MALKIEL, Y., "The Spanish nominal augments reconsidered", *Romance Philology* 43 (1989), pp. 90-112.

MARAVAL, P. (ed.), *Égérie, Journal de voyage (Itinéraire)* (Paris, 1997: *Sources chrétiennes* 296).

MARCOS MARÍN, F., *Reforma y modernización del español* (Madrid, 1979).

MÁRQUEZ VILLANUEVA, F., *El concepto cultural alfonsí* (second edition; Madrid, 1995).

MARSILI, A. (ed.), *Alcuini Orthographia* (Pisa, 1952).

MARTIN, G., "Gestas de arena", in: *Textos épicos castellanos: problemas de edición y crítica*, ed. D. PATTISON (London, 2000), pp. 23-33.

MARTÍN MARTÍN, J.L., *e.a.* (ed.), *Documentos de los archivos catedralicio y diocesano de Salamanca (S.XII-XIII)* (Salamanca, 1977).

MARTINELL GIFRE, E., "Formación de una lengua hispánica en América", in: *Actas del Primer Congreso Anglo-Hispano*. I. *Lingüística*, ed. R. PENNY (Madrid, 1993), pp. 3-24.

McKITTERICK, R., *The Frankish Church and the Carolingian Reforms 789-895* (London, 1977).

McKITTERICK, R., *The Carolingians and the Written Word* (Cambridge, 1989).

McKITTERICK, R. (ed.), *The Uses of Literacy in Early Medieval Europe* (Cambridge, 1990).

McKITTERICK, R., "Latin and Romance: an historian's perspective", in: WRIGHT (ed.), *Latin and the Romance Languages*, pp. 130-145.

McKITTERICK, R. (ed.), *Carolingian Culture: Emulation and Innovation* (Cambridge, 1994).

MEIER, H., "Sobre la historicidad del lenguaje", in: *Actas del coloquio hispano-alemán Ramón Menéndez Pidal*, ed. W. HEMPEL and D. BRIESEMEISTER (Tübingen, 1982), pp. 181-207.

MEIER, H., *Notas Críticas al DECH de Corominas/Pascual* (Santiago de Compostela, 1984).

MELLADO, J., and M.J. ALDANA, *Concordantia in Eulogium Cordubensem* (Hildesheim, 1993).

MENÉNDEZ PIDAL, R., *Orígenes del español* (Madrid, 1926; seventh edition, 1972).

MENÉNDEZ PIDAL, R., *Cantar de Mio Cid*, 3 volumes (Madrid, 1944-1946).

MENÉNDEZ PIDAL, R., *Poesía juglaresca y orígenes de las literaturas románicas* (Madrid, 1957).

MENÉNDEZ PIDAL, R., "Colonización suritálica de España según testimonios toponímicos e inscripcionales", in: *Enciclopedia Lingüística Hispánica*, I, ed. M. ALVAR *e.a.* (Madrid, 1960), pp. 49-68.

MENÉNDEZ PIDAL, R., *Documentos Lingüísticos de España*. I. *Reino de Castilla* (Madrid, 1966).

MICHAEL, I. (ed.), *The Poem of the Cid*, with English translation by: R. HAMILTON and J. PERRY (Manchester, 1975).

MICHELENA, L., "La langue ibère", in: *Actas del II Coloquio sobre lenguas y culturas prerromanas de la Península Ibérica*, ed. A. TOVAR *e.a.* (Salamanca, 1979), pp. 23-39; reprinted in: IDEM, *Lengua e Historia* (Madrid, 1985), pp. 341-356.

MICHELENA, L., "Sobre la posición lingüística del ibérico", in: IDEM, *Lengua e historia* (Madrid, 1985), pp. 334-340.

MICHELENA, L., *Sobre historia de la lengua vasca* (San Sebastián, 1988).

MIGLIORINI, B., *Storia della lingua italiana* (Firenze, 1960).

MIGNE, J.P. (ed.), *Patrologia Latina* (Paris, 1878-1890).

MILROY, J., *Linguistic Variation and Change: on the Historical Sociolinguistics of English* (Oxford, 1992).

MILROY, J., and L. MILROY, *Authority in Language: investigating language prescription and standardization* (London, 1985).

MILROY, J., and L. MILROY, "Linguistic change, social network and speaker innovation", *Journal of Linguistics* 21 (1985), pp. 339-384.

MOHRMANN, C., *Études sur le latin des chrétiens*, 4 volumes (Rome, 1961-1977).

MOLINER, M., *Diccionario de Uso del Español* (Madrid, 1966).

MONTANER FRUTOS, A., *Cantar de Mio Cid* (Barcelona, 1993).

MONTANER, A., and A. ESCOBAR, *Carmen Campidoctoris o poema latino del Campeador* (Madrid, 2001).

MONTEAGUDO, H., "Aspectos sociolingüísticos do uso escrito do galego, o castelán e o latín na Galicia tardomedieval (SS.XIII-XV)", in: *Estudios Galegos en homenaxe ó Profesor Giuseppe Tavani*, ed. E. FIDALGO and P. LORENZO GRADÍN (Santiago de Compostela, 1994), pp. 169-185.

MORALA RODRÍGUEZ, J.R., "Norma gráfica y variedades orales en el leonés medieval", in: *Estudios de grafemática en el dominio hispano*, ed. J.M. BLECUA *e.a.* (Salamanca, 1998), pp. 169-188.

MORIN, G. (ed.), *Sancti Caesarii Arelatensis sermones*, 2 volumes (Turnhout, 1953: *Corpus Christianorum. Series Latina* 103-104).

MOSTERÍN, J., *La ortografía fonémica del español* (Madrid, 1981).

MOUNTAIN, W.J., and F. GLORIE (ed.), *Augustini de Trinitate libri XV* (Turnhout, 1968: *Corpus Christianorum. Series Latina* 50).

MULLER, H.F., "The passive voice in Vulgar Latin", *Romanic Review* 15 (1924), pp. 68-93.

MULLER, H.F., *A Chronology of Vulgar Latin* (Halle, 1929).

MULLER, H.F., *L'époque merovingienne* (New York, 1945).

NARBONA JIMÉNEZ, A., and R. MORILLO-VELARDE PÉREZ, *Las hablas andaluzas* (Córdoba, 1987).

NELSON, J., "Public *histories* and private history in the work of Nithard", *Speculum* 60 (1985), pp. 251-293.

NICHOLS, J., *Linguistic Diversity in Space and Time* (Chicago, 1992).

NIEDEREHE, H.-J., *Alfonso X, el Sabio, y la lingüística de su tiempo* (Madrid, 1987).

NIELSEN, H., and L. SCHØSLER (ed.), *The Origins and Development of Emigrant Languages* (Odense, 1996).

NOBLE, T.F.X., *The Republic of St Peter: The Birth of the Papal State, 680-825* (Philadelphia, 1984).

NOBLE, T.F.X., "A new look at the Liber Pontificalis", *Archivum Historiae Pontificiae* 23 (1985), pp. 347-358.

NOBLE, T.F.X., "The declining knowledge of Greek in Eighth- and Ninth-Century Papal Rome", *Byzantinische Zeitschrift* 78 (1985), pp. 56-62.

NOBLE, T.F.X., "Literacy and the papal government in Late Antiquity and the Early Middle Ages", in: MCKITTERICK (ed.), *The Uses of Literacy*, pp. 82-108.

NORBERG, D., *Introduction à l'étude de la versification latine médiévale* (Stockholm, 1958).

NORBERG, D., *Manuel pratique de latin médiéval* (Paris, 1968).

NORBERG, D., *L'accentuation des mots dans le vers latin du Moyen Age* (Stockholm, 1985).

NOVATI, F., *Storia letteraria d'Italia: le origini* (Milano, 1926).

O'CRÓINÍN, D., "The Irish as mediators of antique culture on the continent", in: *Science in Western and Eastern Civilization in Carolingian Times*, ed. P.L. BUTZER and D. LOHRMANN (Basle, 1993), pp. 41-51.

O'DONNELL, J., "Alcuin's *Priscian*", in: *Latin Script and Letters, A.D. 400-900*, ed. J. O'MEARA and B. NEUMANN (Leiden, 1976), pp. 222-235.

OROZ RETA, J. (ed.), *San Isidoro de Sevilla: Etimologías*, 2 volumes (Madrid, 1982: *Biblioteca de Auctores Cristianos*).

PANHUIS, D., *The Communicative Perspective in the Sentence: A Study of Latin Word Order* (Amsterdam, 1982).

PASCUAL, J.A., "Del latín a las lenguas romances. La complicada gestión – sobre el papel – del castellano", in: *De Roma al Siglo XX*, ed. A.M. ALDAMA (Madrid, 1996), I, pp. 447-471.

PASSALACQUA, M., *I codici di Prisciano* (Rome, 1978).

PASSALACQUA, M., "Priscian's *Institutio de nomine et pronomine et verbo* in the Ninth Century", in: LAW (ed.), *History*, pp. 193-204.

PEDERSON, E.W., *Subtle Semantics: Universals in the Polysemy of Reflexive and Caustive Constructions* (doctoral thesis, Berkeley, 1991).

PELLEN, R., *Los milagros de Nuestra Señora: étude linguistique et index lemmatisé* (Paris, 1993).

PENNY, R., *Patterns of Language Change in Spain* (London, 1987).

PENNY, R., "The Old Spanish graphs 'i', 'j', 'g' and 'y' and the development of Latin $G^{e,i}$ and J-", *Bulletin of Hispanic Studies* 65 (1988), pp. 337-354.

PENNY, R., *A History of the Spanish Language* (Cambridge, 1991).

PENNY, R., "Labiodental /f/, aspiration and /h/-dropping in Spanish: the evolving phonemic value of the graphs *f* and *h*", in: *Cultures in Contact in Medieval Spain: Historical and Literary Essays Presented to L.P. Harvey*, ed. D. HOOK and B. TAYLOR (London, 1990), pp. 157-182.

PENNY, R., "El árbol genealógico: ¿modelo lingüístico desfasado?", in: *Actas del III Congreso Internacional de Historia de la Lengua Española* (Madrid, 1996), pp. 827-839.

PENNY, R., "The Language of Gonzalo de Berceo, in the context of peninsular dialectal variation", in: *The Medieval Mind: Hispanic Studies in Honour of Alan Deyermond*, ed. I. MACPHERSON and R. PENNY (London, 1997), 327-345.

PENNY, R., "La grafía de los textos notariales castellanos de la Alta Edad Media: ¿sistema logográfico o fonológico?", in: *Estudios de grafemática en el dominio hispano*, ed. J.M. BLECUA *e.a.* (Salamanca, 1998), pp. 211-223.

PENNY, R., *Variation and Change in Spanish* (Cambridge, 2000).

PENSADO, C., *Cronología relativa del castellano* (Salamanca, 1984).

PENSADO, C., "How was Leonese Vulgar Latin read?", in: WRIGHT (ed.), *Latin and the Romance Languages*, pp. 190-204.

PENSADO, C., "Sobre el contexto del cambio F > h en castellano", *Romance Philology* 47 (1993), pp. 147-176.

PENSADO, C., "Sobre los límites de la mala ortografía en romance. ¿Por qué el inglés *fish* no se escribe *ghoti* después de todo?", in: *Estudios de grafemática en el dominio hispano*, ed. J.M. BLECUA *e.a.* (Salamanca, 1998), pp. 225-242.

PÉREZ GONZÁLEZ, M., *El latín de la Cancillería Castellana (1158-1214)* (Salamanca, 1985).

PÉREZ GONZÁLEZ, M. (ed.), *Actas del I Congreso Nacional de Latín Medieval* (León, 1995).

PÉREZ GONZÁLEZ, M., *Actas del II Congreso Hispánico de Latín Medieval*, 2 volumes (León, 1998).

PINKSTER, H., *Latin Syntax and Semantics* (London, 1990).

PINKSTER, H., "Evidence for SVO in Latin?", in: WRIGHT (ed.), *Latin and the Romance Languages*, pp. 69-82.

PIRENNE, H., "De l'état de l'instruction des laïcs à l'époque mérovingienne", *Revue Benédictine* 46 (1934), pp. 165-177.

Poema de Mio Cid; edición facsímil (Burgos, 1988).

POSNER, R., "Latin or Romance (again!): change or genesis?", in: *Papers from the 10th International Conference on Historical Linguistics*, ed., J. VAN MARLE (Amsterdam, 1993), pp. 265-279.

POSNER, R., *The Romance Languages* (Cambridge, 1996).

POUNTAIN, C.J., "Copulas, verbs of possession and auxiliaries in Old Spanish: the evidence for structurally interdependent changes", *Bulletin of Hispanic Studies* 62 (1985), pp. 337-356.

RAU, R. (trans.), *Briefe des Bonifatius – Willibalds Leben des Bonifatius* (Darmstadt, 1968: *Ausgewählte Quellen zur deutschen Geschichte des Mittelalters* 4B).

REILLY, B.F., *The Medieval Spains* (Cambridge, 1993).

REYNOLDS, L.D., and N.G. WILSON, *Scribes and Scholars* (Oxford, 1968).

RIBERA, J., *Historia de los jueces de Córdoba por Aljoxaní* (Madrid, 1914).

RICHÉ, P., *Education et culture dans l'occident barbare, VIe-VIIe siècles* (Paris, 1962).

RICHÉ, P., *La vie quotidienne dans l'empire Carolingien* (Paris, 1973).

RICHTER, M., "A quelle époque a-t-on cessé de parler latin en Gaule? A propos d'une question mal posée", *Annales* 38 (1983), pp. 439-448; reprinted in: IDEM, *Studies in Medieval Language and Culture* (Dublin, 1995), chapter 7..

RICHTER, M., *The Formation of the Medieval West: Studies in the Oral Culture of the Barbarians* (Dublin, 1994).

RICKARD, P., *A History of the French Language* (London, 1974).

RIDRUEJO, E., "¿Un reajuste sintáctico en el español de los siglos XV y XVI?", in: *Actas del Primer Congreso Anglo-Hispano.* I. *Lingüística*, ed. R. PENNY (Madrid, 1993), pp. 49-60.

DE RIQUER, M., *Los trovadores: historia literaria y textos*, 3 volumes (Barcelona, 1975).

ROBSON, C.A., "L'*Appendix Probi* et la philologie latine", *Le Moyen Age* 69 (1963), pp. 39-54.

ROHLFS, G., "Oskische Latinität in Spanien?", *Revue de Linguistique Romane* 19 (1955), pp. 221-225.

ROMÁN DEL CERRO, J.L., *El desciframiento de la lengua ibérica en "La Ofrenda de los Pueblos"* (Alicante, 1990).

ROMÁN DEL CERRO, J.L., *El origen ibérico de la lengua vasca* (Alicante, 1993).

RONCONI, A., *Il verbo latino: problemi di sintassi storica* (second edition; Firenze, 1968).

ROTHWELL, W., "Adding insult to injury: the English who curse in borrowed French", in: *The Origins and Development of Emigrant Languages*, ed. H. NIELSEN and L. SCHØSLER (Odense, 1996), pp. 41-54.

RUIZ ASENCIO, J.M., "Hacia una nueva visión de las Glosas Emilianenses y Silenses", in: *Las Glosas Emilianenses y Silenses. Edición crítica y facsímil*, ed. C. HERNÁNDEZ ALONSO and J.M. RUIZ ASENCIO (Burgos, 1993), pp. 83-118.

SABATINI, F., "Dalla *scripta latina rustica* alle *scriptae* romanze", *Studi Medievali* 9 (1968), pp. 320-358.

SABATINI, F., "Prospettive sul parlato nella storia linguistica italiana", in: *Italia linguistica: Idee, Storia, Strutture*, ed. F.A. LEONI *e.a.* (Bologna, 1983), pp. 167-201.

SAGE, C., *Paul Albar of Córdoba: Studies on his Life and Writings* (Washington, 1943).

SALA, R., *La lengua y el estilo de Gonzalo de Berceo* (Logroño, 1983).

SALVADOR, G., "Hipótesis geológica sobre la evolución F- > h-", in: *Introducción Plural a la Gramática Histórica*, ed. F. MARCOS MARÍN (Madrid, 1982), pp. 11-21.

SALVADOR, G., "Lexemática histórica", in: *Actas del I Congreso Internacional de Historia de la Lengua Española*, ed. M. ARIZA *e.a.* (Madrid, 1988), pp. 635-646.

SALVADOR PLANS, A., "La adecuación entre grafía y fonema en los ortógrafos del Siglo de Oro", *Anuario de Estudios Filológicos* 3 (1980), pp. 215-227.

SAMPSON, G., *Writing Systems: A Linguistic Introduction* (London, 1985).

SANGA, G., and S. BAGGIO, "Il volgare nei *Placiti Cassinesi*: vecchie questioni e nuove acquisizioni", *Rivista Italiana di Dialettologia* 18 (1994), pp. 7-30.

SAS, L.F., *The Noun Declension System in Merovingian Latin* (Paris, 1937).

SCHIAFFINI, A., "Problemi del passaggio dal latino all'italiano (evoluzione, disgregazione, ricostruzione)", in: *Studi in onore di Angelo Monteverdi*, ed. G. GERARDI MARCUZZO, II (Modena, 1959), pp. 691-715.

SCHLIEBEN-LANGE, B., "L'Origine des langues romanes: un cas de créolisation", in: *Langues en contact, Pidgins – Creoles*, ed. J.M. MEISEL (Tübingen, 1977), pp. 81-101.

SCHØSLER, L., "Permanence et variation de la valence verbale: réflexions sur la construction des verbes en latin, en ancien français, en moyen français et en français moderne", in: *Actes du XXIIe Congrès International de Linguistique et de Philologie Romanes*, 9 volumes, ed. A. ENGLEBERT *e.a.* (Tübingen, 2000), II, pp. 407-418.

SCRAGG, D.G., *A History of English Spelling* (Manchester, 1974).

SELIG, M., *Die Entwicklung der Nominaldeterminanten im Spätlatein* (Tübingen, 1992).

SELIG, M., *e.a.* (ed.), *Le passage à l'écrit des langues romanes* (Tübingen, 1993).

SERBAT, G., "Quelques traits d'oralité chez Anthime, *De Observatione Ciborum*", in: *Les structures de l'oralité en Latin*, ed. J. DANGEL and C. MOUSSY (Paris, 1996), pp. 85-91.

SILVA CORVALÁN, C., *Sociolingüística: teoría y análisis* (Madrid, 1988).

SILVA CORVALÁN, C., *Language Contact and Change: Spanish in Los Angeles* (Oxford, 1994).

SIMONET, F.J., *Historia de los mozárabes de España* (Madrid, 1897-1903; reprint Amsterdam, 1967).

SMITH, C., "The vernacular", in: *The New Cambridge Medieval History*, V, ed. D. - ABULAFIA (Cambridge, 1999), pp. 71-83.

STELLA, F., "Gotescalco, la 'Scuola' di Reims e l'origine della rima mediolatina", in: *Il verso europeo*, ed. F. STELLA (Firenze, 1995), pp. 159-165.

STENGAARD, B., "The combination of glosses in the *Códice emilianense* 60 (*Glosas emilianenses*)", in: WRIGHT (ed.), *Latin and the Romance Languages*, pp. 177-189.

STRAKA, G., *Les sons et les mots* (Paris, 1979).

SZÖVERFFY, J., *A Concise History of Medieval Latin Hymnody* (Leiden, 1985).

TALBOT, C.H., *The Anglo-Saxon Missionaries in Germany* (London, 1954).

TEJADA Y RAMIRO, J., *Colección de Canones de la Iglesia española*, 7 volumes (Madrid, 1849-1862).

THORSBERG, B., *Études sur l'hymnologie mozarabe* (Stockholm, 1962).

TOON, T.E., *The Politics of Early Old English Sound Change* (New York, 1983).

TORREBLANCA, M., "La 'f' prerromana y la vasca en su relación con el español antiguo", *Romance Philology* 37 (1984), pp. 273-281.

TORREBLANCA, M., "En torno a las Glosas Emilianenses y las Silenses", in: *Scripta Philologica in Honorem Juan M. Lope Blanch*, ed. E. LUNA TRAILL (Mexico, 1991), pp. 469-479.

TORREBLANCA, M., "Isoglosas riojano-castellano-leonesas en la Edad Media", in: *Linguistic Studies in Medieval Spanish*, ed. T.D. CRAVENS and R. HARRIS-NORTHALL (Madison, 1991), pp. 135-147.

TOVAR, A., "Discurso inaugural", in: *Actas del I Coloquio sobre lenguas y culturas prerromanas de la Península Ibérica*, ed. F. JORDA e.a. (Salamanca, 1976), pp. 11-24.

TOVAR, A., "La inscripción del Cabeço das Fráguas y la lengua de los lusitanos", in: *Actas del III Coloquio sobre lenguas y culturas paleohispánicas*, ed. J. DE HOZ (Salamanca, 1985), pp. 227-253.

TRASK, R.L., *A Dictionary of Grammatical Terms in Linguistics* (London, 1993).

TRASK, R.L., *The History of Basque* (London, 1997).

TRASK, R.L., "Why should a language have any relatives?", in: *Nostratic: Examining a Linguistic Macrofamily*, ed. C. RENFREW and D. NETTLE (Cambridge, 1999), pp. 157-176.

TRASK, R.L., *The Dictionary of Comparative and Historical Linguistics* (Edinburgh, 2000).

TRASK, R.L., and R. WRIGHT, "El 'vascorrománico'", *Verba* 15 (1988), pp. 361-373.

TRUDGILL, P., *Dialects in Contact* (Oxford, 1986).

UNTERKIRCHER, F., *Alkuin-Briefe* (Graz, 1969).

VALCÁRCEL, V., *La "Vita Dominici Silensis" de Grimaldo* (Logroño, 1982).

VAN DER WURFF, W., "Gerunds and their objects in the Modern English period", in: *Papers from the 10th International Conference on Historical Linguistics*, ed. J. VAN MARLE (Amsterdam, 1993), pp. 363-375.

VAN KONINGSVELD, P.S., *The Latin-Arabic Glossary of the Leiden University Library* (Leiden, 1977).

VAN UYTFANGHE, M., "Le latin des hagiographes mérovingiens et la protohistoire du français", *Romanica Gandensia* 16 (1976), pp. 5-89.

VAN UYTFANGHE, M., "L'hagiographie et son public à l'époque mérovingienne", *Studia Patristica* 16 (1985), pp. 54-62.

VAN UYTFANGHE, M., "Les expressions du type *quod vulgo vocant* dans des textes latins antérieurs au concile de Tours et aux serments de Strasbourg", *Zeitschrift für romanische Philologie* 105 (1989), pp. 28-49.

VAN UYTFANGHE, M., "The consciousness of a linguistic dichotomy (Latin-Romance) in Carolingian Gaul: the contradictions of the sources and of their interpretation", in: WRIGHT (ed.), *Latin and the Romance Languages*, pp. 114-129.

VAN UYTFANGHE, M., "Mère latin et ses filles", in: *Acta Selecta Octavi Conventus Academiae Latinitati Fovendae*, ed. I. IJSEWIJN and T. SACRÉ (Rome, 1995), pp. 651-681.

VARVARO, A., "Latin and Romance: fragmentation or restructuring?", in: WRIGHT (ed.), *Latin and the Romance Languages*, pp. 44-51.

VELÁZQUEZ SORIANO, I., *Las pizarras visigodas: edición crítica y estudio* (Murcia, 1989).

VERSTEEGH, C., "The debate concerning Latin and Early Romance", *Diachronica* 9 (1992), pp. 259-285.

VILLAREAL, J., "Las Glosas", in: *Hymnarium Oscense*, ed. A. DURÁN *e.a.* (Zaragoza, 1987), pp. 125-146.

WALKER, R., *Views of Transition: Liturgy and Illumination in Medieval Spain* (London, 1998).

WALLACH, L., *Alcuin and Charlemagne* (Ithaca, 1959).

WALTMAN, F.M., *Concordance to Poema de Mio Cid* (Penn State, 1972).

WANG, W.S.-Y., "Competing changes as a cause of residue", *Language* 45 (1969), pp. 9-25.

WASSERSTEIN, D.J., "The language situation in Al-Andalus", in: *Studies on the Muwassah and the Kharja*, ed. A. JONES and R. HITCHCOCK (Oxford, 1991), pp. 1-15.

WEBSTER, N., *A Dictionary of the English Language* (London, 1852).

WEXLER, P., "Marrano Ibero-Romance: classification and research tasks", *Zeitschrift für romanische Philologie,* 98 (1982), pp. 59-108.

WILLIAMS, L., "The act of reading: how straightforward is it?", *Bulletin of Hispanic Studies* 74 (1997), pp. 265-274.

WINTERFELD, P. (ed.), *Monumenta Germaniae Historica. Poetae Latini Aevi Carolini,* IV, 1 (Berlin, 1899).

WIREBACK, K., "The relationship between lenition, the strong word boundary, and sonorant strengthening in Ibero-Romance", in: *Essays in Hispanic Linguistics dedicated to Paul M. Lloyd,* ed. R. BLAKE *e.a.* (Newark, 1999), pp. 155-172.

WOLF, H.J., *Las Glosas Emilianenses* (Hamburg, 1991); Spanish translation by: S. RUHSTALLER (Seville, 1996).

WOLF, K.B., *Christian Martyrs in Moslem Spain* (Cambridge, 1988).

WOOD, I., "Modes of communication: an afterword", in: *East and West: Modes of Communication. Proceedings of the First Plenary Conference at Merida,* ed. E. CHRYSOS and I. WOOD (Leiden, 1999: *The Transformation of the Roman World* 5), pp. 279-282.

WOODCOCK, E.C., *A New Latin Syntax* (London, 1959).

WOUTERS, A., *The Grammatical Papyri from Graeco-Roman Egypt. Contributions to the Study of 'Ars Grammatica' in Antiquity* (Brussels, 1979).

WRIGHT, R., "Semicultismo", *Archivum Linguisticum* 7 (1976), pp. 13-28.

WRIGHT, R., "Speaking, reading and writing Late Latin and Early Romance", *Neophilologus* 60 (1976), pp. 178-189.

WRIGHT, R., *Late Latin and Early Romance in Spain and Carolingian France* (Liverpool, 1982).

WRIGHT, R. (ed.), *Latin and the Romance Languages in the Early Middle Ages* (London, 1991; reprinted, Penn State, 1996).

WRIGHT, R., "Introduction: Latin and Romance, a thousand years of incertitude", in: WRIGHT (ed.), *Latin and the Romance Languages,* pp. 1-5.

WRIGHT, R., "Status Quaestionis: el estudio diacrónico del español", *Lingüística* 5 (1993), pp. 77-126.

WRIGHT, R., "Versatility and vagueness in Early Medieval Spain", in: *Hispanic Linguistic Studies in Honour of F.W. Hodcroft*, ed. D. MACKENZIE and I. MICHAEL (Oxford, 1993), pp. 207-223.

WRIGHT, R., *Early Ibero-Romance* (Newark, 1995).

WRIGHT, R., "La sintaxis reflexiva con semántica no agentiva", in: *Actas del primer congreso nacional de latín medieval*, ed. M. PÉREZ GONZÁLEZ (León, 1995), pp. 415-431.

WRIGHT, R., "Translation between Latin and Romance in the Early Middle Ages", in: *Medieval Translation Theory and Practice*, ed. J. BEER (Kalamazoo, 1997), pp. 7-32.

WRIGHT, R., "Reading a will in Twelfth-Century Salamanca", in: *Latin vulgaire – latin tardif* V, ed. H. PETERSMANN and R. KETTEMANN (Heidelberg, 1999), pp. 505-516.

WRIGHT, R., *El Tratado de Cabreros (1206): estudio sociofilológico de una reforma ortográfica* (London, 2000).

WÜEST, J., *La dialectalisation de la Galloromania* (Bern, 1979).

WÜEST, J., "Latin vulgaire et créolisation", in: *Actes du XXe Congrès International de Linguistique et Philologie Romanes*, II (Tübingen, 1993), pp. 656-661.

ZAMBONI, A., *Alle origini dell'italiano* (Rome, 2000).

ZANNA, P., "Lecture, écriture et morphologie latines en Irlande aux VIIe et VIIIe siècles", *Archivum Latinitatis Medii Aevi (= ALMA)* 56 (1998), pp. 180-191.

ZUMTHOR, P., *Langue et technique poétique à l'époque romane (XIe-XIIIe siècle)* (Paris 1963).

Index

[Note: this index does not include topics that occur in every chapter, such as Latin, Romance, Pronunciation, Phonetics, Morphology, Syntax, Vocabulary, Orthography, Sociolinguistics.]